DICKENS STUDIES ANNUAL
Essays on Victorian Fiction

DICKENS STUDIES ANNUAL
Essays on Victorian Fiction

EDITORS

Michael Timko
Fred Kaplan
Edward Guiliano

DICKENS STUDIES ANNUAL

Essays on Victorian Fiction

VOLUME
19

Edited by
Michael Timko, Fred Kaplan,
and Edward Guiliano

AMS PRESS
NEW YORK

DICKENS STUDIES ANNUAL
ISSN 0084-9812

International Standard Book Number
Series: 0-404-18520-7
Vol. 19: 0-404-18539-8

Dickens Studies Annual: Essays on Victorian Fiction welcomes essay and monograph-length contributions on Dickens as well as on other Victorian novelists and on the history of aesthetics of Victorian fiction. All manuscripts should be double-spaced, including footnotes, which should be grouped at the end of the submission, and should be prepared according to the format used in this journal. An editorial decision can usually be reached more quickly if two copies are submitted. The preferred editions for citations from Dickens' works are the Clarendon and the Norton Critical when available, otherwise the Oxford Illustrated or the Penguin.

Please send submissions to the Editors, *Dickens Studies Annual*, Room 1522. Graduate School and University Center, City University of New York, 33 West 42nd Street, New York, N.Y. 10036: please send subscription inquires to AMS Press, Inc., 56 East 13th Street, New York, N.Y. 10003.

Manufactured in the United States of America

All AMS books are printed on acid-free paper that meets the guidelines
for performance and durability of the Committe on Production Guidelines
for Book Longevity of the Council on Library Resources.

Contents

List of Illustrations

Preface

The editors continue to be grateful for the services of the members of the editorial and advisory boards. Special thanks go to those who wrote the comprehensive review essays. We also thank the participants in the annual Santa Cruz Dickens Coference, especially John Jordan. Alicia Carroll, the editorial assistant from CUNY, and Jack Hopper, AMS Press, deserve special commendation.

We note and express our graditude to those in administrative posts in different institutions who continue to provide supports of various kinds: Chancellor Joseph Murphy, CUNY; President Harold Proshansky, Provost Stephen Cahn, and Executive Officer, Ph.D. Program in English, Martin Stevens, the Graduate School and University Center, CUNY; Dean of Humanities Michael Spitzer, The New York Institute of Technology; Ptesident Shirley Strum Kenny, Dean John Reilly, and Chair, English Department, Charles Molesworth, Queens College, CUNY; and Gabriel Hornstein, President, AMS Press, whose encouragement has always been a constant source of strength.

—THE EDITORS.

Notes on Contributors

MURRAY BAUMGARTEN is the Founding Director of the Dickens Project of the University of California. He has just published *Understanding Philip Roth* (with Barbara Gottfried). He is also Editor-in-Chief of the Essential Carlyle.

CHIARA BRIGANTI recieved a Laurea in Lingue e Letterature Straniere Moderne form the Università degli Studi di Pisa in 1976, her M.A. in English Literature from the University of California at Davis, and her Ph.D. from Pennsylvania State University in 1988. She teaches Victorian Literature and Women's Studies at Carleton College in Northfield, Minnesota.

CAMILLE COLATOSTI received her Ph.D. in Language and Literature form the University of Michigan, Ann Arbor, in 1990. She is a staff reporter, assistant editor, and researcher of the Detroit-based labor journal, *Labor Notes*.

PHILIP COLLINS, Emeritus Professor of English at Leicester University, is author of *Dickens and Crime*, *Dickens and Education*, editor of *Dickens: The Critical Heritage*, *Dicken's Public Reading*, *Dickens: Interviews and Recollections*, and many other books, monographs, collections, bibliographies, essays, etc. relating to Dickens, Thackerary, Trollope, Tennyson, Hardy, and other authors of the period.

C. R. B. DUNLOP is Professor of Law at the University of Alberta. Besides teaching creditor-debtor law and labor relations, he offers a course in the Law Faculty on law in literature. He is the author of *Creditor-Debtor Law in Canada* and has written about the law in Theodore Dreiser's novels.

SIMON EDWARDS is Head of the English Department at Roehampton University in London. He has also taught at Michigan State University, and recently at the University of Sofia in Bulgaria. He has published articles and papers on Dickens, Thackeray, Scott, and the city in English literature. His current research is on Scott and his European reception. (As an unreconstructed Lukacsian, his interest in food does not include the "nouvelle cuisine.")

RICHARD T. GAUGHAN is an Associate Professor at the University of Central Arkansas.

MARCIA RENEE GOODMAN teaches in the English Department at the University of California, Davis. She also coordinates the publications program for the office of University-School Programs in the Division of Education. She writes on literature and on teaching.

BARBARA GOTTFRIED is Assistant Professor of English at Bentley College in Waltham, Massachusetts. A feminist teacher and critic, she is concerned with nineteenth and twentieth century fiction, gender studies, and film. She has recently co-authored *Understanding Philip Roth* with Murray Baumgarten.

SUSAN R. HORTON is Professor and Chairperson of the English Department at the University of Massachusetts at Boston, and President of the Dickens Society for 1990. She has published three book-length studies, including two on Dickens, as well as articles on such topics as the politics of literacy and surveys of contemporary literary theory. She is currently working on a book-length study of Olive Schreiner and Isak Dinesen, a theoretical study of white women in Africa.

PATRICK J. MCCARTHY is Professor of English at the University of California at Santa Barbara, has written a variety of studies on Victorian subjects, including *Matthew Arnold and the Three Classes* (1964). He has published extensively in scholarly journals, including *Dickens Studies Annual*.

CYNTHIA NORTHCUTT MALONE is Assistant Professor of English at the College of St. Benedict, St. Joseph, Minnesota. She has published articles on Dickens and Carlyle, and she is working on a book-length study of self-representation in Dickens' novels.

PATRICK O'DONNELL is the Eberle Professor of American Literature at West Virginia University. He is the author of *John Hawkes, Passionate Doubts: Designs of Interpretation in Contemporary Fiction* and co-editor of *Intertextuality and Contemporary American Fiction*. He is also an Associate Editor of the Arizona Quarterly, and of "the Columbia History of the American Novel" (forthcoming). Currently, he is completing a book entitled "Echo Chambers: Figuring Voice in Modern Narrative," of which his essay on Dickens' *Our Mutual Friend* is a part.

ALEXANDER PETTIT is a Teaching Assistant and an Assistant Director of expository writing at the University of Washington. His article on the *Grub Street Journal* is forthcoming in Philological Quarterly.

HILARY M. SCHOR is Assistant Professor of English at the University of Southern California. She has published articles and reviews on Victorian fiction and narrative theory, and has completed a book-length study of Elizabeth Gaskell. She is currently at work on a study of women and narrative in the novels of Charles Dickens.

Male versus Female Self-denial: The Subversive Potential of The Feminine Ideal in the Fiction of Charles Dickens

Camille Colatosti

One way of looking at the entire feminist theoretical enterprise would be to see it as the examination of the construction of woman as the object of discourse—and the reorientation of this discourse to create a new object—women—with women themselves as the reason behind the discourse.

Claire Duchen, *Feminism in France*

"You're never safe with 'em, Mr. Pickwick, ven they vunce has designs on you; there's no knowin' vere to have 'em; and vile you're a-considering of it, they have you."

Tony Weller, speaking of women

In *The Pickwick Papers* women work in mysterious and dangerous ways. Without understanding what he has done to prompt her, Mr. Pickwick finds himself sued for breach of promise by Mrs. Bardell, a woman he never courted and to whom he never proposed. Mr. Tupman falls in love with old maid Rachael Wardle only to discover that her affections are easily gained by any man willing to marry her. Though she declared herself to him, she runs off with Mr. Jingle. Mr. Weller's wife, Susan, comes to oppress him, devoting her energy to the drunken cleric Mr. Stiggins, who takes advantage of her financially and encourages her to belittle her husband for his lack of religious fervor. Not until after her death, as Tony Weller recounts Susan's final words, do we learn that she regrets neglecting her duties as a wife.

1

Significantly, Dickens does not allow his readers to hear this apology from Susan herself. By placing her language in Mr. Weller's mouth, Dickens restores the husband to his "rightful" place as master of his home. Mr. Weller controls his wife's words and behavior after she dies as he could not while she lived. On her death-bed, so Tony Weller relates, Susan finally admits that he was right to mistrust Stiggins: "I begin to see now . . . ven it's too late, that if a married, 'ooman vishes to be religious, she should begin with dischargin' her dooties at home, and makin' them as is about her cheerful and happy. . . . I hope ven I'm gone, Veller, that you'll think on me as I was afore I know'd them people, an as I raly wos by natur' " (PP, ch. 52).

Susan Weller's final speech, as translated by her husband, implies that the older Weller subscribes to the doctrine of separate spheres—men function in the public realm while women's "natur" qualifies them for domestic work. However, even with her sphere, woman must not be as concerned with the satisfaction of her own goals as with fulfilling her husband's desires, establishing her home in a way that suits him, whatever the personal cost involved. When male characters in Dickens lose control of "their" women, as Mr. Weller does of Susan, they also relinquish command of their homes and may, as in Tony Weller's case, have to bear criticism from other men. After watching Mr. Weller submit to his wife's wishes and passively agree to entertain Stiggins, Sam tells his father that he is ashamed of him: "[I]f *I* was the proprietor of the Markis o' Granby, and that 'ere Stiggins came and made toast in *my* bar, I'd. . . . [p]ison his rum and water. . . . I wouldn't be too hard upon him at first. I'd drop him in the water-butt, and put the lid on . . ." (PP, ch. 27). Impressed by his son's fortitude, Mr. Weller does eventually follow the latter part of Sam's advice, immersing Stiggins in a horse-trough full of water—but not until after his wife's death (PP, ch. 52). Though on her deathbed Susan tells her husband that she really is self-sacrificing, submissive and "womanly" "by natur,' " the story of her relationship with Tony suggests that woman's "nature" is easily perverted and needs to be carefully controlled by men.

While Edgar Johnson attributes *Pickwick*'s presentation "of husbands lashed by the sharper sides of their wives' tongues" to Dickens' early dissatisfaction with his own wife (I: 266), I investigate Dickens' depiction of female figures not simply in terms of the author's biography, but in other to explore the complex desires that Victorian domestic—and, in fact, all patriarchal—ideologies have for women. [1] By presenting Susan Weller's deathbed speech as he does, Dickens attempts to reconfirm both male power and female submissiveness. To do so, he must deny the force of Susan's female voice that has, throughout her marriage to Tony, insisted upon her independence from her husband as well as her right to participate in the activities she chooses. Tony's re-telling of Susan's final words masks tensions within Dickens' construction of the widow that undermine the ideology of male dominance which Tony—and ultimately Dickens himself—want to uphold.

The author's efforts to close his fictions with an illusory unity reveal his fear of changing gender relations despite his liberal, reformist politics.[2] Not only have feminist critics of Dickens largely ignored his efforts to resolve artificially tensions within his construction of female figures, but most have also failed even to note the existence of ambiguity in his depiction of women and of "feminine" virtue.[3]

I

Dickens' ambiguous depictions of women depend upon the system of economic and political values that he promotes, values that privilege the bourgeoisie above all other classes.[4] His desires for women never escape the overlapping boundaries of capitalism and patriarchy. While he implies that "feminine" virtue transcends the material realm, he nevertheless structures women's moral influence so that it comes exclusively into the control of his middle-class heroes, men, who, though not as greedy as Ralph Nickleby, Mr. Merdle, or Josiah Bounderby, do support and succeed at capitalist economic practices. Nicholas Nickleby, and David Copperfield, for example, are, by their novels' end, as a result of their "honest" labor, comfortably middle class. Though Arthur Clennam momentarily succumbs to the Merdle "epidemic," he realizes his error before the novel closes and, returning to his old place as Daniel Doyce's business partner, "[w]ent down" with Little Dorrit, "into a modest life of usefulness and happiness" (II, ch. 34, 895). And the novel makes Arthur, despite his class differences from the heroine, appear a far more likely and more natural lover for Amy than the working-class Young John Chivery, a man Little Dorrit has known all her life and who, like her, has struggled in relative poverty.

Raymond Williams touched upon this paradox thirty years ago when, in *Culture and Society,* he noticed that Dickens, like many of his contemporaries, separates morality from bourgeois industrialism, and attempts to favor the former, alongside the realm of "culture," over "the processes of practical social judgment," offering it as a "mitigating and rallying alternative" (XVIII). But Williams's observation implies a separation that does not acknowledge the complicity between the two realms. Dickens' fictions reveal not the opposition but the interconnectedness of the "moral" and the "industrial." The spirituality Dickens pits against capitalism functions within a set of symbolic distinctions that the bourgeoisie can easily appropriate. Morality, like housekeeping and childraising, appears in Dickens' fictions to be women's work, existing outside of the marketplace, quietly and nebulously influencing the men who control Victorian society (Armstrong 44). Through an appeal to the ascetic or spiritual signs of culture—many of which are embodied in women's selflessness—the bourgeoisie legitimates its economic materialism.[5]

In *The Rape of Clarissa,* Terry Eagleton reminds us of a precept Antonio Gramsci outlines in his *Prison Notebooks*: "any revolutionary class, in addition to seizing political power, must secure *cultural* hegemony over its opponents" (1). Every social class creates alongside itself a group of intellectuals who give it "homogeneity and an awareness of its own function not only in the economic but also in the social and political fields" (Gramsci 5). The Victorian era saw the middle class solidify its economic power, as well as its control over cultural institutions. Popularly and critically acclaimed, Dickens' fictions—constituting and not simply reflecting social interests—promote the imagined universality of bourgeois values. Transvaluing economic and social conflicts into personal and psychological ones, his fictions repress the historical specificity of the oppressions on which their plots turn, emphasizing instead "feminine" or domestic values and romantic plots. The problem of the workhouse as an institution, for example, is raised but quickly displaced in *Oliver Twist*. When Dickens creates Agnes Fleming, the sister of Mrs. Maylie, as Oliver's mother, he transforms the poor orphan boy into a gentleman, and converts a novel about the effects of poverty upon children into a story about one gentlewoman's fall and one child's estrangement from his family (Marcus 54–91, *passim*).

Likewise, the real class differences separating Pip from Estella appear, by the end of *Great Expectations*, less significant than the personal effects Miss Havisham's psyche have upon her ward. The old woman's desire for revenge against all men, a rejection of the feminine selflessness that initially prompted her to love the penniless and deceitful Compeyson, emerges as the cause of Estella's coldness to Pip—and class differences between the hero and his lover fade. Estella tells Pip that her "suffering has been stronger than all other teaching, and has taught me to understand what your heart used to be" (ch. 59, 493).[6] Suppressed are the facts that Pip initially desired Estella over Biddy not because of the purity of his heart, but because of her class status, and that she disdained him as "a stupid, clumsy labouring-boy" (ch. 8, 90).

History seems to disappear from Dickens' novels. They apparently focus on specific material problems—the workhouse, the debtors' prison, the incompetence of government bureaucracies. But finally they privilege middle-class notions of sympathy that the author associates with a set of ideal feminine heroines whose guidance serves as a corrective to a Victorian society facing rapid industrial change, a society whose citizens honor appearances and displays of wealth—worship Ruskin's "Goddess of Getting-on"—rather than sincerity and truth.[7]

Establishing "feminine" virtue as both an essential female quality and an illusory corrective to "Society"—including bureaucratic governmental departments such as the Circumlocution Office and the Court of Chancery, fanatical religious and philantropic groups, and socialites like the Merdles and the Podsnaps—enables Dickens to criticize social standards without dismantling them. Because the "feminine" deviates from those standards, embodying everything they are not, it appears to exist as a viable alternative. Yet, if women's moral influence remains confined to the private realm, it women lack autonomous political and economic power, and if women do not exercise their "goodness" in ways that directly benefit themselves, feminine sympathy will not seriously threaten the dominant order which produced it.

At the same time, however, inherent contradictions embedded within ideologies of femininity may—despite their limitations—provide a liberating opening for women who take seriously the rhetoric of female goodness. Such women may employ their moral influences not only to reform the men in their lives but to empower themselves, either psychologically or politically. While Dickens, along with other advocates of the philosophy of separate gendered spheres of action, intends the idealization of feminine morality to illustrate women's natural aptitude for domestic duties, early feminists used this ideology subversively by extending it to its logical conclusion. Rather than assert the equality of the two sexes, they insisted that women enter the public sphere in order to compensate for men's moral deficiency (Vicinus 249).

For, as Janet Murray contends, "in a culture in which women were brought up to pride themselves on their selflessness, the creation of any standard by which they could affirm a strong moral character was one of the most basic ways to resist the limitations of their position" (20) The self-contradictory definition of woman's naturally transcendent character confines women to the domestic sphere and denies them political and economic power at the same time that it provides idealized feminine figures a moral superiority over men which makes women appear more apt—because more compassionate—for public work.

Critics like John Kucich and Nancy Armstrong, drawing on the work of Michael Foucault, argue that because "self-denial" and "human sympathy" are constructed by the dominant social order and essential to the middle-class "self," they cannot be used subversively.[8] For, they reason, an ideology produced to privilege one class over another cannot be manipulated by an oppressed group in a revolutionary way. However, they do contend that ideological contradictions may force a dominant class to concede reforms that ultimately leave exploitative structures intact.

Such arguments remind us that struggle at the level of ideology, struggle which does not focus upon economics, will remain primarily reformist. But this logic unnecessarily minimizes the extent to which social change, beginning on an ideological front, may develop into a struggle that transforms an oppressive material structure in the direction of a politically and economically democratic society.

The demand for female suffrage, for example, born from women's desire to extend their moral influence from the private sphere into the public realm—a demand that the dominant order was forced by the feminist suffrage movement to concede—had subversive political and economic consequences. Middle-class women entered the professions; many refused their subordinate familial position. Once in the professions, feminists demanded economic equality with men. Equal pay for equal work led to a demand for comparable worth, a demand that threatens one of the fundamental social divisions that capital seeks to exploit in its effort to perpetuate its own domination.

Likewise, the demand for *de jure* democratic rights for all may be born, as were the Chartists' six planks, from the ideological contradictions of capitalist societies that profess the possibility of "success" for anyone who works hard. But this struggle for democracy, taken to its logical conclusion, necessitates not only universal suffrage, not only significant social welfare legislation, but an end to the economic exploitation of one class by another—that is, an end to all political and economic inequality—and, eventually, an end to capitalism. For as Marx never tired of arguing, the "completion" of the bourgeois democratic revolution remains the indispensible precondition for those oppressed groups, who are now supposedly equal to their oppressors, to recognize the contradiction between their ostensible liberation and their ongoing economic exploitation.[9]

Whenever oppressed people probe the ideological contradictions promoted by the dominant order, they challenge that order—especially if it wishes to see itself as benign—to construct new arguments justifying its dominance. When Dickens allows his heroines to take seriously the moral authority with which Victorian bourgeois society endows them, he begins to lose control of his creations. Virtuous Dickensian women who exercise their own moral judgment gain a degree of psychological and emotional independence that leads them to question their dependence on men. Recognizing the limitations of her Uncle Ralph, for example, Kate Nickleby learns self-reliance. Likewise, Madeline Bray's confidence in her feminine morality leads to an emotional self-dependence that conflicts with Nicholas's desire to make her his wife. To minimize the subversive potential of female figures who exercise their goodness, Dickens must periodically undermine the power of his heroines' moral authority at the same time that he honors it. Thus his presentation of idealized heroines remains contradictory, and leaves him with a real dilemma. Even as he promotes their morality—the ideological prop for his disingenuous "alternative" to capitalism—he must also limit their ability to influence their world if he is to justify his decisions to marry them off and to confine them within the domestic realm. But to the extent that he limits their authority, he fails to offer even a temporary solution to the economic exploitation of which he cannot help but be aware.

Dickens' fictions favor traditionally feminine values while simultaneously revealing a fantasy of male autonomy—the myth of a world where women pose no threat because they make no demands. Alexander Welsh argues that Dickens wishes to embrace "the myth of woman who possesses powers without any threatening aspect" because faith in the "unchanging female principle makes death and history acceptable" (*Copyright,* 99–100). But belief in the "feminine" ideal serves a greater purpose than Welsh suggests. It allows men like Dickens, servants of the bourgeois social order that characterizes modern industrial societies, to make essential their social privilege, especially in terms of the power they possess over women. In Dickens' novels, women's voices become incoherent and their personalities and moral fortitude become increasingly more nebulous to the extent that they adhere to the ideal of "feminine" self-denial without crossing the thin line into a potentially liberating space of "feminine" assertiveness, Victorian style. And Dickens makes sure that his heroines toe that line, whatever the narrative or political costs to himself.

II

To become a "true" person with a "pure" heart involves, for Dickens, repressing selfish passions, denying personal desires and, in a sense, agreeing to relinquish independence in order to help others. But the repression of personal desires functions differently for Dickens' male characters than for his women. Ironically, the self-denial of male characters usually strengthens their self-image.[10] The embodiment of traditionally feminine qualities by bourgeois men allows them to think better of themselves. Women, by contrast, are not to gain self-confidence from selflessness, but are, according to Dickens, simply to recognize such behavior as natural. For female characters, self-denial exists less as a choice than as a necessity, and serves to confuse their goals and their sense of self.

Compare, for example, Nicholas Nickleby's repression of his love for Madeline Bray with his sister's denial of her love for Frank Cheeryble. When Nicholas decides not to declare his love to Madeline, he congratulates himself for behaving selflessly. Realizing that the Cheerybles brothers may think he has taken advantage of their confidence by falling in love with a woman they asked him to protect, he chooses to leave Madeline free to marry their nephew Frank, a match the brothers have wanted for years. Both because he wants to please his employers and because Kate hasn't any fortune, Nicholas tells his sister that she is right to refuse Frank's marriage proposal. Kate, however, wonders whether she really should reject Frank's "disinterested love" (NN, ch. 61). But Dickens muffles the force of her opposing voice, leaving Nicholas secure in the value of his own selflessness.

While Nicholas's self-sacrifice increases his estimation of himself, Kate's confuses and depresses her. Nicholas tries to console his sister by assuring her that their self-denial will ultimately strengthen them, and he fantasizes melodramatically about the comfort their virtuous decisions will yield in their old age: "[W]hen we are quaint old folks and talk of the times when our step was lighter and our hair not grey, we may even be thankful for the trials that so endeared us to each other, and turned our lives into that current down which we shall have glided so peacefully and calmly" (NN, ch. 61).

Kate's vague response to her brother's musings takes the form of tears. When she tells Nicholas that she feels pleased to have acted "as you would have had me," her self-denial appears to be motivated more by her desire to make him happy than by her sense of doing what is right. Asked by her brother if she regrets her decisions, she lacks the facility to express her feelings as eloquently as he does, and answers with a stutter:

N—n—no . . . I don't regret having done what was honourable and right, of course, but I do regret that this should have ever happened—at least sometimes I regret it, and sometimes I—I don't know what I say; I am but a weak girl Nicholas, and it has agitated me very much.

(NN, ch. 61)

Dickens' task as author remains a difficult one insofar as he tries to create women who are self-abnegating and submissive, but who are also able to express in "sincere" language their willingness to be so. Just one year before Dickens' death, John Stuart Mill explained that men require from women a great deal more than the actual service that most masters demand from their subjects: "Men do not want solely the obedience of women, they want their sentiments. All men, except the most brutish, desire to have, in the woman most nearly connected with them, not a forced slave but a willing one, not a slave merely, but a favourite . . ." (141).

Because Dickens wants to create heroines who feel affection for the men with whom they are connected, who are—in Mill's terms—"willing slaves," he needs to provide space within his narratives for his women to, if not proclaim, at least hint at the satisfaction they find in their submissive roles. By doing so, Dickens inadvertently reveals a paradox embedded within Victorian notions of "true womanliness": it is impossible for a speaker, no matter how incoherent her language, to appear, or for that matter to *be,* completely selfless. To speak is to posit oneself, even if only temporarily, as a subject, as a distinct identity. To quote from Monique Witting, "[W]hen one becomes a locutor, when one says "I" and, in so doing, reappropriates languages as a whole, it is then and there . . . that there occurs the supreme act of subjectivity . . ." (66)

Dickens tries to solve the problem by structuring his heroines as "false" subjects, granted the illusion of an "I" with only a limited possession of the power that accompanies the act of locution. In his efforts to qualify the possibility of female subjectivity, he limits women's speech—as illustrated in the abovementioned conversation between Nicholas and Kate Nickleby—and minimize the value of female self-denial. Because he creates his women to be inherently self-abnegating, sacrifice demands less from them than from his male characters. Numerous scenes in Dickens' fictions reveal instances when the suppression of personal desires potentially could offer women the same opportunities for ego development that it provides men. But Dickens attempts to discredit female self-denial as a "natural" force that women do not control and that, therefore, lacks the power of male repressions which, because consciously chosen, appear dynamic.

Natural "feminine" virtue, implies Dickens, is passive by definition. The womanly ideal stands as a "retiring beauty that must be sought out, for it cannot vaunt itself; if it could, it would be what it is, no more" (DS, ch. 33). "Feminine" greatness goes unnoticed by most unless it is reflected through "the great ones of the earth, when it becomes a constellation" (DS, ch. 33). A "slight, small, patient figure," Harriet Carker's "household virtues . . . have so little in common with the received idea of heroism and greatness" (DS, ch. 33). Though she does nothing to make the world notice her, or to make herself into an active, virtuous hero, her natural influence leads her brother John to reform his dishonest ways and to repay his "old lost debt" by dispensing to Mr. Dombey the interest of his inheritance from James (DS, ch. 58).

In contrast to this passive, natural virtue stands the active process through which Dickens' middle-class men learn both to deny their desires and thereby to re-create themselves as noble heroes. The younger Martin Chuzzlewit learns self-denial through his experiences with illness and poverty, and by actively analyzing the differences between himself and Mark Tapley as well as between himself and Mary Graham.

Ironically, heroes achieve selflessness only through an active process of self-discovery and self-control. Not until Martin Chuzzlewit the Younger comes to terms with his own development—"discern[s] the truth" of his selfishness—can he begin to deny his desires (MC, ch. 33). But Dickens refuses heroines this kind of self-knowledge. Though an understanding of himself enables Martin to recognize finally the selflessness of Mary Graham, it is Mary's lack of self-awareness—her absence not only of selfishness but of any sort of individual self—that prevents her from correctly analyzing Martin's selfish behavior: "That heart where self has found no place and raised no throne, is slow to recognize its ugly presence when it looks upon it. As one possessed of an evil spirit was held in old time to be alone conscious of the lurking demon in the breasts of other men, so kindred vices know each other in their hiding-places every day, when Virtue is incredulous and blind" (MC, ch. 14). Mary embodies the ignorance of innocence.

Struck ill, appropriately enough, in the City of Eden, Martin gains knowledge from his sins and, in a kind of reverse story of Adam and Eve, learns how to behave *as if* he were innocent.[11] He actively determines to act selflessly. As John Harmon of *Our Mutual Friend* feigns his death and re-creates himself as John Rokensmith, so the younger Martin experiences a symbolic death and rebirth in Eden. Resolved to root out selfishness from his breast, he determines to tell no one of his decision to change "but steadily to keep his purpose before his own eyes solely" (MC, ch. 33). This independence results from "humility and steadfastness" and "not a jot of pride," explains the narrator. But the effect increases Martin's vanity by enabling him to credit himself alone with his reformation. He denies the value of the emotional support he receives from Mary and Mark, and of the financial assistance his grandfather gives him. Though certainly a more sensitive character than Mr. Bounderby of *Hard Times,* Martin Chuzzlewit the Younger could, like the "banker, merchant, manufacturer, and what not" of Coketown, declare: "Here I am . . . and nobody to thank for my being here but myself" (HT, ch. 4).

Likewise, David Copperfield, narrating his own story, emphasizes the extent to which his private pain led to his self-creation: "That I suffered in secret, and that I suffered exquisitely, no one ever knew but I. How much I suffered, it is, as I have said already, utterly beyond my power to tell" (DC, ch. 11). But of course it is not beyond his power to tell, "as [he] ha[s] said already," over and over again. His "secret" suffering serves as the focal point of his narrative; for deprivation, he tells us, enables him to develop into the man he becomes, one capable of teaching himself shorthand, of working as a reporter, and of writing several favorably received novels. All this he accomplishes, so his story recalls, despite the lack of love he received as a orphan, and despite his work at Murdstone and Grinby's warehouse. In order to accentuate his solitude, David likewise represses the positive aspects of his childhood; and in his account of his self-creation he neglects to measure the effects the maternal love of Betsy Trotwood and of Peggotty have had upon him.[12] Though Dickens criticizes Josiah Bounderby for a similar refusal to acknowledge the help he has received from his mother, Mrs. Pegler, the author does not question David's denial of his female guardians.

Translating Agnes's letters into his own words, much as Tony Weller restates his wife's deathbed speech, David disguises praise of himself as the thoughts of a friend and strengthens his image as a self-made man who succeeds despite adversity:

> She knew (she said) how such a nature as mine would turn affliction to good. She knew how trial and emotion would exalt and strengthen it. . . . As the endurance of my childish days had done its part to make me what I was; so greater calamities would nerve me on, to be better yet than I was. . . .
>
> (DC, ch. 58)

As Martin Chuzzlewit, isolated in Eden with a delirious Mark Tapley, discovers self-knowledge, so David, alone in Switzerland for three years after

Dora's death, works to "penetrate the mystery of my own heart," and "to get a better understanding of myself" (DC, ch. 58). David's inner quest implies his belief in an essential self whose secrets, once exposed, will provide a key to his desires. The shape of this self remains relatively stable despite social circumstances. Thus, it is not further contact with Agnes that changes the contours of David's relationship with her. Rather, introspection apart from the women he has, until now, considered a sister, leads him to realize that "he has long loved her" (DC, Appendix C, 736).

Not until he exposes the desires he has unconsciously repressed can David consciously choose to deny their fulfillment and, through a dynamic self-denial that parallels those of Nicholas Nickleby and Martin Chuzzlewit, the Younger, "convert what might have been between myself and Agnes, into a means of making me more self-denying, more resolved, *more conscious of myself,* and my defeats and errors" (DC, ch. 58, emphasis added). Despite the temporary nature of David's decision not to pursue his longing for Agnes—he does propose to her soon after he returns to England—this repression increases his self-awareness while it enables him to mold himself into a better man. Although Tony Weller mocks his wife's religious belief that she has "god hold o' some inwention for grown-up people being born again . . . the new birth I think they calls it" (PP, ch. 22), Dickens accepts the possibility that heroic male characters can, with the help of neither mortals nor gods, create themselves anew.

While *David Copperfield* provides ample space for its narrator and hero to recount his suffering, David himself repeatedly complains about Mrs. Gummidge's inability to keep her sorrows to herself: hers was "rather a fretful disposition, and she whimpered more sometimes than was comfortable for other parties in so small an establishment" (DC, ch. 3). Despite her self-indulgence, however, her "feminine" virtue, which she does not need to develop as David does his selflessness, "naturally" appears when Emily elopes and Mr. Peggotty needs a woman to organize his household: "What a change in Mrs. Gummidge in a little time! She was another woman. She was so devoted, she had such a quick perception of what it would be well to say, and what it would be well to leave unsaid, she was so forgetful of herself, and so regardful of the sorrow around her . . ." (DC, ch. 32).

Without effort, without a struggle to gain self-knowledge, Mrs. Gummidge behaves like all of Dickens' selfless heroines do—naturally. As Lizzie Hexam was "[a]ccustomed from her very babyhood promptly to do the thing that could be done [for her home, her father and her brother]—whether to keep out weather, to ward off cold, to postpone hunger, or what not—" (OMF, I, ch.

6), as Little Dorrit, from an early age, keeps family accounts, cares for her father, and provides schooling for her brother and sister (LD, I, ch. 7), as Little Nell takes the place of mother to her grandfather, soothing "him with gentle and tender words, smil[ing] at his thinking that they could ever part, and rally[ing] him cheerfully" (OCS, ch. 15), so Mrs. Gummidge instinctively acts as ideal housekeeper.

Dickens' narratives appear to reject the idea of direct confrontation with one's enemies, aspiring instead to develop a society where moral people patiently wait for the good in everyone to reveal itself. Still, male characters frequently resort to the direct expression of the passions they have repressed, especially when indirect influence proves an ineffective method by which to gain power. Though Martin Chuzzlewit, Senior represses his disgust for Pecksniff throughout most of the novel, he overtly displays his anger before the close of the narrative, beating Peckniff with his stick and declaring him to be a scoundrel. Likewise, John Harmon and Mr. Boffin suppress their ill feelings towards Silas Wegg throughout most of *Our Mutual Friend* only to enjoy, finally, the pleasure of actively participating in his downfall by instructing Sloppy to literally throw him into the street. In *Little Dorrit,* quiet, self-denying Uncle Fred vindicates Amy in a way that Dickens would never allow a virtuous woman to defend herself; Fred objects to the pride and ingratitude of the newly wealthy Dorrits that enable them to forget all that Amy did in their poverty: "I protest against any one of us here who have known, and have seen what we have seen, setting up any pretension that puts Amy at a moment's disadvantage, or to the cost of a moment's pain" (LD, II, ch. 5). Immediately following his outburst he returns to his "usual weak condition" (LD, II, ch. 5). The most submissive of men may, in certain situations, actively express himself.

Even Nicholas Nickleby, a young man so conscious of his duty to his employer that he admits he would have told the evil Squeers of innocent Smike's plans to run away had he himself known of them (NN, ch. 13), eventually reaches a point where he can no longer repress his true feelings for the Yorkshire schoolmaster. When Squeers begins to whip the captured Smike, Nicholas cries, " 'Stop!' in a voice that made the rafters ring." Realizing the futility of his humble attempts to exert a moral influence upon his master—Squeers had "disregarded all my quiet interference in the miserable lad's behalf"—he opts for a more active approach to end Squeers' injustice: "Concentrating into that one moment all his feelings of rage, scorn, and indignation, Nicholas sprang upon [Squeers], wrested the weapon from his hand, and, pinning him by the throat, beat the ruffian till he roared for mercy" (NN, ch. 13). Despite the intensity of the violence and Nicholas's "unpleasant doubts"—soon proved unwarranted—that he has killed his employer (NN, ch. 13), the narrator assures his readers that the hero is innocent of all wrongdoing. His subsequent separation from his family by his uncle exists as an injury to a man whose actions were justified.

<h1 style="text-align:center">III</h1>

The direct expression of repressed feelings allowed heroes is a privilege Dickens denies his female characters, who must depend solely upon their moral influence to right the injustices they experience. Often, however, heroines have more success exerting this influence than do the male characters who are given a comparatively wider latitude with which to develop it. While the revenge women effect against those who harm them is not as definitive as that of Dickensian heroes, it still exists as a powerful force in Dickens' fiction, revealing one way in which ideal "femininity" exceeds male control and provides individual women the moral authority needed to assert themselves while they degrade abusive men. Kate Nickleby, for example, uses her "feminine" authority to confront and scold her Uncle Ralph, causing him to question his behavior in a way he has never done before. Though she becomes meek and silent once Nicholas returns home to "protect" her, she manages to care for herself effectively while her brother is away.

Kate actually suffers more trials than her brother, including the attentions of Mr. Mantalini and Sir Mulberry Hawk, as well as the jealousy of Miss Knag and Mrs. Wititterly. Ralph Nickleby places both his niece and nephew in situations where their duties to their employers prohibit honorable action. But after leaving Squeers, Nicholas manages to free himself from his uncle's power by finding employment without Ralph's aid. Kate's gender, however, denies her the opportunity to make her own fortune. Though unhappy at Madame Mantalini's establishment, she leaves only when Miss Knag, acquiring the business, dismisses her. Likewise, she does not leave the Wititterlies, where she has been "so very, very miserable," until her brother rescues her (NN, ch. 33). In revealing her inability to effect change in her own life, Dickens appears to understand some of the limitations placed upon young Victorian gentlewomen who found themselves in need of money.

"Respectable" employment for a middle-class woman living in the Victorian period—work that would not harm her innocence by unduly exposing her to harsh social realities—consisted primarily of needlework, serving as a lady's companion, or working as a governess. Kate Nickleby holds successively the former two jobs. Despite her inability to leave her situations on her own initiative, Kate does succeed in making her dissatisfaction known to the man acting as her paternal guardian—her Uncle Ralph. Without convincing him to change significantly his behavior towards her, she exerts her "feminine" virtue in a way that discomfits him and forces him to realize that he has neglected his duty to her. Perhaps because Kate recognizes her moral superiority to her uncle, she speaks to him without the hesitation with which she addresses her brother, and she eloquently expresses her righteous anger.

Leaving Ralph's dinner party after suffering Sir Mulberry's insults, Kate, "violently agitated," tells her uncle "that beneath the roof where I, a helpless girl, your dead brother's child, should most have found protection, I have been exposed to insult which should make you shrink to look upon me." Implied in Kate's outburst to her uncle is the sense of shame he should feel for subjecting her to a situation that would force her to listen to a sexual proposition. Her knowledge of the extent to which he has neglected his responsibility as her guardian encourages her articulate discourse and enables her, temporarily, to gain power over him. Under the eyes of the "indignant girl," states the narrator, "Ralph *did* shrink" (NN, ch. 19).

Peter Cominos tells us that daughters of respectable Victorians were thought to exist in a state of innocence or inherent purity dependent upon their ignorance of their own sexuality. When exposed to sexual knowledge, the chastity of the young girl became vulnerable (Cominos 157). Neglecting to keep Kate from men who force her to become dangerously aware of her sexuality, Ralph pushes her towards her potential fall. Kate's "feminine" virtue, her just sense of having been abused, shames Ralph and leads the greedy old man actually to put Kate's feelings before profit. Momentarily gaining control over the usurer, Kate leads him not simply to turn Sir Mulberry, an important business connection, from his house, but to feel reluctant to pursue his plan to use his niece to strengthen his ties with Lord Frederick Verisopt. When Hawk confronts Ralph, asking him to deny "that your pretty niece was not brought here as a decoy for the drunken boy [the Lord]," the powerful money-lender reveals his fear of his brother's daughter. Before answering he "looked involuntarily round to ascertain that Kate had not moved her position so as to be within hearing." Recognizing her as one "who has patiently yielded to all his wishes; who had tried so hard to please him," he feels "awkward and nervous" (NN, ch. 19).

Kate's "feminine" virtue forces Ralph to acknowledge the injustice of his "masculine" business practice in a way that Nicholas's outbursts do not. After Ralph accuses his nephew of unjustly attacking Wackford Squeers, Nicholas threatens that "a day or reckoning" will arrive "sooner or later." But the hero does not unnerve Ralph or lead him to question his own morality as Kate does. In response to his nephew's warning "Ralph did not allow a muscle of his face to indicate that he heard one word of this parting address. He hardly knew that it was concluded . . ." (NN, ch. 20). Contrast this rigidity to his reaction when Kate leaves his home after her fateful encounter with Hawk. Her uncle, "who was proof against all appeals of blood and kindred—who was steeled against every tale of sorrow and distress—staggered while he looked, and reeled back into his house, as a man who had seen a spirit from some world beyond the grave." Kate's pained expression recalls for Ralph an image of his dead brother "on some occasion of boyish grief" and forces him to remember the feelings of love he once bore his play-fellow (NN, ch. 19).

In response to Kate's "feminine" influence, Ralph questions momentarily the "two great morals" he has believed since his boyhood: "that riches are the only true source of happiness and power, and that it is lawful and just to compass their acquisition by all means short of felony" (NN, ch. 1). Even the nearly 2,000 pounds he has made from Lord Verisopht do not seem to him to justify "selling a girl—throwing her in the way of temptation, and insult, and coarse speech" (NN, ch. 26). Though he loves none of "God's creatures. . . . there had somehow stolen upon him from time to time a thought of his niece which was tinged with compassion and pity; breaking through the dull cloud of dislike or indifference which darkened men and women in his eyes, there was, in her case, the faintest gleam of light . . . and it showed the girl in a better and purer aspect than any in which he had looked on human nature yet" (NN, ch. 26). Later, Ralph will think about "what his home might be if Kate were there" and he will realize "in that one glimpse of a better nature" that "he was friendless, childless, and alone. Gold, for the instant, lost its lustre in his eyes, for there were countless treasures of the heart which it would never purchase" (NN, ch. 31).

"[F]or the instant," Kate's "feminine" moral authority triumphs over her uncle's greed. Gaining strength from an ideology meant to confine her and Victorian "ladies," Kate asserts herself. She employs her goodness not to promote the interests of a man in her life, but to declare her own anger at a male relative who mistreats her. Defeating her guardian, she proves her ability to "guard" herself.

As if unwilling to pursue the potentially subversive consequences of Kate's show of self-dependence, Dickens quickly disempowers the female character he previously endowed with moral authority. Her victory proves to be shortlived. Ralph resumes his "accustomed business attitude" (NN, ch. 31). Retreating from her formerly bold stance, Kate continues her work as an exploited lady's companion for an unprincipled woman. Unable to escape on her own, or to shame her employer as she does her uncle, she must suffer until her brother Nicholas rescues her and tucks her safely away in a cottage he provides.

Dickens' reluctance to challenge the dominant order of the Victorian society he criticizes becomes especially clear when he robs Kate, the one character who appears capable of affecting Ralph, of further opportunities to exert her influence. For Dickens does not want a woman capable of shaming and proving her superiority to bourgeois men to function as his heroine. Instead, from this point on, he de-emphasizes Kate's moral authority. In order to prevent her from affirming herself as the independent agent she became in the above- mentioned scene with her Uncle Ralph, Dickens transfers Kate to the control of another bourgeois male—her brother. Rather than assert her individual moral worth, Kate now functions only to shore up Nicholas's ego, regressing into a lovely human mirror, a woman "invested by the (masculine) 'subject' to reflect himself, to copy himself" (Irigaray 30). She serves to reassure Nicholas that his decision to leave London was a heroic one—a decision that, to readers, seems questionable at best, especially when we consider the pleasure he finds with the Crummles while Kate suffers without the protection of a man who cares for her. "Tell me," he commands his sister, "that we parted because I feared to bring misfortune on your head; that it was a trial to me no less than to yourself . . ." (NN, ch. 33).

Depriving his sister of the self-assertion that strengthens her character and enables her to disconcert Ralph, Nicholas transforms Kate into a beautiful object of his contemplation, one which reflects his success as a provider: the pride that Kate takes in the cottage is "nothing to the pride with which Nicholas looked at Kate herself; and surely the costliest mansion in all England might have found in her beautiful face and graceful form its most exquisite and peerless ornament" (NN, ch. 43). By the time Madeline Bray enters their home, Kate clearly fulfills her role as her brother's mirror: "Madeline . . . with the image of Nicholas so constantly recurring in the features of his sister . . . could scarcely separate the two" (NN, ch. 55). Kate spends the majority of her time by Madeline's sickbed commending her brother's actions. "What wonder, if with every hour of returning health, there came some stronger and sweeter recognition of the praises which Kate . . . would lavish on her brother; where would have been the wonder even if those praises had found a quick response in the breast of Madeline" (NN, ch. 55). Before she recovers completely, Madeline, like Kate, will acquiesce to enact her role as Nicholas's reflection.

Dickens' narratives frequently transform the strength that woman derive from exercising their own morality into the kind of female mirroring described above. By suppressing the potential power of women who assert their culturally prescribed "femininity"—without necessarily aiding any man—for their own benefit, such fictions will the "truth" of Ralph's statement that women are "easy things to understand and control" (NN, ch. 54). Ralph designs his assertion to convince Arthur Gride that, because women are quickly satisfied, he has no need to fear that "a gallant young rival" will seduce Madeline. Of course, a rival does take Madeline from her fiancé, but both Ralph and Gride underestimate Miss Bray when they imagine that she would "belong" to the old usurer if she ever became his wife. Affiancing herself to Gride, Madeline controls and defines herself in a way that she cannot when her relationship with Nicholas develops. Though Dickens wants to oppose Gride's interested desire for Madeline to Nicholas's disinterested love, the young hero actually demands more from the heroine than does the usurer.

The self-sacrifice Madeline voluntarily makes when she decides to marry the old man will enable her to free her father from debtor's prison. More importantly, this selfless act allows her to develop a self that she may either satisfy or deny, much as Nicholas's later decision not to marry Madeline lest he appear ungrateful to the Cherrybles provides him an opportunity to develop himself as an independent individual. In part, Madeline's self-sacrifice resembles Lizzie Hexam's in *Our Mutual Friend* when she chooses not to become Eugene Wrayburn's mistress but still feels "proud and glad to suffer something for him, even though it is of no service to him, and he will never know of it or care for it" (OMF, III, ch. 9). In order for feminine ideals to feed the dominant power structure—and shore up the bourgeois male—middle-class men must be the recipients of their women's selfless acts. The woman who sacrifices herself without worrying what her man thinks, behaves not subserviently but independently. Lizzie's decision not to fulfill her longing for Wrayburn allows her to develop a self independent of her father and brother, a self that she alone controls.

Marrying Gride would likewise permit Madeline to feel proud of a sacrifice she made without the help of her benefactors. When Nicholas urges her to postpone her marriage for one week, she refuses, speaking forcefully: "I am happy in the prospect of all I can achieve so easily, and shall be more so when I look back upon it, and all is done, I know" (NN, ch. 53). Something in her face, a mysterious expression Nicholas cannot name, "quite unmanned him, and appeared far more touching than the wildest agony of grief. It was not merely calm and composed, but fixed and rigid, as though the violent effort which had summoned that composure beneath her father's eye, while it mastered all other thoughts, had prevented even the momentary expression they had communicated to the features from subsiding, and had fastened it there as evidence of its triumph" (NN, ch. 53).

"Unmanned" before Madeline's determination, Nicholas works to weaken her resolve by speaking of her father's "tricks and wiles" (NN, ch. 53). Imploring her to reconsider, he throws himself in front of her literally to block her passage from him. Here, as in his earlier confrontation with Squeers, he relies upon physical strength when self-denial appears unsuccessful; he allows Madeline to leave him only when his will seems to triumph over hers and her speech becomes hesitant and supplicating. To his pleas, "she *incoherently* replied. . . . 'Have mercy on me, Sir, I beseech. . . . I—I hear him calling; I—I—must not, will not, remain here for another instant' " (NN, ch. 53, emphasis added).

In preventing Madeline Bray from carrying out her self-sacrifice, Dickens stifles the development of her self and prevents her virtue from triumphing over the immoral business practices of Ralph and Gride. On the morning of the wedding ceremony, this struggle between female goodness and masculine usury is transformed into a battle between three men for the possession of one woman. No longer a subject actively involved in a moral conflict, Madeline becomes instead the passive object—the spoils—of masculine combat. After Walter Bray's timely death. Madeline falls into a long swoon and is incapable of speaking for herself. Nicholas, again resorting to a violent expression of the "passion he had restrained till now," pushes Gride and Ralph from his path, "and then taking his beautiful burden in his arms rushed violently out" (NN, ch. 54.)

When Madeline recovers from "the state of stupefaction into which the sudden death of her father happily plunged her," her triumphant self-confidence has vanished, and she suffers an illness that "threatened her reason, and—scarcely worse—her life itself" (NN, ch. 55). The self-determination engendered by her decision to sacrifice marital happiness dissolves into a selflessness not derived from conscious choice, but from a 'literal absence of independent identity. Though the times when Nicholas expresses his repressed emotions enable him to act with violent strength, Madeline's release of restrained feelings weakens her: "When the delicate physical powers which have been sustained by an unnatural strain upon the mental energies and a resolute determination not to yield, at last give way, their degree of prostration is usually proportionate to the strength of the effort which previously upheld them" (NN, ch. 55). But such prostration does not occur when men release restraints they have placed upon themselves. Dickens needs Madeline to reveal extreme weakness after her displays of strength so that he may confine her anew within a stereotype of female frailty from which she had managed, momentarily, to escape.

As they succumb to Nicholas's protection, both Kate and Madeline renounce (or are robbed of) any independence that their morality and self-denials may provide them. Such submissions exemplify the author's desire for heroines whose sacrifices never lead to self-sufficiency. But despite the inherent limitations of any exercise of "feminine" goodness, the power Dickens' women do achieve stems from their ability to embody virtues promoted by Victorian domestic ideologies. Threatening the stability of bourgeois patriarchal power are the very qualities, feminine morality and beauty, that men desire women to possess but never to employ on their own behalf.

In order to uphold the dominant order, Dickens must honor feminine selflessness without empowering the individual women who embody it. His narratives reveal the self-contradictions of patriarchy that insist upon the inherent selflessness of female nature while simultaneously emphasizing the need to stifle women's independence in order to preserve traditional gender hierarchies. His female figures suggest the real and complex demands Victorian bourgeois and patriarchal society makes upon its feminine idols: they must be selfless while simultaneously possessing a powerful moral nature; they must remain ignorant of social and political problems but capable of assuring male relatives of their ability to succeed in the public realm; and they must act virtuously and naively while appearing sexually desirable to men. Such contradictions need to be diagnosed if feminists are to understand the important and various effects models of ideal femininity have had, and to an extent still do have, upon women. Though less powerful now than a century ago, these models continue to exercise control over female identity and to limit women's social and political roles.

NOTES

1. Michele Barrett carefully details one important problem with feminists' use of the term "patriarchy": "[N]ot only is it by and large resistant to exploration within a particular mode of production, but it is redolent of a universal and trans-historical oppression. So, to use the concept is frequently to invoke a generality of male domination without being able to specify historical limits, changes or differences" (14). By repeated references to Victorian ideal of femininity, I attempt to ground my discussion of patriarchy in specific historical circumstances while simultaneously drawing readers' attention to similarities between nineteenth-century and modern sexism. Likewise, I mean to discredit the notion that women's oppression is either universal or biologically determined. With Alison Jaggar, I conceptualize both production and procreation as historical processes "constituted by the ever-changing dialectical relationship between human reproductive biology and the forms of social organization" (76). While capitalist modes of production dictate gender relationships, no complete socialist analysis can disregard the extent to which women's subjection, like racial and homosexual oppression, exceeds capitalist production, depending in part on sexist, racist, and heterosexist ideologies that, whatever their origin and consequences within the material realm, often transcend capitalism as an economic system.

2. For discussions of the limitations of Dickens' attitudes toward class reform— especially of his attempts to transvalue economic complexities into moral principles—see Steven Marcus, *Dickens from Pickwick to Dombey* (esp. 44–8; 54–91, *passim*) and Patrick Brantlinger, *The Spirit of Reform*. See also Badri Raina's analysis of *David Copperfield* in *Dickens and the Dialectic of Growth*. By the time Dickens began work on this autobiographical novel, argues Raina, he has become a professional and financial success within the culture he reproves. At the heart of *David Copperfield* lies the contradiction between the hero's personal class ambitions and his denuciation of the principles of industrialism capitalism: "Throughout his life David wishes he were Steerforth." Nonetheless, he fears his resemblance to Uriah Heep (84–5).

3. For the most part, feminist scholars like Françoise Basch, Carolyn Heilbrun, and Gail Cunningham have rightly emphasized the unreality of Dickens' women. Yet by focusing discussion of Dickens' female figures upon their authenticity, feminist critics have not fully accounted for the effects oppressive and contradictory ideologies of femininity have upon the lived experience of real women.

   Two exceptions to this generalization are Margaret Flanders Darby's "Four Women in *Our Mutual Friend*" and Ruth Bernard Yeazell's "Podsnappery, Sexuality, and the English Novel." Darby notes that the women in Dickens' last completed novel "tend to escape the limitations we expect will confine [them], but at the same time each remains confined" (26). Though she uses her analyses of female characters to draw conclusions about Dickens' ambivalence towards the institution of marriage, she does not explore what I see as a more important issue—Dickens' anxiety about female power and changing gender roles.

   Likewise discussing Dickens' ambiguous depiction of women, Yeazell argues that despite his recognition of the limitations of Podsnappery—its refusal to acknowledge anything that would cause a young woman to blush—Dickens himself, by returning Georgina to Podsnap's protection before she marries Fledgeby and discovers the Lammles' deceit, prevents her from gaining knowledge of the world that could dispell her innocence. Though Dickens mocks

Podsnap for creating an impossible ideal of feminine ignorance, the author himself inadvertently perpetuates that ideal.

4. See Eve Sedgwick's provocative study of sixteenth to nineteenth-century English literature, *Between Men: English Literature and Male Homosocial Desire* (esp. 161–200, *passim*), and Nancy Armstrong's *Desire and Domestic Fiction: A Political History of the Novel*. The attempts of both Sedgwick and Armstrong to correlate sexual and social power have greatly influenced my thinking.

5. For a similar phenomenon in the Victorian U.S. see Ann Douglas, *The Feminization of American Culture* (55–64) and Stephanie Coontz, *The Social Origins of Private Life* (161–286).

6. In Dickens' original ending, Estella claims that her suffering has "been stronger than Miss Havisham's teaching" (ch. 59, 496n).

7. For an analysis of the ways belief in female purity and fidelity helped maintain a Christian ideal of morality in a Victorian culture where Christian faith was waning, see Jenni Calder's *Marriage in Victorian Fiction* (esp. 88). Also see Alexander Welsh's *The City of Dickens* for an exploration of Dickens' construction of "the hearth" as a remedy for social problems in an age of ebbing Christian faith (141–63, *passim*).

8. See John Kucich's *Repression in Victorian Fiction: Charlotte Bronte, George Eliot, and Charles Dickens* (*passim*, esp. 2–40), and Nancy Armstrong's *Desire and Domestic Fiction* (*passim*, esp. 55, 254–5).

9. See Karl Marx, "On the Jewish Question," and *The German Ideology*. For an excellent commentary on the revolutionary potential in what many pejoratively refer to as democratic reforms, see Hall Draper, *Karl Marx's Theory of Revolution*, Vol. I: *State and Bureaucracy* (ch. 5).

10. For many of my ideas about the productive nature of repression, I am indebted to John Kucich, *Repression in Victorian Fiction*. Unfortunately, Kucich does not explore the relationship between the production of repression and gender.

11. Welsh places Dickens' version of the fall within an eighteenth-century tradition that emphasizes both satiric and romantic elements in order to illustrate the hero's movement away from nature toward a definition of the self (*Copyright* 66–73). Raina argues that contradictions embodied in Martin Chuzzlewit's Edenic conversion, which enable him both to recognize the evils of greed and inherit his grandfather's money without ill effect, parallel Dickens' own confused relationship to the bourgeois commercialism he denounced as evil and simultaneously required for his own professional success (58–61).

12. Writing about "the death that men fear from the act of generation, which they imagine women do not fear," Alexander Welsh argues that Dickens, like many male novelists, evades confronting his ambiguous feelings about mothering. Instead, he simply disposes of mothers in his fiction, or he ridicules them (*Copyright* 139).

WORKS CITED

Armstrong, Nancy, *Desire and Domestic Fiction: A Political History of the Novel*. New York: Oxford UP, 1987.

Barrett, Michele, *Women's Oppression Today: Problems in Marxist Feminist Analysis*. London: Verso, 1984.

Basch, Francoise, *Relative Creatures: Victorian Women in Society and the Novel, 1837–67*. London: Allen Lane, 1974.

Brantlinger, Patrick, *The Spirit of Reform*. Cambridge: Harvard UP, 1977.

Calder, Jenni, *Marriage in Victorian Fiction*. New York: Oxford UP, 1976.

Cominos, Peter, "Innocent Femina Sensualis in Unconscious Conflict." *Suffer and Be Still: Women in the Victorian Age*. Ed. Martha Vicinus. Bloomgington: Indiana UP, 1972, 155–172.

Coontz, Stephanie, *The Social Origins of Private Life: A History of American Families, 1600–1900*. New York: Verso, 1988.

Cunningham, Gail, *The New Woman and the Victorian Novel*. New York: Barnes and Noble, 1978.

Darby, Margaret Flanders, "Four Women in *Our Mutual Friend*." *Dickensian* 83 (Spring 1987): 25–39.

Dickens, Charles, *David Copperfield*. New York: Oxford UP, 1986.

———,*Dombey and Son*. New York: Penguin, 1985.

———,*Great Expectations*. New York: Penguin, 1982.

———,*Hard Times*. New York: Penguin, 1981.

———,Little Dorrit. New York: Penguin, 1983.

———,*Martin Chuzzlewit*. New York: Penguin, 1985.

———,*Nicholas Nickleby*. New York: Penguin, 1987.

———,*The Old Curiosity Shop*. New York: Penguin, 1984.

———,*Our Mutual Friend*. New York: Penguin, 1984.

———,*The Pickwich Papers*. New York: Penguin, 1987.

Douglas, Ann, *The Feminization of American Culture*. New York: Avon, 1977.

Draper, Hal, *Karl Marx's Theory of Revolution, Vol. 1: State and Bureaucracy*. 3 vols. New York: Monthly Review Press, 1977.

Duchen, Claire, *Feminism in France: From May '68 to Mitterand*. Boston: Routledge & Kegan Paul, 1986.

Eagleton, Terry, *The Rape of Clarissa*. Minneapolis: U of Minnesota P, 1982.

Gramsci, Antonio, *Selection from the Prison Notebooks*. Trans. Quintin Hoare and Geoffrey Nowell Smith. New York: International Publishers, 1987.

Heilbrun, Carolyn, *Toward a Recognition of Androgyny*. New York: Knopf, 1973.

Irigaray, Luce, *This Sex Which Is Not One*. Trans. Catherine Porter. Ithaca: Cornell UP, 1985.

Jaggar, Alison, *Feminist Politics and Human Nature*. NJ: Rowman and Allanheld, 1983.

Johnson, Edgar, *Charles Dickens: His Tragedy and His Triumph*. 2 vols. New York: Simon and Schuster, 1952.

Kucich, John, *Repression in Victorian Fiction: Charlotte Bronte, George Eliot, and Charles Dickens*. Berkeley: U of California P. 1987.

Marcus, Steven, *Dickens from Pickwick to Dombey*. New York: Norton, 1985.

Marx, Karl, *The German Ideology, The Marx-Engels Reader*. Ed. Robert C. Tucker. New York: Norton, 1978, 146–200.

———,"On the Jewish Question." *The Marx-Engels Reader:* 26–52.

Mill, John Stuart, "The Subjection of Women." *Essays On Sex Equality*. Ed. Alice S. Rossi. Chicago: U of Chicago P, 1970.

Murray, Janet, *Strong Minded Women and Other Lost Voices from Nineteenth-Century England*. New York: Pantheon, 1982.

Raina, Badri, *Dickens and the Dialectic of Growth*. Madison: U of Wisconsin P, 1986.

Sedgwick, Eve Kosofsky, *Between Men: English Literature and Male Homosocial Desire*. New York: Columbia UP, 1985.

Vicinus, Martha, *Independent Women: Work and Community for Single Women, 1858–1920*. Chicago: U of Chicago P, 1985.

Welsh, Alexander, *The City of Dickens*. Oxford: Oxford UP, 1971.

———, *From Copyright to Copperfield*. Cambridge: Harvard UP, 1987.

Williams, Raymond, *Culture and Society: 1780–1950*. New York: Columbia UP, 1983.

Wittig, Monique, The Mark of Gender." *The Poetics of Gender*. Ed. Nancy K. Miller. New York: Columbia UP, 1986.

Yeazell, Ruth Bernard, "Podsnappery, Sexuality, and the English Novel," *Critical Inquiry* 9 (1982): 339–57.

Debtors and Creditors in Dickens' Fiction

C. R. B. Dunlop

1.

A recurring situation in the novels of Charles Dickens is that of the debtor who owes money to a harsh and unforgiving creditor. When the debt is not paid, the creditor may sue, go to judgment for the amount owing, and resort to execution against the property or the person of the hapless debtor. The creditor-debtor relationships and the process of debt collection are significant, often crucial, elements in Dickens' plots and are also important in establishing the station or place of characters in the world of the novels.

In this paper, I want to look first at the commercial and legal situation of debtors and creditors in Victorian England. I then want to turn to the novels and see how Dickens makes use of this material. My argument will be that Dickens' fiction reflects a Victorian ambivalence about and fear of debt as a dangerous personal and social activity.[1]

2.

Debt was an important part of commercial life in the nineteenth century.[2] Businesses and factories needed initial and continuing supplies of capital. Wholesalers and retailers frequently obtained their stock in trade on credit.

Some forms of retailing, especially door-to-door sales of clothing by so-called tallymen or Scotch drapers, were habitually carried out on a credit basis. Pawnbrokers were a common credit-granting agency, particularly in working class districts (Tebbutt). Employees were often paid irregularly, even annually, and were therefore creditors of their employers.

A recently published study of court records for the Courts of King's Bench, Common Pleas, and Exchequer from 1740 to 1840 estimates that between 90 percent and 95 percent of all actions commenced in these courts were brought by contract creditors to collect debts (Francis 810–11). The figures seem high, but there can be no doubt that debt collection was and is a substantial part of the courts' day-to-day business.[3]

Partly as a result of these commercial realities, debt began to be viewed by nineteenth-century writers as an acceptable and necessary element of a market economy (Rubin and Sugarman 43–44). A report by the Commissioners of Bankruptcy, published in 1840, expresses this view:

> Credit must be, or commerce cannot be, and without it, no civilization. All transactions have a claim to credit, from the milk score or the newspaper bill to the State loan.

The attitude here is that debt, whether incurred by businesses or consumers, is not immoral, but may instead be a legitimate and sensible part of a free enterprise society.

Alongside these positive statements can be found very different expressions of fear and hostility towards debt, especially as a personal strategy. Victorian periodical literature, including Dickens' *Household Words* and *All the Year Round*, carried many articles about debt.[4] Their thrust is partly to press for law reform, but they also carry the express or implicit message that debt is a dangerous way to improve one's financial or social position.

There are many descriptions of grasping and heartless creditors and moneylenders[5] and fraudulent or insolvent debtors.[6] Some writers go so far as to repeat Polonius's advice to avoid debt altogether. The flavor can be caught from the opening paragraphs of an essay published in *All the Year Round* in 1864:

> The greatest curse of this land is not, as some imagine drink, but debt. . . . In whatever rank of society you move, from the very highest down to the very lowest, you cannot live long without becoming acquainted with men and women who are a trouble to themselves, and to their friends, through owing money. So completely does insolvency pervade society, that those who are not

in debt are almost as much victims to the consequences as those who are. What does it avail me that I pay on the nail for everything, and owe no man anything, when I have relatives, and friends, and acquaintances who are in debt to every one with whom they deal? They come and carry off the money I have saved by my prudence and economy; they come and vex my heart with distresses, which, in my own case, I have taken infinite pains to avoid. They make their debts my debts, and their troubles my troubles. I might almost as well have incurred debt and trouble for myself.

I have lost all patience with these people, and I intend now to read them a lecture. I trust it may do them good.[7]

The Victorian ambivalence about debt can be illustrated by examining two major law reform debates concerning the repeal of the usury statutes and the reform of creditors' remedies.[8] Many medieval lawyers regarded interest on a debt as forbidden by Scripture and by the common law.[9] But the Bible is unclear on the issue, and the common law vacillated on the propriety of interest. As a result, statutes were passed which, under the guise of forbidding usury, had the effect of legalizing it up to a maximum percentage. The percentage varied but, by the beginning of the nineteenth century, the maximum rate, set in 1713, was 5 percent (1713 statute).

During the Victorian period, there was a major political and social debate about whether the 1713 Act should be repealed, or retained with amendments. Articles were published in the periodicals,[10] and the issue was addressed in four separate statutes (1837, 1839, 1850, 1854). The last of these repealed all preceding usury statutes and left general interest rates without any legal control until the passage of the Money lenders Act in 1900.

The basic argument in favor of repeal was that people should be left free to make whatever bargain on interest that they saw fit, in light of such factors as the reputation and creditworthiness of the borrower. The law does not regulate the price of commodities generally, and money should be no exception. Usury laws are easily evaded and probably hurt the very kinds of borrowers they seek to protect. Bentham's essay in support of repeal was cited with approval in the House of Lords debate on the 1854 bill.

The arguments against repeal were more diverse in character.[11] Repeal would lead to interest rates rising, thus hurting the poor and unsettling the economy. The law has a role to play in protecting people against rapacious and heartless bill discounters and moneylenders, often described as being "of the Jewish persuasion."[12] A maximum interest rate would restrict the profits to be made from moneylending, thus making that business less attractive. As a whole, the arguments for retention were weaker and more incoherent, based in substantial part on racial prejudice. They nevertheless reflect a real sentiment present in the Victorian approach to debt.

The other great legal and political debate in the nineteenth century concerned a creditor's remedies for nonpayment of debt. The creditor could sue the debtor and obtain judgment, but what happened if the debtor still refused to pay? Most people agreed that the law was in need of reform, but the direction which reform should take was the subject of vigorous debate and numerous statutes, again reflecting the Victorian ambivalence about debt.

The Victorian legal system, and most other people, began from the position that debts should be repaid. Assuming that the creditor commenced his action against the debtor and proved the debt and the failure to repay, the courts would give judgment for the amount owing. A twentieth-century law reform committee expressed this policy in suitably Victorian terms as follows (1969 Report 12):

> We start from the assumption that citizens ought to repay legally binding debts and that the community recognizes a social and moral obligation to honour obligations freely contracted. *Pacta sunt servanda* is not only legal doctrine; it is moral precept too.

When the lawyers and judges were not stating their policy in Latin, they could rely on aphorisms to make the point. In an 1870 case involving a fraudulent conveyance, the Lord Chancellor, Lord Hatherley, began his judgment as follows:

> The principle on which the statute of 13 Eliz. c.5 proceeds is this, that persons must be just before they are generous, and that debts must be paid before gifts can be made.[13]

The aphorism is not original; *The Oxford Dictionary of English Proverbs* (416) refers to examples in Sheridan and Marryat. Dickens was aware of it; he put it into the mouth of Montague Tigg, although that experienced debtor misunderstands what he describes as that "most remarkably long-headed, flowing-bearded, and patriarchal proverb."[14]

When the courts enforced a debt contract, they did so generally without examining the terms of the contract for fairness. R.C.B. Risk describes the underlying value system as follows (338):

> Individual responsibility was expressed most dramatically in the unwillingness to review the fairness of bargains and to control the use of economic power.

This was the ultimate meaning of the phrase 'freedom of contract.' Each individual was the best judge, and was to be the only judge, of the value and utility of an exchange, and each individual was to be responsible for his own economic fate, even though one transaction or a lifetime of disadvantage made that fate a cruel one.

Sir Henry Maine's famous dictum (*Ancient Law* 100) that the movement of progressive societies had hitherto been a movement from status to contract was not simply an historical generalization; it was as well a value judgment about the direction in which progress ought to take place.

Assuming that the creditor could obtain a judgment against the defendant for the amount of the debt, the common law offered the creditor two major classes of remedies, the first directed against the property of the debtor and the second directed against his or her person.[15] The principal remedy against the debtor's property was the writ of execution or fi fa.[16] It instructed the sheriff to seize and sell goods and chattels of the debtor, the proceeds of which would be sufficient to satisfy the judgment.

The writ of execution was inadequate, both as to the property it caught and as to its method of realization. The sheriff could seize goods and chattels, leasehold interests in land, and some growing crops. However he could not seize money, bank notes or bills, debts owing to the debtor, future earnings of the debtor, money held by a banker, money in court, shares or securities. Land could also not be seized and sold, although the sheriff could seize any rents and profits of land if empowered to do so by a separate writ of elegit. It could therefore happen that a debtor had substantial assets which were valuable but which could not be touched by the creditor. The vast majority of debtors had little or no property of any sort; the writ of execution was useless against them as well.

When goods of the debtor were seized, they were sold by the sheriff at public auction. This method of sale (which is still widely used) is not calculated to produce much money for the creditor, although it will destroy the life savings of the debtor represented by goods and chattels. The writ of execution was much more effective as a threat than when it actually had to be used. Despite these drawbacks, the writ of execution against goods was the remedy most commonly used by creditors in the nineteenth century (Francis 819–20), a result which would likely continue to be true today.

The other great remedy available to the Victorian common law judgment creditor was execution against the person or imprisonment for debt. Before 1838, there were two forms of imprisonment for debt.

(1) The creditor could before judgment and on his own sworn statement have the debtor imprisoned until judgment was obtained. This process was described as arrest on mesne (or middle) process. Its purpose was theoretically to bring the debtor before the court to respond to the plaintiff's claim. In fact, the purpose was coercive, designed to force the debtor to pay the debt or to get friends or relatives to pay it (Cohen 154–55).

(2) The second form of imprisonment for debt was arrest after judgment or arrest on final process. Once the creditor had obtained judgment against the debtor, the creditor could issue a writ of capias instructing a bailiff to arrest the debtor. The writ of capias issued as of right, and the creditor did not have to establish the debtor's fraud or indeed his capacity to pay.

Once the debtor was arrested, he or she would usually be taken first to a private home or sponging house.[17] The debtor would remain there for a period, sometimes stretching to two or three weeks. The debtor would use the time to try to raise money to satisfy the debt. If these efforts failed, the debtor would be taken to one of the debtors prisons in London or elsewhere. There he or she would remain until one of three events occurred:

(1) The debt was paid by the debtor or, often, a relative, a friend or a philanthropic association.[18]

(2) The creditor forgave the debt or abandoned the imprisonment of the debtor. The creditor was unlikely to follow this generous course of action. The law was clear that, once the creditor had acted against the body of the debtor, he or she had no further remedies against the debtor's property. If the creditor was to release the debtor from prison, that was also an effective release of the debt. As Bruce Kercher notes (60–61), these rules sometimes produced a stalemate in which an imprisoned debtor with assets could remain in jail, living on non-exigible property, the creditor being unwilling to agree to the debtor's release.

(3) The debtor and in limited cases the creditor could apply to the Insolvent Debtors Court for relief. The debtor would supply the Court with a list of all exigible and non-exigible assets and an assignment of those assets for the benefit of all of the creditors. The Court then could order the release of the debtor from prison but not from his or her debts.

The idea of imprisoning debtors to coerce them to pay their debts seems to us misguided and cruel. Imprisonment, like execution against property, worked better as a threat than if it actually had to be carried out. Nevertheless imprisonment was used extensively, even routinely, as a debt collection device in the nineteenth century. For example, nearly 13,400 debtors were committed to prisons in 1838, and this figure underestimates committals because it omits committals to local prisons (Kercher 95). Committals of debtors fell during the century as a percentage of total committals to prisons from 14,339 (10.1%) in 1857 to 11,647 (8%) in 1867 to 5,754 (3.1%) in 1877 (McConville 335, 347). Despite this drop in percentages, substantial numbers of debtors continued to be jailed to the end of the nineteenth century and beyond.

Imprisonment was used or threatened because it worked. Clinton Francis estimates (820–21) that the creditors' remedies system as it operated between 1740 and 1840 was effective in that it achieved partial or total payment of judgment debts in two-thirds of the cases where execution against property or the person was used. There were a large number of prisons devoted partly or entirely to the incarceration of debtors; London alone had at the beginning of the nineteenth century eight jails used for this purpose (Rock 308). Over-crowding of prisons was a great problem,[19] and one which may have been an important pressure on Parliament to reform the law. The administrators of the prisons understood that debtors should be treated differently from prisoners convicted of criminal offences, and there was some attempt to separate the two groups.

The creditor who imprisoned a debtor had no legal obligation to provide for his or her maintenance. Statutes had been passed in earlier centuries providing for a very modest payment for food for prisoners, but these statutes were rarely enforced. Therefore conditions in debtors prisons could be appalling for the very poor, unless ameliorated by private charity. Debtors were allowed extensive visiting privileges, and could carry on their trade so far as their confinement permitted. However Hepworth Dixon (283), writing in 1850, observed that "people do not like to send their work—tailoring, shoemaking etc.—into a gaol; and those who try to support themselves by their prison labour almost always fail."

If a prisoner had money in the form of non-exigible assets, or had generous friends or relatives, he or she could live well in prison. In the eighteenth and early nineteenth centuries, many prisoners received permission (usually purchased) to live outside the walls of some prisons in nearby streets, known as the Rules. Prisoners could apply to court to be moved from one prison to another, and Daniel Defoe observed that "some of the gentlemen that are in for vast sums, and probably for life, choose the [King's Bench] for the summer, and the [Fleet prison] for their winter habitation; and, indeed, both are but the show and name of prisons." The wealthy prisoner could buy a comfortable room, share it with a wife or mistress, and receive substantial numbers of visitors. It was even possible to buy a ticket of release from jail in return for a payment to the jailor, a practice which was much abused. One debtor was released to go on a voyage to France; others were permitted to make trips to Richmond, Gravesend, Hampton Court and even to Cowes to engage in boating (Dixon 115).

The poor prisoner, on the other hand, was dependent on charity or the fitfully paid county subsidy. Writing in 1802, Neild described the Borough Compter as having

> no bedding, or even straw to lie upon. No mops, brooms or pails, to keep the prison clean. No fire in the winter; the casements rotting off their hinges, and scarce a whole pane of glass in the windows. Out of the nine poor wretches who were confined, seven of them were scarce half-cloathed, three were very ill, and without any medical assistance whatever. . . . The men debtors live below stairs totally in ruins.

The jailers extracted fees from prisoners for food, drink, beds and other services. Without the money to pay such fees, poor debtors were condemned to live in the squalid conditions described by numerous observers.

The nineteenth century saw some of the more notorious prisons closed, and the remainder were improved. The state began to provide prisoners with meals in some prisons,[20] although others continued in their pre-nineteenth-century conditions. By the 1860s, the policy of treating debtors differently from criminal prisoners was abandoned, and debtors were subjected to the same rules as sentenced criminal offenders.

The law of creditors' remedies was the subject of repeated and yet inconclusive reform efforts during the Victorian period. The Judgments Act of 1838 extended remedies against property to catch intangibles and land, and placed significant restrictions on imprisonment on mesne process.

Imprisonment on final process proved to be more difficult to deal with. The 1838 Act in bill form had abolished arrest on final process, but this part of the bill was opposed in the House of Lords and was deleted. In 1844, imprisonment was abolished for judgments that did not exceed £20 unless there was evidence that the judgment debtor had obtained credit fraudulently or "without having at the same time a reasonable assurance of being able to pay or discharge the same." The effect of this change was modified by statutes passed in 1845 and 1846 which extended the grounds for imprisonment to include cases where the debtor appeared to have had the means to pay the judgment and had refused or neglected to do so. The two Acts also made it clear that imprisonment was for a period not to exceed forty days, and that imprisonment did not have the effect of satisfying or extinguishing the debt. The statistics assembled by Kercher make it clear that large numbers of debtors continued to be imprisoned during this period, over 9,600 being committed to jail in 1854, the last year of Kercher's statistics (Kercher 95; McConville 335, 347).

Imprisonment for debt on final process was abolished by the Debtors Act of 1869, but the reform was more apparent than real. The Act is entitled in part "An Act for the Abolition of Imprisonment for Debt," and section 4 of the Act does abolish imprisonment. However section 5 promptly resurrects the remedy by giving courts a new power to imprison judgment debtors who have failed to pay a judgment debt or an instalment payment set out in the judgment where the debtor "either has or has had since the date of the . . . judgment the means to pay this sum . . . and has refused or neglected, or refuses or neglects, to pay the same."

It is clear that the Debtors Act was used to imprison substantial numbers of debtors from 1869 to 1970 when the provision was finally repealed. The number of debtors sent to prison was running well over 60,000 a year in the early 1960s, a factor which undoubtedly hastened the repeal legislation. Even after 1970, imprisonment continues in England today for maintenance defaulters (almost 2,900 in 1979) and for debtors owing income tax and rates to the Crown (Rubin, *Law Poverty*; Christopher Harding).

The equity courts developed a separate set of remedies against the property and the body of the judgment debtor in order to enforce equitable decrees and, on occasion, to assist common law judgment creditors. These equitable remedies were less significant than their common law counterparts, and need not be discussed at length (Dunlop, *Creditor* 277–91). One point should however be noted.

Equity relied heavily on imprisonment for contempt of court to enforce all its decrees including those ordering payment of sums of money. The court's discretion to commit for contempt was relatively unfettered, and some prisoners spent months or years in jail. The contempt jurisdiction was much criticized in the nineteenth century by Dickens among others ("Martyrs"), and limits were eventually imposed, especially on the imprisonment of debtors.

Walter Houghton has noted the high value that Victorians placed on financial success (184–89). A corollary was the fear of debt and financial failure that appears throughout the literature of the period (Houghton 60–61; Smith 79–81). John Vernon describes the common situation in nineteenth-century fiction of a character trying to find money to pay a debt (69–74, 110). The situation is urgent, even desperate, and it carries a sense of guilt and retribution. Financial failure becomes the nightmare of a society which worships financial success.

The Victorian response to the phenomenon of debt was inconsistent and contradictory. In an age when many feared and loathed the moneylender, the 1854 Usury Repeal Act removed all legal controls on the interest which the moneylender could demand. As far as imprisonment for debt is concerned, the 1869 Act abolished imprisonment in section 4 only to recreate the remedy in a somewhat altered form in section 5.

Victorian society had good reason to fear and distrust debt. Borrowing money was a means to improve one's business or personal life, but it could just as easily lead to financial ruin and personal disgrace. Imprisonment in a debtor's prison was a frightening penalty for bad judgment, misfortune or poverty. On the other hand, Victorian writers were quick to condemn the young swells who borrowed heavily to live far beyond their means. They were even more critical of the financier who floated share issues or created fake insurance companies which promptly collapsed. For these knaves, punishment was seen as richly deserved. The problem of debt did not have a simple or straightforward answer.

3.

Dickens had ample opportunity during his life to reflect on the dangers of indebtedness (Johnson; Kaplan; Wilson). His father was arrested for debt and imprisoned in the Marshalsea in 1824, was declared insolvent a second time in 1831, and was arrested again in 1834 (Easson 111–12; Paroissien 24–25). Dickens' brother Fred, some of his children, and various artist and writer friends experienced financial troubles and appealed to Dickens for help. The young writer worked as a lawyer's clerk and as a court reporter. The stories about debtors and creditors collected during that period were no doubt supplemented later through discussions with his many friends in business and the law.

As a young writer with expensive tastes, Dickens accumulated his own debts, including advances from publishers on books to be written. However he was a tough businessman and an astute investor and, at his death, left an estate worth 93,000 pounds, over one million pounds in present values (Russell 8). His childhood memories of debt and the resulting hardships would appear to explain in part his continuing efforts to accumulate money through his novels, the editing of periodicals, lecture tours and, despite the threat to health, his public readings.

Dickens made extensive use of his knowledge of debt in his novels and short stories. He describes many debtors and creditors whose activities are basic to the plots of the novels. A good example from *Bleak House* is Mr. George's debt to Grandfather Smallweed which Tulkinghorn uses to force George to give up the letter from Captain Hawdon. People's stations in society are established or modified by their debts. Debts connect up people in widely separated social classes, rather like the lawsuits in *Bleak House*. There are numerous accurate accounts of the debt collection process, cognovit writs, bill discounting, execution, imprisonment, the Insolvent Debtors Court and bankruptcy.[21] The Marshalsea debtors in *Little Dorrit* summarize their experience in terms which may be applied more generally to Dickens' fiction: "It was evident from the general tone of the whole party, that they had come to regard insolvency as the normal state of mankind, and the payment of debts as a disease that occasionally broke out."(88)

Debtors are everywhere in Dickens' fiction. A partial list of characters whose debts have a major, even a crucial, effect on their lives would include Alfred Jingle, Samuel Pickwick, the Mantalinis and Mr. Bray, Little Nell's grandfather, Sir John Chester, Chevy Slyme, Montague Tigg and Mr. Lewsome, Trotty Veck, Michael Warden (in *The Battle of Life*), Solomon Gills and, towards the end of the novel, Mr. Dombey and his firm, Tommy Traddles and Wilkins Micawber, Mr. George and Mr. Jellyby, Harold Skimpole and most of the Chancery suitors in *Bleak House*, Tom Gradgrind, William Dorrit and his fellow prisoners in the Marshalsea, Henry Gowan, Arthur Clennam, Mr. Merdle, the Vennerings and the Lammles, and Pip.

Most of these characters are in financial trouble; they cannot pay their debts and have fallen into legal difficulties. A few work their way out of debt or are otherwise relieved of their obligations, sometimes in miraculous fashion. Mr. Micawber, for example, is perpetually insolvent in England but, after his emigration to Australia, is able to pay off his debts and apparently to lose his habit of indebtedness altogether.

Most debtors are not so lucky. They drift further into trouble or decay into chronic insolvency, much like the litigants in *Bleak House* who collapse into complete dependency on their law suits. The litigants and the debtors are alike in their hopes that something may turn up; except for Mr. Micawber, the hopes usually turn out to be false and empty. This inability to face the facts is made worse when debtors fall under the baleful shadow of the Marshalsea which can sap the will and warp the mind even of strong characters like Little Dorrit.

In the early novels, Dickens was prepared to see some debtors as victims of poverty and misfortune. When people today refer to Dickens as the great champion of debtor-creditor law reform, they are thinking of *Sketches by Boz, Pickwick Papers, Nicholas Nickleby*, and the Christmas books, although they might also point to the inhabitants of Bleeding Heart Yard. There are a few innocent characters like Matthew Bagnet and Melvin Twemlow who get into debt as guarantees of other people's obligations.[22] In the later novels, however, the debtors are more often dishonest, shiftless, or morally culpable in some sense. A good example is Mr. George in *Bleak House*. He comes from the servant class and runs away to be a trooper, thus entering into the service of his country. Neither experience equips him to be a businessman. Then, inexplicably, he decides to embark on the business of running a shooting gallery near Leicester Square. He has no (or not enough) capital, and borrows the balance from Grandfather Smallweed.

So far the picture is one of naiveté and incompetence, especially as the business never makes enough money to pay back any of the principal. But when George has his friend Matthew Bagnet sign the bill as a co-endorser, is this still mere naiveté? Or has George crossed the line and behaved badly by involving his friend in a potentially disastrous situation? Mrs. Bagnet thinks the latter to be the case.

Another example of flawed innocence is William Dorrit whose incapacity to understand his own affairs is increasingly seen as a failure for which he is responsible. Instead of making an effort to gain control over his situation, Dorrit prefers to play the shabby role of the Father of the Marshalsea to the extent of contemplating the sacrifice of Little Dorrit to John Chivery. Dorrit's acceptance of the peace and dull relief of the prison betrays his weakness and lack of resolution in failing to confront and overcome his difficulties.

Victorian commercial history is full of examples of people who borrowed money to set up or expand their businesses or to finance their education. Many failed but many others paid back the loans and went on to business or professional success. The factory owners of the Midlands are a good example. Dickens' debtors who borrow for business or professional purposes fail much more often than they succeed. Traddles is a clear exception, and the

Ironmaster in *Bleak House* may be, although we have no evidence that the latter was ever in debt. Much more common are the businesspeople who borrow and get into trouble as a result. They may be small entrepreneurs like Mr. George or William Dorrit, or big operators like Montague Tigg or Mr. Merdle. Debtors who borrow for business purposes are usually either foolish or dishonest; in either event, they are likely to fail in both the commercial and the moral sense.

Dickens' fiction is full of creditors, moneylenders, bill brokers or discounters, and pawnbrokers who are prepared to lend money to the debtors described above. Almost without exception, these characters are grasping, heartless, and brutal in the pursuit of their victims.[23] There is ample evidence for the conclusion reached in *The Cricket on the Hearth* (174) that credit granting and debt collection are activities best suited to ill-natured and unpleasant people.

The menial operatives of the debt collection system, like Coavinses, the Marshalsea turnkeys, and Riah, are portrayed more sympathetically, perhaps because they have no responsibility except to carry out the creditor's orders. The seedy, lower-class lawyers who do debt collection work are treated with simple contempt. However it is the creditors and moneylenders who are ultimately responsible, and Dickens is very hard on them as individuals and as a class.

There are of course Dickens' "good" businessmen, like the Cheeryble brothers and Scrooge after the conversion. In real life, these characters would no doubt extend credit and on occasion collect overdue debts. But no hint of this activity is given to us, and we are led to conclude either that they never extend credit or that all of their accounts receivable are paid on time or, more likely, forgiven. These paragons of virtue, charity, and benevolence are unconvincing as businesspeople and indeed as human beings.

The image of the skinflint moneylender was a popular one in Victorian fiction, melodrama, and periodical articles, and Dickens uses it consistently to suggest an inhuman pursuit of money at the expense of other values. Norman Russell points out that characters like Anthony and Jonas Chuzzlewit and Scrooge are initially introduced as merchants but are later given the trappings of moneylenders in order to make them blacker and more evil (Russell 194–98). The moneylender frightened Victorian readers because he was thought with good reason to have enormous power to harass and ruin those unlucky enough to fall into his clutches.

Dickens' attitude to his creditors is complex. They are sometimes little more than stock melodrama characters but, when his imagination is fully engaged, they can become grotesque, savage, powerful and exciting people (cf. Carey). Unlike many of the debtors, creditors like Quilp and Smallweed fascinate the reader by the charged and powerful atmosphere which surrounds their joyful pursuit of money.

It is useful to compare Smallweed and his debtor, Mr. George. The conflict between them is a struggle between George's sense of chivalry, honor, and decorum and his somewhat compromised morality, as contrasted with Smallweed's rejection of custom or morality of any sort in favour of a single-minded pursuit of money and an adherence when convenient to the letter of the law. George continues to act as though he wore the military costume which he has in fact abandoned. He insists on a pipe to be smoked whenever a two-month period expires and a new bill is signed. But George does not have the slightest inkling that Smallweed can refuse to accept a new bill and can instead demand payment of the principal as well as the interest.

Smallweed on the other hand knows nothing but business. He understands "the first four rules of arithmetic, and a certain small collection of the hardest facts," (287) but has discarded as unprofitable all amusements, story-books, or levities as well as any sense of reverence or wonder. What Smallweed does know is that he has the power at the end of every two-month period to demand full payment and thereby destroy George and his even more innocent friend, Matthew Bagnet. When Smallweed, apparently at the request of Tulkinghorn, exercises his right to require payment of the debt, we are horrified at the consequences for the two old soldiers but fascinated by the brutally joyful way in which Smallweed announces his decision (481–82).

> "That's what it means, my dear friend. I'll smash you. I'll crumble you. I'll powder you. Go to the devil!"
> The two friends rise and look at one another. Mr. Bagnet's gravity has now attained its profoundest point.
> "Go to the devil!" repeats the old man. "I'll have no more of your pipe-smokings and swaggerings. What? You're an independent dragoon, too! Go to my lawyer (you remember where; you have been there before), and show your independence now, will you? Come, my dear friend, there's a chance for you. Open the street door, Judy; put these blusterers out! Call in help if they don't go. Put 'em out!"
> He vociferates this so loudly, that Mr. Bagnet, laying his hands on the shoulders of his comrade, before the latter can recover from his amazement, gets him on the outside of the street door; which is instantly slammed by the triumphant Judy.

The vigor with which Smallweed dismisses George reflects Dickens' own impatience with pretentious and deluded people who, like William Dorrit, could so easily slip into debt. Dickens was himself a tough and aggressive businessman whose letters reflect his unhappiness with those who could not display the same abilities. If people like George insist on leaving the old world of service to become businesspeople, they must realize that they have entered a very different game played by clear, if unpleasant, rules.

The conflict between George and Smallweed can be tied into other themes in *Bleak House*. George's respect for traditional values and customary patterns of conduct is echoed by Sir Leicester's chivalrous respect for his wife and by the Lord Chancellor's paternal concern for the Wards in Chancery. Smallweed's ties are with the world of business in which the worth of everything must be measured in money, amusement is dismissed as unprofitable, and one's station in society depends entirely on the terms of the contracts one can negotiate.

It is possible now to see why Dickens is of two minds about George and Smallweed. George's adherence to traditional values is appealing as is Sir Leicester's love for Lady Dedlock. But the old values are intermingled with the outmoded law, the unworkable politics and the decaying society which Dickens attacks in *Bleak House*. The creditors are part of the new commercial world of the ironmasters and the strong forceful businessmen who can reshape England. But if the new world will look like a Coketown or, worse, a London peopled by Smallweeds, then perhaps the old values are worth preserving.

4.

The society described by Dickens is pervaded by debtor-creditor relationships. Its dominant characteristics are selfishness and hypocrisy; to paraphrase Ada in *Bleak House*, people are all ruining one another and are in constant doubt and discord all their lives.(58) Ada is of course talking about *Jarndyce v. Jarndyce*, but the parallel between litigation and indebtedness is strong. Both activities emphasize a person's individual situation and his or her separation from the community; both stress a person's individual rights which are legal but not moral. Charity, mercy, and benevolence are secondary virtues, if not completely out of place.

When Sir Henry Maine talked of the movement from status to contract, he was talking of legal contracts in contradistinction to customary or moral obligations. If one's position in a society is determined by one's contracts or, to put it another way, by one's personal balance sheet, then it is crucial, as Mr. Micawber observed, to have an income which exceeds one's expenditures, if only by sixpence. This is a dangerous and chancy world in which people can rise or fall without warning, depending upon the state of their finances and the whims of their creditors.

On the other hand, planned indebtedness is unlikely to lead to success in business and a resulting change of station. One can change one's place in society by inheriting money or receiving charity but not by going into debt. The upshot of Mr. George's venture into business is that he returns to the status of servant with Sir Leicester Dedlock. The novels suggest that George's experience is the rule and not the exception, at least when the business venture is based on borrowed money.

If a world of pervasive indebtedness is frightening for the debtors, it is equally disturbing for the creditors who are threatened by the possibility of nonpayment and resulting personal financial difficulty. The Victorians, including Dickens, were haunted by the spectre of political revolution. Widespread default on the payment of financial obligations is a kind of commercial revolution which strikes at the heart of a market society. Default is more obviously a challenge to the state when the debts not paid are debts enshrined in judgments of the court. This political dimension helps to explain the passion which informed fictional and non-fictional treatments of debt and law reform in the nineteenth century.

Dickens shared the view of most Victorians that, once a debt was incurred, the debtor's responsibility was to pay it off as quickly as possible. Harold Skimpole's incomplete moral vision is the opposite of Dickens' views. Martin Chuzzlewit speaks for the author when he describes the payment of one's debts as a great personal and social obligation.(537) If this was all Dickens had to say about debt, his conclusions would hardly be startling. But the more radical idea which seems to underlie the novels is that indebtedness is a dangerous and destructive activity which should be avoided entirely. Debt has no place in Dickens' ideal society which is typified by kindness, benevolence, and charity, and not by business, litigation, and debtor-creditor relationships.

Being a debtor means accepting and using another person's money rather than relying on one's own resources. Dickens' debtors are irresponsible, evasive, confused and usually morally flawed; they are rarely heroes or even positive figures. Dickens seems to prefer the sturdy, if unrealistic, self-reliance of Betty Higden who flees not only the workhouse but financial assistance of any sort. Debt in contrast is the symptom of a disease like dry rot which leads to "a tendency to lurk and lounge . . . a certain slovenliness and deterioration . . . a looseness respecting money . . . a looseness respecting everything . . . a trembling of the limbs, somnolency, misery and crumbling to pieces." (*The Uncommercial Traveller* 131).

Dickens' creditors do not come off any better. When they grant credit or exercise their rights to collect their debts, they are seen as grasping and cruel in their exercise of power over fellow human beings. The implication is that business, insofar as it involves credit granting and debt collection, is not an activity for good people.

Dickens viewed indebtedness with suspicion throughout his life, but his views became more pessimistic as he grew older. In the early novels, some debtors actually do pay their debts, and others are exempted from moral culpability because of their poverty. In the later books, however, Dickens drifted towards the more extreme position that debt itself is wrong. Debtors and creditors alike are engaged in an unproductive and degrading activity which empowers some at the expense of others and runs counter to more positive values.

In light of Dickens' changing views on the morality of debt, it is not surprising that his discussion of law reform is found in his earlier much more than his later writing. If debt is in part caused by poverty instead of bad judgment or dishonesty, then the barbaric system of creditors' remedies existing before 1838 is bad law and should be reformed. As Dickens moved towards the view that debt itself was offensive, law reform would cease to be as important an issue. The fundamental, if unlikely, solution would be a moral revolution in which people learned to avoid indebtedness entirely. The result is a vague call to people to be responsible, charitable, forgiving, and benevolent, without explaining how these virtues can be squared with either the logic of business or the grim facts of poverty (cf. Dvorak).

The declining interest in reform of debtor-creditor law in the later novels can also be explained by changes in public sentiment. *Sketches by Boz* and *Pickwick Papers* were written between 1833 and 1837, at the height of the public debate over the reform of creditors' remedies which led to the Judgments Act of 1838 (Easson; Kercher). The specific issues raised in these books were addressed, if not solved, in the Judgments Act and in the legislation of the 1840s. As public opinion turned to other matters, such as court reform, so did Dickens' reformist efforts. In the later novels, Dickens moved away from the discussion of specific abuses towards a more general critique. As Angus Easson observes (111), the focus in *Little Dorrit* is on a flawed society rather than on specific reformable institutions like the

Marshalsea prison which had in any event been closed in 1849, eight years before the novel was published.

The situation of the ineffectual and morally flawed debtor in the clutches of the heartless creditor clearly held a strong attraction for Dickens; he returned repeatedly to the story long after discussions of specific law reform issues disappeared from his novels. What remains is to try to understand why the theme of indebtedness exercised so strong a pull on his imagination. One obvious explanation is biographical. Dickens was the son of a chronic debtor who caused his family considerable misery through his failure to live within his means. As a result, Dickens was forced to work in the blacking factory, an experience which appears to have hurt him deeply. Therefore, like an alcoholic's child, he may have reacted against his father's failings to the point of rejecting debt in any form. Another explanation can be drawn from literary history. The story of the hapless debtor pursued by the savage creditor is a familiar one in English literature as in Victorian periodical articles on debt. The literary convention of the grasping moneylender not only has a long history; it aroused strong feelings in the Victorian audience which Dickens always kept in mind. It was a good story which bore retelling, and it was told again and again in Dickens' fiction.

The theme of indebtedness can also be related to broader questions about Victorian society. The world described in Dickens' novels is one in which human and communitarian values are pushed aside by a single-minded and selfish pursuit of wealth and power. Debtors and creditors are caught up in this struggle for money to the exclusion of more important goals. Their plight symbolizes the dessicated and degraded world of business which Dickens came increasingly to question (cf. Welsh 86–137).

The Victorians discussed at length the perplexing problem of debt, but they faltered and hesitated in their efforts at law reform. In our age of instant loans and plastic credit cards, the vacillation continues. The politicians still hesitate to grapple with difficult issues. The Canadian Parliament has been considering for fifteen years a series of bills to reform the Bankruptcy Act without making a decision except on minor matters. Law reform commissions in England, the Commonwealth, and elsewhere have published extensive reports on creditor-debtor law which have been ignored or dismembered because of their political sensitivity. On the question of debt as on so many other matters, Dickens still speaks to us. What he says may be disturbing, one-sided, or subversive, but no one can deny its relevance.

WORKS CITED

A. *General*

Alexander, David. *Retailing in England During the Industrial Revolution*. London: Athlone-University of London, 1970.

Atiyah, P.S. *The Rise and Fall of Freedom of Contract*. Oxford: Oxford University Press, 1979.

Bentham, Jeremy. "Defence of Usury." *The Works of Jeremy Bentham*. Ed. John Bowring. Vol. 3. Edinburgh, 1843. 1–29.

Bernstein, J.L. "Background of a Grey Area in Law: The Chequered Career of Usury." *American Bar Association Journal* 51 (1965): 846–50.

Carey, John. *The Violent Effigy: A Study of Dickens' Imagination*. London: Faber, 1973.

Cohen, Jay. "The History of Imprisonment for Debt and Its Relation to the Development of Discharge in Bankruptcy." *Journal of Legal History* 3 (1982–83): 153–71.

Defoe, Daniel. *Tour Through the Whole Island of Great Britain*. London: 1772. Quoted in Rock 311.

Dixon, Hepworth. *The London Prisons*. London, 1850.

Duffy, Ian P.H. "English Bankrupts: 1571–1861." *American Journal of Legal History* 24 (1980): 283–305.

Dunlop, C.R.B. *Creditor-Debtor Law in Canada*. Toronto: Carswell, 1981.

———. *The Operation of the Unsecured Creditors Remedies System in Alberta*. Research Paper No. 16. Edmonton: Institute of Law Research and Reform, 1986.

Dvorak, Wilfred P. "Dickens' Ambivalence as Social Critic in the 1860s: Attitudes to Money in *All the Year Round* and *The Uncommercial Traveller*." *Dickensian* 80 (1984): 89–104.

Easson, Angus. "Imprisonment for Debt in *Pickwick Papers*." *Dickensian* 64 (1968): 105–12.

Francis, Clinton W. "Practice, Strategy and Institution: Debt Collection in the English Common-Law Courts, 1740–1840." *Northwestern University Law Review* 80 (1985–86): 807–955.

Friedman, Lawrence M. "The Usury Laws of Wisconsin: A Study in Legal and Social History." *Wisconsin Law Review* (1963): 515–65.

Harding, Alan. *A Social History of English Law*. London: Penguin, 1966.

Harding, Christopher, Bill Hines, Richard Ireland, and Phillip Rawlings. *Imprisonment in England and Wales: A Concise History*. London: Croom Helm, 1985.

Holdsworth, W.H. *Charles Dickens as a Legal Historian*. New Haven: Yale University Press, 1928.

Houghton, Walter E. *The Victorian Frame of Mind*. New Haven: Yale University Press, 1957.

Johnson, Edgar. *Charles Dickens: His Tragedy and Triumph*. Revised edition. Harmondsworth: Penguin, 1986.

Kaplan, Fred. *Dickens: A Biography*. New York: William Morrow, 1988.

Kercher, Bruce. "The Transformation of Imprisonment for Debt in England, 1828 to 1838." *Australian Journal of Law and Society* 2 (1984): 60–109.

Maine, Sir Henry. *Ancient Law*. 1861. London: Everyman-Dent, 1917.

McConville, Sean. *A History of English Prison Administration: 1750–1877*. Vol. 1. London: Routledge, 1981.

Munro, Hector. "Curious Affair of the Cognovit." *Dickensian* 74 (1978): 88–90.

Neild, J. *An Account of the Society for the Relief and Discharge of Persons Imprisoned for Small Debts*. London: 1802. Quoted in Rock 309.

Oeltjen, Jarret C. "Usury: Utilitarian or Useless?" *Florida State University Law Review* 3 (1975): 167–235.

The Oxford Dictionary of English Proverbs. 3rd ed. Oxford: Clarendon Press, 1970.

Paroissien, David, ed. *Selected Letters of Charles Dickens*. Boston: Twayne, 1985.

Risk, R.C.B. "The Golden Age: The Law About the Market in Nineteenth-Century Ontario." *University of Toronto Law Journal* 26 (1976): 307–46.

Rock, Paul. *Making People Pay*. London: Routledge, 1973. 296–316.

Rubin, G.R. "The County Courts and the Tally Trade, 1846–1914." Rubin and Sugarman 321–48.

———"Law, Poverty and Imprisonment for Debt, 1869–1914." Rubin and Sugarman 241–90.

Rubin, G.R., and David Sugarman. "Introduction: Towards a New History of Law and Material Society in England, 1750–1914." Rubin and Sugarman 1–123.

Rubin, G.R., and David Sugarman, eds. *Law, Economy and Society, 1750–1914; Essays in the History of English Law*. London: Professional, 1984.

Russell, Norman. *The Novelist and Mammon: Literary Responses to the World of Commerce in the Nineteenth Century*. Oxford: Clarendon Press 1986.

Simpson, A.W.B. *A History of the Common Law of Contract*. Oxford: Oxford University Press, 1975.

Smith, Grahame. *Dickens, Money and Society*. Berkeley: University of California Press, 1968.

Tebbutt, Melanie. *Making Ends Meet: Pawnbroking and Working-Class Credit*. Leicester: Leicester University Press, 1983.

Vernon, John. *Money and Fiction: Literary Realism in the Nineteenth and Early Twentieth Centuries*. Ithaca: Cornell University Press, 1984.

Weiss, Barbara. *The Hell of the English: Bankruptcy and the Victorian Novel*. Lewisburg, London and Toronto: Bucknell University Press, 1986.

Welsh, Alexander. *The City of Dickens*. Oxford: Clarendon Press, 1971.

Wilson, Angus. *The World of Charles Dickens*. New York: Viking, 1972.

B. *Nineteenth-Century Periodical Literature*

"Bankruptcy in Six Easy Lessons." *Household Words* 17 (1858): 210–12.

"Behind the Bars." *Temple Bar* 12 (1864): 249–58.

"City Spectres." *Household Words* 4 (1852): 481–85.

"Debt." *All the Year Round* 11 (1864): 463–66.

"Debt." *Household Words* 17 (1858): 319–21.

"Debt." *Temple Bar* 19 (1867): 487–92.

"Debt and Credit at Home and Abroad." *Chamber's Journal* 21 (1854): 385–88.

"Defence of Usury." *Edinburgh Review* 27 (1816): 338–60.

"The Great Penal Experiments." *Household Words* 1 (1850): 250–53.

"In Difficulties: Three Stages." *All the Year Round* 18 (1867): 92–96, 105–08, 136–39.

"The Martyrs of Chancery." *Household Words* 2 (1850–51): 250–52, 493–96.

"Poverty A Crime." *Temple Bar* 12 (1864): 341–51.

"The Queen's Guest." *Household Words* 16 (1857): 421–23.

"Rich and Poor Bankrupts." *All the Year Round* 19 (1868): 540–45.

"Shadowless Men." *Household Words* 17 (1858): 294–99.

"Usury and Usurers." *Bentley's Miscellany* 30 (1851): 275–81, 370–77.

"Usury and Usurers." *Once a Week* 5 (1861): 186–88.

C. *Great Britain Statutes*

An Act to Reduce the Rate of Interest (1713) 12 Anne, c. 2.

An Act to exempt certain Bills of Exchange and Promissory Notes from the Operation of the Laws relating to Usury (1837) 1 Vict., c. 80.

Judgments Act (1838) 1 & 2 Vict., c. 110.

An Act to Amend, and Extend until Jan. 1, 1842, [1 Vict., c. 80] (1839) 2 & 3 Vict., c. 37.

Insolvency, Bankruptcy and Execution Law Amendment Act (1844) 7 & 8 Vict., c. 96, ss. 57–59.

An Act for the Better Securing the Payment of Small Debts (1845) 8 & 9 Vict., c. 127, ss. 1–7.

An Act for the More Easy Recovery of Small Debts and Demands in England (1846) 9 & 10 Vict., c. 95, ss. 98–103.

An Act to Continue [2 & 3 Vict., c. 37] (1850) 13 & 14 Vict., c. 56.

An Act to repeal the Laws relating to Usury and to the Enrolment of Annuities (1854) 17 & 18 Vict., c. 90.

Debtors Act (1869) 32 & 33 Vict., c. 62.

Moneylenders Act (1900) 63 & 64 Vict, c. 51.

D. *Parliamentary Debates*

House of Lords Debates, *Hansard,* 3rd Series, vol. 134 (July 24, 1854), cols. 581–84.

House of Commons Debates, *Hansard,* 3rd Series, vol. 134 (August 4, 1854), cols. 1341–47.

E. *Great Britain Government Reports*

Great Britain. *Report of the Commissioners on Bankruptcy and Insolvency.* London: 1840. Quoted in Rubin and Sugarman 44.

Great Britain. *Report of the Committee on the Enforcement of Judgment Debts.* Cmnd 3909. London: 1969.

NOTES

1. I want to thank the British Council for its financial support of the research which led to this paper.
2. See generally Alexander; Rubin, *County Courts*; Alan Harding 315–18; and Kercher.
3. This is the impression of the writer gained from a study of court and sheriffs' files in Alberta during the early 1980s. See Dunlop, *Operation*.
4. In *Household Words* and *All the Year Round*, see "The Great Penal Experiments;" "The Queen's Guest;" and "In Difficulties: Three Stages." In other periodicals, see "Debt and Credit at Home and Abroad;" "Behind the Bars;" and "Poverty a Crime." See also Weiss 13–65; and Atiyah 229–30.
5. "Usury and Usurers," *Bentley's Miscellany*; and "Debt," *Temple Bar*.
6. "City Spectres;" "Bankruptcy in Six Easy Lessons;" "Shadowless Men;" "Debt," *Household Words*; and "Rich and Poor Bankrupts."
7. "Debt," *All the Year Round* 463. See also "Debt," *Temple Bar*.
8. Other examples might have been taken, e.g., the reform of bankruptcy law and the creation of the limited liability company. On both, see Weiss.

9. See Simpson 113–17, 510–18; Atiyah 65–67, 130–31, 302, 324–25, 381–82, 550–51, 708–13; Bernstein; Friedman 515–23; and Oeltjen 167–80.
10. The basic repeal essay is Jeremy Bentham's *Defence of Usury*, published in 1787. For a summary of Bentham's arguments, see "Defence of Usury." For a virulent essay against repeal, see "Usury and Usurers," *Once a Week.*
11. House of Commons Debates; "Usury and Usurers," *Bentley's Miscellany;* "Debt," *Temple Bar;* and "Usury and Usurers," *Once a Week.*
12. E.g., see "Usury and Usurers," *Bentley's Miscellany* 280. For a corrective to the use of anti-Semitic rhetoric, see Bentham 16.
13. *Freeman* v. *Pope* (1870), 5 Ch. App. 538, 540.
14. Charles Dickens, *Martin Chuzzlewit* (The New Oxford Illustrated Dickens) 221. All references to Dickens' novels henceforth will be to the New Oxford Illustrated Dickens. Page references will be noted parenthetically in the text.
15. There are several recent discussions of Victorian creditor-debtor law. See Cohen; Francis; Kercher; Rock; Duffy; Rubin, *Law, Poverty;* and Dunlop, *Creditor* 91–98, 125–34, 277–91.
16. "Fi fa" is an abbreviation of "fieri facias," words found in the writ of execution and meaning that one should "cause (it) to be done or made." The words came to be used as the name of the writ itself.
17. Legislation was passed as early as 1728 to prohibit bailiffs' sponging houses, but they continued until at least the 1840s. See McConville 56–57, note 28.
18. Prison welfare charities like the Thatched House Society assisted thousands of debtor prisoners to obtain their releases in the eighteenth and nineteenth centuries. See Kercher 62–63; and Cohen 163.
19. The following account is drawn from Christopher Harding 134–35; Rock; and McConville.
20. For a description of the diet served to prisoners in Whitecross Street Jail, founded in 1815, see Dixon 281–82.
21. As to Dickens' accuracy on legal detail, see Holdsworth; Munro; and Easson.
22. A borderline example of an innocent debtor may be Mr. Jellyby who goes "through the Gazette," mostly because of his wife's neglect of the family. Mrs. Jellyby is clearly criticized, but Dickens comes close to letting Mr. Jellyby off the hook entirely.
23. Dickens occasionally described moneylenders and their employees as Jewish, as in *Dombey and Son* (830), but he was able to turn the anti-Semitic cliché inside out in *Our Mutual Friend.*

Anorexia Nervosa versus the Fleshpots of London: Rose and Nancy in *Oliver Twist*

Simon Edwards

While everyone recognises the importance of food in Dickens' novels, there are, to my knowledge, only two essays which have attempted to assess its role critically. Barbara Hardy has discussed the moral significance of feasting and hospitality in *Great Expectations*. Ian Watt, noting the same lack of critical interest in the subject, offers a suggestive psychoanalytic account of Dickens' sensitivity to various aspects of oral behavior, finding a connection between eating habits and the impulse towards verbal display and performance. He rightly stresses that the putatively "regressive" nature of oral fixation is an effective strength of Dickens's art, enabling him to identify imaginatively with kinds of human behavior that are marginalised or excluded by a psychological order governed by a "mature" genitality (Hardy 351–63, Watts 165–81).

Thus, in spite of the psychoanalytic orientation of so much Dickens criticism, it seems that the recurrent, detailed observation of food, meals, and eating habits, has been read and, presumably, enjoyed as simply a device within the strategy for the concrete representation of the reality of social life characteristic of nineteenth-century fiction as a whole. Roland Barthes suggests

> the novelist by citing, naming, *noticing* food (by treating it as notable), imposes on the reader the final state of the matter. What cannot be transcended, withdrawn. . . .

> (Barthes 45)

One might have expected a more speculative account from a French critic discussing the "pleasure of the text." In making specific connections between food and sexuality in *Oliver Twist* I am concerned not only with how food can powerfully suggest repressed sexual appetite, a frequent enough motif in Victorian fiction, but a more general politics of the body. By examining the enigma of the typically insipid heroine, Rose Maylie, and the contrasting figure of Nancy, it should be possible to indicate how food and sexuality interact symbolically in the acquisition of human identity. The acquisition of identity may be seen as the common feature of a number of overlapping projects within the novel: the pursuit of Oliver's real name and social class coincide with Dickens' own pursuit of status as a professional novelist and his inquiry into the lineaments of a new class society in the wake of the Reform Act of 1832 and the Poor Law Amendment Act of 1834. Given the thematic centrality of starvation in the workhouse, the pervasive presence of the hungry poor, it follows that the representation of food throughout the novel forms part of Dickens' exploration of wider issues in the satisfaction and control of physical appetite in the civilization of early industrial capitalism, its distribution of energy and pleasure, and its creation of material wealth and human waste. A frequently noted feature of the novel is the tension between the tone of measured political radicalism and the haunting mythic resonance of its treatment of the criminal world. I want to suggest that its myth is politically and historically specific, as well as identifying some aspects of the development of Dickens' narrative art in relation to the gendering of fictional narrative as a whole. No doubt a stronger psychoanalytic or folkloric reading would generate further meanings that might contribute to an understanding of how this novel has been ingested by our culture. The image of the imprisoning and predatory ogre, for example, occurs throughout Dickens' work and invites such readings. Here, however, I shall want to stress only the literary historical significance of the image in aligning the novel with the immediate tradition of "female gothic."

The interaction between food and sexuality is focused most explicitly in a scene of characteristically grotesque comedy. Mr. Bumble, fresh from his own courtship of Mrs. Corney at the tea table, catches Charlotte and Noah Claypole *in flagrante delicto*. Charlotte feeds Noah from a barrel of oysters. If oysters are conventionally aphrodisiac (there is, of course, the classic myth of the birth of Venus) it may be because they suggest both male and female sexual pleasure. Certainly Noah here enjoys a curiously passive role.

> Mr. Noah Claypole lolled negligently in an easy chair with his legs thrown
> over one of the arms, an open clasp-knife in one hand, and a mass of buttered

bread in the other. Close behind him stood Charlotte, opening oysters from a barrel, which Mr. Claypole condescended to swallow with remarkable avidity.

Charlotte denies she enjoys oysters, that her pleasure is watching Noah eat them.

> "Here's a delicious fat one, Noah, dear!" said Charlotte; "try him, do; only this one."
> "What a delicious thing is a oyster!" remarked Mr. Claypole, after he had swallowed it. "What a pity it is, a number of 'em should ever make you feel uncomfortable; isn't it, Charlotte?"
> "It's quite a cruelty," said Charlotte.
> "So it is," acquiesced Mr. Claypole. "Ain't yer fond of oysters?"
> "Not over much," replied Charlotte. "I like to see you eat 'em, Noah dear, better than eating them myself."
> "Lor!" said Noah, reflectively; "how queer!"
> "Have another," said Charlotte. "Here's one with such a beautiful, delicate beard."
>
> (OT 251)

This dialogue implies a complex exchange of sexual roles and pleasures, especially when read along Cruikshank's illustration of the scene (OT, 252). Here Charlotte's vigorous right forearm displays an oyster, while with her left she holds a knife which, rather than prising the shell, seems delicately to caress the beard. Noah's left hand fingers the well-buttered piece of bread, and the open clasp-knife in his right hand seems almost to anticipate the detail that accompanies Bill Sikes's death by hanging: "and there he hung, with the open knife clenched in his stiffening hand"(OT, 453). (Popular myth had it that the mandrake was formed from the semen of the executed criminal at the foot of the gallows [Thomas 79].) There seems a conspicuous absence between Noah's legs as he lolls submissively in the chair. He and Charlotte are locked, however, in a gaze of mutual gratification, in a world of secret pleasure, illuminated by a solitary candle. Secret were it not for the phallic tilt of the chair back, pointing to the cocked head of Mr. Bumble peering voyeuristically over the drapery that conceals the lower half of the window, prior to his "bursting into the room," when Noah, unable to eat another oyster, offers to kiss Charlotte. In spite of the apparently gratuitous play of this scene it is a significant one. Mr. Bumble, already familiar as monitor of the diet of the working class, is now monitor of its sexuality. "Kissing . . . the character of the peasantry gone forever"(OT, 253). His exclamation is unwittingly correct. The character of the peasantry is exactly what is being remodeled by the laws of political economy embodied by the workhouse.

It is to a wholly implausible world of ideal peasant labor that Rose Maylie is removed after the attempted burglary at Chertsey and it is there that she nearly dies from some mysterious unnamed disease. I do not want to propose that Rose, or any other early Victorian heroine, may be retrospectively diagnosed as an anorexic, rather that the "meaning" of anorexia has some bearing on the meanings of the novel.

The movement toward treating the female body as a commodity is a process that is intensified and transformed during the early nineteenth century. James Laver describes the demise of the Empire line (a mode of female dress we may associate with Jane Austen's heroines who are always involved in frank economic exchanges, not least as members of a rural *haute-bourgeoisie* with a long history of sexual-marital trading).

> The same year [1822] was a turning point for female dress. The waist, which had been high for a quarter of a century, now resumed its normal position, and when this happens it inevitably becomes tighter and tighter. As a result, the corset once more became an essential element of female dress, even for small girls. A contemporary advertisement advises a mother to make her daughter lie face down on the floor in order that she might then place a foot in the small of the back to obtain the necessary purchase on the laces.
>
> (Laver 15)

While the female body has been subjected historically to many constraints in which mothers and daughters have colluded, the spread of the fashion advertisement on which Laver draws here, is a major means by which fashion becomes a more general bourgeois preoccupation in a culture of conspicuous consumption. Advertising was one medium of generalizing a discourse of class and sexuality in which young women found themselves increasingly inscribed. (Indeed, the popular success of Dickens' own early work is part of the same process of making a commodity of female adolescence.) This remains the context in which anorexia nervosa has become such a common "disease" of the Western world. The disease was not diagnosed definitively until the 1870s, by two doctors, William Gull and E. C. Lasegue, working independently in, respectively, London and Paris. Lasegue's paper *On Hysterical Anorexia* (1873), based on an individual case study, drew attention to the patient's home life as another crucial factor in the syndrome.

> Both the patient and her family form a tight-knit whole, and we obtain a false impression of the disease if we limit our observation to the patient alone.
>
> (MacLeod 15)

(Once again Dickens's own work may be seen as contributing to, as well as reflecting, a major reconstruction and revaluation of family life in the early nineteenth century.) Both Sheila MacLeod in *The Art of Starvation* (1981) and Susie Orbach in *Hunger Strike* (1986) have stressed the role of the mother in the life of the anorexic. We may then note the first gesture of Mrs. Maylie in the novel. Although only Rose's adoptive mother, her eyes are "attentively fixed upon her young companion", as they sit "at a well-spread breakfast table." Rose already bears some ominous signs although she is "in the lovely bloom and spring-time of womanhood."

> She was not past seventeen. Cast in so slight and exquisite a mould; so mild and gentle; so pure and beautiful; that earth seemed not her element, nor its rough creatures her fit companions . . . above all, the smile, the cheerful happy smile, were made for Home, and fireside peace and happiness.
>
> (OT, 264)

Sheila MacLeod writes:

> The connection and confusion with "consumption" are both inter-esting . . . . Because anorexia nervosa has typically been a disease of the upper or middle classes I am led to wonder how many young ladies of the eighteenth and nineteenth centuries who wasted away or "went into a decline", were not in fact suffering from tuberculosis, which is often associated with poor social conditions, but from anorexia in protest against the narrowness of their social roles and the lack of stimulation in their over-protected lives.
>
> (MacLeod 13)

Rose is kept by her foster-mother in just such an over-protected suburban seclusion, surrounded by a group of apparently impotent old men—the bungling Giles, the "slow boy" Brittles, the fat Dr. Losberne (who isn't averse to making Rose a leering proposition). Later they are joined by the bland Brownlow and the similarly leering Mr. Grimwig. When Chertsey, after the burglary, seems over-stimulating, Rose has to be removed to an even more remote village where there is little else to do but pick flowers. It is here that she enters her decline and we learn that in fact she is being guarded from the attention of her adopted brother, Henry. We may reconstruct for her a childhood made up of feelings of deep obligation mixed with anxious emotional and sexual awakening. Additionally, although Rose believes she returns Henry's feelings, she must deny them because of her own tainted origins, about which, after her recovery, she can be perversely and priggishly eloquent. The extravagant qualities of Rose's self-renunciation and guilt ("there is a stain upon my name . . . I will carry it into no blood but my own" [OT, 317]) are accompanied by fulsome testimonies to her goodness and dutifulness from all around her. Taken together they suggest a highly distorted self-image, an impossible load of family responsibilities, and a contradictory knowledge of sexuality to carry. Conventionally criticism hardly considers her a convincing "character." We may now, however, get beyond both the immediate post-Victorian contempt for her type and the orthodox feminist critique of Dickens' absurd idealizing of young women and begin to find her more sympathetic, more interesting.

The anorexic experience focuses a wider crisis of the body, its needs and desires. It may help account for the contrast between the strangely disembodied social milieu that is supposed to provide the novel's moral center, the Brownlow/Maylie axis, and the delighted, passionate, playful rendering of the physical sensations, the bodily experience of those who are outlawed from domestic enclosure to the "cold, wet, shelterless midnight streets of London," or consigned to the "tender mercies" of the Poor Law. The psychological and physiological drama of anorexia, in which the female body becomes the site of a contradictory articulation of relations between pleasure and power, a means to deny and assert oneself simultaneously in a world of ambiguous freedoms, is all the more baffling when it is set amongst nutritional excess. (This setting may partly account for presence of bulimia within the contemporary syndrome.) The sheer quantity of food, the scale of its production and marketing, the fetishization of its consumption, the deodorizing and marginalizing of both human excretory functions and the butchery of animals, the obsessive paramedical discourse on health and diet all contribute to the anorexic condition in a culture where the marketing of sexuality itself is centered on the representation of the female body. If anorexia has a "meaning" it seems to lie in a series of splittings, doublings, projections and displacements in the sufferer's understanding of these facts about her world. The "meaning" is shocking as well as baffling when seen from the outside, as a response to a hyperproductive global economy where the supply of food is taken for granted and, at the same time, predicated upon the destitution of whole communities and societies, denied nutritional variety and continuously subject to famine and disease.[1]

Oliver Twist as a novel seems characterized by a similar succession of splittings and doublings. Its starting point is the same paradox that Orbach identifies in her chapter, "Starving amidst plenty"(Orbach 50–70). Dickens wants to expose both the intimate pathos and the wider scandal of this. He creates a significant pattern in the representation of various anxieties about the body, in which eating and drinking are symbolically central in the assumption of social and sexual identity.

In his first novel, *Pickwick Papers*, the feast had been the staple of shared pleasure, not merely between the characters, but between author and reader. The detailed inventory of meals sets the "Dickens myth" on the road. *Pickwick* derives from the picaresque English novel developed by Fielding in ways explicitly analagous to the pleasures of the table. Natural appetites are healthily roused by a day of travel, followed by a night at an inn, first consulting the bill-of-fare. Each chapter of *Joseph Andrews* is intended to provide a local narrative satisfaction of just this kind.

> those little spaces between our chapters may be looked upon as an inn or resting-place where he may stop and take a glass or any other refreshment as it pleases him.
>
> (*Joseph Andrews*, 60)

The appeal to the male reader insinuates that "any other refreshment" includes sexual pursuit and conquest. Fielding's version of natural appetite is based on male desire for woman as a tasty dish, dressed (in the double sense of clothed and cooked) so as to be devoured with relish. Also at work in Fielding is a larger principle of narrative health, part of the critique of the Richardsonian malaise. Pamela's efforts are slight in comparison to Clarissa's later heroic and fatal determination to control her own body. Fielding's journey are to find one's "natural" sexual partner, a country girl like Fanny or Sophia, and to elude the temptations of a deviant metropolitan sexuality where women like Lady Booby and Lady Bellaston openly express their appetite. (The last device is parodically present in Mrs. Bardell's pursuit of Mr. Pickwick.) The first chapter of *Tom Jones* is titled "The Introduction to the Work, or Bill of Fare to the Feast" where the metaphor of healthy eating underpins a coherent theory of relations of social class, narrative propriety and moral responsibility, and "the whole . . . consists in the cookery of the author" (*Tom Jones* 1–3). Fielding's suggestion that "true nature is as difficult to be met with in authors, as the Bayonne ham, or Bologna sausage, is to be found in the shops" is found playfully echoed in Dickens's apologia for the melodramatic texture of *Oliver Twist*.

> It is the custom on the stage, in all good murderous melodramas, to present the tragic and comic scenes, in as regular alternation, as the layers of red and white in a side of streaky bacon.
>
> (OT, 168)

Popular versions of the novel, like Lionel Bart's musical, all acknowledge the centrality of food. Crucial to such an understanding is the scene of the starving little boy in the workhouse "asking for more." Students reading the novel for the first time often express their surprise that this incident occurs so early, a feeling that it ought to be climactic in some way.

> The master was a fat, healthy man; but he turned very pale. He gazed in stupefied astonishment on the small rebel for some seconds, and then clung for support to the copper. The assistants were paralysed with wonder; the boys with fear.
>
> (OT, 56)

The melodrama mixes the ingredients of woe and wonder to be found in the authentic tragic perepeteia. Our perception, like the gaze of the "fat, healthy" master, is "stupefied," and, like his assistants, we are "paralysed with wonder" or, like the boys, "with fear." At the same time we see the true relations of things with the utmost clarity, the whole "system" laid bare by the intervention of a "small rebel." That phrase, both sentimental and political, contributes decisively to the centrality of the moment in the novel's mythic account of the criminalization of bodily appetite. The revolution in the social relations of production and consumption inaugurated by industrial capitalism is accompanied by forms of surveillance and policing of the body, transforming among much else, as Foucault has suggested, both medical and penal theory.

Dickens had clearly identified the Poor Law Amendment Act of 1834 as the central plank in the program of the post-Reform Act parliament for the reconstruction of the "body politic" through the liberation of certain "natural" economic laws. He recognizes the full irony of an economic, social, and ideological revolution that guarantees new levels of production and the potential satisfaction of all basic human needs and which, at the same time, erects into a principle of social regulation and control the fact of hunger. The abolition of outdoor relief and the notorious "less eligibility" clause are intended to strip away all the historical, social, and cultural meanings that have accreted, protectively, to the body, in order that it shall find its "real" value as a tool for the production of wealth it is not destined to enjoy. Such a redefinition of the relations between needs and desires, communities and individuals, is also the redefinition of the human as a group of raw appetites to be deployed in the form of a conscious animal cunning. Thus Fagin, the most articulate spokesman of the new *laisser-faire* order, with his watchword,

"Look after number one!", is presented most typically "crawling forth . . . in search of some rich offal for a meal"(OT, 186). There is much fairly heavy-handed irony at the expense of the "philosophical gentlemen" who make up the board of poor law guardians "sitting in solemn conclave"(OT, 58). The theological pretensions of the board are beautifully conveyed in the only individually named member—Limbkins. This name suggests a self-regarding but diminished body, its combination of limb and little lamb, a parody of the qualities of affection and concern consumed in narcissistic self-communion.

The force of Dickens' critique is checked by his own class position. His bourgeois radicalism is modified by his aspiration towards gentility, the acquisition of a tone of voice that is achieved by Mr. Brownlow, "speaking like a gentleman," in his insistently quiet rebuke to the savage magistrate, Mr. Fang (OT, 120). This aspiration serves to intensify the mythic relation of the novel to modern urban and, importantly, suburban society. Yet Dickens' avowed intention had been to demythologize a popular tradition of the criminal hero running from Gay's *The Beggar's Opera* to the Newgate Novels of the 1830s and which included the Dick Turpin legend. This was, however, a road and street mythology belonging to an earlier stage of social modernization, with which Fielding may be connected and which it was Dickens' achievement to domesticate.

Oliver Twist stands in relation to urban industrial society as the adventures of Robin Hood did to late medieval England. The continuing vitality of film, comic book, television, and musical versions of the novel (adaptations had started before the novel was finished) testify to this. Robin Hood balladry postulates an ideal feudal order, a version of pastoral in Sherwood Forest. Important functions of this bandit game are merry-making and feasting, as well as redistributive justice, robbing the rich to give to the poor. The sporadic dearth to which the medieval agricultural economy was always subject is countered by images of plenty consumed in a world where chivalric codes of conduct and distinctions of rank are normally observed. No one needed to be literate to know the names of Robin's companions.

> In this our spacious isle I think there is not one
> But he hath heard some talk of him, and little John,
> And to the end of time the tale shall ne'er be done
> Of Scarlock, George a Green, and Much the Miller's son.
> Of Tuck the merry Friar, which many a sermon made
> In praise of Robin Hood, his outlaws, and their trade.[2]

Similarly everyone knows about Fagin, the Artful Dodger, Bill Sykes, and Nancy. Mr. Bumble stands to Oliver as the Sheriff of Nottingham to Robin. The difference is that Fagin's gang, as a form of collective resistance to a social system it also echoes, is consigned not to the forest but an inner city jungle. They are the secretive and desperate inhabitants of collapsing slums, the decayed houses of an urban bourgeoisie that has decamped to a genteel suburbia. By the end of the novel they have all been eliminated in the interests of a social hygiene with which Dickens is complicit. The pastoral elements within the Robin Hood tradition are hived off to re-appear: first, as the Islington garden home of Mr. Brownlow; then in Chertsey, a day and a night by foot from the capital (to reach which Sykes and Oliver pass through the great metropolitan food markets of Smithfield and Covent Garden at dawn); finally, as the country retreat where Rose nearly dies amidst a community of laborers who only appear, conspicuously clean, at church on Sundays. Later, just once, we see them as an emblem of mortality at the side of the road as Oliver races to fetch the doctor, when the "mowers and haymakers were busy at their work". Strikingly the wasting of Rose's life is juxtaposed by an image of agricultural production (OT, 296).

There is, however, another form of female waste. Rose's other name, Maylie, echoes nothing so much as one of the terms in the irascible Mr. Grimwig's distinction between different kinds of boy in response to Mr. Brownlow's query whether Oliver is a "nice-looking boy."

> "I only know two sorts of boys. Mealy boys, and beef-faced boys."
> "And which is Oliver?"
> "Mealy. I know a friend who has a beef-faced boy; a fine boy they call him: with a round head, and red cheeks, and glaring eyes; a horrid boy; with a body and limbs that appear to be swelling out of the seams of his blue clothes; with the voice of a pilot, and the appetite of a wolf. I know him! The wretch!"
>
> (OT, 148)

Rose will overcome her mealy pallor to recover "all the bloom and grace of early womanhood" (OT, 479). Just as boys form opposing types, Rose has her opposite in the "wretch," Nancy, who meets another fate. She is described intitially as "stout and hearty" when she and her friend Bet appear with "a good deal of colour in their cheeks"(OT, 111). Nancy, in contrast to Rose, tucks into "a plate of boiled beef"(OT, 155). If she too has the raucous "voice of a pilot," it is a misleading one that we hear in her drunken exclamation— "Never say die!"—a theatrical assumption of pleasure in her job as well as a taunt to her wilting clientele. With these dangerous indications of the "appetite of a wolf," she meets an ugly apotheosis when her own blood is let in an act of brutal vengeance by her pimp Sikes. Sikes has always testified to the stoutness of her heart, but he is quick to notice the signs of her wasting away and loss of appetite as she may be on the verge of recovering "something of the woman's original nature" (OT, 360), by renouncing her past and shopping the gang. Such a recovery is impossible and her murder is presented terrifyingly as a half-invited sexual assault. Sikes enters the house "softly" and goes "lightly up the stairs."

> The girl was lying, half dressed, upon it. He had roused her from her sleep, for she raised herself with a hurried and startled look.
> "Get up!" said the man.
> "It *is* you, Bill!" said the girl, with an expression of pleasure at his return.
>
> (OT, 421)

By the next morning light and blood have become interchangeable, "the reflection of the pool of gore . . . quivered and danced in the sunlight"(OT, 423). Dickens' imagination appears now wholly identified with the "murderer" Sikes, while the formal unravelling of the plot that finally casts light on the purity of Oliver's blood feels like an attempt to erase these guilty stains on the narrative. Sikes acquires those heroic qualities that Oliver was incapable of sustaining. It is as a hero, confirmed by his actions in the fire, that he returns to London, drawn by the magnetic power of the city. When Dickens tells us that his attempt at flight takes him past the Dick Whittington stone on Highgate Hill, it is a certain portent of his fatal destiny. His death by hanging will be a great act of public theater before the London crowd. The scene brings together so many of Dickens' own obsessions that it is important to examine closely the setting—Jacob's Island and Folly Ditch. It is Dickens' first treatment of the excremental vision found in earlier poets of the city—Jonson, Dryden, Pope, and Swift. London is the center of a great cycle of production and consumption, analagous to that of the human body, from which consciousness is alienated as capitalist development adds new dimensions of both wealth and waste, the sublime and the grotesque. Jacob's Island lies at the center of an intestinal labyrinth of city streets, its description, like that of the pit in Defoe's *Journal of the Plague Year* (78–80), pointing to a moment of impossible metaphysical revelation, some black hole in space. The name also refers us to the vision of Jacob's Ladder in Genesis 28.

> And Jacob awaked out of his sleep, and he said, Surely the Lord is in this place; and I knew it not.

> And he was afraid, and said, How dreadful is this place! this is none other but the house of God, and this is the gate of heaven.

The chapter locates the site in the rear of the church.

> Near to that part of the Thames on which the church at Rotherhithe abuts, where the buildings on the banks are dirtiest and the vessels on the river blackest, with the dust of colliers and the smoke of close-built low-roofed houses, there exists the filthiest, the strangest, the most extraordinary of the many localities that are hidden in London, wholly unknown, even by name, to the great mass of its inhabitants.
>
> (OT, 442)

We read of the difficulty with which this place is reached "through a maze of close, narrow and muddy streets"; how "the coarsest and commonest of wearing apparel . . . stream from the house-parapet and window"; of the human "raff and refuse of the river"; "offensive sights and smells from the narrow alleys." At the same time the "visitor" is "deafened by the clash of ponderous wagons that bear great piles of merchandise from the stacks of warehouses that rise from every corner." Dickens is determined to rub our noses in the "muddy ditch" and,

> a stranger, looking from one of the wooden bridges thrown across it at Mill Lane, will see one of the inhabitants on either side lowering from their back doors and windows, buckets, pales, domestic utensils of all kinds, in which to haul the water up; and when his eyes turned from these operations to the houses themselves, his utmost astonishment will be excited by the scene before him. Crazy wooden galleries common to the backs of half a dozen houses, with holes from which to look upon the slime beneath; . . . rooms so small, so filthy, so confined, that the air would seem too tainted even for the dirt and squalor which they shelter; wooden chambers thrusting themselves out above the mud, and threatening to fall into it—as some have done; dirt-besmeared walls and decaying foundations; every repulsive lineament of poverty, every loathsome indication of filth, rot and garbage;—all these ornament the banks of Folly Ditch.
>
> (OT 443)

This animated mass seems a giant and foetid latrine where we find three men "with powerful motives for a secret residence," in a house "strongly defended at door and window—of which house the back commanded the ditch in the manner already described." They are "regarding each other every now and then with looks expressive of perplexity and expectation" as they sit "in profound and gloomy silence." The scatological implications of the whole sequence are bizarrely reflected in the names of the three men, each suggesting a different potential performance. Toby *Crackit* has already been characterised as a type of anal-retentive dandyism; Mr. *Chitling* suggests perfect formations from the pig's intestine, and the third is an otherwise inexplicably introduced returned transport, "and his name was *Kags*." The bravura performance will be that of Sikes before the roaring crowd. What is striking is how fully Dickens elaborates the setting for the climax of Sikes's heroic role in a novel devoted to the exploration of bodily appetites as they are determined by the new social order. The physical allure and urgent pleasures of the underworld stand obliquely for the whole of the modern city which is epitomized here between "piles of merchandise" and the open sewer. The representation of Nancy as a full-blooded and full-bodied creature of appetite, "whose life had been squandered in the streets, and among the most noisome of the stews and dens of London" (OT, 360) is consistent with this troubled perspective in which, as a prostitute, she embodies the treatment of human relations by the metropolitan market as a commodity. While the contrast between Rose and Nancy at first sight reflects a conventional Victorian male ambivalance, it is subtly bound up with a more complex account of the social processes that generate this ambivalence. More importantly we may see Dickens struggling to find a *subjectivity* for these two figures. Dickens' sense of visual theater and his indebtedness to the arts of caricature mean that he arrives at such a possibility through observing the mutations of the body. His comic inventiveness can tap the spirit of carnival with its surrender and distortion of conventional shapes and forms, while his narrative art attends to elements of growth and development.

It is part of the vitality of the early nineteenth century novel that it mutates itself in response to the market. The previously noted demise of Oliver's unlikely heroism may be linked with his loss of appetite and the subduing of his blood. When he reaches the outskirts of London he meets the Artful Dodger, who will lure him to Fagin's kitchen, where the old fence is discovered toasting sausages. These are the basis of a diabolic communion that Oliver will learn to deny. Sausages are also one of the ways offal is made edible for the squeamishly civilized. The cooking of the waste product may be an emblem of how the human "refuse" of a wealthy society is processed and devoured, as so many of the gang are transported or hanged. Yet the earlier breakfast with the Dodger seems to have a true sacramental status. It is offered in response to Oliver's simple statement: "I am very hungry and tired . . . I have walked a long way."

Assisting Oliver to rise, the young gentleman took him to an adjacent chandler's shop, where he purchased a sufficiency of ready-dressed ham and a half-quartern loaf. Or, as he himself expressed it, "a fourpenny bran!", the ham being kept clean and preserved from dust, by the ingenious expedient of making a hole in the loaf by pulling out a proportion of the crumb and stuffing it therein. Taking the bread under his arm, the young gentleman turned into a small public-house, and led the way to a tap-room at the rear of the premises. Here, a pot of beer was brought in, by direction of the mysterious youth; and Oliver, falling to, at his new friend's bidding, made a long and hearty meal. . . .

(OT, 101)

It may be hard to situate this little miracle of prose in relation to the great miracles and parables of the road within the Christian tradition. That Dickens had some such effect in mind is evidence by the novel's sub-title "The Parish-Boy's Progress." Yet this meal also marks the effective end of his role as plucky little *picaro*, the small boy, who when his blood was roused could lay into both Noah Claypole and Mr. Bumble. He takes no more initiatives from this point. He will be either captive or convalescent. Once he has been rescued from Fagin's clutches we note that he can hardly sip the thin gruel offered by Mrs. Bedwin. After the Chertsey expedition Sikes too will undergo a brief convalescence. Charley Bates brings him a bundle of food.

"Sitch a rabbit pie, Bill", exclaimed that young gentleman, disclosing to view a huge pasty; "Sitch delicate creeturs, with sitch tender limbs, Bill, that the wery bones melt in your mouth, and there's no occasion to pick 'em; half a pound of seven and sixpenny green, so precious strong that if you mix it with biling water, it'll go nigh to blow the lid of the tea-pot off; a pound and a-half of moist sugar that the niggers didn't work at all at, afore they got it up to sitch a pitch of goodness, - oh no! Two half-quartern brans; pound of best fresh; piece of double Glo'ster; and. to wind up all, some of the richest sort you ever lushed!"

(OT, 349)

The delicious comic *brio* of this passage is inseparable from its vein of violence and cruelty. The promise of immediate and complete gratification from the "very bones" of the anthropoid rabbits complements and contrasts with the slave labor that produces the sugar. If this is food fit for a hero it is noticeable that the dominant narrative mode has shifted from a masculine to a femine emphasis. Oliver's submission to captivity and carriage identifies him with the heroines of female gothic as described by Ellen Moers (esp. part II).

In *Oliver Twist* the road from which he is seduced is not replaced by the turreted and dungeoned castle of Mrs. Radcliffe with its alluring passages and stairways down which an unchaperoned woman may adventure. Rather it leads to that labyrinth of city streets, of which Folly Ditch is the dark center, endlessly turning on themselves. The Radcliffe heroine may have access to romantic vistas, sublime or picturesque, to console her captivity. Oliver's views are confined either to dark townscapes, stifling rooms and, at the last, astonishingly, Fagin's condemned cell; or, on the other axis of his being, those libraries, parlors, and gardens that typify a new suburban ideal.

Such a shift in narrative mode reflects a wider "feminization" at work in bourgeois culture which will have consequences for Dickens' later fiction: the troubled passage from "Daisy" to David Copperfield; the dainty table manners Pip will have to learn from Herbert Pocket in *Great Expectations*. This shift in narrative mode has to do not only with the problem of conceiving a new kind of "gentleman-hero" of everyday life, the passive recipient of reward. It is crucial to those extraordinary stories in which Dickens attempts to imagine female adventure. There is, of course, *The Old Curiosity Shop*, with its plump heroine fading away, and, more challengingly, the angry refusal of Miss Wade's "History of a Self-Tormentor," itself refusing to be integrated into the mainstream of *Little Dorrit*. Most striking of all is the decision to give two-thirds of the narration of *Bleak House* to a young woman. Esther begins *her* story with a chapter called "A Progress." A strangely wrapped man speaks to and touches her in a coach. Then he exposes himself.

> After a little while, he opened his outer wrapper, which appeared to me large enough to wrap up the whole coach, and put his arm down into a deep pocket in the side.
> "Now, look here!" he said. "In this paper", which was nicely folded, "is a piece of the best plum-cake that can be got for money—sugar on the outside an inch thick, like fat on mutton chops. Here's a little pie (a gem this is, both for size and quality), made in France. And what do you suppose it's made of? Livers of fat geese. There's a pie! Now let's see you eat 'em."
> "Thank you, sir," I replied, "thank you very much indeed, but I hope you won't be offended; they are too rich for me."
>
> *(Bleak House 71)*

NOTES

1. See, for example, Susan George's *A Fate Worse than Death*.
2. From Michael Drayton's *Polyolbion*, cited in Henry B. Wheatley's Preface to Thomas Percy's *Reliques of Ancient English Poetry*.

WORKS CITED

Barthes, Roland, *The Pleasure of the Text*, trans. Richard Miller. London: Jonathan Cape, 1976.

Defoe, Daniel, *A Journal of the Plague Year*, eds. Anthony Burgess and Christopher Bristow. Harmondshire: Penguin, 1983.

Dickens, Charles, *Bleak House*. ed. Norman Page. Harmondshire: Penguin, 1983.

————, *Oliver Twist*, ed. Peter Fairclough. Harmondsworth: Penguin English Library, 1966.

Fielding, Henry, *Joseph Andrews*. London: Dent, 1910.

————, *Tom Jones*. London: Dent, 1909.

George, Susan, *A Fate Worse than Death*. Harmondshire: Penguin, 1983.

Hardy, Barbara, "Food and Ceremony in *Great Expectations*," in *Essays in Criticism* 13 (1963). 351–63.

Thomas, Keith, *Man and the Natural World: Changing Attitudes in England, 1500–1800*. Harmondshire: Penguin, 1983.

Laver, James, *A Concise History of Costume*. London: Virago, 1981.

MacLeod, Sheila, *The Art of Starvation*. London: Virago, 1981.

Moers, Ellen, *Literary Women*. London: The Women's Press, 1978.

Orbach, Susie, *Hunger Strike*. London: Faber, 1986.

Percy, Thomas, *Reliques of Ancient English Poetry*. London: Swan Sonnenshein, 1891.

Watt, Ian, "Oral Dickens" in *Dickens Studies Annual* 3. New York: AMS, 1974. 165–81.

Railway/Reading/Time:
Dombey & Son and the Industrial World

Murray Baumgarten

The railroad "starts the new era," Thackeray wrote in 1860, "and we of a certain age belong to the new time and the old one. . . . We elderly people have lived in that pre-railroad world, which has passed into limbo and vanished from under us. I tell you it was firm under our feet once, and not long ago." The nostalgia in his voice evokes the stagecoach world so important for Dickens and other novelists of the era. "They have raised those railroad embankments up, and shut off the old world that was behind them. Climb up that bank on which the irons are laid, and look to the other side—it is gone." An elegy for a landscape that had changed very little since the Middle Ages, Thackeray's comment also comprehends the passing of the lumbering passenger and mail coaches that traversed it, horse-drawn vehicles stopping at inns which cared for animals, passengers, and goods in accordance with age-old traditions. Dependent upon the old modes, the inns would come to be replaced by a new species of what Richard Altick calls "traveler-serving buildings, imposing yet bustling 'termini' (the elegant Latin is characteristic of the time), often with large hotels under the same roof." These structures came to define the entryways to the new cities, serving as the portals to Victorian industrial civilization. "When Queen Victoria came to the throne in 1837," Asa Briggs reminds us, "there were only five places in England and Wales outside London with a population of 100,000 or more . . . [while] by 1891 there were 23." The iron rails Thackeray berated led, as he well knew, out of the rural civilization of the country into the increasingly numerous and populous cities, which were creating a host of new social relationships, institutions, and values (Altick 74, Briggs 59). His comment articulates half the story: manifest sadness is balanced by the youthful optimism of his listeners. Together, latent and manifest functions define the situation. Whatever their tone, the doubled image of the train bearing down upon the past like a Juggernaut implicit in Thackeray's remarks and taking England into the future like a prophecy was the common starting point of most mid-Victorian explorations of the railroad world.

Among the most famous and important of these is Turner's steam engine—a figure to conjure with. In his striking painting, *Rain, Steam, & Speed*, done in 1844, two years before Dickens was to write *Dombey & Son*, he evokes the railway's dynamic qualities. Color, line, and light conspire to bring the train forward in the painting like a god emerging from his natural realm. The locomotive in motion toward us, the impressionistic treatment, and the barely discernible visual panorama create a fitting emblem for a technology about to transform the world. The viewer experiences both the shock and awesome beauty of this new event in human history as we enter the liminal moment of an historical threshold. Our curiosity to know more is stirred by this powerful painting: we desire as we fear the future.

Ruskin, who championed Turner's work, repudiated the railroad world so brilliantly portrayed in this painting, the contradictions of his stance under-lining the difficulties of a transitional era. Like Thackeray, for whom the world was divided by the railroad, Ruskin regarded attitudes toward it as touchstones for artistic judgment. Thus, after Dickens' death, Ruskin called him "a pure modernist" and "leader of the steam-whistle party." And, he noted with disdain, Dickens' "hero is essentially the ironmaster."[1] Much of the critical commentary on *Dombey & Son* depends upon a similar negative view of the industrial world. Motivated like Ruskin by a sense of overwhelm-ing loss, many critics project into the past world of crafts and hand manufacture an esthetic wholeness it has only in retrospect. Rousseau, not Marx or Freud, animates their critique of Dickens; thereby they miss the importance of his charting of the transformation of time and space brought about by industrialization. One way to avoid this confusion is to look at some aspects of the historical context, most readily available in this instance in a group of central images drawn from the record of the past.

For the moment it is important to note that Turner's achievement in *Rain, Steam, and Speed* finds appropriate parallels in the railroad lithographs of Currier & Ives. Later, photographic images of steam engines and railroad trains became a conventional way of marking passages through time and space, especially in the American motion picture film. Celebrating the power of industrial civilization's heroic conquest of previously impassable barriers, these images enshrine the iron linkages of the railways in an icon that for our Victorian forebears articulated the idea of one world, visual counterparts to the literary narrative of Phineas Fogg's 80 days' journey. Without knowing what the future had in store for them, Victorian views of the train and of modernity were nevertheless multi-layered. Though the triumphant mood captured in the photograph of the driving of the golden spike at Promontory Point, Utah, on 10 May 1869 to mark the completion of the first North American transcontinental railway is echoed in Walt Whitman's invocation to the steam-engine, his poem also raises questions about the amoral qualities of this new force.

For us railroads are no longer the vehicles of world-conquering optimism. Their fuller representation includes the acquiescence in racial discrimination that made separate compartments standard in this country for a century and more, and that still continues in South Africa. Furthermore, their presentation as engines of history also evokes the grisly negative after-images of the trains used by the Nazis to herd Jews to the death-camps, boxcars that were themselves instruments of genocide. Of course, Victorian ambivalence to trains did not extend to these extremes. For the Victorians the slaughter of aristocracy lurked in their past, the terror of the French Revolution reminding them of the shapes revenge might take. Carlyle's great portrait was a warning of what the mob might do. The Crimean War and the American Civil War, with their mass carnage on a vast new and impersonal scale with unimagined magnitudes of destruction made possible by industrial technology, were but proleptic hints of what our century of a world at war would bring.

Industrialism changed England; where it destroyed, it also rebuilt. When Humphry House notes that the railroad civilization created the sense of English neatness which was the pride of the Victorians, he reminds us how the strength of Victorian England grew from its industrial civilization. "It is hardly fanciful to associate the neater hedging and ditching of the middle and later Victorian age with the necessary primness of railway works. More scientific farming played its part; but there was also a new pride in neatness for its own sake, which abolished the tangled hedgerows of Constable." And, as he notes earlier, "The growth of home consumption was enormously accelerated by improved transport: diet, furniture, fireplaces, and all the physical appurtenances of life changed character more rapidly; the very landscape was given a new aesthetic character—even perhaps a new standard—by embankments, cuttings, and viaducts" (House 138). Punctuality, for example, is one of the qualities connected with neatness in the emerging middle-class world of nineteenth-century England. Thus, in *Dombey & Son*, traditional views of time-keeping are presented satirically. Here the comedy of time results from the fact that an impersonal and regular order is perceived subjectively and altered for individual needs. Though the watch Cap'n Cuttle gives Walter works, it is with the proviso that the hands be moved back a half hour every morning and "about another quarter towards the afternoon" (chapter 19), thereby placing this sense of time in a pre-industrial context. This world of leisurely time, linked to the inns and coaching world of *Pickwick* that Cap'n Cuttle evokes, brings a gentle laughter. In *Dombey*, it gives way to harsher strictures, as we encounter a different view of time in which an iron schedule rules. The clocks in Dr. Blimber's establishment in chapter 11, their heavy tick-tock rendered mimetically ("how, is, my, lit, tle, friend? how, is, my, lit, tle, friend?") have much to do with education as a system of forcing, but little with an effective sense of punctuality. In 1846, Dickens was able to hope that the punctuality so important for the new railroad civilization would be informed by the personal ease of Cap'n Cuttle, for he was still part of a transitional era. Despite the establishment, with the founding of the Greenwich Observatory in 1675 of a standard chronometer for nautical purposes, even railroad time was approximate until it was linked directly to Greenwich Mean Time in 1884. And it is worth noting that one way in which the regions of England were to lose their temporal identity was a result of the railroads, which by the 1870s were to deprive them of their local time, with the coming of standard train schedules (Schivelbusch, 42–43). Nevertheless, it is important to recognize that punctuality as an abstract and impersonal idea became a national ideal only in the twentieth century with the establishment of radio broadcast networks and the hooking up of the BBC to the Greenwich time signal. In fact, the three beeps before the hour characteristic of the BBC became a nationwide phenomenon only in the 1920s. People set their watches by the tones and became in our sense "punctual."

The speed with which the iron horse conquered the landscape transformed it: perception changed reality in a pre-figuring of Einstein's relativity theorem. The shock of moving at gale-force and hurricane speed in a railroad when a stage coach travelled at barely the pace of a brisk breeze was registered throughout the culture: the world was changed for all by speed. Transformed by the coming of the railroad, the novel opened to encompass its experiences, becoming a loose baggy monster that included the picaresque adventures of the stagecoach world and the directness of the enterprise of the iron horse riding on iron grooves. The heroic paintings and full-face portraits of

Reynolds and Gainsborough gave way to Constable's broad canvases and Turner's experiments with light. The clickety-clack of the rails now became an ever-present metronome measuring the time of this new world. Thus railroad music—that splendid mixture of nostalgia and eager anticipation— lets us recover the rhythmic intricacies and impersonal regularities which the coming of the railways bestowed upon us. The change in the auditory landscape echoed the transformation of the English countryside brought by the iron rails. Embankments, viaducts, right-of-ways, tunnels, and roundhouses redefined the English landscape and endowed it with a new sense of order. Cathedral-like terminals at St. Pancras and Paddington Station proclaimed their allegiance to the new industrial gods, erected with the new technology that mounted in 1851 its triumphant exhibition, the first world's fair in the Crystal Palace.

Written at the height of the railway boom of the 1840s, *Dombey & Son* articulates the transition from the stagecoach world to the railroad civilization. As Steven Marcus has noted, in this novel "the railroad is the great symbol of social transformation. . . . By the time [Dickens] was finishing *Dombey & Son*, more than 5,000 miles of railway were open in the United Kingdom and

Cruikshank, *The Railway Dragon* (detail). Possible image of Carker's death in *Dombey and Son*.

2,000 more miles were under construction. A railway *system* had sprung into existence and had imposed itself on the life of society." And one of the central achievements of this novel as of the mid-Victorian novel in general, Marcus reminds us, is that of bringing the complex "rhythms" and visual transformations "of the industrial revolution" into the "living language" (Marcus 306-07, 295).

Perhaps that is why Dickens, the virtuoso of English, makes his *Dombey* prose so clearly do the work of painting and of music. His railroad scenes include onomatopoetic passages that punctuate the novel. "Away, with a shriek, and a roar, and a rattle, from the town, burrowing among the dwellings of men and making the streets hum, flashing out into the meadows for a moment, mining in through the damp earth, booming on in darkness and heavy air, bursting out again into the sunny day so bright and wide; away, with a shriek, and a roar, and a rattle, through the fields, through the woods, through the corn, through the hay, through the chalk, through the mould, through the clay, through the rock. . . ." In this novel the representation of train travel is brilliant—and brilliantly paradoxical and ambivalent. Ironically, there is only one illustration in *Dombey* where a train appears, the frontispiece of the novel, originally included in the final monthly number. Here the locomotive that kills Carker has a humorous look and is part of an otherwise happy, even sensually rendered, scene. How then can we comprehend the function and nature of Dickens' (and of course Phiz's) representation of the railroad in *Dombey & Son* in these musical, visual, and narrative terms? If the ironmaster is his hero and Dickens is indeed, to adapt Blake's phrase, of the railroad party, why is this treatment of the railroad ambivalent?[2]

In this passage from chapter 20, we encounter the railroad through the eyes of Dombey. The Birmingham train that is taking Dombey and Bagstock to the encounter with Cleopatra and Edith becomes to his imagination—in a brilliant act of narrative compression and condensation—the funeral train bearing his dead son home for burial. Dombey interprets what he sees and feels on this journey in the teleological terms of his previous trip: the rhythms of train travel register for him as signs of death. Looking out the window, he sees a world he cannot seize, "objects close at hand and almost in the grasp, ever flying from the traveller, and a deceitful distance ever moving slowly with him: like as in the track of the remorseless monster, Death!" For Bagstock, of course, the train is taking his friend and potential gull to the trap he has laid for him, a journey essential to the realization of his schemes. For Dombey, death and the railroad are linked: the question posed by many critics, particularly those who argue with Marcus's view, is whether this link expresses Dickens' view of his industrial world.

I think it important to see how Dickens emphasizes that the linkage is subjective and takes place in Dombey's stunted imagination. The mimetic rendering of train travel takes up six astounding paragraphs, four of which conclude in the same refrain: for Dombey, we are in the hands of the vengeful god. What is for him a personal reading of this power in the terms of his inability to respond to anything that opposes his monumental will, we see as well as an impersonal force. Dickens' prose renders Dombey's fear and the "sheer exhilaration at the monster's unswerving power and speed," a response not "unique to Dickens; in the late 1830s and early 1840s it was shared by most people" (Lucas 103).

Let us acknowledge that there was danger in travelling by train, then and now. For Dickens' time, train travel had the edge that airplane flight was to have a hundred years later. Like all new and unfamiliar technologies, the railroad produced an entire new class of accidents. To fear it and to take precautions was an entirely appropriate response. In 1865, Dickens himself was in a train accident, and his account of what happened illuminates the dangers of this new world.

> I was in the only carriage that did not go over into the stream. It was caught upon the turn by some of the ruin of the bridge, and hung suspended and balanced in an apparently impossible manner. . . . Fortunately, I got out with great caution and stood upon the step. Looking down I saw the bridge gone, and nothing below me but the line of rail. Some people in the two other compartments were madly trying to plunge out of window, and had no idea that there was an open swampy field fifteen feet down below them, and nothing else! . . . Suddenly I came upon a staggering man covered with blood (I think he must have been flung clean out of his carriage), with such a frightful cut across the skull that I couldn't bear to look at him. I poured some water over his face and gave him some drink, then gave him some brandy, and laid him down on the grass, and he said, "I am gone," and died afterwards. . . . No imagination can conceive the ruin of the carriages, or the extraordinary weights under which people were lying, or the complications into which they were twisted up among iron and wood, and mud and water.
>
> (Paroissien 150–01)

To connect death and the symbolic representative of the new order, the railroad, as Dombey does, however, is to displace fear of the future and of change onto a human product. It is to make train travel into a phobia and thus construct a traumatized self. Dickens does not dismiss railroad travel because of his accident. Rather, he incorporates it into the postscript of *Our Mutual*

Friend in a tone that reveals how the railroad has become one of the familiar spirits of the nineteenth-century world:

> On Friday the Ninth of June in the present year, Mr & Mrs Boffin (in their manuscript dress of receiving Mr & Mrs Lammle at breakfast) were on the South Eastern Railway with me, in a terribly destructive accident. When I had done what I could to help others, I climbed back into my carriage—nearly turned over a viaduct, and caught aslant upon the turn—to extricate the worthy couple. They were much soiled, but otherwise unhurt. The same happy result attended Miss Bella Wilfer on her wedding day, and Mr. Riderhood inspecting Bradley Headstone's red neckerchief as he lay asleep. I remember with devout thankfulness that I can never be much nearer parting company with my readers for ever, than I was then, until there shall be written against my life, the two words with which I have this day closed this book: The End.

By contrast, Dombey, the character, taints the new technology. On his train journey he registers its impact, but refuses to acknowledge its full meaning, for that would require him to confront his own act of bad faith. Note how Dickens' use of the present tense brings us into Dombey's experience of the railroad: "Louder and louder yet, it shrieks and cries as it comes tearing on resistless to the goal: and now its way, still like the way of Death, is strewn with ashes thickly. Everything around is blackened. There are dark pools of water, muddy lanes, and miserable habitations far below. There are jagged walls and falling houses close at hand, and through the battered roofs and broken windows, wretched rooms are seen, where want and fever hide themselves in many wretched shapes, while smoke, and crowded gables, and distorted chimneys, and deformity of brick and mortal penning up deformity of mind and body, choke the murky distance" (Pope 221–22).

Then Dickens moves us out of Dombey's mind, offering us a view of what he has projected onto this landscape: "As Mr. Dombey looks out of his carriage window, it is never in his thoughts that the monster who has brought him there has let the light of day in on these things: not made or caused them. It was the journey's fitting end, and might have been the end of everything; it was so ruinous and dreary." Like Werther, Dombey responds to the landscape by experiencing his own subjective dreary and depressing thoughts. Ironically, Dickens' phrase here reminds us that "the monster who . . . has let the light of day in on these things," the railroad, performs the function of the spirit whom he asks in chapter 47 to come and take the rooftops off.

Looking at these two passages side by side, we notice that the first prefigures the second: "Oh for a good spirit who would take the house-tops off, with a more potent and benignant hand than the lame demon in the tale, and show a Christian people what dark shapes issue from amidst their homes, to swell the retinue of the Destroying Angel as he moves forth among them!" What will follow in the novel, as Florence is banished, Edith leaves, and Carker rushes off, does not appear to Dombey to be the work of the good spirit but of the Destroying Angel, another figure perhaps for the work of the railroad. To Dombey's eyes the railroad is the monstrous modern mythological vehicle bearing him into the underworld; for us as for Dickens, who did not think the past a record of the "good old days," the railroad as the representative of the future may also be the good spirit letting in the light.

For Dombey, the railway journey he takes with Bagstock turns out to be fateful, but not in ways in which he (or the reader at that point in the serial publication of the novel) had expected. Death will indeed result from a railway journey but it will be Carker, Dombey's managerial double, who is killed at the climactic beginning of the penultimate monthly number, as part of the ironic and powerful playing out of the complex plot of the novel. Dombey will live. What is at stake is not the railroad but Dombey's incomplete and subjective experience of it. Dombey's trip is not into the underworld but into the fullness of the industrial civilization of the nineteenth century.

THE TERRIBLE RAILWAY ACCIDENT ON THE SOUTH EASTERN.—SEARCHING FOR THE DEAD AND WOUNDED AT STAPLEHURST.

In these astounding passages, virtuoso Dickens provides us with an example of *panoramic* vision, the new mode of perception brought by the railroad and industrial civilization. On his railway journey, Dombey sees

The Railway Dragon

things in motion which are separate from him. In *The Railway Journey*, Wolfgang Schivelbusch notes that "the railroad choreographed the landscape. The motion of the train shrank space, and thus displayed in immediate succession objects and pieces of scenery that in their original spatiality belonged to separate realms. The traveler who gazed through the compartment window at such successive scenes, acquired a novel ability . . . the synthetic philosophy of the glance . . . the ability to perceive the discrete as it rolls past the window, indiscriminately"(60–61). Because of his self-absorption, which makes him refer all events over and over again to himself, Dombey registers the discrete bundles but cannot make the quantum jump to perceiving the whole. What he is missing is the "concept of panorama: 'In a few hours [the railway] shows you all of [a country], and before your eyes it unrolls its infinite panorama, a vast succession of charming tableaux, of novel surprises. Of a landscape it shows you only the great outlines, being an artist versed in the ways of the masters. Don't ask it for details, but for the living whole. Then, after having charmed you thus with its painterly skills, it suddenly stops and quite simply lets you get off where you wanted to go.'" (Schivelbusch 61)

Because of his pride, Dombey cannot achieve a vision of the whole.[3] It is not that he is fixed in the details of the stagecoach world. Would he have been happy with Ruskin's exhortation "to be content with as little change as possible? If the attention is awake, and the feelings in proper train, a turn of

Rural English landscape with railroad. Unidentified artist.

a country road, with a cottage beside it, which we have not seen before, is as much as we need for refreshment; if we hurry past it, and take two cottages at a time, it is already too much . . ." (Schivelbusch 57). Dombey does not have Ruskin's interest in the foreground; he is not concerned with the details of objects and the perception of depth and volume which enables the stage-coach traveller "to relate to the landscape" through which he travelled as if he were part of it. For Dombey, the smells and sounds as well as the synaesthetic perceptions that were part of stagecoach travel had disappeared: for him, all reality is abstract, as it is for train travellers. The dreamlike experience of train travel, on which Emerson like many others comments, turns Dombey in upon himself. The "evanescent landscape" that he observes shocks him into thoughts of death. "Panoramic perception, in contrast to traditional perception, no longer belonged to the same space as the perceived objects: the traveler saw the objects, landscapes, etc., *through* the apparatus which moved him through the world. That machine and the motion it created became integrated into his visual perception: thus he could only see things in motion" (Schivelbusch 64).

And motion in all its aspects is what monumental Dombey avoids and fears. It is there in his response to young Paul's famous question about money. "Mr Dombey was in a difficulty. He would have liked to give him some explanation involving the terms circulating-medium, currency, depreciation of currency, paper, bullion, rates of exchange, value of precious metals in the market, and so forth; but looking down at the little chair, and seeing what a long way down it was, he answered: 'Gold, and silver, and copper. Guineas, shillings, half-pence. You know what they are?'" As the rest of this wonderfully realized exchange in chapter 8 makes clear, Dombey's answer to Paul, rationalized as something adapted to a child's level of understanding, is really directed to himself. What he is doing thereby is refusing to acknowledge here (as he does for most of the novel) that the essential quality of his world is motion. Dombey, the figure of pride, is Dombey the Static Man, in a world where everything else, even the means of his livelihood, is in movement.

Schivelbusch's analysis of the railroad journey is also a brilliant study of nineteenth-century culture. His richly documented work marshalls an astounding range of evidence, showing that "while the railroad caused the foreground to disappear, it also replaced looking at the landscape with a practice that had not existed previously. Reading while traveling became almost obligatory." Here too the railroad brings new social forms, for "the dissolution of reality and its resurrection as panorama thus became agents for the total emancipation from the traversed landscape: the traveler's gaze could then move into an imaginary surrogate landscape, that of his book. By the mid-nineteenth century, reading while traveling had become an established custom" (Schivelbusch 66). And, it is worth noting that "what the opening of major railroads provided in reality—the easy accessibility of distant places—was attempted in illusion, in the decades immediately preceding that opening, by the 'panoramic' and 'dioramic' shows and gadgets. These were designed to provide, by showing views of distant landscapes, cities, and exotic scenes, 'a substitute for those still expensive and onerous journeys' " (Schivelbusch 62). What the railroad did, to look once more at Turner's picture, was make train travellers into impressionist painters.

Railway travel created a new way of viewing the world that, as was the case with impressionist painters, often produced beauty in scenes previously considered ugly (and the photographer with his new technology was there to construct a record of this new way of seeing). By abstracting the whole from the parts through the velocity of its passage, the train helped all travellers to experience the idea of the whole, of totality. Thus they became participants in this phenomenon, something that might result, it is clear, if the good spirit did indeed remove the housetops and gave them a vision of the way everyone lived, a hope shared by the founders of social science, among them John Stuart Mill and Max Weber.

As we explore the meanings that accumulate around railways in *Dombey & Son* it is worth glancing at how other nineteenth-century writers dealt with them. The index of modernity, the railroad helped to establish new modes of behavior. In *Cranford* (1853) Mrs. Gaskell focuses on the ritual experience of commuting, defining a world in which the railroad is the necessary link between men and women: "In the first place, Cranford is in possession of the Amazons; all the holders of houses, above a certain rent, are women. If a married couple come to settle in the town, somehow the gentleman disappears; he is either fairly frightened to death by being the only man in the Cranford evening parties, or he is accounted for by being with his regiment, his ship, or closely engaged in business all the week in the great neighbouring commercial town of Drumble, distant only twenty miles on a railroad." The humorous tone, the echo of the mock-epic, make fun of this new phenomenon. The satire leads to the realization that the train makes possible that intercourse between the sexes which in the novels of Jane Austen, for example, depended upon neighbors, neighborhoods, and the locations of the baths, thereby replacing the *places* of social encounter with the process of travel itself. And it is worth noting how in the opening pages of Gaskell's novel, we quickly reach the scene where a reader of Dickens, the good Captain, in saving a young child's life is himself struck and killed by a train. In *Cranford*, published originally in Dickens' *Household Words*, the railroad is both a life-giving and a life-consuming force.

Just before he began to write *Dombey*, Dickens helped found and briefly edited *The Daily News*, which depended upon special trains for a national circulation. And of course these trains were the vehicles by which his own work spread throughout the nation and the world. As Schivelbusch notes, "In the late 1840s, English booksellers established stalls in railway stations, as well as a peculiar kind of lending library, to meet the general demand for things to read while traveling." We are reminded (in the words of J. W. Dodds) that "the development of railways encouraged the sale of books of all kinds. Until 1848 no systematic attempt had been made to supply passengers with either books or papers at the railway stations. In that year W. H. Smith got the exclusive right to sell books and papers on the Birmingham Railway. His first bookstall was at Euston Station. Shortly he had the franchise for the entire London and Northwestern System. By 1849, the station library at Paddington terminus contained one thousand volumes, chiefly works of fiction. Here, for the charge of one penny, a passenger had free access to the use of the library while waiting for trains, and for slightly more could take a volume with him on his journey, turning it in at his destination . . ." (Schivelbusch 65). In 1837 Bernhard Tauchnitz began to publish "the best contemporary literature" of England for "residents and travellers on the Continent of Europe." Dickens was his second author, Bulwer Lytton holding pride of place as the first in an enterprise that was to publish over five thousand volumes in a hundred years. For continental travelers, it was Dickens in the Tauchnitz edition that they purchased at railroad stations to serve as a companion on their railway travels.[4] Industrial civilization had transformed not only the passage through space and time but the production of books. Both were now machine processes. Lending libraries were made possible by the fact that books were now standard, mass-produced, commodities. Each copy of a given book was for most intents and purposes the same as every other.

The impersonal order of the iron rails had its necessary counterpart in other aspects of life. Because of the mania of railway speculation in the 1840s, Parliament passed an act establishing joint-stock companies, thereby creating the modern corporation. In an ironic stroke, *Dombey*'s Staggs's Gardens, a random collocation of houses and byways transformed into an orderly place of bustling commerce by the coming of the railroad, takes its name from the word "Stag" which was introduced by Thackeray in 1845 to refer to a speculator in railway stocks. Dickens even plays with the origin of its name: "Some were of opinion that Staggs's Gardens derived its name from a deceased capitalist, one Mr Staggs, who had built it for his delectation. Others, who had a natural taste for the country, held that it dated from those rural times when the antlered herd, under the familiar denomination of Staggses, had resorted to its shady precincts. Be this as it may, Staggs's Gardens was regarded by its population as a sacred grove not to be withered by railroads . . ." (chapter 6).

What the rural population regards with awe, the railroad will destroy, and in its place put Camden Town, a prosperous London suburb and business center (Steig 145–58). By the topical reference to speculators in stock contained in the name, Staggs's Gardens, Dickens reminds us that people who dealt in paper—not Dombey, the mercantilist who trades in goods, reputation, and honor—wielded the power of the new god of the railroad. Dickens himself wielded a similar power in the institution of literature and public opinion, here too the invisible force of writing on paper—of his signature, if you will—producing tremendous effects in everyday life. Note that what Dombey fears is an impersonal power. It is homologous to his fear of the circulation of money, and masks a fear about the circulation of print: that is, it is the fear of writing as mass literature, what in another context I have called writing as impersonal, general code.[5]

It is worth noting at this point that the availability of cheap paper in the nineteenth century, through the use of wood-pulp and the use of steam power in the production of newsprint, was an essential ingredient in the industrial civilization that shaped English life. Until 1818 it was a punishable offense in England, Scott Cook notes, "to print newsheets or broadsides larger than 22 by 32 inches (roughly the size of *The New York Times*)." In 1776 the Massachusetts General Court "required . . . that in each community a person be appointed to collect rags . . . and an early New England periodical . . . suggested that each housewife make a rag bag and keep it next to the family Bible—a wonderfully symbolic connection emphasizing the value placed on paper. . . ."[6] How ironic that cheap paper was the prerequisite for the Bank of England Act which in 1844 created a national currency that was to remain a byword for stability and value throughout the century.

The impact of standard money, standard business units, the standard business day, and the carving out of the units of time—most notably in railway schedules—as well as the development of the newspaper and the new technologies of lithography and roller/metal printing reinforced the rising literacy rate. Reading material was in demand; newspapers were founded and prospered; the great age of the novel was under way. The joint-stock company, also created by paper shares, and as a unit with limited liability functioned as an impersonal and collective fiction, was analogous to the limited and impersonal knowledge imparted by the products of the printing press (by contrast with the hand-crafted book or story-teller), and was also connected to labor unions with their impersonal standards that were formed to deal with the impersonal demands of employers and the marketplace. And, by the end of the century, schedules, standards, and impersonal work had also brought about the contemporary meaning of *tea-time*, for example, which was fixed at 4:00 in the afternoon throughout the country.

Humphry House reminds us that it was the railroad which made it possible for the English woman to travel wherever she chose, by contrast with the world of public coaches which were inaccessible to the middle class. Without a private vehicle of her own, she walked or, more often, stayed at home. For women, then, the railroad with its impersonal standards (that led among other things to a more general civility and tone of politeness), tickets for a fixed price, and regular schedules, provided the condition for mobility and personal liberation.[7] Thereby it also had a major impact on the formation of modern sexuality and desire. The railroad and desire became in effect a covert subject of the novel—for example, Sister Carrie arriving in Chicago and meeting Drouet on the train—awaiting John Fowles and Erica Jong's explicit articulation in our own time of the "zipless fuck" in the railway carriage.[8] What better evidence to reinforce the point that by the 1840s the human possibilities brought by industrial civilization were manifold, complex, and inescapable.

One effect of railway travel commented on by early train travellers was boredom. As Schivelbusch notes, "dullness and boredom resulted from attempts to carry the perceptual apparatus of traditional travel, with its intense appreciation of landscape over to the railway. The inability to acquire a mode of perception adequate to technological travel crossed all political, ideological, and esthetic lines. . . . Flaubert wrote to a friend in 1864: 'I get so bored on the train that I am about to howl with tedium after five minutes of it. One might think that it's a dog someone has forgotten in the compartment; not at all, it is M. Flaubert, groaning'" (Schivelbusch, p. 58). And Humphry House notes how boredom and hurry alternate in "The Lazy Tour of Two Idle Apprentices," which Dickens wrote for *Household Words* and published on October 3, 1857 (volume xvi). Reinforced by the physical arrangement of the European and English railway carriage, which was divided into class-bound compartments (by contrast with the open American saloon car that was modelled on the river steamship), this phenomenon of boredom further encouraged reading on the train. Reading was now becoming, by contrast with so much of its past history, a private act. Privacy on the railroad paralleled the general increase of private domestic and "public" spaces for the middle classes, and thus encouraged access to their personal fantasy world for contemplation, examination, and reenactment.

That private world of the feelings is what Tolstoy's Anna Karenina, perhaps the most famous train traveller in nineteenth-century literature, explores. Her misfortunes and the railroad are linked. Anna first meets Vronsky, her lover, in the passenger compartment of a train that has just arrived at the station. Their encounter is punctuated by an accident in which a guard "had not heard a train being shunted and had been run over." The "mangled corpse" distresses Anna's brother, Oblonsky, and brings Anna to the edge of tears. The comments of the other passengers about the accident strike her as an omen.

> "What a horrible death," said someone passing by. "They say he was cut in two."
> "On the contrary, I think it's the easiest, it's instantaneous," said someone else.
> "How can they be so careless!" said a third. (67)

This scene will echo for her years later, and encourage her to put an end to her unhappiness by throwing herself under a train. Modernity, in the guise of the railroad, makes possible the search for personal happiness. It drives Anna out of her husband's cold world into Vronsky's embrace. Multiplying desires, it also makes it impossible to sustain them. Only Levin can make a happy marriage, as he leaves the expensive, overwhelming city for the pastoral haven of his love and country estate. In the light of Anna's suicide, the famous opening statement of the novel becomes part of the pastoral repudiation of modernity. "Happy families are all alike; every unhappy family is unhappy in its own way." The only model for happiness is the traditional way; all the modern options bring only suicide and the death of desire. The railroad, a Russian doctor commented, "increases the number of rented apartments, rented carriages . . . and rented women'" (Engelstein 171). Tolstoy is clearly not interested in John Stuart Mill's project for "the culture of the feelings," so central to the aims and purposes of liberal education. He repudiates the world Mill explored, which includes the new possibilities for women outlined in "On the Subjection of Women." Tolstoy does not want to confront the meanings of the development of impersonal relations brought on by the industrial world.

Anna Karenina concludes with Levin's return to his farm and grainfields. With Anna's death, Tolstoy can return his hero to the mythic cycle of the pastoral world. This tone is sounded at the ending of *Dombey & Son*, which concludes with the drinking of the last bottle of the old Madeira wine. Together, the beginning of the novel—the birth of the heir of Dombey—and this closing ritual moment of celebration, bracket and thus limit the impact of the impersonal values of the industrial world. The drinking of the wine also marks the formal transfer of authority to Walter. His power is not that of Dombey's, who moved in a time, Cousin Feenix reminds us, "when men lived very freely" (chapter 61). Whatever he acquires in the romance ending results from his own enterprise, luck, and, most of all, from his marriage to Florence. At the end of the novel, Sol Gills's shop prospers (chapter 62); the extended family, which includes the grandfather, congregates at the seashore. It is not an accident that Florence goes by coach to the final meeting with Edith. Her story, however, is not transmitted orally to Florence, but written out on paper, made into a manuscript, for future reading. The power of the impersonal world is limited by such reticence, which allows the muted though still resonant personal voice of the new family of Walter and Florence its hearing.

Like *Dombey & Son*, *Anna Karenina* is a domestic novel, occupied with the fortunes of a family. Like *Dombey*, it also was published in serial form, appearing in eight parts in *The Russian Messenger*, a new magazine, over the course of two years, beginning in 1875. Just as *Dombey* does not end with Carker's death, so the novel *Anna Karenina* does not conclude with hers. Almost at the same time that Anna commits suicide, Kitty, her sister-in-law, gives birth to her first child. After Anna's death, the narrative continues for another sixty pages. As is the case in Dickens' novel, here too death is transition. In Dickens' as well as Tolstoy's novels, death is the place where feeling erupts. For "Dickens is attempting purposely to arouse his readers' innate moral sentiments, reminding them that the more emotionally sensitive they are to death the more morally attentive they will be to the values of life" (Kaplan 50). From his letters and reported conversation, we know that Tolstoy had read Dickens. In *Anna Karenina*, Count Oblonsky responds to Levin, who criticizes his interest in "fallen women," by reminding him of Podsnap: "It's easy for you to talk that way—just like that character in Dickens who tossed all difficult questions over his right shoulder with his left hand. But denying a fact is no answer. What am I to do?" (Ch. 11) For Podsnap here, read Dombey. But the rush of feeling with which we regard, through Dombey's eyes, the mangled body of Carker differs from the horror evoked by Anna's suicide. With Dombey we experience the relief that he is alive, while his rival and double is dead; in Tolstoy's novel, Anna's act is dramatized: "And just at this moment she was horror-struck by what she was doing. Where am I? What am I doing? Why? She tried to get up, to throw herself back, but something huge and implacable struck her on the head and dragged her down. 'Lord, forgive me for everything!' she murmured, feeling the impossibility of struggling . . .." The section ends with a eulogy: "A little peasant was working at the rails muttering something to himself. And the candle by which she had been reading that book that is filled with anxiety, deceit, sorrow, and evil flared up with a brighter flame than ever before, lighted up everything for her that had previously been in darkness, flickered, dimmed, and went out forever." In both novels, the difficulties of transition between traditional and modern is exemplified in images of death.

Tolstoy's defamiliarizing the everyday by "making it strange" suggests a comparison between the two novels. On the level of plot, the railroad suicide of Anna Karenina and the train sequences are all ways of defamiliarizing and thus renewing the pastoral world of the novel, the modern world thereby giving new life to the traditional. This opposition makes Levin valuable, Anna and the train world wrong—and echoes Shperk's sneer at modernity. In *Dombey*, by contrast, Dickens makes the familiar strange by his perspectivism—that is, we see railroad travel through the subjective eyes of the characters involved. Toodles' view, as well as that of Dombey and Carker, is part of our understanding of the railroad world. In effect, their comprehension of the railroad reveals more about them than it does about the object of their responses. Unlike Tolstoy's, in Dickens' novel we have theatrical presentation rather than narrative exposition, and, like a play which unfolds before us, we take the information presented to be part of the character's temperament rather than a statement about the nature of reality. Both Tolstoy and Dickens work in relatively small units in these novels. For Tolstoy there is a theory of accumulation, defined most clearly in the meditation on history in *War and Peace* where every bit is as large or important as any and every other; for Dickens, each bit is subjective, articulating character theatrically rather than through the world-defining narrative of the omniscient narrator.

In both *Anna Karenina* and *Dombey and Son* we have entered a world in motion. Tolstoy's heroes repudiate the urban world, reject change, and seek the true and the good amid unchanging values. By contrast, Dickens evokes not only the positive force of the railroad world but the new possibilities provided by the expanding cities of Victorian England. His novels provide us with examples of the achievements of industry and commerce as well as the self-alienation of the underground man, which Dostoevsky, who read Dickens avidly, was to explore. Dickens' novels offer us the world of "the streets" and the libidinous impersonal crowds, leading us to the analysis of urban anonymity and the overstimulation of Georg Simmel, providing us with the materials for an analysis of the social construction of self, sexuality, and gender in the industrial world that Tolstoy does not.[9] In making the growth of the city possible, the railroad brought about the ceaseless change of modern life. Bringing the capital city within reach of all, it made possible the movement in culture that removed the hero from the center of the picture. *Dombey & Son*, which began serial publication three months before Thackeray's *Vanity Fair*, "a novel without a hero," has a daughter as its main character. *Anna Karenina*, by contrast, vainly struggles to keep Levin at its center.

One literary strategy by which to represent this moving world is to contrast past and present, and thereby suggest the dynamic experience of history, as Carlyle did in 1843. Another is to use the tableau as a theatrical and literary device. While Thackeray makes good use of it in *Vanity Fair*, the illustrations to Dickens' novel, as well as his narrative exposition, eschew those qualities of tableau. Rather, like the picture of the rescue of Rob from the attack of the Charitable Grinders, they are all of characters in motion, images in search of a moving picture. Once the center of the picture is vacated by the hero, all the other characters start to move: pictures become dynamic. What some critics see as loss of focus is also new human possibility.[10] Perhaps this is just another comment on the greatness of Turner's achievement and the importance of impressionism.

Like Turner, Dickens is self-conscious about his artistic methods, and calls attention to them in *Dombey* as well as in his brilliant journalistic writing. As the wonderful rhythms of "A Flight" take us on a train trip from London to Paris in less than a day, we realize with the narrator that like a magician the train has transformed his world by casting a spell upon it (echoed of course by Dickens' prose). "So, I pass to my hotel, enchanted: sup, enchanted; go to bed, enchanted; pushing back this morning (if it really were this morning) into the remoteness of time, blessing the South Eastern company for realising the Arabian Nights in these prose days, murmuring, as I wing my idle flight into the land of dreams, 'No hurry, ladies and gentlemen, going to Paris in eleven hours.' It is so well done, that there really is no hurry."[11] Toodles is this sorcerer's apprentice. Unlike Levin, Toodles is at home in the world of the railroad; he is also someone who knows how to feel. The ease with which he stokes the hungry locomotive is reflected in the pleasure he has in giving his son the name of Biler, in an analogy that links his work and his sexual habits and warm family life. Toodles is a figure from the folk vocabulary. He springs from the stagecoach world of Sam Weller fully formed into the ironmaster's civilization. He is as well an indicator of Dickens' ability to meld the narrative habits of the stagecoach novel with that of the enterprise of the tale that rides on iron grooves. He parallels the imagery that links Walter to Dick Whittington in this novel; Toodles is the inspiration for *The Little Engine That Could* bringing into the impersonal modern world the episodic, picaresque, and folk world of the personal enchantment of Don Quixote. Into the modern, Dickens brings the traditional and transforms it, for the iron rails that smash Staggs's Gardens and teach Dombey about transition also bring a new order in which change is now part of everyday life.

William Dean Howells joked in 1871 about Dickens' fictional methods, "there's nothing like having railroads and steamboats transact your plot for you." But in *A Wedding Journey*, his respectable honeymooners note with dismay that "you saw people who ought to know better, well-dressed, stylish people, flaunting their devotion in the face of the world and going to sleep on each other's shoulders on every railroad train. It was outrageous, it was scandalous, it was really infamous. Before she would allow herself to do such a thing she would—well, she hardly knew what she would not do; she would

THE RAILWAY JUGGERNAUT OF 1845

have a divorce, at any rate. She wondered that Basil could laugh at it; and he would make her hate him if he kept on" (Howells 57). The passage from Howells suggests that there are two narrative models at work here, one formed on stagecoach travel and suggested in *Dombey & Son* in the country-travel passages (echoing those in *Nicholas Nickleby* and the "yo-ho" passages of *Martin Chuzzlewit*), the other modelled on train travel of which I have already cited some examples.[12] The stagecoach world is characterized by a personal narrative voice. The pleasures of interpolated stories, and the tales of the landlord at the inn, with their digressive, winding style, dominate this world. By contrast, the railroad narrative model is characterized by purposefulness. Its voice is impersonal and objective. We hear the accents of the social scientist and the marshalling of facts, as the *system* of life is analyzed. Like walking in Camden Town, the creation of the railroad-enterprise world which replaced Staggs's Gardens, it is directional, oriented to the valuing, purchase, and use of a world of industrial production by the use of paper currency: "The miserable waste ground, where the refuse matter had been heaped of yore, was swallowed up and gone; and in its frowsy stead were tiers of warehouses, crammed with rich goods and costly merchandise. The old by-streets now swarmed with passengers and vehicles of every kind; the new streets that had stopped disheartened in the mud and waggon-ruts, formed towns within themselves, originating wholesome comforts and conveniences belonging to themselves, and never tried nor thought of until they sprung into existence. Bridges that had led to nothing, led to villas, gardens, churches, healthy public walks." The episodic story-telling coin of the realm of the leisurely world of Fielding's countryside, in which feudal politics and rural sexuality are intertwined, has given way to the directed plot ruled by measured and impersonal time, another way of counting money, in whose terms the enterprise of industry, desire, and political action are implicated.

The final paragraph of Dickens' account of the Staplehurst railway accident provides a coda that recalls the complexities of the human situation brought by the coming of the railroads. The letter concludes on an uncharacteristic, abrupt note: "I don't want to be examined at the inquest and I don't want to write about it. I could do no good either way, and I could only seem to speak about myself, which, of course, I would rather not do. I am keeping very quiet here. I have a—I don't know what to call it—a constitutional (I suppose) presence of mind, and was not in the least fluttered at the time. I instantly remembered that I had the MS of a number with me, and clambered back into the carriage for it. But in writing these scanty words of recollection I feel the shake and am obliged to stop." The emotional trauma Dickens suffered as a result of this accident reminds us that the coming of the railroad and its world of transition and panoramic vision had its unexpected costs.[13]

NOTES

1. Note also Ruskin's comments in "The Lamp of Beauty," about "the strange and evil tendencies of the present day" in the "decoration of the railroad station." The passage goes on to contrast leisurely travel "over hills and between hedges, instead of through tunnels and between banks" and the hurry of railroad travel, which "transmutes a man from a traveller into a living parcel."
2. The question is, of course, central to many studies of *Dombey*, and proves a stumbling block for, among others, John Lucas (103) and A. O. J. Cockshut (VII).
3. The concept of totalization is an important one for this novel; Raymond Williams comments on it in his introduction to the Penguin edition, and Jonathan Arac has a sustained discussion in chapter 5, "The House and the Railroad," in *Commissioned Spirits*.
4. See *The Harvest, Being the Record of One Hundred Years of Publishing, 1837–1937*, by Bernhard Tauchnitz et al., Leipzig, 1937, including the letter from Dickens expressing complete confidence in Tauchnitz. My thanks to Rosemarie Milazzo for her help in locating these and other recondite sources.
5. See my essay "Calligraphy and Code: Writing in *Great Expectations*."
6. "The *Boston News Letter* . . . encouraged" readers to fulfill their civic duty in 1769 "with the following poem:

> Rags are beauties which concealed lie,
> But when in paper, how charms the eye!
> Pray save your rags, new beauties to discover,
> For of paper, truly, everyone's a lover;
> By the pen and press such knowledge is displayed
> As wouldn't exist if paper was not made.
> Wisdom of things, mysterious, divine,
> Illustriously doth on paper shine.

The availability of rag and the cost of paper were clearly serious obstacles to printing on a mass scale well into the nineteenth century" (Cook 10,11). I have also benefited from personal discussions on this subject with Professor Cook.
7. "To the railways also must partly be attributed the greater uniformity of manners which becomes apparent in Dickens's later books. It was said as early as 1844: 'We cannot help noticing the visible, and in general beneficial, influence of railroad travelling upon public manners. . . . The bringing of various ranks and classes of mankind into more familiar intercourse and better humour with each other—the emancipation of the fair sex, and particularly of the middle and higher classes, from the prohibition from travelling in public carriages, which with the majority was a prohibition from travelling at all—the opportunities, so frequently improved, of making agreeable acquaintances—the circulation, as it were, of the current coin of the intellect—and the general tone of mutual frankness and civility

so observable in railroad travellers, and *so new in the English character*, are producing rapid and important effects. . . .' " (*The Dickens World* 151).
8. Also see Steven Marcus's *The Other Victorians* on the rise of pornography in the Victorian era, and its creation as a mass market.
9. Rates of maternal death at childbirth decreased in Victorian England during the nineteenth century from just over 6/1,000 in 1847 to less than 4/1,000 in 1901. It would be interesting to correlate the decrease in the maternal childbirth death rate and the railroad accident rate in the nineteenth century, and to compare the English and Russian rates, but accurate statistics especially on railroad accident rates are hard to come by.
10. See Praz for the negative view.
11. *Household Words*, volume III, August 30, 1851; also see the discussion by Humphry House (140–142). He notes that the description of train travel in *Dombey* set a standard for this kind of writing, echoed in other passages like the one in *Our Mutual Friend*, Book IV, chapter 11. "The method of the description as a whole is to combine the more immediate effects of speed upon the sight and hearing . . . with a quick kaleidoscopic view of passing scenes, which compel in their succession a number of social contrasts."
12. My thanks to David Nordloh for calling my attention to this passage in Howells. I owe the insight about the two narrative models to Hilary Schor; its elaboration owes much to discussions with John Jordan.
13. For a fuller discussion of the problem of trauma, see Schivelbusch (IX).

WORKS CITED

Altick, Richard, *Victorian People and Ideas*. New York: Norton, 1973.

Arac, Jonathan, *Commissioned Spirits*. New Jersey: Rutgers UP, 1964.

Baumgarten, Murray, "Calligraphy and Code: Writing in Great Expectations, in *Dickens Studies Annual* 11, 61–72.

Briggs, Asa, *Victorian Cities*. New York: Harper, 1970.

Cockshut, A. O. J., "Dombey and Son" in *The Imagination of Charles Dickens*. New York: New York UP Gotham Library, 1962.

Cook, Scott, "On Technology and Words: Gutenberg and the Myth of Moveable Type." Unpublished.

Engelstein, Laura, "Morality and the Wooden Spoon: Russian Doctors View Syphilis, Social Class, and Sexual Behavior, 1890–1905" in *Representations* 14. Berkeley: U of California P.

Fielding, K.J., *Studying Charles Dickens*. London: Longman, 1986.

House, Humphry, *The Dickens World*, London: Oxford UP, 1960. Paperback Edition.

Howells, William Dean, *A Wedding Journey*, ed. J.K. Reeves. Indiana: Indiana UP, 1968.

Kaplan, Fred, *Sacred Tears: Sentimentality in Victorian Literature*. New Jersey: Princeton UP, 1987.

Lucas, John, "Dickens and Dombey and Son: Past and Present Imperfect" in *Tradition and Tolerance in Nineteenth-Century Fiction,* ed. David Howard, John Lucas, and John Gross. New York: Barnes and Noble, 1967.

Marcus, Steven, *Dickens from Pickwick to Dombey.* New York: Simon and Schuster, 1965.

Marcus, Steven, *The Other Victorians.* New York: Basic Books, 1966.

Paroissien, David, ed., *Selected Letters of Charles Dickens.* Boston: Twayne, 1985.

Pope, Norris, *Dickens and Charity.* New York: Columbia UP, 1978.

Praz, Mario, *The Hero in Eclipse in Victorian Fiction.* tr. Angus Davidson. London: Oxford UP, 1956

Ruskin, John, "The Lamp of Beauty" in *The Seven Lamps of Architecture.* New York: Noonday Rpt, 1970.

Schivelbusch, Wolfgang, *The Railway Journey.* Berkeley: U California P, 1986.

Steig, Michael, "Dombey and Son and the Railway Panic of 1845" in *The Dickensian* 67, 1971.

Tolstoy, Leo, *Anna Karenina,* tr. Rosemary Edmonds. New York: Penguin, 1954.

Dombey and Son:
Language and the Roots of Meaning

Patrick J. McCarthy

Dickens' language embodies a personal yet primal vision that subsumes and undergirds his novelistic world. It is a vision he deals with and modulates novel by novel, but it is always present. The fable of *Dombey and Son* centers on a type of Victorian businessman, but the language in which it is cast draws story into myth, and shapes particulars of incident and character into typological configurations.

Judged by standards of the plausible, the ordinary, and the received, Dickens' language deserves the complaints lodged against it as extravagant, falsely intense, or simply idiosyncratic. Its oddity, however, has reasons that the reason may be slow to recognize, and in his odd habitual language, its expressive energies, its repetitive turns and quirks, and its special metonomic and metaphoric cast Dickens has his purposes. "There's magic in the web of it."

What that language is, what it serves to body forth, and what happens to both myth and characters in the final disposal of forces will concern me here. But first I shall state candidly what I take to be the mythical burden of the novel and also, if I may, point to a recurrent, insistent idea working in Dickens' mind during the second half of 1846. The idea occurs just as he is beginning *Dombey* and at the same time starting to plan the Christmas story, *The Battle of Life*, which he wrote while engaged on the novel.

On the basis of its language I read *Dombey and Son* as a secular and Christian version of a morality play worked out in a particularizing, middle-class art form. Its hero, Paul Dombey, is both Victorian capitalist and

91

representative man whose salvation is at stake. He is involved in a complex personal psychomachia at the center of a warring universe. He must realize himself in the face of inner conflicts and a world bursting with self-asserting energy. The struggle goes on at every level of existence, is conducted under the resistless force of time, and is forced to points of awareness and judgment by the fact of death. One force alone, love, unaccountably survives, even prevails, and certainly comforts. At the end, in the general resolution of forces a partial deflationary effect takes place and certain principles of exclusion as well as inclusion appear to be at work.

As he gave himself both to novel and Christmas book, Dickens' mind was haunted by notions of struggle, death, and eventual survival. He describes himself as "racking [his] brain between Dombeys" and the Christmas book he had promised his publishers for the coming season. His letters to John Forster that summer and fall suggest the state of his thinking: "An odd shadowy undefined idea," he wrote, "is at work within me, that I could connect a great battle-field somehow with my little Christmas story." Four times more, with *Dombey* under way and until he actually set to work, he mentioned his "notion" and also the difficulty of fitting it into "any natural socket." Meanwhile he was planning and writing the first two numbers of *Dombey and Son*. When the title *The Battle of Life* came to him—an odd one for a Christmas story—he said it was a title he had not "conned at all . . . except in connection with [his] foggy idea."[1] The story opens on a battlefield, an unspecified English field strewn with dead, reddened with blood, and layered with the shattered fragments of conflict, then shows the field generations later as a vision of "repose and peace . . . with the corn and grass growing over the slain, and people singing at the plough" (*Letters* IV 56). Ruins of the conflict lie deep under the countryside where the characters of the story live, and though Dickens has one of them urge another to "forget this battle-field . . . in the broader battle-field of Life on which the sun looks every day," the lurid and portentous symbol, like the detritus of battle, remains in the memory throughout (*The Battle of Life* 252). Its relation to the tale he then tells, though clear, is so distant in time as to be strikingly inappropriate, and the conjoining of pastoral atmosphere and blood-drenched soil suggests the strength of Dickens' fascination with the notion of embattlement, of the perennial struggle deep down in things.

That the notion of battle also subsumes *Dombey and Son*, under way at the same time, is clear from its opening paragraph. Typically, and engagingly, its serious intention passes itself off as comic domestic story:

Dombey sat in the corner of the darkened room in the *great* arm-chair by the bedside, and Son lay tucked up warm in a *little* basket bedstead, *carefully* disposed on a low settee *immediately* in front of the fire, and close to it, as if his constitution were analogous to that of a muffin, and it was *essential* to toast him brown while he was *very* new.

(Italics mine)(1).

Re-reading it, we feel that the double-directedness of the ensuing chapter has already begun. Dombey and Son are together and yet firmly apart; the apparent unity manages to suggest a fracture. Balanced independent clauses express a contrast which is heightened by connections to the universe of things. Father's chair befits his greatness, the lowness of the settee befits Son, and the littleness of the basket connotes, as so often in Dickens, loveableness and vulnerability. The positioning of the principals relative to the fire carries the contrast further and predicts the future. Dombey, we will learn, prefers to sit apart in darkness and cold, and Son will sit before the fire and closely interrogate its meanings. The intensifying words of the passage stress the juxtapositioning and underline the odd analogy between Son and a toasted muffin. At first reading we smile at its homely facetiousness, but later we may think of Little Jack Horner who sat in a corner to eat, and of Chronos who devoured his young.

That we think of Chronos at all is surely a critical back-formation, for Dickens calls our attention to Time as Devourer, *tempus edax rerum*, in the very next paragraph. But there Time is the enemy not just of son but of father as well, and what is introduced thus early in the novel is greater than either and is in fact the supervenient power of the novel, Time as universal enemy. Its introduction here is to place Dombey in relation to an absolute power and to place his assumptions of power in a defining context. Again, however, it is a context that we do not at first see, for Dickens speaks comically, and it is not until Mrs. Dombey dies at the end of the chapter that by another back-formation we understand that everyone in it is held by Time, green and dying.

The chapter thus asserts a principle of radical dangerousness and the terrible predictability of doom. Dombey, the would-be chtonic god who makes the languages of religion, cosmology, and law his own, who sees the universe as created primarily for his own uses is ignorant of his own plight. Though the doctors appear to hold Time captive, a golden trinket at their waistcoats, the instruments disagree and trip up one another. In his cold and terrible singlemindedness, Dombey does not show even the same compassion the doctors do as they stand beside his wife's deathbed. Son, wisely sensing danger, has squared his fists against his prospects, Daughter has "crouched timidly" before Father's power and insensibility, and Mother has "drifted out upon the dark and unknown sea" on which the ships of Dombey and Son do not sail.

The tone of the chapter shifts with chameleon rapidity amid a shimmering play of allusion through a wide range of expressiveness. Dombey is made to seem powerful and mock-mighty at the same time; he is surrounded by serio-comic sychophants, and his own stiffness is made a joke of. While his neglected daughter is pure forlornness and pathos, and his broken-spirited wife slips into death, the comic doctors are shocked into compassion, and Dombey's sister takes to droll yet macabre hectorings of the dying woman. References range from court to pincushion, from the Christian God and the Bible to eighteenth-century abstractions like Nature and Care, from children as angels to daughters as pieces of base coin. Rhythms are equally various, rolling out fine cadences, tinkling with light repetitions, beating soft alliterations and firm anaphoras, snapping out short climactic phrases, and ever shifting—from formal to colloquial, from pun to reworked cliché, from metonymic absurdities to solemn Johnsonian fulsomeness. Dickens has in effect reinforced the denotation of words by reenacting their conflicting, multi-directional energies. Dombey's battle of life has found a syntax opulent with instability and uncertainty.

Contemporary criticism has tended to pass over the radical struggle at the heart of *Dombey and Son* while it has tested its symbols and image clusters for their validity and coherence and studied its social and cultural implications. Dickens taught us to look in the latter direction when he expressed to Forster his fear that the "very name" of his projected work getting out "would be ruinous." (*Letters* IV 586). As *Martin Chuzzlewit* had earlier been a Jonsonian study of selfishness, here was a study of pride exposing an egregiously self-satisfied mercantile community. And so it is, being precisely up to date as Humphry House long ago pointed out, and brilliantly awake to social relations as Leavis, Cockshut, and Williams—among others—have observed.[2] But such views make us forget that Dombey is from the outset an archetypal figure of power amid a world of oppositions who has risen and will fall. His story is closer to *Everyman* and *King Lear* than to *Père Goriot* or *The Way We Live Now*. He is a man of the times, a man recognizably of the City and "the region between Portland-place and Bryanstone-square"(24), but his connections are only secondarily with the great world, more crucially with his domestic life, and centrally with his innermost self.

In *Dombey and Son* the oppositional nature of the world interfuses every element, and we first see it clearly (but of course not completely) as it pertains to the characters. In the prospective letter Dickens wrote to Forster outlining his plans, Dombey is conceived in conjunction with and in opposition to his son and then at long variance with his daughter, and only finally is he to be reconciled and united with her. Dickens knew then—he had reached the end of the fourth chapter—that the title of the book would be fulfilled "after all," with Dombey and daughter in one another's arms. But, as planned, the book proceeds through sets of oppositions beginning, as Dickens says, with Dombey's "struggle with himself" (IV, 590). This initial pattern of character disjunction, its system of differences, encourages other sets of pairings and oppositions to spring up at every point. In time we find Dombey opposed by Carker and Edith; Carker by Florence, Edith, and Alice Brown; Paul by the Blimbers and Mrs. Pipchin; while, further, Mrs. Brown terrorizes Florence and Rob; and Mrs. MacStinger victimizes Captain Cuttle and Captain Bunsby. Almost all the characters slip into the established oppositional pattern to the point that in the act of writing Dickens actually lets certain decisions depend upon the way the pattern works itself out. The fate of Walter Gay, for example, remains for a time undecided and that of Edith Dombey even longer, but Dickens notes that in the "branches and offshoots and meanderings that come up," characters will go over to a particular side. They line themselves up with the pattern.

That opposition rather than cooperation characterizes the pattern follows from the elemental nature of things. Dazzlingly anarchic energies roam their world. A will to power and domination seeks to impose itself on the passive, the inoffensive, and the complacent, while death threatens an untimely termination to life and continually judges its quality. But let me now sort out the verbal pressures in order to gauge their force.

They exist first of all at the simpler levels of language intensity, frequently charging the medium to fullest voltage. Words expressive of absolutes or ultimates abound; adjectives prefer their superlative degrees, and itemized lists burst with fullness.[3] There is a kind of percussive insistence, particularly at the beginning of chapters, that the language be extremest of its kind, and that it push its referents to the edge of things. Attendant on these insistencies is a pervasive unexpectedness. Clichés and proverbial expressions set themselves up and then spin into new formulations. Puns shift the focus of a sentence and complicate meanings: an aquiline nose determines "never to turn up at anything" (7); when Miss Tox is being importunate toward Toodle, he says to her, "You *are* suppressing" (21). Frequent syllepses achieve surprising verbal collocations and suggest curious interactions: Mrs. Skewton puts on "paralysis with her flannel gown" (383), Miss Tox thinks of her mother, "of her virtues and her rheumatism" (396), and Susan Nipper shakes "her head and a tea canister" (259). The commonest verbal reference may subvert itself into oddity: "I lost money by that man," says Mrs. MacStinger, "and by his guzzlings and his muzzlings" (532); the language of religion may move from clinker to clincher: Walter, says Captain Cuttle, "is what you may call a out'ard and visible sign of a in'ard and spirited grasp" (322). The world is tilted, sliding into unpredictability.

The quicksilver surprisingness of language extends itself, as so often in Dickens, to its referents, most particularly the ordinarily sullen, inanimate commonalty of things.[4] Everything from chandeliers to violoncellos, from buttons, boxes, books, and busts, to windows, watches, winds, weather-glasses, walls, waves, wardrobes, and wooden midshipmen shimmers with will and self-ness. The result is not the dissolution of what Emerson called "the solid seeming block of matter," but its breakdown into dynamic and unruly elements. Anarchic energy courses freely through all matter, part and whole alike, small and large. A house (Dombey's), a district (Staggs's Gardens), a city (London), may tumble into disarray, disappear into non-existence, or turn into "a wide wilderness" (638).

In its larger embodiments, so to speak, this independent, omnipresent vitality confronts man as both real and symbolic threat. The railroad may crush him and the sea drown him. But they offer opportunities as well. One may be a hero in a storm and a guide through uncharted streets. What Conrad calls "the immense indifference of things" exists in *Dombey and Son* as a continuum of energy translating the world into a huge testing ground. It forces humans to be wary, to react, and to adapt to the uncertainties and mysterious otherness of the inanimate world.

Similarly, energy mindful only of itself invades humans, eluding intellectual control, dismembering and fragmenting the central self. Miss Tox's hands, the legs of Cousin Feenix, Dr. Blimber, and Captain Cuttle, and the simper of Mrs. Skewton all act with apparent independence. Mrs. Brown's mouth chatters of itself, and Mr. Chick's whistling is quite beyond his volition. Integrated characters are the less wont to suffer such rebellions of parts but are not immune. It is as though contrary impulses rise from a verbal substratum of unpredictables, from the vagrant, untrammeled energy in the world of things, and escape control.

Multiple references to animals and animal behavior help further constitute and characterize the novel's groundwork of licentious independence.[5] Dickens ranges here as freely and broadly as he had in the Eden scenes of *Martin*

Chuzzlewit: fish, birds, insects, and reptiles—everything from minnows to monsters crowd his pages, not however, as actual animals (there are only three of those), but as referents to humans. Animal images bridge the gap to the human world, but while some few such references are harmless (Florence, e.g., as startled fawn or foreign bird) the great majority are to animals of a predatory sort: sharks, reptiles, wolves, foxes, and so on. Dickens' birds may nestle, soar, and coo, but they more typically swoop, peck, and scratch, and his beasts claw, snarl, bite, wallow, and writhe. The principal emphasis is on wildness and ferality even when the context is relatively neutral. After Dombey is injured, for example, and doctors are called in, the narrator sees them coming "as vultures are said to gather about a [dead] camel" (576).

Names of characters also help Dickens connect the human with the realms of fish and animal. We think of John and Louisa Chick and the Game Chicken, Withers, and MacStinger; Morfin, Nipper, and Glubb perhaps; and certainly Cuttle, Gills, and Perch. Of these, only the Game Chicken and Mrs. MacStinger are aggressive animal-humans, and that of a comic sort. The darker feralities are reserved to Carker, Bagstock, Mrs. Brown, and less insistently, to Mrs. Pipchin and Mrs. Skewton. Some dozen and a half references and of course his dazzling dentures connect James Carker to a variety of biting animals; Bagstock's animal analogies confirm him as a devourer and engorger; Mrs. Brown searches out, claws, and tears in the manner of a ferret, a crab, or a bird of prey. They belong with the punishers and exploiters of the novel, with the Bagstock who abuses his Native and the Mrs. Brown who sells her daughter, Alice. The hammering repetitiveness of such attributions confirms the continual presence of energies for which *fierce* is the precise root word.[6] Appropriate actions for such human beasts are never tentative or blunted. By rough count some thirty images of striking, stabbing, stinging, and wounding, of penetration and violation occur. Certain characters, themselves wounded or damaged—Edith, Rob, Alice Marwood—are induced to partake of the ferocity, and for all it is a constant near-presence and threat.

Still other language forms have been declaring all along that forces seeking to contain, control, or impinge upon others are simply everywhere. *Dombey and Son* is in fact so fascinated by incarceratory prose as to rival *Bleak House* and *Little Dorrit*, long noted for their tropes of imprisonment. More specifically, in *Dombey and Son* verbs expressive of compunction (*force, drive, coerce, bend, fix*) connect with or lead into a wide range of verbs of enclosure (*bind up, bury, button up, cage, close on* and *in, confine, constrain, coop, encase, enslave, ensnare, entrap, hem round, immure, impound, imprison, inter, pen, possess, shut up, snare, steep in, tie, yoke*). These appear in other verbal and nominative forms and join together with words of similar import without verbal forms (e.g., *cell, dungeon, mesh, pitfall, web*). In addition, various periphrastic expressions of control (e.g., *under guard, make a property of*, and so on) interlard the prose, particularly when the belligerent forces confront potential victims.

Clusters of images of forcing and containment bring in turn contrary images of shutting out, by which the outcast is forced to seek a retreat or sanctuary. Most often the imprisoning or excluding forces are represented as hard, frozen into unfeelingness. Dombey is of course the prime example here, striking victims into his own killing stoniness. But the power to control is often too a power to enchant, the mysterious imposition of one will on another. Carker and Edith are most often credited with such power, but fear of spells, charms, and enthralment is general. Even aggressors like Bagstock and Mrs. Chick fear the entrancing power of Miss Tox. At the most obviously comic level, Captain Cuttle is right to bury himself in his "fortified retreat" (437) against the imprisoning and entrancing will of Mrs. MacStinger, and Captain Bunsby foolishly self-confident in leaving the protecting confines of the "Cautious Clara."

Though Bunsby had seemed a man of rebellious parts—his eye, hand, and voice given to acting independently of his central self—we had thought him the most protected by self-repression, the least assailable of characters. Vagrant inner energies require control; even the harmless Mr. Toots, good-natured Cousin Feenix, and outspoken Susan Nipper learn this lesson (524, 748, 825, 750). Dombey, early forcing himself into self-containment, deplores Mrs. Chick's emotional agitations and admires Carker's apparently complete, cool restraint. Florence learns self-management early and withholds all manner of complaint against her father (244). Edith has "garnered up her heart" (358) and wounds herself physically to maintain self-mastery.

But self-control may fracture when tried too hard or when foiled of its object. Like Dombey, Carker expects a reward for his self-suppression, but when Edith denies him "voluptuous compensation" (736) his inner self cannot deal with external terrors. Florence bursts out when Mr. Dombey deals a physical blow to her hopes of love, and, however much she is justified, and however successful her flight, she regrets her failure of control. Edith loses her two reasons for self-suppression, her mother and Florence, and gives way to raging hatred and self-loathing. The result is that she is cast into permanent exile and incompleteness, the novel's version of outer darkness.

Wariness and self-control then may not be enough in the face of so many destructive energies, themselves both outer and inner. Though the central figure of his world, Dombey regards himself as impervious to its various sorts of expressive and threatening energy. He has hardened himself against consideration for others and sought to elevate himself above local contentions. By virtue of the position accorded him by his social order he sees himself as man against the sky, man whose place is with the stars and planets moving through eons of time. Having chosen to live within a fiction of superiority to all others and self-sufficiency unto himself, he derives from the choice both strength and blindness.

Supremely confident, he employs agents to enforce his will (Mrs. Chick, Carker, Bagstock, Pipchin, and Blimber) but totally fails to see in them any threat to himself. They exist for him only as they confirm and support his position. Since they apparently recognize the simple fact of his pre-eminence and observe the gulf between them, in his eyes they act neither with servility nor self-interest. When hiring Mrs. Pipchin, for example, it is enough for him to know that she has society's approval and that her husband died in its economic service. She knows what proper conduct is within the order and is therefore "respectable." She knows what belongs outside the order and so practices the arts of "exclusion" (99).

Nothing could be more attractive to Dombey whose obsessive pride desires exclusiveness to the point that he wishes, in the company of his son, to "shut out all the world as with a double door of gold" (275). Self-isolated, he has succeeded also in excluding himself from the knowledge of his own subordinates and their dangerousness.[7] Consider how totally unaware he is of the Mrs. Pipchin who lives within the imagistic patterns on one level as witch, ogress, and dragon, on a second as a series of animals (bear, bull, cat, crow, horse, and lion) and creeping things (crocodile, snake, and spider), on a third as metalic object and machine.

The warnings of the universality of battle are all around him, and the other characters hear them, but not he. Messrs. Chick and Toodle, for example, sense the presence of threat and fear being possessed by the wills of others. Mr. Chick remains in memory as a model of empty-headed amiability, yet for him family squabbling is not comic byplay. When he is "in the ascendant himself," we are told, he "punishe[s] Louisa roundly" (15). Mr. Toodle registers himself as an amiable illiterate, and the narrator blunts the edge of his responses by dubbing them "allegorical," but Toodle knows enemies when he meets them. His replies during the interview at Dombey house are warily defensive. He "couldn't hardly afford" losing his sons, he says to Dombey. No, he is a "stoker" not a "choker"; no, he is not happy to leave his wife: "Here's wishing of her back again," he says. "Hold up your head and fight low," he warns her, and does so not once but three times. His is an elementary apprehension but an accurate one. "Do it now," that is "defend yourself," he says, "or Bricks is no longer so" (16, 19, 21, 22fn).

Dombey's obliviousness also contrasts sharply with what we might call the novel's verbal and structural alertness to the conditions of battle. Amid the uncertainty and surprisingness, in the presence of predator and punisher, the weak and vulnerable provide themselves with local and individual defenses. In the Wooden Midshipman, which houses the novel's alternative society, the potential rowdiness of things is thwarted by an all-subduing order of arrangement so that should there be "an unexpected launch" for its ship-like interior, it would move "securely" (37). In the famous sequence after she is struck by her father, Florence flees through "the wide wilderness of London" (638) and takes refuge at the Midshipman under the watchful protectiveness of Captain Cuttle.

When outside the Midshipman, the centrally non-aggressive characters acquire sets of guardians against the predators. It is always a special element in his pathos that Paul understands his own drift toward death and sees that no protector, least of all money, can help him. Paul first gets and then loses Polly Toodle, keeps Florence throughout, and acquires the largely uncomprehending Toots. He takes to the madcap mongrel Diogenes, who knows that enemies are about in all guises, and that constant attack is a kind of prudence.[8] Florence early attracts Polly Toodle, later acquires Toots, inherits Diogenes, and except for one important period has the protection of the human counterpart of Diogenes, Susan Nipper. Like Diogenes who constantly watches Florence so that "nothing harm[s] her" (313), the Nipper by name and nature "perpetually wage[s] war . . . with society" (315) in behalf of her mistress.

Actually, Susan has only limited effectiveness in defending Florence, but no one is more alert to the novel's dynamic patterns. She partakes in its pugnacious animality, its verbal extravagance, and its barely controlled energies. She can bristle against friend and foe alike as is shown by her ready resentment of Polly Toodle, of Miss Tox, and the Skettleses. Her "Nipperisms" work by bracketing the norm within two unacceptable extremes: "I may not wish to live in crowds . . . , but still I'm not a oyster" (244). The effect is to affirm the mean while admitting the existence of unacceptable alternatives. Susan's conduct works the same way. Flying out against Mr. Dombey as she finally and injudiciously does, she expresses Florence's genuine grievances while at the same time providing room for the latter's patient, wordless devotion. In the middle sections of the novel, she—along with Diogenes—is necessary to the roundedness of Florence: they are together in the Dombey house, but the house is described as "deserted" and "bleak" and Florence lives "alone" (242).

Some characters, Edith and Alice Marwood the most important of them, take ambiguous places in the large pattern I have been describing. Edith is a resentful and self-resentful member of the Dombey set, one of its victims as a property for sale, an enchained slave, and a snared bird. That she loves Florence and melts into tears as she first leaves her are signs of grace. But she is also an enchantress and a punisher on her own—of Dombey, Carker, and of course herself, particularly of the self she has allowed herself to become. Her energy in symbolically breaking her bonds, literally tearing from her arms her diamond bracelets, and dismissing Carker contumeliously, is wonderfully self-assertive but not restorative. Her revenge accomplished and her passion spent, she tells Florence she "will try . . . to forgive" Dombey (827), but apparently she does not merit full forgiveness herself. She is relegated to a kind of limbo, but she calls it quite bluntly "the grave" (828). The pattern makes no room for her in the loving society and in effect casts her out.

For Alice Marwood, Edith's first cousin and lower-class clone, another pattern takes over, the explicit pattern of Christian salvation. As proud as Edith, as fierce, self-hating, and vehement, and a would-be stabber (718), Alice also takes revenge on Carker by betraying where he and Edith have fled. Like Edith, too, she accepts responsibility, but the terms of her repentance are different, and with Harriet Carker to direct her she seeks nothing less than divine compassion. Introduced as a "fallen angel" she dies as a "ruin," fallen irrecoverably into the Victorian category of "ruined woman," but also a repentant Magdalen figure (470, 786). Dickens has in effect cast her out as well, into another world perhaps, in which the Christian view of life and death is more consistently honored.

But once Florence flees to the Wooden Midshipman, at the same time as Edith decamps to Dijon, the pattern I have been describing has begun to shift, or, more accurately, an element of the pattern largely present only in its ineffectiveness begins to assert itself. Such a shift, not noted earlier, also takes place, almost proleptically, in *The Battle of Life*. There the attractive young medical student, Alfred, notes that though even loving mothers and girls of "the Christian world" are "mad for a battle-field," there are "quiet victories and struggles, great sacrifices of self, and noble acts of heroism," many of them private and unchronicled and done in people's hearts (*Christmas Books*,

252). As it happens, one of the young women of the story, Marion, achieves such a private victory through love and devotion to her sister.

Florence, as we know, also achieves a private victory, and also does so in the face of terrifying forces. Before she can work her salvationary magic on Mr. Dombey, however, the fiercer human energies of the book lose their power and dissolve into entropy. What happens is not so much that the oppressed group conquers as that the important oppressors self-destruct. The shift is prepared for by the blind assurance of Mr. Dombey, the surprising tunnel vision of Carker, and, as we have noted, the vengeful strategies of Edith.

Of the former two, Carker's is the more satisfying case. As shark, cat, reptile, and worm, as forger of chains and weaver of webs, he is formidable enough, and as master game player and conniving intelligence, he surpasses such earlier Dickens villains as Daniel Quilp and Jonas Chuzzlewit. But he misreads Edith, who entraps the would-be trapper and makes impotent his ferocity with a ferocity of her own (731, 736). His confidence is "shattered at a blow," he cannot think, his mind is muddled with wine and weariness, and finally fascinated by a "fiery Devil," the fierce, red-eyed monster of the rails. The suddenness of it all is just right, terrific, supremely suitable to the brutal harshness of Carker's verbal etiology.

As for Dombey, there had been further preparation for his fall in the delicate place given him among the self-imprisoners and social products: the man so long armored in wood, steel, and ice, the protagonist the book *gives* to us as fully formed, a victimizer and victim, now turns on himself in wounded self-hatred.[9] Alone, powerless, and disgraced, he torments himself to the point of suicide, reducing his vivid energies to a spectral image of himself and into thoughts of his blood tracked by the feet of others. A miracle of sorts is necessary to save him, and it comes, predictably compounded of Victorian melodrama, salvationary myth, and Christian repentance: the darkness of Dombey house gives way to the "glorious sunshine" of Florence (802). It is all, of course, extravagant, and the once powerful figure of Dombey must pay the price. His old self virtually melts away, dissolving into impotency amid a flood of watery symbols: tears, Madeira wine, and of course the circumambient sea.

While this is going on, the loving group has reconstituted itself to fight the continuing battles of life. Free at last from the wildness and enchantment of her father's house, Florence has proposed to a Walter almost magically restored from the wild sea. Now with him as effective protector, she no longer needs Susan or Toots, her comic knight errant. Since for his part Toots has dismissed his professional bodyguard—the Game Chicken who had turned into a vulture—he now needs Susan and thus marries her forthwith. He does so, as he tells Mr. Feeder, for her sense, which suggests what the future will require. Yet however much of a winding down into domestic stability we expect, the verbal energies of the book, its residential sense of power, danger, and excitement do not disappear. The fate of Dombey is the final but not the only word; the text in fact effects no closure on its energies and uncertainties.

Two weddings are described in the latter sections of the novel. Contrasted brilliantly, they affirm the continuing presence of the dynamic dangerousness on which so much of the novel has been predicated. On their wedding day Florence and Walter walk on "enchanted ground," such as their "childish feet of long ago, did not tread" (768). What follows is compounded of the joy and sadness, hope and acceptance, appropriate to moral and artistic seriousness. First they visit the memorial tablet to Paul in the church where Mrs. Miff and her "mortified" bonnet still attend. Together they walk through labyrinthine ways, from light into shadow, through narrow streets, and past a burying ground to another church. It is a place largely given over to darkness and dust and "has a strange smell like a cellar." Here amid the purlieus of dusty death Walter unites Florence "to the uncertainties and dangers" of life (772). They are joined, as Captain Cuttle predicted they would be, "in the house of bondage" (747). The joke, as so often in Dickens, is a serious one. Their enchantment is the enchantment of love in the face of the terrible certainties that lie ahead; it stands in marked opposition to the enchantments and imprisonments, the ferocities and dangers, of the world they inhabit. Here the aggressive energies so richly embodied in the novel's language are clearly recognized by the party of peace and love, and not denied but effectively confronted.

The second wedding takes place in the novel's alternative society, the world of the Wooden Midshipman, and particularly that of Captain Cuttle, its resident cheerleader, attendant good spirit, and Bible-overhauling Christian. Broadly comic as it is, however, it is not an independent world. It functions within the same structural patterns and responds to the same verbal energies as its more serious counterpart. One would not want to make too much of Cuttle, but Dickens clearly thought it essential to emphasize his verbal exuberance and to counter his high-spirited optimism with a wariness of the terrors proper to his sphere.

Essential, too, is the role of Captain Bunsby and the redoubtable Mrs. MacStinger in providing late in the novel a parodic example of contending powers. Bunsby had reduced himself to "one stationary eye in [a] mahogany face" (325) and his speech to Delphic utterance, all we presume to protect himself. But Mrs. MacStinger is not only a "terrible fire-ship," "an avenging spirit," and a "savage" (314, 182, 528) but a wily opponent as well, for the Bunsby who first appears able to melt her into tears becomes "a captive borne into a foreign land" and his wedding to her "a procession of sacrifice" (813). Here, too, there is no suggestion of energy winding down as the plot winds up. The observing presence of young Juliana MacStinger assures its longevity. In her Cuttle sees "a succession of man-traps stretching out infinitely" (815).

What I have been arguing for throughout this essay is the presence in *Dombey and Son* of a subsuming myth made evident to us by—and in a sense co-extensive with—Dickens' language. Far from being simply intensifying or heightening rhetorical counters. Dickens' language turns *require* expression. All those superlatives, all those animal ferocities, all those self-willed energies within and outside humans, all the signs of strain and cracking to express or defend the self, all the divisions into predator and prey, aggressor and victim, all the nervous tonal variations rise out of and enact a central anarchy. While it is true that love effects an evening peace, the disturbing dangerousness remains.[10]

At this juncture of his career, however, Dickens is still willing to trust his optimistic faith somewhat more than he fears the dangers to it. Carker, like Ralph Nickleby, Daniel Quilp, and Jonas Chuzzlewit before him, self-destructs. Though shadowed by death and reduced by experience, the happy company at the end has moved from being the alternate society to the central society, and its alternate society is comic MaStinger-dom, present and future. All in all, the salvationary legend and imaginative vitalities serve as effective counterbalances to all the ferality and darkness. *Dombey and Son* is still middle rather than late Dickens. The heedless, noisy streets of *Little Dorrit* into which Amy and Arthur Clennam step, the blood-tainted, rotten worlds of Little Britain and Tom All-Alone's, the self-satisfied Veneering society of *Our Mutual Friend*, all of which dominate the endings of the later novels are not yet at hand. In *Dombey and Son* a favorable issue in the continuing battles of life is still not in doubt. Even the sea, whispering of death, whispers also of change, transformation, and continuity.

NOTES

1. See *Letters* (IV 610, 569, 574, 579, 590, 623, 586).
2. In House, see especially the chapter entitled "The Changing Scene."

3. Gaston Bachelard is helpful here: "To enter into the domain of the superlative, we must leave the positive for the imaginary. We must listen to poets." (88–9).
4. Dorothy Van Ghent's evocation of the "forbidden" life of things in her essay "The Dickens world: A View from Todgers'" has had deserved attention, but contemporaries of Dickens noted his extraordinary penchant for animalism.
5. Dickens' use of animal imagery has caught the eye of commentators since David Masson in mid–19th century. Noteworthy among moderns are R. D. McMaster (354–61) and (on birds) John Carey (100–01, 116–19).
6. For a cluster of such uses, see 722, 723, 729, 731 and 736.
7. John Romano (160–7) notes that Dombey mistakenly trusts an individual's powers to interpret the world, and that Florence's choice of interdependence, love, and community eventually prove the stronger.
8. Paul tries to extend his own protection to the animal as later he also does for Walter Gay (203, 204).
9. Though Chesterton (92) calls the idea "rubbish," Tillotson (167–71) admirably gives the evidence for its validity. Unless Dombey had feelings to be crushed, he would be impossible; crushing them, he becomes the blind, exclusive enforcer who cooperates in destroying himself.
10. For a modern treatment of the redeeming effects of love in *Dombey and Son*, see Welsh (185–91).

WORKS CITED

Bachelard, Gaston, *The Poetics of Space*, tr. Maria Jolas. New York: Orion Press, 1964.

Carey, John, *The Violent Effigy*. London: Faber and Faber, 1973.

Chesterton, G. K., *Charles Dickens*. London: Methuen, 1906.

Cockshut, A. O. J., *The Imagination of Charles Dickens*. London: Methuen, 1965.

Dickens, Charles, "The Battle of Life" in *The Christmas Books*. London: Oxford UP, 1954.

Dickens, Charles, *Dombey and Son*, ed. Alan Horsman. Oxford: Clarendon Press, 1974.

House, Humphry, *The Dickens World*. London: Oxford UP, 1941.

Leavis, F. R., and Q. D., *Dickens the Novelist*. London: Chatto and Windus, 1970.

Letters of Charles Dickens. Eds. Madeline House, et al. Pilgrim Edition. 6 vols. Oxford: Clarendon Press, 1977–88.

McMaster, R. D., "Man and Beast in Dickensian Caricature," in *UTQ* 31 (April 1962).

Romano, John, *Dickens and Reality*. New York: Columbia UP, 1978.

Tillotson, Kathleen, *Novels of the Eighteen-Forties*. Oxford: Clarendon Press, 1954.

Van Ghent, Dorothy, "The Dickens World" in *SR* (Summer 1950), reprinted in *The Dickens Critics*, ed. George Ford and Lauriat Lane, Jr. Ithaca: Cornell UP, 1966.

Welsh, Alexander, *The City of Dickens*. Oxford: Clarendon Press, 1971.

Williams, Raymond, "Introduction" to *Dombey and Son* by Charles Dickens. Harmondsworth: Penguin, 1970.

"Flight" and "Pursuit": Fugitive Identity in *Bleak House*

Cynthia Northcutt Malone

Prowling the streets of *Bleak House*, Jo is confronted with an unfathomable mystery. The veiled lady whom he once led to the "berryin ground" returns like a recurrent nightmare, each manifestation almost—not quite—identical with the last (485). First Jo, then Inspector Bucket attempts to puzzle out the mystery: who *is* this elusive figure? As we make our way through this diffuse and densely populated novel, we wait expectantly for the revelation of a name; we depend upon proper names and personal pronouns to designate identity, to distinguish one figure from another. But the flight of the veiled lady through *Bleak House* challenges the designating power of the name, for the novel represents a substitutive chain of veiled ladies whose track through the dual narrative involves movements of conflation, division, and dissolution. Beginning with the fugitive lady, I want to show that proper names and pronouns designate identity in the novel only as they reveal its flight.

After Jo guides the mysterious lady to the "berryin ground," each appearance of a veiled figure provokes an unanswerable question: is it that lady or another one?[1] The figure that appears in Tulkinghorn's chambers, "the forenner," seems to be both: "It is her and it an't her. It an't her hand, nor yet her rings, nor yet her voice. But that there's the wale, the bonnet, and the gownd, and they're wore the same way wot she wore 'em, and it's her height wot she was, and she giv me a sov'ring and hooked it" (369).

Surfacing and vanishing with terrifying stealth, the veiled lady glides in and out of the plot. The watchful "eye" of the present-tense narration tracks her steps through the pursuing figure of Inspector Bucket, but the lady slips out

107

of sight only to turn up in the first-person narration, in the guise of the "I."
Hearing of illness at the brickmaker's cottage, Esther puts on her bonnet and
veil and goes to visit Jenny. It is Jo who is ill, of course, and he is deeply
shaken by this reappearance of the veiled lady.[2] "The boy staggered up
instantly, and stared at me with a remarkable expression of surprise and
terror," Esther reports (485). "Ain't the lady the t'other lady?" Jo asks (486).
But no; this lady is neither the one nor the other: "If she ain't the t'other one,
she ain't the forenner. Is there *three* of 'em then?" (488).

That Jo should be perplexed by misleading appearances is hardly surprising, since he "don't know nothink" (274). It is the institutions of law and
police, Chancery Court and the Detective Police, that penetrate veils and
establish names; the representatives of these institutions are confident that the
mystery of identity will be solved when the veiled figures are correctly
named.[3] Back in Tulkinghorn's chambers, Inspector Bucket's tidy mind sorts
out the problem of the veiled lady into the two logical possibilities. Logic
dictates that Hortense must be either the same lady Jo has seen before, or
another lady. Inspector Bucket settles the confusion; he dismisses Hortense
and informs Tulkinghorn that "[t]here an't a doubt that it was the other one
with this one's dress on" (370)—that it was Lady Dedlock, wearing
Hortense's clothes—who followed Jo to the burying ground.

Inspector Bucket unravels the plot by lifting the veils, uncovering concealed identities. Working from the traces left behind by this vanished figure,
Bucket ingeniously sorts out "appearance" from "reality," this veiled lady
from that one. Beneath the surface of the plot, however, the text surrepti-
tiously erodes his distinctions. Appearing now as Esther, now as Hortense,
now as Lady Dedlock, the veiled lady figuratively dissolves the boundaries
that appear to contain the self. Indeed, it is the illiterate Jo who most aptly
formulates the logic of the text: in *Bleak House*, one figure always "is and
an't" another.

Thus, while the detective plot of *Bleak House* suggests that the mystery of
identity can be solved, and identity can be established, the plot itself functions
as a concealing surface. The plot indicates that the truth about identity is to be
discovered beneath the veil, but in fact it is the veiled surface itself that
metaphorically figures the condition of identity in this novel; identity is
slippery, multiple, and impenetrable. It is in her veiled condition, as an
unnamed, three-faced figure in flight, and not as an uncovered face, that the
lady signals the status of the self. In *Bleak House*, the self is always
anonymous, multiple, and fugitive; and both narratives, in their different
registers, bear the tracks of fugitive identity.

"SOME ONE ELSE"

When the veiled lady penetrates into Esther's narration, she seems to peer out of the "I" at the bewildered Jo. A moment later, Charley assures Jo that Esther is not the veiled lady he remembers, but someone else. This confusion of figures is telling, for the difference between self and other is deeply problematic in *Bleak House*. As I will show, the distinction between the "I" and "other" figures in the first-person narration is always unstable. Esther always seems to be someone else, even when she is apparently alone, for the "I" of this narration is intractably plural.

Of course, the dual narrative structure of *Bleak House* seems to establish the boundaries of the "I", for the shifts in pronoun and verb tense seem to assert a firm distinction between the "I" and the "other," unnamed narrator. The "I" seems safely contained within the first-person narration, while the other narration seems to be the voice of an anonymous, third-person narrator.[4] However, as the movement of the veiled lady across this boundary suggests, this apparently stable formal distinction is untenable. Indeed, careful scrutiny of the relationship between these narratives demonstrates that the dual narrative structure of *Bleak House* recapitulates, at the level of narrative form, the division that always operates within the "I."

The illness that scars Esther's face creates a visible sign of this division within the "I"; the new, scarred Esther, the fictive narrator, begins her story looking back at the old, beautiful Esther. This event in the plot metaphorically represents the distinction that is always implied in the stance of retrospection, the distinction between an old self and a new self, a narrated "I" and a narrating "I."[5] From her illness until the closing page of the novel, Esther wears a new face. At the close, the plot pretends to merge the two figures into one by lifting the veil of that new face and finding the old beauty concealed beneath it—finding a stable, unified identity concealed under difference. But the unfolding of the narrative reveals the impossibility of a final unity.

For there is also a more widespread, more intractable division within the "I" that is repeatedly marked in the narrative. This division is often read in psychological terms. Zwerdling argues, for example, that Esther's discovery of her illegitimacy is the "childhood trauma" whose "long-range effects" are traced in her narrative; and he suggests that her disfigurement symbolically marks her sense of guilt.[6] I would like to recast the problem in narratological terms, however. Esther's scarred face may represent the difference within the "I," but it is crucial to notice that this difference is registered in the narrative discourse even before Esther's illness. Just before the encounter with Jo, Esther signals her self-division in an enigmatic remark: "I had for a moment an undefinable impression of myself as being something different from what I then was" (484–485). Already, before the disfiguring illness, Esther's face both is and is not her own: "She looks to me the t'other one," Jo insists (486). As the encounter with Jo makes clear, Esther's face seems not to be her own even before she is disfigured by her illness. This sense intensifies when Esther first sees her mother's face. Esther is startled when she sees Lady Dedlock at church, for Lady Dedlock's face seems to her "in a confused way, like a broken glass to me, in which I saw scraps of old remembrances" (304). Those "old remembrances" recall a painful past:

> . . . *I——I*, little Esther Summerson, the child who lived a life apart, and on whose birthday there was no rejoicing—seemed to arise before my own eyes, evoked out of the past by some power in this fashionable lady, whom I not only entertained no fancy that I had ever seen, but whom I perfectly well knew I had never seen until that hour.
>
> (305)

The sight of Lady Dedlock's face prompts Esther to remember not only her past self, but also her now-dead godmother, so that the revelation of blood ties among these three figures is all but announced. In terms of the plot, then, the function of this passage is to prepare us for the revelation of Esther's identity, to rationalize that discovery.

But it is important to notice what arises before Esther's "own eyes" in this scene: an absent face, the face of Esther's past self. The narrated Esther takes the fictive posture of the narrating Esther. Sitting in church, the narrated Esther becomes for a moment the "author," recalling her past self, "little Esther Summerson." This scene figures the restrospective stance of the narrator, for it represents an older Esther looking back at a younger version of Esther. But the posture of retrospection which the narrated Esther assumes here does not point toward an eventual unification of the "I" that would represent achievement of identity. The "author" names the face that arises before "my own eyes" as "*I*," as "Esther Summerson," but this act of naming also calls attention to temporal difference: the other face of the "I," the face of "little Esther Summerson," is "evoked out of the past." Thus, the mirror-like moment offers no steadily reflected image of the self that might confirm a coherent and unified identity; instead, this moment splinters the "I," exposing its division and multiplicity, refracting it in "a broken glass."

By establishing a reflexive relationship between different faces of the "I," this scene graphically illustrates the specular structure of Esther's narrative.[7] And the structure of specularity involves still other faces of the "I," faces that wear different names. The first-person narrative locks together the faces of mother and daughter in a reflexive relationship: "I had a fancy, on more than one of these Sundays," Esther says, "that what this lady so curiously was to me, I was to her—I mean that I disturbed her thoughts as she influenced mine, though in some different way" (372). Esther's "unaccountable agitation" grows still more acute with the addition of the third face—that other face of the veiled lady, the face of Hortense—whose "observation" leaves Esther "distressed" (305). The rhetoric of disturbance, agitation, and distress aptly describes the vertiginous structure of specularity.

Far from consolidating or affirming Esther's identity, then, the moment of retrospection dissociates the "I." Here, even before Esther loses her beauty, the text calls attention to an irremediable division within the "self." The scene points back to a part of the "I" that is irrecoverably lost, the face of "little Esther Summerson." Esther's illness only intensifies this sense of loss and absence of identity. After her recovery, Esther recalls "watching what was done for me, as if it were done for some one else whom I was quietly sorry for" (545). That "some one else" gazes back at Esther when she goes to the mirror:

> There was a little muslin curtain drawn across it. I drew it back: and stood for a moment looking through such a veil of my own hair, that I could see nothing else. Then I put my hair aside, and looked at the reflection in the mirror, encouraged by seeing how placidly it looked at me. I was very much changed—O very, very much. At first, my face was so strange to me, that I think I should have put my hands before it and started back, but for the encouragement I have mentioned.
>
> (559)

Here is a case to trouble Bucket's logic: the face that the "I" discovers behind the veils, the "muslin curtain" and "my own hair," is "strange to me"; it is not "I" in the glass, but "it." Probing beneath the veils, one does not uncover identity; instead, one uncovers another radical loss of identity.

According to Lowry Pei, the mirror scenes in Esther's narrative figure her psychological condition; these scenes represent her "unknown self," the repressed "Other within Esther which her conscious mind cannot reach" (148, 151). While that reading might account for the self-division that Esther's narration so frequently registers, it fails to account for the circulation of identity between different figures—between the multiple figures of the veiled lady. Conflation of the "I" with "another" figure is most clearly marked in the relationship between Esther and Ada Clare. When Esther becomes ill, the narrative discourse literally displaces the lost, beautiful face of the "I" onto "some one else," onto Ada Clare. Zwerdling has suggested that Ada is a kind of "second self" for Esther, "as the girl she might have become if she had not been born 'different from other children' and 'set apart' " (431). Zwerdling is right to point out the very close relationship between Esther and Ada, I think, but I would like to argue that he takes too literally the rhetoric of difference that he adopts from Miss Barbary. In the text, Esther is not "set apart"; that is, there are no clearly defined borders around the "self" to set her apart. Thus, Esther not only "might have been" Ada, but, more radically, the self and this other are all but indistinguishable.

The relationship between Esther and Ada replays the scene before Esther's mirror, exposing again the division and loss suffered by the "I." The reflexivity of "Ada" and the suggestion of light in "Clare" mark Ada's function as a reflection of the "I"; furthermore, both Ada and the mirror are banished from the sickroom until Esther's recovery. When Esther begins to recover, she thinks of Ada "[a] little in connexion with the absent mirrors, but not much; for I knew my loving girl would be changed by no change in my looks" (549). The scarred face promises to set Esther apart, to establish the boundary between the "I" and "she." But when Ada returns and "my beauty and I" walk together in the garden, that boundary disappears (670).[8] The possessive pronoun anchors "my beauty" to "me," so that the two faces are involved in a specular structure. It is as if Esther had been disfigured, yet her reflection had retained its beauty. Ada represents the face of the "I" that Esther has lost. Thus, when Esther begins to think that she has no right to keep the flowers that Allan gave "to one so different" (559), it is Ada's lips that bestow the farewell kiss on the faded flowers: "I took the withered flowers out, and put them for a moment to her lips" (669). Furthermore, when Ada leaves Bleak House to join Richard, the "I" seems to register Ada's absence. "I was so lonely, and so blank without her, and it was so desolate to be going home with no hope of seeing her there, that I could get no comfort for a little while," Esther says (755). As the distance increases between the "I" and "my beauty," Esther is literally dis-figured.[9]

Jarndyce's marriage proposal threatens to arrest the "I" in its condition of loss. According to Esther, his proposal is addressed specifically to the new, scarred face, the face that points to the loss of identity; "he did not hint to me," Esther says, "that when I had been better looking, he had had this same proceeding in his thoughts, and had refrained from it. . . . But *I* knew it, I knew it well now." Esther reads the letter, weeping and feeling "as if something for which there was no name or distinct idea were indefinitely lost to me" (668). That nameless, lost something is nothing less than the self: "By and by I went to my old glass. My eyes were red and swollen, and I said, 'O Esther, Esther, can that be you!' I am afraid the face in the glass was going to cry again at this reproach, but I held up my finger at it, and it stopped" (668). The "I" may well ask if the dis-figured face, the some one else in the glass, can be Esther.[10] It is difficult to name a "self" as fragmented as this.

Of course, the formal structure of *Bleak House* seems to attribute a great deal of authority to names. The mystery form implies that the closure of the narrative will unravel the plot and resolve the confusion. In the case of *Bleak House*, that means penetrating disguises, bringing to light concealed identities, revealing the relations between figures—discovering names. Furthermore, the fiction of a retrospective stance positions the "I" "after" the story, so that Esther has "already" learned her name and her birth-story. Ostensibly, it is the knowledge of her identity that authorizes Esther to recount her story. If accurate naming is the key to identity, however, Esther's case demands close attention. The circumstances of Esther's birth preclude the possibility of a legitimate name; and her proper name, "Esther Summerson," is only a pseudonym—only one pseudonym among others. When Esther first comes to Bleak House, she accrues a wealth of nicknames. Jarndyce christens her "Little Old Woman" after the figure in the "Rhyme": "This was the beginning of my being called Old Woman, and Little Old Woman, and Cobweb, and Mrs. Shipton, and Mother Hubbard, and Dame Durden, and so many names of that sort, that my own name soon became quite lost among them" (148). Esther's "own name" is only one more nickname, "quite lost among" the countless other names. The point is made again when the text establishes the allegorical appropriateness of Esther's "own name," "Summerson"—a name that is inscribed and erased in the same act: "I must write it, even if I rub it out again, because it gives me so much pleasure. They said there could be no East wind where Somebody was; they said that wherever Dame Durden went, there was sunshine and summer air" (482). This playful remark may grant significance to Esther's name, but it also equates "Summerson" with another playful name, "Dame Durden." As Ragussis observes, the "symbolic names" attributed to Esther "seem finally to make more apparent that her proper name is unknown" (90).[11] The point is underscored when the passage clears all the nicknames out of the way for a moment, revealing what lies behind them: an indefinite "Somebody."

The text which Esther fictively authors, then, exposes "Esther" to be an anonymous "Somebody," and it exposes the "I" as "some one else." The same confusion between the "I" and a nameless "some one else" is mirrored at the larger level of narrative form, in the dual narrative structure. Readers of *Bleak House* have generally assumed an absolute difference between the narratives and an internal coherence within each narrative—though Harvey argues that "Dickens" occasionally slips, and "his" voice intrudes into "Esther's" narrative.[12] But the internal coherence of the first-person narration is clearly under severe strain, and the dissociation of the "I" should make us question the assumption of an absolute boundary between the narrations.

Certainly, the shifts in verb tense and pronominal person between the narratives seem to suggest a marked difference in the positions of the narrators. The past-tense verbs in Esther's narration seem to position her at a point after the story, retrospectively recounting the events, while the unnamed narrator's present-tense account seems to follow events as they unfold. Each narrative also acknowledges the other, signalling both a sense of participation in a larger whole and a sense of the integrity of parts. Esther refers to "my portion of these pages," suggesting that there is at least one other "portion" (62); and the "other" narrator seems to distinguish himself or herself from Esther, taking up the story "while Esther sleeps, while Esther wakes" (131).

Given Esther's habit of self-address, however, reference to Esther by name hardly constitutes a firm distinction between the "I" and the "other." That is, the "I" of Esther's narration frequently adopts the stance of another toward herself. Not only does she address herself by "you" or by name; her narration also figures the "I" in the third person in its textual reflections: the face in the mirror, habitually referred to as "it"; and "my beauty," Ada Clare. Thus, the "other" narrator merely sustains a posture that the "I" occasionally takes. The distinction suggested by the shift in verb tenses is no more definite. The present-tense verbs evoke a sense of unfolding history:

> Fog everywhere. Fog up the river, where it flows among green aits and meadows; fog down the river, where it rolls defiled among the tiers of shipping, and the waterside pollutions of a great (and dirty) city. Fog on the Essex marshes, fog on the Kentish heights. Fog creeping into the cabooses of collier-brigs; fog lying out on the yards, and hovering in the rigging of great ships; fog drooping on the gunwales of barges and small boats.
>
> (49)

The events of the narrative seem to take place under the attentive eye of an unknown observer. Though reported in present tense, these events are contemporaneous with those that Esther recounts from a retrospective position; thus, the effect of the present-tense verbs is to create a sense of a resurrected past. In fact, the present-tense narration recalls the encounter between Esther and her mother, when "little Esther Summerson . . . seemed to arise before my own eyes, evoked out of the past by some power in this fashionable lady." In the "other" narration, figures from the past seem to arise before the observer's eyes, evoked out of the past by some power in this unknown narrator.[13] Here again, the present-tense narrative sustains a stance that Esther takes momentarily. Perhaps, after all, this "some one else" is a posture of the "I."

"NO ONE"

Even as names and pronouns destabilize the "I," the plot seems to move steadily toward the revelation of Esther's familial identity, as if the self might congeal around that core of revelation. Esther's parentage functions as the great secret of *Bleak House*, the discovery that effects narrative closure. The plot reaches its end when the mysteries have been solved and identities have been established in familial terms. But the text also militates against its own ending, for the narrative discourse affirms identity only by negating it. That is, to identify this "Somebody" with "so many names" is the great effort of the plot; but *Bleak House* defies any comprehensible notion of identification. "Somebody" turns out to be "no one."

Esther's dream at the Jellyby house traces the pursuit of identity, and it figures the end of the quest. At the beginning of the passage, the "I" is apparently intact. Esther is sitting before the fire, with the sleeping figure of Caddy resting against her. But the "I" that asserts self-recognition gives way to an indefinite "some one," and at last, to "no one":

> At first I was painfully awake, and vainly tried to lose myself, with my eyes closed, among the scenes of the day. At length, by slow degrees, they became indistinct and mingled. I began to lose the identity of the sleeper resting on me. Now it was Ada; now, one of my old Reading friends from whom I could not believe I had so recently parted. Now, it was the little mad woman worn out with curtsying and smiling; now, someone in authority at Bleak House. Lastly, it was no one, and I was no one.
>
> (94)

At the beginning of the passage, it is "the identity of the sleeper" that is in question. But as Esther grows drowsy, the "I" and "the sleeper" are no longer distinguishable; the "I" is gradually absorbed into the procession of figures, for the "some one in authority at Bleak House," of course, is Esther herself. When the passage ends, the identity of the "I" is posited—but only by negation: "I was no one."

At one level, this moment in the text signals the discovery of Esther's identity, for Esther is indeed "no one": she is the child of Nemo. But this formulation of discovered identity repays reflection. Even as the narrative discourse foreshadows the revelation of Esther's father, the revelation that will solve the central mystery of the plot, it also points to a more deeply concealed secret: discovery of identity, in this novel, always constitutes its negation. The mystery of Esther's identity hinges not on the shameful secret of illegitimacy, but on the more troubling problem, absence of identity. The plot turns on the discovery that Nemo and Lady Dedlock bore a child, but beneath the plot the text reveals that Nemo has fathered "no one," a verbal echo of his own absence.

Nemo first appears in the text as a kind of track pointing to his own absence. He first appears in the text already dead, as a corpse. He has already assumed "that last shape which earthly lodgings take for No one—and for Every one": "And all that night, the coffin stands ready by the old portmanteau; and the lonely figure on the bed, whose path in life has lain through five-and-forty years, lies there, with no more track behind him, that any one can trace, than a deserted infant" (196). There need be "no more track . . . than a deserted infant," of course; the law and the police "can trace" the "track" that links Nemo to the "deserted infant," Esther. Esther is not only the evidence that points to an absent Nemo, however. The explicit translation of "Nemo" as "No one" conflates father and daughter, so that the two figures are linked in absence and in denial of identity.

The text establishes the "I" as a virtual absence from the opening of Esther's narration. The first-person narration corroborates the supposedly false account of Esther's birth-story, an account that negates the "I": "So strangely did I hold my place in this world, that, until within a short time back, I had never, to my own mother's knowledge, breathed—had been buried—had never been endowed with life—had never borne a name," Esther muses (569). The "I" holds its "place" very strangely indeed, for the text represents that place as a blank. The first appearance of the "I" is an act of self-erasure; Esther begins her narration by staging her own disappearance. The narrating "I" remembers confiding "every one of my secrets" to a doll, who "used to sit propped up in a great arm-chair, with her beautiful complexion and rosy lips, staring at me—or not so much at me, I think, as at nothing—" (62). At me, at nothing; Esther's formulation makes these terms grammatically equivalent, so that the "I" seems to vacate the very sentence that represents it. And this linguistic form of self-erasure is recapitulated in the plot when Esther buries herself by proxy, wrapping the doll in her own shawl and burying her in the garden. Thus, the "I" can be said to "hold my place" in the text only as a signal of its own absence. Although Esther suffers a deeply troubling sense "of filling a place" at Miss Barbary's "which ought to have been empty," that "place" operates in the text as an emptiness to be filled.

The "I" is literally absent from the "other" narration, of course; at least, an "I" recognizable as Esther is absent from this narration. A mysterious "I" does surface like the veiled lady, cloaked in anonymity and vanishing quickly. The first-person pronoun takes plural form, and takes flight, when Krook dies: "we run away" from the awful scene of his death (511). Later, the "I" passes more sedately, but just as mysteriously, from a Chesney Wold "with no inhabitants except the pictured forms upon the walls." The "I" identifies here with the ghost of a painted Dedlock, who might "find it, as I find it, difficult to believe that it could be, without them; so pass from my world, as I pass from theirs, now closing the reverberating door; so leave no blank to miss them, and so die" (620). The portraits of deceased Dedlocks fill the "blank" spaces at Chesney Wold, and the text fills the "blank" space of absence, in this passage, with a ghostly "I."

The present-tense narration also points to the absent "I" that we associate with Esther. Nemo and Lady Dedlock, for example, function in this narration as indices to Esther's "identity."Esther's name does appear in the present-tense narration—in a chapter that is significantly titled "The Ghost's Walk." This moment links Esther directly with the ghostly "I" that haunts Chesney Wold. Like that ghost, she appears only to pass from the world of the present-tense narration. But the ghost appears again, or is reflected, in the first-person narration; the "I" explicitly figures itself as the ghost of Chesney Wold:

> . . . my echoing footsteps brought it suddenly into my mind that there was a dreadful truth in the legend of the Ghost's Walk; that it was I, who was to bring calamity upon the stately house; and that my warning feet were haunting it even then. Seized with an augmented terror of myself which turned me cold, I ran from myself and everything, retraced the way by which I had come, and never paused until I had gained the lodge-gate, and the park lay sullen and black behind me.
>
> (571)

This metonymic association of Esther with the ghost sets the "I" in desperate motion. The remarkable syntax of Esther's statement, "I ran from myself," sends the first-person pronouns in hot pursuit of a fugitive identity. Reading this remark as a "grammatically reflexive index to self-division," Garrett Stewart includes this passage in his discussion of the many moments of death and absence that surround "Esther's quest for herself." (445, 447). Yet *Bleak House* represents a trajectory that is at once a quest and a flight; the novel projects a self from the evidence of its flight, from its "echoing footsteps." In this narrative, the "self" is always an extrapolation, traceable from the signs of its departure.

The narration of Krook's end offers a horribly graphic illustration. Seeking the evidence that will establish Esther's identity, Mr. Guppy arranges to receive papers from Krook. Krook misses the appointment, however, so Mr. Guppy and Tony descend to investigate:

> Here is a small burnt patch of flooring; here is the tinder from a little bundle of burnt papers; but not so light as usual, seeming to be steeped in something; and here is——is it the cinder of a small charred and broken log of wood sprinkled with white ashes, or is it coal? O Horror, he *is* here! and this from which we run away, striking out the light and overturning one another into the street, is all that represents him.
>
> (511)

Krook "*is* here"; that is, Krook's "presence" is established by the evidence of his combustion, the "foetid effluvia" that creeps down the walls (513), and the small pile of ashes on the "burnt patch of flooring." "Krook literalizes the death of the self, the idea of being no one," according to Ragussis; in Esther's writing, on the other hand, "anonymity" has a different value, for the representation of the "I" as "no one," "someone," or "everyone" joins the self with others, demonstrating that "one's life is never simply one's own"(106–7). Here again, I want to question the firm distinction between the narratives, to suggest that Esther's narrative replays Krook's combustion in another register: the Spontaneous Combustion of the self is linguistically represented in the textual moments that expose the "I" as "no one." Esther "*is* here," in the narrative, because smoldering figures offer evidence of her flight.

The flight of the self is thematized in the plot in the chapters called "Flight" and "Pursuit." The veiled lady turns fugitive, with Detective Bucket on her trail—or on their trails: all three faces of the veiled lady are caught up in flight, so that the fugitive lady seems to flee from herself. Hortense, through her accusing letter, sets Lady Dedlock on the run, and Esther joins Bucket in the futile pursuit. The lady's flight is arrested at the grave of Nemo, but when Esther lifts the veil, putting "the long dank hair aside," she finds only emptiness and absence (869). The fugitive is apprehended—but only as a corpse.

The union of Esther's family is the climax of the plot, the moment that should establish both the identity of the "I" and the relations of the figures. As D. A. Miller points out, however, the "closural moments" in this novel repeatedly "end by producing a corpse, as though the novel wanted to attest, not just the finality, but also the failure of a closure that, even as it was achieved, missed the essence of what it aspired to grasp"(96–97). Instead of affirming identity, the scene reveals an absence or negation of identity. At the grave of Nemo lies "the mother of the dead child," and "the dead child" herself bears witness (868).[14] The apparent confirmation of identity is subverted, or perhaps inverted, in a moment of utter emptiness, as the dead father, the "mother, cold and dead," and "the dead child" meet at last (869). The plot arrests the fugitives and strips away their disguises, only to find "no one" at the end of the trail.

"THE MISTRESS OF BLEAK HOUSE"

The "dead child" who spent her early years conscious of "filling a place . . . which ought to have been empty" does find a place at Bleak House.[15] Jarndyce defines Esther's social identity, giving her a place as housekeeper, and then as mistress, of Bleak House.[16] As Esther takes up the housekeeping keys, she seems to identify herself fully with her new responsibilities: "Esther, Esther, Esther! Duty, my dear!" (131). In this hortatory self-address, "Duty" seems to function as another of Esther's many names. But the narrative fragments the "I" once again, projecting the "I" into other places. Fantasies of higher social status are played out opposite Esther in her doll and in Ada Clare, in specular relation to the "I." In these reflexive moments, the face of the housekeeper is intent on duty; but that face is positioned opposite the reflected face of an idle beauty.

The opposition of beauty and duty is established in Esther's first narration, long before the illness that mars her beauty. The text figures the child busily sewing, determined "to be industrious, contented, and kind-hearted," (65) while her doll, her surrogate self, sits idly by, "with her beautiful complexion and rosy lips" (62). This opposition is adumbrated in Esther's relationship with Ada Clare. On one page, Esther addresses her "own" face, reflected in the mirror, as "my plain dear," and she exhorts herself to cheerful industry. Two pages later, Esther walks in the garden with "my beauty" (668, 670). And after Esther relinquishes a youthful idea that she might hold the place of daughter, dismissing "the possibility of his being my father" as an "idle dream," that place is filled by Ada (131). "Dear cousin John," Ada tells Jarndyce, "my father's place can never be empty again. All the love and duty I could ever have rendered to him, is transferred to you" (232).

The closure of *Bleak House* enacts a substitutive exchange of these faces. Jarndyce directs the substitution of Ada for Esther at the old Bleak House after Richard Carstone's death, and he also directs Ada to take up Esther's customary title of address. Thus, in verbal acknowledgment of the exchange, Ada trades her customary "cousin John," for Esther's term, "guardian." "He was her guardian hence forth," Esther says, "and the boy's; and he had an old association with the name" (932). The exchange constitutes a sanitized, novelized Shakespearean bed-trick, as Esther finds herself the mistress of Bleak House, but the wife of Allan Woodcourt.[17]

This plot device has attracted critical outrage, for the substitution of husbands at the end of *Bleak House* seems both farfetched and disturbing.[18] But the exchange also forces us to acknowledge the impossibility of distinguishing between figures in this text. The apparent indifference with which figures are redistributed at the end of the novel is the effect of this indistinguishability. And it is worth pointing out that the plot breaks down and the boundaries between the "I" and the "other" dissolve completely just here, at the end of the novel—at the very moment when Esther supposedly achieves a unified and coherent identity.

The relationship between the "I" and the "other" in the narrative structure is suspended in the same "undecidability" in the final chapters of *Bleak House*. The forward movement of the present-tense voice is arrested at Chesney Wold, "[a] labyrinth of grandeur, less the property of an old family of human beings and their ghostly likenesses, than of an old family of echoings and thunderings which start out of their hundred graves at every sound":

> Thus Chesney Wold. With so much of itself abandoned to darkness and vacancy; with so little change under the summer shining or the wintry lowering; so sombre and motionless always—no flag flying now by day, no rows of lights sparkling by night; with no family to come and go, no visitors to be the souls of pale cold shapes of rooms, no stir of life about it;—passion and pride, even

to the stranger's eye, have died away from the place in Lincolnshire, and yielded it to dull repose.

(931–932)

Here, in the graveyard of echoes—as in that other graveyard in London—arrested movement reveals a "vacancy," a blank place filled with a ghostly "family of echoings and thunderings," pointing to departed presence. With these "hundred graves" to mark the echoing footsteps of absent figures, the present-tense voice passes from their world, as they have passed from Chesney Wold.

But on the following page, the "I" picks up the narration in the present tense, abandoning the customary retrospective stance. The distinction between the two narrations becomes most pointedly blurred at this closing moment, when the "I" takes up the tense of the "other" narrator. And this tense shift, along with the suggestion of recovered beauty, signals the impossibility of distinguishing between the "narrating" Esther and the "narrated" Esther. The text ends with a virtual erasure of the boundaries between author and subject, the "I" and the "other." It also ends with another moment of vacancy, for the "I" leaves a family of visual "echoes," a ring of beautiful faces surrounding its absence. The narration comes to a halt as the "I" passes from their world, leaving no blank—or leaving precisely that, a blank that marks its place:

> . . . I know that my dearest little pets are very pretty, and that my darling is very beautiful, and that my husband is very handsome, and that my guardian has the brightest and most benevolent face that ever was seen; and that they can very well do without much beauty in me—even supposing—

(935)

NOTES

1. In his "Introduction" to *Twentieth Century Interpretations of Bleak House: A Collection of Critical Essays* (Englewood Cliffs, NJ: Prentice-Hall, 1968), Jacob Korg attributes the widespread doubling in *Bleak House* to a "restless indecision" that prompted Dickens to "embody each of his ideas in various forms, and to rehearse each of his ideas in a different key or with a second cast of characters" (p. 19). See also Taylor Stoehr, *Dickens: The Dreamer's Stance* (Ithaca, NY: Cornell Univ. Press, 1965; rpt. in *Dickens Bleak House: A Casebook* (London: Macmillan and Co., 1969), p. 236. I want to argue that the doubled figures in *Bleak House* call into question the apparent distinction between "self" and "other."

2. Robert Newsom explores such "déjà vu" experiences in *Dickens on the Romantic*

Side of Familiar Things: Bleak House and the Novel Tradition (New York: Columbia Univ. Press, 1977), pp. 47–92. Newsom's treatment of characters as psychological subjects limits the mobility of his argument, however, for it reifies the boundaries between figures in the text.

3. According to Robert A. Donovan, in "Structure and Idea in *Bleak House, ELH* 29 (1962); rpt. in *Twentieth-Century Interpretations of Bleak House*, p. 35, "the main mystery" of the novel is "the question of establishing the identity of all the characters involved, and in the world of *Bleak House* one's identity is defined according to his relations to other people" (p. 35). I want to explore the moments in the text that counter or subvert the movement of the plot toward establishing these identities.

4. The differences between the narratives have led some critics to argue that they are irreconcilable. In a recent article, "The Two Worlds of *Bleak House*," *ELH* 43 (Winter, 1976), Ellen Serlen argues that the "worlds" of the *Bleak House* narrators "are intended to be two totally separate entities rather than two halves of a whole fictional world" (p. 551). See also Jacob Korg, p. 18; John R. Reed, "Freedom, Fate, and the Future in *Bleak House*," *Clio* 8 (Winter, 1979), 175.

   Among those who argue for a greater cohesiveness is J. Hillis Miller, who asserts in *Charles Dickens: The World of His Novels* (Cambridge: Harvard Univ. Press, 1958) that the "third-person anonymous spectator" discovers "that he must seek the help of an *involved* spectator" to solve the mysteries of the novel, so that Esther is enlisted as a kind of subordinate, assistant narrator. While I cannot help noticing Miller's tacit assumption that the directing narrator, the "anonymous spectator," is male, I will let it pass without comment. Donovan, pp. 31–44, generally shares Miller's view, arguing that the novel demands both a panoramic and a personal view. See also W. J. Harvey, in "*Bleak House*: The Double Narrative," *Character and the Novel* (Ithaca, NY: Cornell Univ. Press, 1965); rpt. in *Dickens Bleak House*, calls the two narrations the "systole" and "diastole" of the narrative system (p. 230). See also Leonard Deen, "Style and Unity in *Bleak House*," *Criticism* 3 (1961), 206–218; D. W. Jefferson, "The Artistry of *Bleak House*," *Essays and Studies*, NS 27 (1975), 40; and Ned Lukacher, *Primal Scenes: Literature, Philosophy, Psychoanalysis* (Ithaca, NY: Cornell Univ. Press, 1986), p. 322. I would like to argue that the relationship between parts of the narrative structure is far more dynamic than either of these critical views would suggest.

5. As this terminology demonstrates, I am drawing on recent work in theory of autobiography in order to mark the division of the "I" in the first-person narration. On the implied temporal stance of retrospection in autobiographical narration, see James Olney's treatment of the "autobiography of memory" in "Some Versions of Memory/Some Versions of *Bios*: The Ontology of Autobiography," in *Autobiography: Essays Theoretical and Critical* (Princeton: Princeton Univ. Press, 1980), pp. 240–248. In the same collection of essays, Jean Starobinski offers a statement of the argument for the convergence of narrated and narrating "I"; see "The Style of Autobiography," pp. 78–79. While these models for understanding the difference "within" the "I" offer a helpful beginning point, I want to show that the elusive "I" of *Bleak House* demands a model that is more sensitive to mobility and plurality.

6. Alex Zwerdling, "Esther Summerson Rehabilitated," *PMLA* 88 (May, 1973), 430. "Her scarred face is the outward and visible sign of an inward and spiritual sin," according to Zwerdling (p. 435). See also William Axton, who sees in

Esther "an objective study of a character divided against herself by contending forces clearly discernible in her personal history; and her portion of the narrative illustrates this inner conflict," in "The Trouble With Esther," *MLQ* 26 (1965), 546; and Judith Wilt, "Confusion and Consciousness in Dickens' Esther" *Nineteenth Century Fiction* 32 (1977), 285–309.

7. On the specular structure of self-cognition in autobiography, see Paul de Man, "Autobiography as De-Facement," *MLN* 94 (1979), 919–923. The model of specular structure illuminates the relationships of reflexivity and reflection that I want to examine.

8. In his discussion of Esther's relationship with Ada, Zwerdling notes, "When, after her disfigurement, she calls Ada 'my beauty,' as she frequently does, the phrase is charged with meaning" (p. 431). It is precisely this phrase that suggests the instability of the boundary between these figures, and gives the lie to Miss Barbary's "you are set apart."

9. Examining the original illustrations of *Bleak House*, Michael Steig finds that Esther's face is frequently averted. He argues that "the averted face is clearly a symbol of disgrace," a symbol that connects Esther with the pervasive social corruption in the novel. See "The Iconography of the Hidden Face in *Bleak House*," *Dickens Studies* 4 (March, 1968), 22. But the averted face also figures this loss of identity Esther describes as a "blank."

10. On the marked difference between the "self" and the image in the glass, see Pei, pp. 144–156, and Lawrence Frank, in *Charles Dickens and the Romantic Self* (Lincoln: Univ. of Nebraska Press, 1984), pp. 97–123.

11. See also Axton, p. 550.

12. "Only rarely does [Esther's] style slip and allow us to glimpse Dickens guiding her pen," Harvey states (p. 226). Albert J. Guerard refutes this view in *"Bleak House*: Structure and Style," *Southern Review* NS 5 (April, 1969), 339, but Guerard does not examine fully the narrative interpenetration that I want to explore.

13. Wilt suggests the possibility that the voice of the present-tense narrator is the voice of the "I" "in another mode," p. 295. She also notes the similarity between the present-tense chapters in *Bleak House* and the present-tense retrospects in *David Copperfield*, a point that reinforces both her argument and mine.

14. Pei comments on the psychological appropriateness of the phrase "the dead child" as a description of Esther, arguing that this death is the consequence of her "childhood of unlimited guilt," p. 154. However, it is not Esther's condition of death, but the acknowledgment of familial identity, that is crucial here; when father, mother, and child are united in death, as throughout *Bleak House*, the discovery of identity occurs in a moment of negation.

15. The *OED* lists two meanings of "place" that are pertinent here: "Position or standing in the social scale, or in any order of estimation or merit; rank, station, whether high or low." (III.9) "An office, employment, situation; sometimes *spec*. a government appointment, an office in the service of the crown or state" (IV.14).

16. According to Axton, the "pet names" associated with Esther's function "obscure her given names," and "they tacitly deprive Esther of a measure of identity and reduce her to the relative anonymity of a housekeeper" (p. 550). But Esther's "given names" provide a slender hold on identity, since they do not signify familial identity; thus, her function as housekeeper seems to shore up identity. As Steig argues, "it is through her association with Mr. Jarndyce, and her role as

housekeeper of Bleak House that Esther gains her identity as a human being" (p. 20).

17. Serlen dismisses this exchange with a brief comment: "Ada is now Esther to Jarndyce, Esther is 'Dame Durden' to her husband . . . Roles have shifted, but that is all" (p. 565). That is all, indeed; this closing gesture of the plot fully exposes the specular relation of Esther and Ada throughout *Bleak House*.

18. For a survey of the vituperative commentary on the closure of *Bleak House*, see Marianna Torgovnick, *Closure in the Novel* (Princeton: Princeton Univ. Press, 1981), pp. 37–40.

WORKS CITED

Dickens, Charles. *Bleak House*. Norman Page, ed. Harmondsworth: Penguin Books Ltd., 1971.

Miller, D.A. "Discipline in Different Voices: Bureaucracy, Police, Family, and *Bleak House*," *Representations* 1 (1979); reprinted in *The Novel and the Police.*, Berkeley: U of California P, 1988.

Pei, Lowry. "Mirrors, the Dead Child, Snagsby's Secret, and Esther." *English Language Notes*, 16 (1978): 144–56.

Ragussis, Michael. *Acts of Naming*. Oxford: Oxford UP, 1986.

Stewart, Garrett. "The New Mortality of *Bleak House*." *ELH* 45:3 (Fall 1978): 443–87.

Zwerdling, Alex. "Esther Summerson Rehabilitated." *PMLA* 88 (May, 1973): 429–39.

Some Narrative Devices
in *Bleak House*

Philip Collins

The readers for whom Dickens wrote *Bleak House* in 1852–53 were—if reviews of the novel are a fair guide—much less interested than we have become in its having two narrators. For better or worse, they read fiction differently then, and their interest in narrative techniques, point of view, and suchlike, fell short of ours. Only two of the many reviews of *Bleak House* known to me say much about the dual narration. Both of them identify the present-tense narrator with Dickens—"the author speaking in his own person"—which may now strike us as a somewhat rough-and-ready handling of the narratorial-persona question. Both approved of Dickens' experiment. "We do not know," wrote *Bentley's Monthly Magazine*, "of any similar instance in our literature of the mixture of autobiography and ordinary narrative" (and, I might add, I too know of no precedent for Dickens' method here). But, the reviewer continued,

> though the idea is novel, the effect is good. It affords the writer a wider range of character and scene than a single autobiography would have done, while its partaking partly of the nature of the latter, gives an additional interest to the character of the Heroine.
>
> (66–67)

Dickens had succeeded admirably, thought the American *Eclectic Magazine* reviewer:

> The work is Dickens throughout; but in parts it is the Dickens whose portrait we have seen; while, in others, it is Dickens disguised in a sisterly form . . . but

a stream of womanly thought and feeling seems to have passed into his very
heart. We know of none but himself who could have exhibited, in this respect,
such a delicate conception of the human mind.

(666)

Dickens would have appreciated that compliment. As recorded conversations show, he specially valued reassurance about his presentation of Esther.
"I see you understand me! I see you understand me!" he exclaimed, with his
face taking on "a pensive, tender aspect" when an American interviewer
praised his "insight into the heart of woman" and instanced the episode when
Esther accepts John Jarndyce's proposal of marriage (Collins *Interviews* II:
327–78). It is well that Dickens did not see the letter written after reading the
current Number by Charlotte Bronte, herself an expert in female first-person
narration (and Dickens owed a debt to her *Jane Eyre* in *Bleak House*): "I liked
the Chancery part, but when it passes into the autobiographic form . . . it
seems to me too often weak and twaddling; an amiable nature is caricatured,
not faithfully rendered, in Miss Esther Summerson" (Collins *Heritage* 273).
I must acknowledge that, to use Dickens' term, I have not yet fully
"understood" him here. By the standards of world literature, Esther is at best,
I think, a very modest achievement. *Bleak House* is one of the great
nineteenth-century novels not because of Esther, but despite her. Even John
Forster, who must have known how greedy Dickens was for praise in this
area, held that he had not succeeded with Esther.

Dickens himself never even mentions that "autobiographic form" nor
indeed the dual narration in his preface or in any letters or recorded
conversations known to me. Like almost all his prefatory statements, the
Bleak House preface is concerned with verisimilitude, his assertion that
characters, institutions, and episodes *are* the way he has depicted them (here,
the Chancery Courts and the medical evidence for spontaneous combustion).
He does however, add one tantalizing brief literary-critical remark: "In *Bleak
House*, I have purposely dwelt upon the romantic side of familiar things." He
is a very inadequate guide to his own work: but then, he held that, as he said
in one general preface, "It is not for an author to describe his own books. If
they cannot speak for themselves, he is likely to do little service by speaking
for them." Often he has been compared to Shakespeare, for this range and
amplitude of his imagination, and they are akin, too, in this reticence about
aims and methods; we have no word from Shakespeare about his verse
techniques, dramatic construction, or artistic development.

Wisely, inside the novel itself, Dickens does not explicitly draw attention to the dual narration. Esther begins her first chapter: "I have a great deal of difficulty in beginning to write my portion of these pages, for I know I am not clever" and, opening her final chapter, she refers to "the unknown friend to whom I write"; but sensibly Dickens leaves it at that, not raising questions about why Esther is writing or who that unknown friend might be—any more than he invites readers of *Great Expectations* to ask why Pip is telling his story or why, being so good at doing so, Pip does not give up being a small-time merchant in the Orient and take up novel-writing as a career. Only once does the Narrator betray any consciousness of Esther and her narrative: she goes to bed at the end of Chapter 6, and Chapter 7 opens with "While Esther sleeps, and while Esther wakes . . . ." Dickens might have been wiser to omit this momentary breach of the decorum he has established. Then in Chapter 56, the Narrator records that Esther, in bed again, is coming downstairs at one in the morning to assist Mr. Bucket, but it is she who narrates her arrival downstairs. The Narrator never sees Esther, though it could have been interesting to have his account of her appearance and his impressions of her personality—not that I shall argue that any such glimpse would have been likely much to extend or modify our view of her. Otherwise, the two narrators ignore each other and are unaware of what the other one has told the reader. Thus, in Chapter 1 the Narrator notices in the Chancery Court "a little mad old woman in a squeezed bonnet" with a reticule full of documents. In Chapter 3 Esther encounters "a curious little old woman" who haunts the Chancery Courts, lodges at Krook's (to whom she introduces Esther and her friends) and has a "little bag of documents." In Chapter 10, the Narrator records Tulkinghorn's visit to a shop "kept . . . by one Krook" (evidently he has never heard of him before). In the next chapter, the Narrator observes "a crazy little woman" who is Krook's female lodger and whose name is Miss Flite: three chapters later, Esther visits her and "for the first time" learns her name.

This is one simple example of how Dickens, with almost complete consistency, keeps the two narratives separate, while at the same time alerting the reader to their numerous connections. The opening number offers a simple example of the latter. The first two chapters belong to the Narrator, their echoing titles "In Chancery" and "In Fashion" providing a first indication of how this many-worded novel is to be read—an indication made explicit in the first of his "sign-post" pronouncements, those opening paragraphs to Chapter 2 when the Narrator adverts us to the links between these apparently diverse worlds: both are "things of precedent and usage: over-sleeping Rip Van Winkles . . . ; sleeping beauties, whom the Knight will wake one day . . . ." A major social theme of the novel is here announced: Dickens, it is evident, is not merely joining in the vociferous contemporary agitation against the Chancery scandal, but is broadening his vision to present a Britain that is complacently inefficient and unjust, "deadened" by archaic procedures but threatened by the present "rushing of the larger worlds" ignored by the "Fashionable" (and politically dominant) world; no wonder that the next character introduced is surnamed Dedlock. Chapter 1 begins, memorably, with London in a November fog and moves to Chancery where *Jarndyce and Jarndyce* is droning along. In Chapter 2 we learn that the first major character introduced, Lady Dedlock, is involved in that case: also that she is childless (and manifestly disturbed by that fact) and that something in her past, evoked by some handwriting, is so disturbing that it makes her swoon. Esther takes over in Chapter 3 with, as I remarked, minimal authorial explanation. Her dead aunt, it transpires, was also a party in *Jarndyce and Jarndyce*, and Esther is to be a companion to a Ward of the Court involved in the same case, and she arrives in London while the same November fog is prevailing, and she is taken before the Lord Chancellor. Also, we learn, Esther is parentless and illegitimate, and we thus get the first of the hints that rapidly accumulate about possible connections between her and Lady Dedlock.

Number I ends with Esther and her new friends lodging overnight, most uncomfortably, at Mrs. Jellyby's. "What a strange house!" Ada remarks. "How curious of my cousin Jarndyce to send us here!" This is the first of John Jarndyce's "strange," indeed dotty, actions (he is often more a narrative device than a character), though in Chapter 6 he somewhat explains himself: "I may have sent you there on purpose"—and Esther rises to the occasion with the correct reply: "We thought that, perhaps, it is right to begin with the obligations of home, sir . . . ." With Mr. Skimpole's "childishly" nonchalant attitude to the adult world's duties to the young, later in that chapter, it becomes evident that here we have another theme:

> "We will not call such a lovely young creature as [Miss Clare] . . . an orphan. She is the child of the universe."
> "The universe," [Mr. Jarndyce] observed, "makes rather an indifferent parent, I am afraid."
> "O! I don't know," cried Mr. Skimpole, buoyantly.
> "I think I do know," said Mr. Jarndyce.

Two chapters later, another notably inadequate parent, Mrs. Pardiggle, is introduced, and soon after that, in the other narrative, the orphans Guster and Jo; then, from afterwards in Esther's narrative, we have the Turveydrop household and the orphaned Neckett children. The domestic theme of the responsibility which parents, and other elders, should feel (but mostly don't) for the young is fully, though inexplicably, launched in both narratives, and it is manifestly paralleled in the larger social institutional world by the Chancery Courts', and in Chapter 12 by the Chesney Wold's Dandiacal political and other associates' abject failure to fulfill their responsibilities—to be "in earnest, or to receive any impress from the moving age."

It was with reference to *Bleak House*'s opening number that E.M. Forster in his *Aspects of the Novel*, to describe how novelists must command their readers' attention, used the agreeably unpretentious term "bounce." Far-off days, when literary discourse could be thus conducted with the critic, like Wordsworth's poet, being "a man speaking to men" or a "person," instead of a pedagogue speaking to other operative or would-be pedagogues. Forster, referring to Percy Lubbock's then-classic discussion in *The Craft of Fiction* of "*the point of view*—the question of the relation in which the narrator stands to the story," remarks that

> for me the whole intricate question of method resolves itself not into formulae but into the power of the writer to bounce the reader into accepting what he says. . . . Look how Dickens bounces us in *Bleak House*. Chapter 1 of *Bleak House* is omniscient. . . . In Chapter 2 [Dickens] is partially omniscient. We still use his eyes, but for some unexplained reason they begin to grow weak; he can explain Sir Leicester Dedlock to us, part of Lady Dedlock but not all, and nothing of Mr. Tulkinghorn. In Chapter 3 he is ever more reprehensible: he goes straight across into the dramatic method and inhabits a young lady, Esther Summerson. . . . At any moment the author of her being may snatch [the pen] from her, and run about taking notes himself, leaving her seated goodness knows where, and employed we do not care how. Logically, *Bleak House* is all to pieces, but Dickens bounces us, so that we do not mind the shifting of the view point.
>
> (107–8)

As I have begun to suggest, there *is* an artistic logic underlying Dickens' superficially arbitrary shifting of pen-holders: the two narrators manifestly, though inexplicitly, converge both chronologically and in plot-concerns and thematically. But their perspectives differ.

Esther, we eventually discover in the final chapter, is writing seven years after the novel's climactic events, which had followed hard upon one another: the death of Jo on the afternoon of the day which ends with Tulkinghorn's being murdered in Lincoln's Inn Fields, a mile or so away "as the crow flies" (one of many examples of the novel's tightness in time and place): the death of Lady Dedlock soon after the disclosure that it was not she nor George, but Hortense, who was the murderer; the marriage of Esther and Woodcourt; the death of Richard on the same day as the *Jarndyce and Jarndyce* case concludes (another instance of the narrative's killing two birds with one stone); and the incidental sorting-out of the final fates of Skimpole, Guppy, Rosa and Watt, Miss Flite, Sir Leicester and Volumnia, Boythorn, George and other minor characters. In her fictionally-conventional seven-years'-later final round-up, Esther tells us how life has treated Ada and her boy, John Jarndyce, Charley and her siblings.

Esther's narrative is sometimes preluded by special warnings, for instance, "I had not thought, that night . . . of what was soon to *happen to me*" just before Charley, and then herself, come down with fever (and the weather that evening is ominously bad too). Or, "I could have no anticipation, and had none, that something very startling to me at the moment, and ever memorable to me in what ensued from it, was to *happen to me* before this day was out," preluding the scene when she tells Jarndyce that Lady Dedlock is her mother. (As the italics which I have added remind us, Esther is a character to whom things *happen*, rather than an initiator of events.) Normally, however, she maintains narrative suspense by telling her story chronologically without giving the game away. Dickens, I might register, is more skillful here in first-person narration than in his previous novel, *David Copperfield*, where, for instance, David has to be the concealed and inactive observer of the episode where Rosa Dartle cruelly lays into Emily; if David had intervened, there would have been no scene, and if he had not been present there would have been no record. Similarly the existence of the second Narrator saves Dickens from having to use such clumsy messenger-scenes as Peggotty's lengthy accounts of his overseas wanderings. Esther is plausibly present at all the episodes that need to be in her narrative. Only once, in Chapter 51, does she have to rely on somebody else's account (Woodcourt's, of his London encounters with Vholes and Richard.)

The other Narrator, whom Albert J. Guerard in a fine essay on the novel's "Structure and Style" names the "Roving Conductor," lives in the present tense (a common narrative device for communicating urgency and hotting up the action) and his basic stance is that of a keen, intelligent, and knowledgeable observer. His knowledgeability is established, on the second page, for instance; he knows that Chancery proceedings involve "bills, cross-bills, answers, rejoinders, injunctions, affidavits, issues, references to masters, masters' reports," a density of information which the young lady narrator lacks. But he is a lesser man than Dickens who, as creator, knows more about where the story is heading and what the characters are up to, though this Narrator is in full command of Dickens' intelligence, informedness, eloquence, vivacity, rhetoric, and ideology. He is highly opinionated, too: that list continued with "mountains of costly nonsense." Esther's voice is generally subdued, as befits her age, sex, station, experience, period, and repressed personality. Often she is diffident in passing judgment, or is at a stage in the action when the information available to her is too incomplete or incomprehensible. Sometimes, rather cleverly, Dickens makes her, in her innocence or diffidence, unconsciously ironic. Thus on her very first page she says of Miss Barbary that "She was so very good herself, that the badness of other people made her frown all her life." Had a more fully Dickensian narrator said that, it would obviously have been an ironic attack on a kind of censorious self-righteous religiosity that Dickens always abominated. But Esther, who has very little irony in her make-up, has been cowed into wholly unjustified feelings of guilt and inadequacy by her appalling aunt, and actually takes her at face value. The reader, however, gets Dickens' point about Miss Barbary, despite Esther's inability at this stage to see through her. Sometimes, of course, Esther does make judgments on the Chancery Courts, for instance, or on the position and duties of women-judgments that are never at odds with the Narrator's, nor, as we know on the evidence of Dickens' other pronouncements in or outside his fiction, with his.

The Narrator, by contrast, uses—to adopt Sir Walter Scott's handy phrase—a "Big Bow-wow strain." In this first of what have been called Dickens' "dark novels," the Narrator can be endowed with extra sonority and fierceness because the other half of the story is being told in a quieter voice. He handles more of the larger public issues: the law, politics, housing and sanitation, the "shameful testimony to future ages, how civilization and barbarism walked this boastful island together" (Chapter 11), an unmistakably Dickensian narratorial comment, for none of his contemporaries was capable of producing a severity so incisively concise. On such matters, the Narrator can pronounce more forcibly than Esther, and with powers of generalization which her modest nature and limited experience preclude her from deploying. Thus it is he who utters that eloquent "Dead, you Majesty" paragraph which follows the death of Jo and concludes, inevitably in blank verse, "And dying thus around us every day" (Chapter 47).

Though knowledgeable, and firm in his opinions, the Narrator is far from omniscient, though many lazy commentators call him that. He reports the characters' actions and speeches, he notes significant gestures, and makes intelligent surmise or asks pertinent questions about their motives or thoughts. For instance, "Has Mr. Tulkinghorn any idea of this himself? It may be so, or it may be not" (Chapter 2), or, again wondering about Tulkinghorn's knowledge and intentions in Chapter 29, a series of three "It may be"s followed seven "Whether"s, as various possibilities are mooted. Similarly a nudge is given to the reader as the Narrator meditates over Nemo's corpse:

> O, if, in brighter days, the now-estinguished fire within him ever burned for one woman who held him in her heart, where is she, while these ashes are above the ground!
>
> (Chapter 11)

The question is (just) plausible, but the reader will realize why it has been asked and has probably, by this early stage of the narrative, have guessed that the mystery of this decayed gentleman-scrivener is akin to the mysteries of Lady Dedlock's past and of Esther's unfortunate origins.

Two pages after that, the Narrator notices that the sunbeams shining through the gallery at Chesney Wold throw athwart Lady Dedlock's portrait "a broad bend-sinister of light that strikes down crookedly into the hearth, and seems to rend it." It is in the Narrator's chapters, too, that the ominous ghost's walk episodes occur, the ghost being that of an earlier Lady Dedlock who, like the present one, differed from her husband in age and character, "and they had no children." These omens point only in one direction, but the Narrator, while reporting them, has no consciousness of that direction. Esther too, I should interject, is receptive of omens. She experiences strange tremors and heightened emotions when in the proximity of the people who turn out to be her parents when passing the room where her father had died (Chapter 14) and when seeing Lady Dedlock before meeting her (Chapters 18—three "strangely"s on one page—and 23), a psychic sensitivity which she shares with Oliver Twist, whose heart beats faster when he sees a portrait of the mother whom he never knew (*Twist*, Chapter 12). But, like most fictional narrators, Esther abstains from evaluating these omens fully for her readers. The other Narrator can be equally sparing of information (or, as the British Secretary of the Cabinet lately confessed to having been, "economical with the truth"). "I think, Small," says Guppy to Young Smallweed in Chapter 33, "you might have mentioned that the old man [Krook] was your uncle." The reader might feel inclined to reproach the Narrator for being similarly silent, and the Narrator is likewise uncommunicative about the surprising identity of Mr. Bucket's twice mentioned "amiable lady" lodger.

Only once does Dickens depart from the convention he has established for his Narrator—breach his decorum—when he cannot resist drumming up excitement after Tulkinghorn's last interview with Lady Dedlock. The lawyer walks home alone, with the Narrator evoking a big set-scene of that "very quiet" moonlit night and punctuating the description with the six-times-repeated "Don't go home!" Three pages later Tulkinghorn is discovered, "shot through the heart."

In the episodes leading up to that, Dickens had also allowed the Narrator to become briefly semi-omniscient about Tulkinghorn's thoughts (in Chapters 51, 52, 58). The range of Tulkinghorn's reported thoughts is, however, limited to his immediate mental responses to Lady Dedlock in what Dickens in a running-title in the 1868 edition calls their "Diamond Cut Diamond" encounters. The Narrator never finds occasion to pluck out the heart of Tulkinghorn's mystery: what is he really up to, and why? In his penultimate meeting with Lady Dedlock, Tulkinghorn had said: "I am not clear what to do, or how to act next. . . . The sole consideration in this unhappy case is Sir Leicester. . . . Therefore, I have much to consider. This is to be hushed up, if it can be." Of course it can be; all that Tulkinghorn has to do is to shut up, as any family solicitor must often recognize a need to do; and unless he is here lying to Lady Dedlock, it is wildly implausible that, at this stage of the game, so wily an old laird as Tulkinghorn does not know what to do or how to act. Here, I think, Dickens' narrative method, by which the Narrator has only fitful access to Tulkinghorn's mind, lets him down or rather, in fact, lets him *off* from the tougher job of elevating Tulkinghorn from being a plot-mechanism threat to Lady Dedlock, who will thus soon become the prime suspect as his murderer, to his standing fullsquare as a credible and explicable human being. The Tulkinghorn-centered action has its good moments and contributes to the plot-momentum, but never, I think, gets close to being a serious literary achievement. George Eliot, who was to re-write and improve upon parts of *David Copperfield* in *Middlemarch*, had already rewritten and improved upon parts of *Bleak House* in her *Felix Holt*: the relationship, centering upon guilty sexuality, between the gentlewoman Mrs. Transome and the malign lawyer Jermyn, is explored with an intelligence and to a depth which makes the interplay between Lady Dedlock and Mr. Tulkinghorn look gimcrack. (The heroine of *Felix Holt*, incidentally, is another Esther who makes surprising discoveries about her parentage; there is much scope for comparing and contrasting these two novels). (1)

Later in *Bleak House*, in Chapter 55 for instance, which ends with Lady Dedlock's flight from the marital home, the Narrator has some access to her mind too: "The horror that is upon her, is unutterable" though she feels a "wicked relief" over the opportune sudden death of her tormentor, and the account of "her murderous perspective" ambiguously connives at the reader's encouraged suspicion that she is the murderer. (Though of course Dickens, in this first English detective-novel, has hit upon what was to become the classic fictional murder solution, there is more than one suspect and the least likely one, or a character not under suspicion, proves to be the perpetrator.) The brief late disclosure of Lady Dedlock's thoughts again does not amount to much. Dickens is finally pressed into making his Narrator breach decorum by gaining access to the minds of Tulkinghorn and Lady Dedlock in their penultimate moments, because they are solitaries with secrets; neither of them can use dialogue to inform the reader. For similar reasons, Inspector Bucket is allowed to soliloquize, as he begins his quest for Lady Dedlock (Chapter 61) and indeed Dickens had used the same theatrical device for Lady Dedlock after Mr. Guppy had told her what he knew:

> "O my child, my child! Not dead in the first hours of her life, as my cruel sister told me . . . ! O my child, O my child!"
>
> (Chapter 29)

This does not make one wish that she had been given ampler opportunity to soliloquize.

Neither Lady Dedlock nor her tormentor Tulkinghorn is ever plumbed: and in the other narrative Esther, for reasons that more plausibly relate to her psychological condition, never attempts to give us a candid and heart-searching account of her feelings over, for instance, her abandoning hope of becoming Allan's husband or agreeing to become John Jarndyce's. Even after another emotional crisis, her finding her mother "cold and dead" at the end of Chapter 59, she begins Chapter 60 with "I proceed to other passages of my narrative," not a single word being recorded about her emotions, immediate or subsequent, over this bereavement. Here, alas, Esther repeats an exactly similar, and artistically damaging, reticence on the part of her predecessor in Dickensian first-person narration, David Copperfield. My mentioning him prompts me to record my surmise that a main reason for the novel's being half-told by a young woman was Dickens' justified pride in having done so well in his first substantial attempt at first-person narration, and his commendable determination to up the artistic bids by creating a first-person narrator who was not, so easily, a young man who becomes a successful novelist after enduring several of Dickens' own most significant experiences, but a young woman of a character and background markedly different from his. Still, as I said, both first-person narrators cop out spectacularly (though their novels seem not to notice it) at what should be big emotional crises. The comparable moment to Esther's "proceeding to other passages" of her narrative is David's following his wife Dora's death with a chapter about Mr. Micawber's comic misadventures, preluded with the get-out emotional-postponement statement: "This is not the time at which I am to enter on the state of my mind beneath its load of sorrows." He never does find the right time, nor does Esther find the occasion to reflect upon her joining the novel's long list of orphans. This, like the inadequate presentation of Lady Dedlock and Tulkinghorn, badly dents Dickens' achievement in this area of the novel. One of the perils of the Victorian multi-plot novel is that the novelist, having other actions to keep going, can shift, or finds himself forced to shift, to one of these instead of adequately developing a tricky situation. Such evasions remain, however, artistic dishonesties.

I remarked that the two narrators hold similar ideas and attitudes, which are strongly akin to the novelist's. They share linguistic habits too, imagery, for instance. Thus, Vholes is first met in the Esther narration (Chapter 37) and she establishes the two images which constantly accompany him: he is seen as a carnivorous animal, or snake, preparing to gobble up Richard, and, always dressed in black, he is associated with death. Two chapters later, Vholes and Richard appear in the other narrative, the attorney "always looking at his client, as if he were making a lingering meal of him" and, assuring him that "This desk is your rock, sir!" he "gives it a rap, and it sounds as hollow as a coffin." The predatory image recurs in our last sight of him, which occurs in Esther's narrative (Chapter 65): "As he gave me that slowly devouring look of his, . . . he gave one last gasp as if he had swallowed that last morsel of his client, and his black buttoned-up unwholesome figure glided away." In these Vholes episodes, there is only one significant divergence in the two narrators' presentation: Esther is unable to rise to so confident a generalization as the Narrator can make after contemplating this "man of undoubted respectability" who unscrupulously uses the law to provide handsomely for his family: "The one great principle of the English law is, to make business for itself . . . viewed by this light it becomes a coherent scheme, and not the monstrous maze the laity is apt to think it" (Chapter 39).

"As if he had swallowed the last morsel of his client": Esther is fond of "*as if*" remarks, which are of course a great Dickens trademark, to introduce a simile, generally a surprising one. Recall page 1: "As much mud in the streets, as if the waters had but newly retired from the face of the earth, and it would not be wonderful to meet a Megalosaurus, forty feet long or so, waddling like an elephantine lizard up Holborn Hill." The next sentence mentions snowflakes "as big as full-grown snowflakes—gone into mourning, one might imagine, for the death of the sun." Esther is fond of that common Dickensian locution too, "*one might imagine*" and of "*it was easy to fancy that*. . . ." Many virtues are attributed to Esther by other characters but never, I think, wit or humour: nor do those qualities appear in her speeches: but, as narrator, she has both in abundance and along the regular Dickensian lines. I sometimes give Dickens-readings, which include Esther-excerpts (such as her account of the visit by Mrs. Pardiggle and her children to the brickmakers), and I find that, although I must of course soften my narration voice to suggest a young woman's, the speech-rhythms, the joke-patterns, and the forms of wit are exactly the same as those in impersonal-narrator passages from various novels: and they produce the same effect on audiences. Dickens thought of devising a Mrs. Pardiggle public-reading and a Mr. Turveydrop one, but attempted neither. But, here in the introduction of Mr. Turveydrop (Chapter 14) we surely have indeed, as that reviewer said, "Dickens disguised in a sisterly form"—not heavily disguised either, and with his skirts well tucked up—

> He was a fat old gentleman with a false complexion, false teeth, false whiskers, and a wig. He had a fur collar, and he had a padded breast to his coat, which only wanted a star or a broad blue ribbon to be complete. He was pinched in, and swelled out, and got up, and strapped down, as much as he could possibly bear. He had such a neckcloth on (puffing his very eyes out of their natural shape), and his chin and even his ears so sunk into it, that it seemed as though he must inevitably double up, if it were cast loose. He had, under his arm, a hat of great size and weight, shelving downward from the crown to the brim; and in his hand a pair of white gloves, with which he flapped it, as he stood poised on one leg, in a high shouldered, round-elbowed state of elegance not to be surpassed. He had a cane, he had an eye-glass, he had a snuff-box, he had rings, he had wristbands, he had everything but any touch of nature; he was not like youth, he was not like age, he was not like anything in the world but a model of Deportment.
>
> "Father! A visitor. Miss Jellyby's friend, Miss Summerson."
>
> "Distinguished," said Mr. Turveydrop, "by Miss Summerson's presence." As he bowed to me in that tight state, I almost believe I saw creases come into the whites of his eyes.
>
> (Chapter 14)

The surprising perception or surmise in that final phrase reminds one of the opening description of Doctor Blimber, in *Dombey and Son* (Chapter 11) who had "a chin so very double, that it was a wonder how he ever managed to shave into the creases." The whole passage of course is typically Dickensian in its perceptions and in its rhetoric: three "falses"s, "in"/"out," "up"/"down," six "He had"s, and three "he was not"s. I recall Shelley's remarking how every line of Wordsworth bore his imprint—so much so, he said, that if he had come across three lines of his verse, unattributed, in the middle of a desert, he would have immediately shouted out "Wordsworth!" Similarly, this passage could only have been written by Dickens. No one, reading it, would surprise the desert air by shouting "Esther Summerson!"— but I am not complaining about Dickens' craft at this point.

It would be easy to replicate instances of Esther's writing with Dickensian verve, pith, and wit a hundredfold (and much more amusing that would be than the rest of my paper). But so what? What does it matter, how does it count, that Esther is so constantly endowed with Dickensian perceptions, wit, and stylistic resources that do not belong to her posited character? Not overmuch, I think; these linguistic skills do not exhibit, sustain, or enlarge his character, which is developed through the less frequent, but pointed, "feminine" touches and the specifically Summersonian hesitancies and obliquities; in fact, her writing Dickensese militates against her characterization; but any reader will welcome this display of the familiar Dickensian insights and phraseology, and few would will to trade them for a duller, penny-plain instead of a twopence-colored, style more consonant with a determined effort by the novelist to maintain narratorial verisimilitude. It would indeed have been the most Pyrrhic of victories if Dickens had succeeded consistently in narrating half of his novel in a style wholly appropriate to his heroine's character. A (half-) novel written by Miss Summerson might have some curiosity value, but Dickens can safely be relied upon to write a better novel in his own accustomed style.

Readers of first-person narratives are inured to granting a large latitude to their narrators, including a willingness to accept a sacrifice of verisimilitude to expressiveness; as I said, one does not regard Pip, or Jane Eyre, or Emily Brontë's Nelly Dean as fine potential novelists, any more than one lists among Macbeth's character traits a remarkable capacity for extemporizing splendid blank verse. The problem arises with Esther more acutely than with Jane or Nelly because, Dickens being Dickens, she had a much fancier and more ostentatious narrative style than theirs, and because her character is specifically modest, undemonstrative, unself-asserting, and none ·of these are adjectives one would ever use to describe Dickens' forms of discourse. Dickens offers a few gestures towards verisimilitude by making Esther attribute some of the witty remarks she records to Richard or Skimpole or Jarndyce, and of course he inserts a quiet Estherian hesitancy or feminine touch from time to time (once every ten pages, perhaps?), but mostly he lets her write in his own accents, though more quietly than the other Narrator, and, to use E. M. Forster's word, he "bounces" us into contentedly accepting this convention.

Though Esther's latitude of experience is smaller than that of the "Roving Conductor," she has the same knack of running into Dickensian grotesques and eccentrics such as Krook and Miss Flite. Both of these characters appear in the Narrator's chapters too, little different, though, as we saw, the Narrator forthrightly calls Miss Flite "mad" and "crazy" while Esther contents herself with "curious." Some characters appear in only one narrative. Thus Esther has a monopoly of Ada, the Jellybys, Pardiggles, Bayham Badgers, and Turveydrops, of Boythorn and Mrs. Woodcourt and "Conversation" Kenge, while the Narrator alone sees Tulkinghorn, Chadband, Mrs. Smallweed, and Young Smallweed, most of the Chesney Wold group such as Mrs. Rouncewell, her ironmaster son and his son Walt, and Volumnia Dedlock and Bob Stables, and most of the Took's Court people. Esther briefly glimpses some characters who predominantly belong to the other narration, such as Gridley, Jo, Sir Leicester, the Bagnets, the Snagsbys, Grandfather Smallweed, and Jobling, and the Narrator has similar glimpses of Richard and Jarndyce and others from Esther's *dramatic personae.* Characters who have a more substantial presence in both narratives include, besides those already mentioned, Lady Dedlock, Guppy, George Rouncewell, Bucket, Jenny, Hortense, and Woodcourt.

Here, I think, Dickens singularly fails to exploit the potentialities of the form he has devised, for none of the characters are seen differently by the two narrators. Thus, Esther might have been made to find Inspector Bucket's mannerisms rather irritating, but instead she wholly shares the Narrator's awed admiration for him. She does of course see Lady Dedlock with her defenses down—"I am your wicked and unhappy mother!" (Chapter 36)—as Tulkinghorn and the Chesney Wold and town house characters in the other narrative never do, though the Narrator had glimpsed the unhappiness implicit in her gestures. (And, as I have suggested, the narrative method has deprived us of knowing how wicked she felt herself to be: she had not abandoned her baby but thought her dead, though she does indeed reproach herself for "dishonoring" her husband by arriving at the altar in less than pristine virginal condition.) What Dickens fails to do may be suggested by the only analogue to his method in earlier British fiction known to me, James Hogg's *Confessions of a Justified Sinner* (1824), where events in the first half, told by an impersonal so-called "Editor," are retold from a very different perspective in the first-person second half. Or think of how Browning, in the decade after

Bleak House, plays off his ten narrative voices in *The Ring and the Book* against one another.

I would be happy to be proved wrong on this, for I would sooner think well of Dickens than otherwise, but here, I cannot but judge, he missed a rather obvious trick. I have (alas) been mostly drawing attention to flaws in Dickens' achievement in this enterprising but difficult new form. But then, as Dr. Johnson sagely said, "We must confess the faults of our favorite [he was writing about Shakespeare], to gain credit to our praise of his excellences. He that claims either for himself as for another the honors of perfection, will surely injure the reputation which he designs to assist." Not all lectures that I have heard at Dickens conferences have heeded this good counsel; as I think, their "praise" would have been more impressive if they had done so. Let me now end by proceeding to some of Dickens' "excellencies" in the *Bleak House* narrative.

Pacing and spacing is one area of conspicuous success. Dickens has set himself difficult technical problems, not only intermeshing two narrators, but also telling through them (and neither holds all the clues) half-a-dozen plotlines: These are ably summarized by Graham Storey in his fine recent booklet on this novel: the Esther parentage plot ("the most complicated Dickens had by then written," Storey asserts), the Esther/Woodcourt and Ada/Richard and Caddy/Price courtship plots, the "who-killed-Tulkinghorn?" one, and the Trooper George/Rouncewell family one—and, enveloping them all, as Storey says, the *Jarndyce and Jarndyce* case. (16) (There are minor actions too, such as Sir Leicester/Mr. Rouncewell and Rosa/Walt, and Storey's summary has failed to mention Jo, whom "Fate," as the Narrator points out (Chapter 47), has so "strangely . . . entangled . . . in the web of very different lives.") Dickens' handling of these problems which he has set himself impresses me as consummately skillful. The novel-reader, confident that he/she is not being presented with a random collection of documents, quickly cottons on to the connections between the two narratives in Number I: they converge upon the *Jarndyce and Jarndyce* hearings on a November day, and its aftermath. "Time and place," to half-quote Lady Macbeth, henceforth "cohere" remarkably. The Chancery Court action entails, of course, many characters living and working in close contiguity (no wonder they keep running into one another). Thus, Coavinses' is visible from Snagsby's, which has Krook's just over the road, and Took's (or Cook's) Court runs into Cursitor Street, which runs into Chancery Lane just opposite Lincoln's Inn Fields where Tulkinghorn lives and dies. "London" is the novel's first word, indeed its first sentence, and all its London locations are within easy walking distance of one another. Dickens doubtless selected the St. Alban's area as the location for *Bleak House* because it was within commuting distance of London (just over twenty miles away) and because in 1852 it was notorious for electoral corruption. Lincolnshire he probably chose because it was a highly conservative county, with hardly any industrial development; by one of the coincidences that criss-cross the novel, Boythorn lives there, thus giving an excuse for Esther to get within range of Lady Dedlock, near Sir Leicester, who had married the sister of Boythorn's once-beloved. This, of course, is another plot-device, the credibility-aspect of which Dickens does not invite the reader to contemplate. (However could a man so generous-souled as Boythorn have given a second glance to the frigid Miss Barbary?)

As for the pacing of the novel, Dickens, well practised by now in the special art of serial fiction, manages to keep all the actions moving forward in echelon, with none of them being lost sight of for too long, and with major developments in several actions converging to crisis-points at, for instance, Numbers X and XV (half-way and three-quarters-way through the narrative, facts which would not have escaped Dickens' consciousness). Number X ends with the novel's most spectacular event, Krook's death by spontaneous combustion—an explicitly prophetic event (the Chancery Courts are threatened with a similar end) and one which has obvious plot implications too (if the letters he was due to hand over to Guppy have perished with him, the threat to Lady Dedlock may have receded). By now, both Guppy and Tulkinghorn are pressing hard upon her. One minor action culminates in this Number—Caddy and Prince Turveydrop get married—and there is also an important development in the Esther story: she encounters Jo, and thus Caddy and she catch his fever, and she goes blind. Number XV, none of which is narrated by Esther, contains a similar congeries of episodes: Jo dies in Chapter 47, Tulkinghorn is murdered that evening in Chapter 48, and Chapter 49, after starting unexpectedly, not with a follow-up to the Tulkinghorn murder but with Mrs. Bagnet's birthday, ends with George's being arrested; he was, he acknowledges, at Tulkinghorn's at around the time of the murder—but then we know too that Lady Dedlock, who expected her secret to be exposed the next day, was also out, alone, in the area at the same time. A few chapters later, we discover that on the day of Jo's and Tulkinghorn's deaths, Ada announced her secret marriage to Richard, and her departure from the Jarndyce household—another climax (Chapter 51).

It shows my ignorant insensitivity, or Dickens' compelling qualities as a narrator, or both, that it was only recently that I noticed not only that Mrs.

Bagnet's birthday was a highly unpredictable sequel to Mr. Tulkinghorn's assassination—rather like "Mr. Micawber's Transactions" immediately following Dora's death in *David Copperfield* (Chapters 53–54)—but also that, plot-wise, it is a wholly superfluous episode. All that Dickens needs, hereabouts, is a plausible occasion for Mr. Bucket to arrest George with, preferably, a customary display of his professional skills and oddities—though, as we later learn, he does so on the most dubious of legal grounds, for (as he admits) he did not actually believe that George was the murderer—"but he might be, notwithstanding." (George could have sued Bucket and obtained substantial damages for wrongful arrest. The reader indeed might feel inclined to sue Bucket for subsequently dropping so many hints that Lady Dedlock is guilty, and the Narrator could be sued for failing to notice Hortense's presence in Lincoln's Inn Fields on the fatal night.) But why four pages of Mrs. Bagnet's birthday, with Lignum Vitae's ritual pair of fowls, as a preliminary? Well, one could avail one's self of George Orwell's remark that "The outstanding, unmistakable mark of Dicken's writing is the *unnecessary detail*" (493) or of Albert Guerard's in his essay on *Bleak House* that

> we know that much of any Dickens novel is simply entertainment for its own sake. A great deal of irrelevance will turn out to be truly irrelevant. Yet we also know that any event, any chance scrap of conversation, . . . may prove to be important."
>
> (333)

Or we might think about *Bleak House* in the light of these phrases from letters that Dickens wrote, two years earlier, to potential contributors to his forthcoming magazine *Household Words*, for there are many similarities in spirit as well as in content and opinion between Dickens' novels, particularly *Bleak House*, and his weekly journal:

> *To* Georgina Ross: "we can't be too wise, but we must be very agreeable."
> *To* Mrs. Gaskell: "the general mind and purpose of the journal . . . is the raising up of those that are down, and the general improvement of our social condition."
> *To* Revd. James White: "We hope to do some solid good, and we mean to be as cheery and pleasant as we can."
> *To* Mary Howitt: "All social evils, and all home affections and associations, I am particularly anxious to deal with well."
>
> (Letters)

Or we may recall John Forster's summary judgment that "His leading quality was humour . . . He was conscious of this himself," and Forster quotes a letter in which Dickens agrees that sometimes he goes over the top, though he does "constantly restrain" his invention:

> I think it is my infirmity to fancy or perceive relations in things that are not apparent generally. Also, I have such an inexpressible enjoyment of what I see in a droll light, that I dare say I pet it as if it were a spoilt child.
>
> (Forster *Life* 721)

He somewhat resembled Doctor Johnson's friend Oliver Edwards who "tried . . . to be a philosopher; but, I don't know how, cheerfulness was always breaking in." Also, as a narrator, he enjoyed a mix of moods, if only on the "sugaring the pill" principle: the mix succinctly and memorably summarized in his plan for *David Copperfield*, Number X: "First chapter funny/Then on *to Emily*."

The Bagnet episode could be explained along these lines (and, if one is determined to find thematic unity, I suppose one *could* relate it to the novel's domestic theme—the Bagnets are one of its few happy, fully-functioning families). Guerard takes the matter a little further when he continues: "Reading, then, we experience life as unorganized often incoherent flow, rich in digression, yet all the while we remain alert for open or secret connections" (333). As the Narrator prompts us, in another of those "sign-post" indications, "What connexion can there be between the place in Lincolnshire, the house in town, the Mercury in powder, and the whereabouts of Jo the outlaw with the broom?" (Chapter 16). As we have seen, the novel is criss-crossed by plot and thematic connections. When, to use Guerard's terms, no significant connections can be discovered, but simply "we experience life as unorganized often incoherent flow," the apparent irrelevance can, I think, be justified in the way that Samuel Johnson indicated in his claim that Shakespeare's plays—and again the comparison with Dickens is historically inevitable as well as suggestive—were not "in the rigorous or critical sense" (he meant the critically conventional sense) "either tragedies or comedies,"

> . . . but compositions of a distinct kind; exhibiting the real state of sublunary nature [we might say "life as it really is"], which partakes of good and evil, joy and sorrow, mingled with endless variety of proportion, and innumerable modes of combination; and expressing the course of the world, in which the loss of one is the gain of another; in which, at the same time, the reveller is hasting to his wine, and the mourner is burying his friend; . . . and many mischiefs and many benefits are done and hindered without design.
>
> (*Preface to Shakespeare*, 1765)

At another conference recently in Spain, on "Comedy," I gave a talk on narrators in Victorian Fiction entitled "A Twinkle in the Narratorial Eye," in which I took three deeply serious, disillusioned in some ways despondent novels about the state and prospects of mid-nineteenth-century British society, *Vanity Fair*, *Bleak House* and *Middlemarch*, and I pointed out that, nevertheless, all three frequently adopted witty and humorous narrative accents.[3] *Bleak House* encompasses eleven deaths, besides making grave judgments on Victorian society and on human fate. But that twinkle in Dickens' eye, in both narrations—and here we see another reason why Esther the *narrator* must have verbal and humorous powers that are no attribute of Esther the *character*—lets cheerfulness keep breaking in. It helps to establish that friendly relation between author and reader which then was so valued; it views human imperfections from the reductive critical perspective of wit and irony, seeing that (to alter Dr. Johnson's aphorism) there is much to be enjoyed in human life as well as much to be endured, and it reminds readers of the most serious fictional explorations of human fate that life is not all serious but includes also the trivial and the hilarious. Why not, after all, as Dickens said in that letter about his aims, "be as cheery and pleasant as we can," while also remaining mindful of the uncheering and the unpleasant? In the letter where Dickens used that phrase, the advice might be dismissed as merely an adroit editorial commercial maneuver. The maneuver is in touch, however, and is consonant with a highly civilized and eminently sensible apprehension of life, more warmly positive than the (for me) wry cross-Channel phrase "C'est la vie."

Let me end with a final extract from Dickens, about a character who appears on a single page of *Bleak House*. This chapter is being narrated by Esther Summerson but, as often (we have seen), she is here endowed with Dickens' own vision and humor, just as Dickens' other first-person narrators, David Copperfield and Pip, are. Esther's eyes, when they are working (she goes blind at one point), are modest and sympathetic, not twinkling: other characters praise her virtue but not (I have remarked) her wit. All that the plot requires in this incident is for Esther to get a message to go to the local inn, where Richard Carstone is staying, but this is how Dickens manages it. Esther's little maidservant Charley (Charlotte) announced that W. Grubble has brought a message inviting her to go to the Dedlock Arms. "And who is W. Grubble, Charley?" Esther asks.

"Mister Grubble, miss," returned Charley. "Don't you know, miss? The Dedlock Arms, by W. Grubble," which Charley delivered as if she were slowly spelling out the sign.

"Aye? The landlord, Charley?"

"Yes, miss. If you please, miss, his wife is a beautiful woman, but she broke her ankle, and it never joined. And her brother's the sawyer, that was put in the

cage, miss, and they expect he'll drink himself to death entirely on beer," said
Charley . . .

Mr. Grubble was standing in his shirt sleeves at the door of his very clean little
tavern, waiting for me. He lifted off his hat with both hands when he saw me
coming, and carrying it so, as if it were an iron vessel (it looked as heavy),
preceded me along the sanded passage to his best parlour: a neat carpeted room,
with more plants in it than were quite convenient, a coloured print of Queen
Caroline, several shells, a good many tea-trays, two stuffed and dried fish in
glass cases, and either a curious egg or a curious pumpkin (but I don't know
which, and I doubt if many people did) hanging from the ceiling. I knew Mr.
Grubble very well by sight, from his often standing at his door. A pleasant-
looking, stoutish, middle-aged man, who never seemed to consider himself
cozily dressed for his own fireside without his hat and topboots, but who never
wore a coat except at church.

(chapter 37)

I had forgotten Mr. Grubble until a perceptive student mentioned him in an
essay. He, his wife and brother-in-law and inn, have nothing to do with the
novel's great themes or its critique of society. Is then Dickens' inventing this
apparently gratuitous little episode merely an amusing endearment, a pleasant
sideshow, a self-indulgent demonstration of the facility with which he can in
a few words create a memorable character? I think not. The amused delight
with which Dickens contemplates, first Charley's simplicity and non-
sequaciousness, and then the Grubbles and their misfortunes and Mr.
Grubble's attire and manners, and the details of his bar-parlor—including that
hanging object which was "either a curious egg or a curious pumpkin (but I
don't know which, and I doubt if many people did)"—contributes something
to the meaning of the book. The evils of the Chancery Courts and of
unsanitary living conditions and of uncaring and inefficient government and
much else exist ("And dying thus around us every day"), and should worry
and concern the reader. But so also do Mr. Grubble and his relatives and
parlor exist, remote and relatively blamelessly. Matthew Arnold made an
opposite remark in his Inaugural Lecture at Oxford, about maintaining an
awareness of life's multiplicity:

So hard, so impossible for most men it is to develop themselves in their
entireness: to rejoice in the variety, the movement of human life with the
children of the world; to be serious over the depths, the significance of the world
with the wise!

It was patronizing and only half-wise for Arnold to associate rejoicing with
"the children of the world"—can't we elders find good reason, from time to

time, to rejoice a bit, maybe the way that Dickens does, and surely "the variety, the movement of human life" offers an ample spectacle for the most "wise" of observers?—and it might be charged against Arnold and such other major contemporaries in verse that they conspiciously failed to "develop themselves in their entireness." Tennyson was right, though as poet he recked not his own rede, when he said that "It is only men of humour who see things as they truly are" (27). But Tennyson was no more able than Arnold, whose prose writings have plenty of witty "twinkle" about them, to deploy in his verse both a sense of "the depths, the significance of human life" and also an active memory of its "variety" and "movement," including the limping or inebriate Grubbles and the well-meant though ill-chosen and ill-cooked annual pair of fowls in the Bagnet household. These two poets' weakness in this respect was typical of the age's poetry. By contrast Dickens and his other "twinkle-in-the-eye" contemporaries in prose fiction had this rare ability to be serious over the depths and to rejoice over the variety and movement of life—to see its funny side while remaining aware of its evils and its tragic possibilities. Their emotional inclusiveness enabled them to "see things as they truly are"—"the real state of sublunary nature," to requote Johnson's phrase about the Shakespeare whom they thus resembled.

NOTES

1. After writing this paragraph, I discovered that my comparison had been anticipated by Jerome Meckier, "Hidden Relationships in Victorian Fiction: the Case of the Two Esthers," in *The Changing World of Charles Dickens*, ed. Robert Giddings (London: Vision Press, 1983), pp. 216–38. I argued that *Middlemarch* re-treated elements of *David Copperfield* in *TLS*, 18 May 1973.
2. *David Copperfield*, Chapter 54. I have discussed David's evasiveness—or rather Dickens' failure—at this point more fully in my *Charles Dickens: David Copperfield* (London: Edward Arnold) 1977.
3. The remainder of my essay repeats some material from my "Twinkle" paper, published in *Literary and Linguistic Aspects of Humour: The AEDEAM Conference Proceedings* (Universitad de Barcelona) 1984, pp. 9–25.

WORKS CITED

Arnold, Matthew. *The Study of Poetry*.

———. "On the Modern Element in Literature"

Bentley's Monthly Magazine. October 1853, reprinted in *Dickens' Bleak House: A Casebook* pp. 66–67.

Collins, Philip, ed. *Dickens: Interviews and Recollections*. London: Macmillan, 1981.

———, ed. *Dickens: the Critical Heritage*. London: Routledge & Kegan Paul, 1971.

Dickens, Charles. *Dickens' Bleak House: a Casebook*. Ed. A. E Dyson. London: Macmillan, 1969.

———. *The Letters of Charles Dickens*. Ed. Graham Storey et al. Oxford: Clasendon Press, 1965–.

Electic Magazine. Reprinted in *Dickens' Bleak House: a Casebook*. p. 666.

Forster, E. M. *Aspects of the Novel*. London: Edward Arnold, 1927.

Forster, John. *Life of Charles Dickens*. Ed. J. W. T. Ley. London: Cecil Palmer, 1927.

Guerard, Albert. "*Bleak House*: Structure and Style," *Southern Review*. Volume 1, 1969.

Orwell, George. "Charles Dickens," in *Collected Essays, Journals and Letters*. Ed. Sonia Orwell and Ian Angus. Harmondsworth, Middlesex: Penguin, 1970.

Storey, Graham. *Charles Dickens: Bleak House*. Cambridge: Cambridge UP, 1987.

Tennyson, Hallam. *Materials for a Life of Alfred Tennyson*. London: privately printed, 1895.

"I'll Follow the Other":
Tracing the (M)other in *Bleak House*

Marcia Renee Goodman

I

A little over twenty years ago, Taylor Stoehr wrote confidently that no one would mistake Esther Summerson for Charles Dickens. "No one," he wrote, "would argue that Esther's half of *Bleak House* is as vital as the third-person narrator's half, still less that Esther stands for Dickens" (45). And yet, apparently without the prompting of someone who did make the "mistake," Stoehr imagines the possibility of such a reading even as he denies its plausibility. And so he, in a sense, anticipates this article's arrival two decades later, for I will argue that the characterization of Esther portrays many of Dickens' own psychological conflicts, particularly those related to issues of self-revelation and connection to an-other.

Though Esther's character may not tell us much about Dickens' external life, she represents much of his inner experience.[1] Interestingly, David Copperfield, the figure whom almost all critics take to be Dickens' most fully developed stand-in, overtly reveals less about Dickens's feeling about self-revelation, the fear and desire involved in telling one's own story, than does Esther. Though David becomes a professional writer, he says little to explain writing's meaning to him. Esther on the other hand makes her "difficulty speaking" both to us and to her intimates one of her narrative's principal subjects.

If we analyze Esther from the standpoint of her role in Dickens's psychological autobiography, we find aspects of her personality which have been overlooked because of her gender disguise. We also find a story of the male writer that has been overlooked, the tale of the desire for and fear of connection to mother, and a fantasy of mothering that links it to a portrayal of writing.

Before turning to the text of *Bleak House*, I'd like to briefly outline an interpretation of the emergence of male identity which, in its depiction of particularly masculine fears and desires about connection and intimacy, runs parallel to that which we get in Dickens' novel. In the following account, I primarily use the work of Nancy Chodorow.

Chodorow relies on the studies of object relations psychologists, those interested in the earliest mother-child relations. For Chodorow, the characteristics we typically call "feminine" and "masculine" develop out of a nuclear family in which an individual woman provides primary care and love.[2] In discussing feminine and masculine identity, Chodorow looks at psychic constructions that exist within individual differences, and that persist despite some institutional changes—for example, in our own culture, despite the greatly increased number of women now working outside the home. She focuses on structural differences in boys' and girls' formation of gender identity.

At the Oedipal stage of development, in order to identify with his father so as to assume his masculine gender identity, the young boy must rather abruptly separate from his mother. This means breaking off his identification with the person who until this time has been his primary love object, and thus repressing not only his desire for her, but also his identification. In order to identify with his father, the boy insists that she is *other*, different from himself, denying his earliest bond's physical and emotional intensity. Mothers help with this process: seemingly "naturally," they begin to treat their sons differently from their daughters, subtly, and unconsciously, pushing them away as companions and casting them in a more sexualized, differentiated role. Directing their sons toward father and the concerns of the public world, mothers stop responding to them as if they were continuous with themselves.

In what we have come to term "the traditional family," this process raises the difficulty of the boy suddenly identifying with a father who is largely absent. The definition of masculinity, without a day-to-day, fully present, realizable model of maleness, becomes a denial of femininity. The threat created for the male child by his acknowledging his earlier, easier identification and connection with mother resonates powerfully in his unconscious since to remember this stronger, more primitive tie would be to endanger the more fragile, relatively new identification with father.

Because the first all-encompassing relationship is sustained by a female adult, daughters stand a better chance of maintaining their early intimacy with mothers than do sons. Daughters remain in close relation to their mothers beyond the oedipal stage, beyond, that is, their formation of libidinal attachment to their fathers. Chodorow argues, in fact, that women remain libidinally attached to their mothers as well. The daughter, then, is not quickly pushed away from continuous, identified contact with the mother; instead, she may be in intimate relationship with her throughout her resolution of the crisis and afterward. For daughters, gender identity, in fact, grows out of continued identification with their first love (since in traditional families the first caretaker is a woman), while for boys, the definition of maleness arises out of an experience of separation.

As psychologists and sociologists increasingly point out, there are severe consequences of this structure of gender identity formation for both adult male and female development. Carol Gilligan summarizes the general but crucial differences:

> Relationships, and particularly issues of dependency, are experienced differently by women and men. For boys and men, separation and individuation are critically tied to gender identity since separation from the mother is essential for the development of masculinity. For girls and women, issues of femininity or feminine identity do not depend on the achievement of separation from the mother or on the progress of individuation. Since masculinity is defined through separation, while femininity is defined through attachment, male gender identity is threatened by intimacy while female gender identity is threatened by separation. Thus males tend to have difficulty with relationship, while females tend to have problems with individuation. (8)

Gilligan's account here stresses early unconscious fears, but later she goes on to discuss her observations of women's and men's more conscious desires, desires which change as men and women mature. She finds that women come to crave the experience of a separate self, to struggle to articulate their own needs; men, on the other hand, come to want connection, to struggle for some experience of merging. Both women and men, however, often fail to fulfill their desires because of unconscious and conscious fears about loss of identity. Consequently both women and men continue to experience a loss of part of the self. Many women cannot permit themselves the psychic freedom of the self's needs separate from immediate consideration of others, while many men lose the early self who did safely merge, who experienced more fluid personal boundaries. Dickens' *Bleak House*, I will argue, demonstrates a particularly male wish for and fear of merging.

II

Esther Summerson portrays many of the characteristics which our culture still recognizes and reproduces as important constituents of feminine identity. She talks about herself in relational terms, that is, tells us that her meaning and identity are rooted in her connection to others. She takes care of the needs of those around her. She formulates moral issues in a context of helping others, rather than in an arena of abstract notions of law and justice. Gilligan notes, for example, that boys tend to be much more interested in legalistic resolutions to conflicts than girls—girls often try to resolve conflicts by taking into account the feelings and personal conditions of those involved (9–11). Thus Esther says that her voice is a personal one, one not informed by worldly (i.e., "masculine") knowledge, but rather by insight only into those she loves. She acts passively except in the personal service of others, mediating the emotional relationships in Jarndyce's house, as confidante to Richard, Ada, and her guardian himself.

Esther, though, possesses other traits and exhibits particular conflicts that put her in a more profound way in the traditionally masculine camp. One of the reasons her characterization is so confusing and can seem at moments so inconsistent is that she fulfills a double function in the novel. She portrays many characteristics of the angel in the house, but also enacts the conflicts, tensions, angers, fears, and hurt of the masculine constructed psyche. It is primarily in the story of her relationship to her mother that this masculine Esther appears, but, as we shall see, other stories she tells about herself reveal it as well.[3]

In my focus on the masculine aspects of Esther's character, I am particularly concerned with her desire and fear of self-revelation. I read telling about the self as a way of connecting to someone else, of trying to establish an intimate bond. Afraid of connection, but craving it, Esther struggles to find a way to be intimate with us, to allow us to see her; this effort marks Dickens' ambivalent alignment with, and wish for, his own early feminine connection. The unselfconscious expression of needs and demands characterizes the earliest connection to mother. This expression of self without shame is the state to which Dickens longs to return but which he fears will fix him in permanent regression.

"It seems so curious to me to be obliged to write all this about myself," Esther tells us in her first chapter. "As if this narrative were the narrative of *my* life! But my little body will soon fall into the background now" (III, 27). Less an apology to her reader than an effort to appease her own anxiety about writing autobiography, Esther's comment reveals her nervousness about speaking about herself. She tells us—and herself—that she will not have to say much about herself, though, of course, we know that this is precisely what she wants to do.

David Copperfield, her predecessor as first person writer, also expresses anxiety when he begins his novel: "Whether I shall turn out to be the hero of my own life, or whether that station will be held by anybody else, these pages must show" (I, 49). "These pages," cut off from the agency of the authorial "I," would seem to have a mind of their own, separate from the beliefs and wishes of their subject and writer. David-Dickens creates a mystery—the mystery of David's self—which will keep the reader reading; but at the same time he holds out the promise of giving us his identity, he suggests that that might not be his primary purpose, that the book's hero might be somebody else. Thus, even in this self-professed autobiographical novel, Dickens backs away from the spotlight. And indeed, David often, like Esther, tells his emotional story by relating the narrative of other lives; he however does not apologize for this nor call our attention to it as does Esther.

In the terms we've been discussing, the creation of a narrative does seem a feminine activity. (We might think of David's many feminine names and his affiliation with the novel's several emotionally and, in one case, physically battered, women.) Esther, following David, may represent Dickens' effort to confront his longing for and fear of the merging with the mother of infancy as well as his anxiety about the gender meaning of the career at which he was so extremely successful.

Though both men and women may certainly experience tremendous anxiety about revealing themselves and may be ambivalent about their innermost feelings being seen, men tend to fear the connection that self-revelation might entail while women tend to fear the self-assertion of their separate feelings and beliefs. Because the masculine personality fears personal, specific self-revelation as meaning connection to another and regression to identification with mother, what we might call "male discourse" is more comfortable with the abstract, the distant and the logical, than with the immediate, personal, and emotional. We hear Dickens' anxiety about speaking of the personal in

Esther's frequent double messages about her desire to tell her own story, just as we hear it in David's opening sentence. Reading Esther as a woman would take us to her insecurity about speaking, to, that is, the issue of her right to her own authority. Reading Esther as a man, on the other hand, highlights her ambivalence about sharing her inner self because of the fears that she will either be rejected or, just as awful, accepted but encompassed, merged with another. The latter reading of Esther's trouble speaking and writing directly about herself interests me here, but Esther's woman self is certainly operative in the text as well.

The heroine of *Bleak House* provides a voice in which its author can tell us more about his inner struggle to reveal himself and about his conflict over making intimate connections, than can any of his earlier protagonists, including David Copperfield. Esther comes to write so much about herself not, as many have believed, out of a coy egotism, but rather, out of a feeling of contained freedom. Bordered off by the other narrator, and "obliged," as she puts it, to tell us about herself, Esther can give herself to her inner voice without fear of loss of identity. She can reclaim part of herself in the act of writing—or rather, she can feel as if she does as she actually writes.

She finds herself revealing dangerous emotions, then attempts to distract us with apology; through it all, though, she goes on making her inner story known. Esther may be guilty about speaking, as both Alex Zwerdling and Crawford Killian have suggested, but her guilt functions as a screen; she uses it, I suggest, to disguise her fearful desire to speak, to connect intimately with another—here, her projected audience.

Esther's narrative's exploration of her feelings understandably seems naive because she tries to order and condense her emotions, to present in a form "as compact as possible" both her household accounts and her inner life (IX, 111). But her tendency to treat emotions as if the psyche were a closet that periodically needed cleaning and straightening should not cause us to overlook her wish to understand her own and others' inner lives.

She says, in fact, that disorienting feelings and mental images have significant meaning though she herself cannot effectively interpret them. For example, in the metacommunication which surrounds her description of the necklace and staircase dreams, she tries to border off the potential intrusion of difficult feelings even as she brings them to our attention:

> When I was very ill, the way in which these divisions of time became confused with one another, distressed my mind exceedingly. At once a child, an elder girl, and the little woman I had been so happy as, I was not only oppressed by

cares and difficulties adapted to each station, but by the great perplexity of endlessly trying to reconcile them. I suppose that few who have not been in such a condition can quite understand what I mean, or what awful unrest arose from this source. . . . Perhaps the less I say of these sick experiences, the less tedious and the more intelligible I shall be. I do not recall them to make others unhappy, or because I am now the least unhappy in remembering them. It may be that if we knew more of such strange afflictions, we might be better able to alleviate their intensity.

(XXXV, 431–2)

Esther offers her own feelings as instructional, insisting that such "sick experiences" should be understood because doing so will help to alleviate them, thus reformulating in moral terms her personal wish to understand and talk about herself. She argues for attention to the individual's fantasies even as she apologizes for her position; in so doing, she expresses Dickens' own tensions about this subject matter.

Half-heartedly, Esther apologizes to her readers for the dullness of this part of her narrative. As soon as she accuses herself of tedium and unintelligibility, however, she moves to her statement about the importance of reading dreams. Her fear of being "tedious" signals her anxiety about straying to her own psyche, instead of sticking to her ordering, "intelligible" description of events and of the lives of others; the anxiety, however, does not stop her from going astray. Esther's dreams serve no narrative plot purpose; thus to make sense of them we must read them as a sign that her internal life is, in fact, important to her.

The heroine's qualified assertion of the importance of her dreams marks a turning point in Dickens' canon: through the self-doubting voice of its narrator, *Bleak House* argues for the exploration of the inner self. For the first time in his fiction, Dickens details the struggle of an extraordinarily fragmented personality to speak directly to us, though he camouflages his portrait well by the presence of innumerable stories and an omniscient narrator who executes the novel's social function. This is not to say that Dickens was not genuinely interested in the novel's other themes, but to suggest that Esther and the third-person narrator present different versions of the same issues; both narratives focus on revealing connection and on providing detailed knowledge of deprivation, but while Esther concentrates on her personal struggle, her co-writer describes the social forms of abandonment. The poor, for example, have been abandoned by almost everyone, and Sir Leicester Dedlock's aristocratic household cuts itself off from the accomplishments of Mrs. Rouncewell's son, a factory owner in the north of England. My interest being in Dickens' psychological configuration, my account of the novel privileges the individual's emotional concerns. Dickens himself, though, tried to balance in this novel, particularly through the use of the split narration, his interest in the individual self's psychological make-up and his concern for the social conditions and psychological health of England at large.

Esther's omission of an overt record of her feelings at the narrative moments that would seem to promise them resembles Chancery's failure to produce its position. And Nemo, "no one," proves to be the last absent piece of Esther's buried history just as nothing proves to be left of Jarndyce and Jarndyce. Esther finds that there is "no one" where she would like to have a father, and that she has been abandoned by her mother. Like the young boy child who gets pushed away from mother toward a father defined by absence, Esther, too, finds the communication of personal feeling a threatening activity.

While the novel's third-person, wide-ranging narrative disguises the work's great interest in Esther's struggle to speak, and Dickens' use of a female protagonist hides his discussion and demonstration of some particularly male psychological issues, Esther's sympathy for Lady Dedlock camouflages her fear of the anger at this abandoning mother.

As Al Hutter points out, the Lady Dedlock-Esther relationship is the thematic core of the novel: the novel "derives its dramatic impact from a traumatic separation, a subsequent reintegration which cannot be maintained, and the ultimate loss of the mother" (311). From my point of view, Dickens' structuring of the novel around Lady Dedlock's separation from her newborn daughter, momentary rediscovery of each other, and renewed separation allows him the stage on which Esther-the-writer can portray both her desire to know her mother and her anger at and fear of her.

Esther lets us know that it is the search for her mother about which she is writing; she tells us that this is what primarily preoccupies her:

> I had never heard my mama spoken of. I had never heard of my papa either, but I felt more interested about my mama. I had never worn a black frock, that I could recollect. I had never been shown my mama's grave. I had never been told where it was.
>
> (III, 18)

In her commissioned narrative, Esther writes the story of her longing for her mother. She does twice wonder whether or not Jarndyce might be her father, but she primarily ponders her mother's identity, continually returning to memories of her early years with her godmother, the mystery of her relationship to her, and the question about where her real mother might be. Many of her chapter sequences end with her haunted imagination of the mother figure, whether it be the early surrogate mother or the later present but distant Lady Dedlock.

I would put the two climactic moments in the narrative at Lady Dedlock's revelation of herself to Esther and her injunction of distance, control, and carefulness, and the moment in the pursuit of Lady Dedlock by Bucket, when the two narratives catch up with each other. When Bucket arrives at Bleak House to ask Jarndyce for Esther's help in tracing Lady Dedlock, the third-person narrator breaks off, leaving Esther to portray her own involvement. Jarndyce goes upstairs to tell Esther of Bucket's request in the third-person narrative, and Esther comes down in the first. Esther will track down her mother in her own voice (LVI–II, 673–4). Esther's association with Bucket in the chase after her mother reveals her in both aggressive physical and narrative pursuit.

Her search for her mother will only conclude, we know, with Lady Dedlock's corpse, but this final missing of each other culminates the separation that characterizes their relationship throughout the novel—even once they know of each other's identity. The aggressiveness of Bucket and Esther's search, in which Lady Dedlock is driven on before them, suggests the anger the novel directs at the mother figure. Though images of deserted, neglected, and abused orphans run throughout *Bleak House*, suggesting that Dickens wishes for a healthy, loving, primary care, the sub-text tells a tale of primary love that cannot be trusted, of connection that is dangerous; and the novel offers the fantasy of completely separating oneself from it.

The necklace dream, which Esther has during her long illness, portrays this fear of connection:

> Dare I hint at that worse time when, strung together somewhere in great black space, there was a flaming necklace, or ring, or starry circle of some kind, of which I was one of the beads! And when my only prayer was to be taken off from the rest, and when it was such inexplicable agony and misery to be a part of the dreadful thing?
>
> (XXXV, 432)

Esther dreads connection to others because it threatens her own sense of self; this makes some sense if we read her as a woman, given the literal redefinition that will be necessary when she discovers her origins; and she may also dread connection, as Zwerdling suggests (107–8), because it represents onerous duties; but the intensity of the necklace image also conveys an extreme fear of merging, of identity lost through connection.

Esther does literally lose herself because of maternal connection. Her face, the sign of her identity, becomes disfigured after she catches Jo's fever. Jo has come into her life because of his connection to Esther's parents, but in terms of Tulkinghorn's use of him—the plot device that keeps him a key figure in the novel's pages—particularly in connection with Lady Dedlock.

Much earlier in the novel, Esther tells us about the dream she has the night she sleeps at Mrs. Jellyby's:

> I began to lose the identity of the sleeper resting on me. Now it was Ada; now, one of my old Reading friends from whom I could not believe I had so recently parted. Now it was the little mad woman worn out with curtseying and smiling; now, some one in authority at Bleak House. Lastly, it was no one, and I was no one.
>
> (V, 45)

This dream, too, suggests her fear of connection, for with Caddy's head resting on her lap and Caddy's emotional demands upon her, she fears the blurring of individual boundaries and, ultimately, the loss of any individualized identity.

But the novel also portrays the anger at being cast out, at being too separate. Dickens orchestrates the text so that Lady Dedlock abandons her daughter a second time. Esther, even amidst her sympathy for her mother's sorrow—a sympathy made possible to her only retrospectively after her mother's death—expresses her anger at being cast away again.

Her description of her effort to obey Lady Dedlock's injunction to maintain distance and secrecy reveals her extreme disappointment and anger about this second leaving, as well as her discomfort possessing such aggressive feelings. In a passage that Valerie Kennedy also notices, Esther thrice repeats that her feelings about her discovery of and renewed separation from her mother "matter little," although she spends two lengthy paragraphs describing them (XLIII, 520–21). She writes of her "terror" at the possibility of disclosing their connection, admitting to us her present awareness of the excessive quality of her caution: "I am conscious now, that I often did these things where there can have been no danger of her being spoken of." Her reiteration of the dread of exposing her mother reads as her unconscious desire to do so—or, at least, as her fantasy about what it would be like to be publically connected to her.

She confesses "how strange and desolate it was" that Lady Dedlock's voice should be so "new" to her, hinting at the loneliness that characterized her childhood, and that threatens to remain unchanged despite her new knowledge of her mother's existence.

Since her "living mother," as Esther puts it, insists that she "consider her dead," she must face once again the coldness of her aunt's house, and the feeling of abandonment despite presence. Her response underlines her own fragmentation: Esther tells us that she "passed and repassed the door of her house in town, loving it, but afraid to look at it."

She concludes this section of her narrative with a negative statement of disappointment in her mother. She writes: "I can relate little of myself which is not a story of goodness and generosity in others," and quickly moves to a celebration of her guardian's patience with Richard. The statement strongly implies that "the little" that is not a story of others' goodness has been the portion about her mother's separation from her. Esther's anger about maternal abandonment expresses a masculine unconscious anger at the young boy's abrupt separation from identification with his mother. We can also read Esther's anger in the feminine terms of her need to be separate from her mother and her fear of replicating her mother's experience, although it seems to me that the text stresses fears of connection and abandonment more than anxiety about sameness. The heroine's most operative desire is to be connected in a nurturing way rather than to be separate.

Her movement to the subject of the relationship between Jarndyce and Richard reflects Esther's interest in expressed anger toward a parent figure. She devotes her attention to Richard's outspoken distrust and criticism of her guardian because anger at a parent fascinates her. Just as Skimpole represents in her narrative the direct, demanding expression of self that she can so rarely manage, Richard's anger portrays the fury she can not permit herself to feel consciously, but which she can intermittently and indirectly reveal in her writing. And Dickens' doubling of Esther in the figure of Hortense suggests the suppression of anger Esther must manage.

III

The statement "I'll follow the other," echoes several times throughout the novel. It passes principally among Jo, Esther, and Bucket as an expression of both confusion and understanding about individual identity. When Jo, baffled by Esther's resemblance to Lady Dedlock and Hortense, asks for clarification, he indirectly presses Esther for an answer about her connections: "If she ain't the t'other one, she ain't the forrenner. Is there *three* of 'em then?" (XXXI, 383). Esther, unconsciously frightened by anger at the mother who abandoned her as a baby, writes: "Charley looked at me a little frightened. I felt half frightened at myself when the boy glared on me so." Bucket repeats the phrase to Esther: "Miss Summerson," he answered, "back. Straight back as a die. You know me. Don't be afraid. I'll follow the other, by God." And a few lines later, "But I'll follow the other. My darling, don't you be afraid!" (LVII, 689).

Esther, though, is afraid to follow the other—the mother—even as she wants to find her. The novel itself has been following the mother, and showing us a world in which connection to her is dangerous; we have Esther's disfigured face as the sign of harm. Bucket's phrase "straight back as a die," and his assurance not to be afraid, lead to poverty, Nemo's grave, Esther's infancy, and memories of the cold Mrs. Barbary, the punishing mother surrogate; we can also read Bucket's phrase as his injunction to the heroine to find herself, the lost part of her experience that continually haunts her with trace memories and feelings about her relation to mother.

Esther's frequent association of Lady Dedlock with Jenny's dead baby portrays her author's masculine fear of the maternal, as if close association with mother means death, disintegration of identity. Esther's final description of her mother perhaps moves us more because of its image of Esther as a lost child and of her confusion about the relationship to her mother, than it does because of its depiction of Lady Dedlock's lonely death:

> I saw before me, lying on the step, the mother of the dead child. She lay there, with one arm creeping round a bar of the iron gate, and seeming to embrace it. She lay there, who had so lately spoken to my mother. She lay there, a distressed, unsheltered, senseless creature.
>
> (LIX, 713)

The "distressed, unsheltered, senseless creature" describes Esther's memory of herself as a young child. The passage's syntax suggests that Lady Dedlock's arm embraces the imagined dead child in place of the "bar of the iron gate."

In this account, then, the search for other, for maternal connection, brings one to the foot of a diseased graveyard, where bodies are tossed together in a heap, a place where physical and symbolic marks of identity quickly disintegrate. Thus Esther moves between the poles of two experiences of mother: at one, mother is the abandoning parent, distant and unconnected to her; at the other, mother means complete merging, the disintegration of individual identity. These two extreme views of mother reflect characteristic masculine fears about the dangers of intimacy.

But Dickens does attempt to imagine a restorative personal connection. The relationship between Ada and Esther represents his effort to portray an intimate, intense, and honest connection between two people. Esther several times informs us that she tells Ada everything—except, of course, and significantly, her secret about her mother. Their relationship represents Dickens's fantasy of connection and intimacy.

Esther primarily acts as a mother figure for Ada, although she herself experiences Ada's love as maternal. Hired by Jarndyce to be a companion to his cousin, Esther quickly becomes nurturer and proud parent. To be sure, Esther acts as a little mother to many characters in the novel, including Jarndyce himself, but her relationship with Ada is more emotionally charged; Esther is extraordinarily involved with Ada's physical and emotional well-being, and, in fact, often confuses Ada's identity with her own. Thus even this fantasy of mutual love carries the fear of loss of self in connection to another.

Though certainly we see a great deal more of Esther's maternal care than Ada's, Dickens portrays them in a reciprocal mothering relation. Take, for example, this passage describing Esther's meeting with Ada after her long illness:

> O how happy I was, down upon the floor with my sweet beautiful girl down upon the floor too, holding my scarred face to her lovely cheek, bathing it with tears and kisses, rocking me to and fro like a child, calling me by every tender name that she could think of, and pressing me to her faithful heart.
>
> (XXXVII, 456)

Dickens imagines an intimacy that can make some amends for the separations from the missing mother, and that can quell some of the individual's feelings of aloneness. Like David Copperfield's belief that Agnes returns to him a lost part of himself, Esther feels that Ada's presence dramatically compensates for the missing connection of her childhood.

Though Esther's depiction of her relationship with Ada may move us in its representation of the desire for closeness, it can never work as a realistic portrayal because it relies on a fantasy that someone else can restore to one split off parts of one's early self. The fantasy includes an intimate partner or companion who can mind read, that is, understand everything without being told, and who can love one so much that one begins to feel whole. In this fantasy, the other forges connection without any activity on the part of the self; the self remains passive and yet still connected, manages to get taken care of without risking revealing needs, for the other instinctively knows what they are. The intimacy imagined is a primitive one in the sense that it reflects the infant-mother connection. This explains, I think, the frequent perception that Dickens' lovers do not portray realistic relationships. I would say that there is psychological realism here, but it portrays the infant-mother bond as Dickens fantasizes/remembers it rather than adult relationship. That he does imagine intimacy in these terms seems important because in doing so he represents his culture's desperate and ultimately futile effort to heal the early split through the writing of fiction.

From the very beginning of Dickens's description of Esther and Ada's relationship, we see the depiction of an effortless connection, the child's fantasy of return to an adoring, knowing mother:

> She came to meet me with a smile of welcome and her hand extended, but seemed to change her mind in a moment, and kissed me. In short, she had such a natural, captivating, winning manner, that in a few minutes we were sitting in the window-seat, with the light of the fire upon us, talking together, as free and happy as could be.
>
> (III, 30)

Significantly, then, the portrait of the greatest intimacy we see in this novel is that between two young women. This makes sense if we read the relationship as Dickens' projection of closeness, for he would call up the early relationship with mother, the one before gender identity separated them, in which distinctions between self and other blurred, and in which the boy baby, identified with the mother, was, in a sense, feminine.[4]

IV

Esther's description of her desire for love as a girl portrays her author's blending of a wish for acceptance and nurturing with a wish for mastery.

> I often thought of the resolution I had made on my birthday, to try to be industrious, contented, and true-hearted, and to do some good to some one, and win some love if I could; and indeed, indeed, I felt almost ashamed to have done so little and have won so much.
>
> (III, 26)

The belief that if she does "some good to someone" she will be loved, and the notion that love can be "won," that it is an achievement for which one works, rather than a feeling that two people come to share and to nurture between them, mark Esther's masculine gender affiliation, her aspirations in the symbolic, abstract, hierarchical world of the father in which achievement promises acceptance. Love here is something one earns or competes for, a mark of success rather than a reciprocal, shared process.

Esther lets us know, though, that ultimately neither the relationship to Ada nor the winning of love do satisfy her longing for some connection to her mother, or her desire for some reworking of her childhood feelings and images. Thus she continually returns to haunting memories of her early years, and events taking place in the present become emotionally charged and exaggerated by her early pain. We might, for example, consider her hysterical response to Mr. Guppy's first proposal or her reaction to Jarndyce's marriage offer.

A very quick contrast with *Jane Eyre* will highlight my point about Esther's portrayal of Dickens' desires and fears. *Jane Eyre*, like *Bleak House*, contains both several momentous secrets and a heroine who struggles to keep angry feelings under control. Jane's feelings of hostility, however, are much more conscious than Esther's and her effort to control them strikingly less successful. All we need do is think of Jane in hand-to-hand combat with John Reed and her passionate confinement in the Red Room to realize the extent of the difference in the behavior of these two heroines. But Jane, like Esther, does narrate her own story, make friends only after she leaves her childhood home, decide between appropriate and inappropriate marriage partners, and experience a meaningful discovery of lost relatives.

Despite the plot similarities, the differences in the heroines' psychologies are striking: Jane struggles for independence and separateness where Esther looks for dependence and merging; though Jane craves Rochester's love, she loves her independence, her separate sense of self, at least as much. The novel's conclusion troubles many readers because they wonder whether or not Jane really gets what she wants. Even our confusion, though, about her marriage to a maimed Rochester, indicates our conviction that Jane's primary struggle has been for separateness and self-definition, and for the kind of self-fulfillment that comes through this.

On the other hand, at the end of *Bleak House*, we ponder not how separate a self Esther has been able to develop, but how well she can connect to those whom she calls intimates, whether or not she can truly share love. We wonder, for example, if she does share the details of her feelings and thoughts with her husband, the perplexities of her many conflicts and tensions, as she has shared them with us, her readers. Each novel sets in motion some gender specific conflicts: Brontë's portrays an ambivalent struggle for individuation, for the ability to know one's separate needs and feelings and to respond to them; Dickens' depicts an ambivalent longing for connection. Each work, in this sense, describes the desire of the author and the tension about enacting it. The authors' different genders, I am arguing, account for these novels' different psychological motifs.

V

Though we never actually see a portrayal of Esther's intimate connection with anyone other than Ada in this novel (for certainly Woodcourt remains more absent than present), we do hear Esther revealing herself to us in her role of writer. Her audience, or her projected version of audience, becomes her felt confidante; one of the things we may most enjoy about her narrative, I think, is the intimate tone in which she speaks to us, even as she worries over what she may be revealing. In fact, often the worries themselves seem the most intimate revelations, for they go to the center of Esther's identity.

Esther does not consciously want to write about her own feelings; her brief and cryptic allusion to the absent authority who requests that she write, and her omission of any reference to the project of which she is a part—save to note once that she writes only "a portion" of the story—suggest her satisfaction in fulfilling the job. Preoccupied with her own narrative, she does not interest herself in the whole.

Esther expresses her individual needs and desires through a series of projections. A "record of other lives," as she puts it, her narrative consistently focuses on her own psychological issues. She writes about Richard's hostility toward Jarndyce instead of her own, details Ada's longing for Richard instead of her love for Woodcourt, and describes Caddy's anger at Mrs. Jellyby instead of her own anger at Lady Dedlock.

But Esther's account not only provides stories chosen and rewritten according to her private preoccupations, but also a record of her struggle to disguise painful feelings, and an invitation to the reader to interpret them. Thus, of receiving Jarndyce's proposal, she writes, "I was very happy, very thankful, very hopeful; but I cried very much" (XLIV, 538). Esther goes on to tell the reader of her scolding of herself in her mirror. Thus we see her process of conscious self-suppression, and pity her for her self-denial.

In her role of writer, Esther asks for our sympathy and pity for her sense of isolation and separateness, and for her constant efforts of self-suppression. She does so by showing us her obsessive mothering of others, a mothering meant, ultimately, to make up for the separateness from her own mother that she feels. Thus she nurtures and guides Ada, Richard, Jarndyce, Caddy, Peepy, Jenny, Liz, Jo, and Charlie. The only character whom she refuses her maternal solicitations is Skimpole, that self-declared baby, because he threatens her own fantasy of being taken care of by nurturing those around her (he gets nurtured simply by demanding it).

The gender issue may get dizzying here, for it is one thing to imagine Esther as a version of Dickens in her role of busy, efficient housekeeper and conscientious writer, but more difficult to see her as her author in her characteristic mothering persona, the one, that earlier on, I said also represented her feminine affiliation. If we look closely, though, Esther seems more masculine than feminine in the mothering role: her mothering activities are obsessive; she doesn't seem to enjoy the activity but rather calls it her duty or her effort to win love. Mothering for Esther means the achievement of love for herself; she professionalizes mothering in her effort to earn success, which here translates "affection."

But Esther, in so far as she reveals her feelings and imagines her reader's sympathy, does mother herself in the act of writing. She forms an imagined intimacy with her audience, that is, she feels intimate with us *as* she writes. Despite her initial disclaimer, she quickly becomes comfortable in the writer's role. This comes as no surprise if we remember her response to the disorienting chaos at Mrs. Jellyby's home and the depressing neglect of the Jellyby children, especially depressing for Esther because it replays her own neglected childhood on the eve of the beginning of a new life with Jarndyce. To quell her own anxiety as well as the child's, Esther quickly takes to soothing Peepy, the most pronounced victim of Jellyby parental indifference; she does so primarily by telling him a story. Storytelling serves her as a way to comfort and entertain, but also as a method of establishing human connection, just as it served David Copperfield to create a bond with Steerforth and the other boys at school. For both Esther and David, storytelling creates intimacy without overwhelming the self; a narrative about somebody else's life creates the illusion that the writer is not talking about the self, even as we may know that she or he is. David's stories of Robinson Crusoe's ingenuity and solitary power, for example, reveal his own desire to be powerful and to stay intact—to survive Murdstone. David's storytelling allows Steerforth to respond to David's vulnerability, his wish for power, without David feeling too threatened by exposure. And yet the exposure of telling has occurred, represented in the new bond between David and his roommates.

By telling her own story and the story of her self-consciousness about telling this story, Esther asks us to take care of her. We will listen in the right way; we will read between the lines and understand. We will interpret her; she invites us to do so, as the novel as a whole invites us to read it. In the following passage, for example, she provides a series of obvious displacements of her unhappiness about the necessity of abandoning her love for Woodcourt:

> It was weak in me, I know, and I could have no reason for crying; but I dropped a tear upon her dear face, and another, and another. Weaker than that, I took the withered flowers out, and put them for a moment to her lips. I thought about her love for Richard; though, indeed, the flowers had nothing to do with that. Then I took them into my own room, and burned them at the candle, and they were dust in an instant.
>
> (XLIV, 539)

Esther insists on her reason for crying even as she denies it, giving the reader the sympathetic friend's task of absorbing and understanding her minimally disguised message. That Esther rests on the border of an awareness about both her feelings and her need for sympathy surfaces in her provision of interpretive guidelines for the reader: she tells us that she gets continually "weaker" with regard to the flowers; she lets us know that the flowers "have nothing to do" with Ada's love for Richard. She gives us a story about herself with blanks where her feelings should be, with a separate set of extensive clues for filling in the meanings. Thus she encourages us to listen actively, to become energetic participants in the unravelling of her tale.

And we get some rewards. In the novel's final pages, Esther expresses her sense of a warm, intimate bond with her reader, thanking us for our attention:

> Full seven happy years I have been the mistress of Bleak House. The few words that I have to add to what I have written, are soon penned; then I, and the unknown friend to whom I write, will part forever. Not without much dear remembrance on my side. Not without some, I hope, on his or hers.
>
> (LVIII, 767)

As Sylvère Monod notes, Esther here assumes the guise of the nineteenth-century conventional narrator (21). But where Monod reads this moment as

Dickens slipping, I would argue that the words and sentiment are very much within character. For Esther's voice does gradually change over the course of her writing; she comes to speak in a tone of authority. She says, for example, "As it so happened that I never saw Mr. Skimpole again, I may at once finish what I know of his history" (LXI, 729). And she stops apologizing for writing about herself. She begins to call her narrative her own story: "And now I come to a part of my story, touching myself very nearly indeed, and for which I was quite unprepared when the circumstances occurred" (LXI, 729), she says, as she begins to tell us of Woodcourt's marriage proposal.

The nostalgic sound of her last chapter makes clear her regrets at leaving her reader, her sense of loss about concluding her writing:

> It is difficult to believe that Charley (round-eyed still, and not at all grammatical) is married to a miller in our neighborhood; yet so it is; and even now, looking up from my desk as I write, early in the morning at my summer window, I see the very mill beginning to go round.
>
> (LXVII, 767–8)

VI

If writing represents connection for Dickens, and at the deepest level, connection to mother, than the portrait of written expression the novel gives us should be an ambivalent one. And indeed it is. Chancery's innumerable written legal documents collectively author many a death: Gridley, Richard, Tom Jarndyce, Jo, Nemo, Lady Dedlock, even Tulkinghorn—all in some way die as the result of law writing. But personal writing endangers too: the letters Lady Dedlock wrote to her lover bring about her downfall and John Jarndyce's epistolary marriage proposal confines and manipulates Esther even as it offers her affection and security. Mrs. Jellyby's many letters lead to an angry, deprived, ink-stained daughter and in turn to her deaf and mute baby girl. And Skimpole's personal writings defame the characters of those who have helped him. Esther writes:

> He left a diary behind him, with letters and other materials toward his life; which was published, and which showed him to have been the victim of a combination on the part of mankind against an amiable child. It was considered very pleasant reading, but I never read more of it myself than the sentence on which I chanced to light on opening the book. It was this, "Jarndyce, in common with most other men I have known, is the Incarnation of Selfishness."
>
> (LXI, 729)

And Inspector Bucket knows well that to put something in writing is to give evidence against yourself.

I would seem to be discussing two different relations to the issue of connection here: Chancery's writing creates no unity, no contact between part and part, while personal correspondence promises connection. Both, though, demonstrate a fear of merging in that earliest connection to mother, for Chancery causes its victims to get lost; it suffocates them beneath its papers, denying them their identities. Gridley becomes the Man from Shropshire, and Richard gives up any chance of a professional self. Similarly, on the personal level, Skimpole's diary and Jarndyce's written marriage proposal threaten identity: Skimpole slanders Jarndyce's good name, and Jarndyce denies Esther's filial identity and daughterly tie to him by suggesting a sexual connection between them.

As several critics have noted, *Bleak House* is filled with connections and invitations to us to find them and interpret their meanings—a writer's novel.[5] And yet the novel also denies us some intriguing connections, defies us to find unity or wholeness. Dickens never provides us with the final plot connection about Nemo: we never know whether he commits suicide or not, nor why and how he came to lose the identity of Hawdon. And most importantly, Dickens never reconciles the presence of the two narratives; we can only speculate about the relationship between Esther and the other voice and try to create our own wholeness out of the novel's ambivalence and its fragmented world.

Even Esther leaves us with an unfinished story, one that does not make the last connection. She leaves us guessing: she is disfigured or beautiful, depending on how we read her, but she is neither with any certainty. Perhaps even writing that serves as safe self-mothering can never be safe enough, because the reader, even a projected reader, might find out too much, more than the self could stand. And perhaps, too, Esther withdraws mid-sentence so that we can not abandon her.

NOTES

1. There are, however, more external similarities than one might imagine. Dickens, like his heroine, spent a great deal of time keeping his house in order. He left notes in his children's drawers complimenting their tidiness or remarking their need of attention, on vacation rearranged furniture even in rooms where he might be staying for only a short time, supervised decoration and furnishing of his own home, and was generally preoccupied with household efficiency. On a level less mundane perhaps, he shared Esther's interest in dreams, often talked about himself in the third person just as she frequently discusses herself as if she were

someone else, and felt, like his heroine, great anxiety when starting to write a narrative.

2. Someone who gave care without emotional investment in the child would not fill this role. What characterizes the traditional mother is that she serves her infant and also forms an intimate, loving bond with her or him.

3. I am grateful to Catherine Gallagher for pointing out that Esther's relationship to her mother can also be persuasively read in terms of the girl/woman's relationship to her mother: Esther's fear of replicating Lady Dedlock's experience and her anger about the difficulty of being different from her reflect a feminine battle in the traditional family. Though I think the text supports both readings and that it gives us both a masculine and feminine Esther, I believe that the psychological issues of the masculine Esther have greater impact on the text as a whole.

4. This seems to me a particularly male fantasy. I wonder, in fact, if it inspires male pornographers' frequent depictions of Lesbian relationships.

5. See for example J. Hillis Miller's Introduction to the Penguin *Bleak House*, 1980, pp. 11–34.

WORKS CITED

Chodorow, Nancy. *The Reproduction of Mothering: Pschoanalysis and the Sociology of Gender*. Berkeley: U of California P, 1978.

Dickens, Charles. *Bleak House*. Eds. George Ford and Sylvere Monod. New York: Norton, 1977.

Gilligan, Carol. *In a Different Voice: Psychological Theory and Women's Development*. Cambridge: Harvard UP, 1982.

Hutter, Al. "The High Tower of His Mind: Psychoanalysis and the Reader of *Bleak House*." *Criticism* 19 (1977), 296–316.

Kennedy, Valerie. "Bleak House: More Trouble with Esther?" *Journal of Women's Studies in Literature* 1 (1979), 330–47, 337–8.

Killian, Crawford. "In Defense of Esther Summerson," *Dalhousie Review* (1974), 318–28.

Miller, J. Hillis. Introduction. *Bleak House*. By Charles Dickens. Harmondsworth, Middlesex: Penguin, 1980. 11–34.

Monod, Sylvere. "Esther Summerson, Charles Dickens and the Reader of *Bleak House*." *Dickens Studies* (1969): 5–24.

Stoehr, Taylor. *Dickens: The Dreamer's Stance*. Ithaca: Cornell UP, 1965.

Zwerdling, Alex. "Esther Summerson Rehabilitated." *Charles Dickens: New Perspectives*. Ed. Wendell Stacy Johnson. Englewood Cliffs, N.J.: Prentice Hall, 1982. 94–113.

Fathers and Suitors:
Narratives of Desire in *Bleak House*

Barbara Gottfried

In recent collections of source materials and essays on Victorian womanhood, both Erna Olafson Hellerstein and Estelle B. Freedman in *Victorian Women: A Documentary Account*, and Martha Vicinus in *A Widening Sphere: Changing Roles of Victorian Women* cite Dickens as one of the most influential writers to propagate/disseminate the Victorian ideal of women's special domestic mission. According to them, the presentations of female characters in his novels both draw on and help to perpetuate the gender roles to which middle-class Victorians adhered. As his correspondence and non-fiction prose suggest, Dickens would have been the first to admit that he subscribed to all the Victorian pieties, especially the notion that "a woman's place, and her vocation, were in the home." But the polyphony of the Dickens text undercuts, questions, subverts the "givens" of Victorian ideology and suggests a gap between Dickens the man and the texts that bear his name.[1] Paying attention to the tensions and distortions, gaps and elisions engendered by the competition of voices in the text allows us to move beyond the immediate intentions of Dickens as author and authority to the irony and ambivalence in his texts, and demands a more complex assessment of Dicken's familial and sexual politics.

My thanks to my colleague Tom Caramango for his suggestions for editing and revision, and to John O. Jordan and H. Marshall Leicester, Jr. of the University of California, Santa Cruz, for their contributions to the shape of my reading of *Bleak House*.

Esther Summerson's narrative in *Bleak House*, Dickens' only attempt at a "female" voice, invites such a reading. This essay will insist on the "fiction" that Esther has indeed written her "portion of these pages." To do so empowers Esther as narrator, allowing her to "speak" beyond Dickens, so that her narrative can be read as an allegory of the cost and benefits of the daughter's placing of herself in patriarchy.[2] As a figure structurally defined as a victim who wishes retrospectively to empower herself, Esther is caught. Although she does, like Dickens' autobiographer-sons Pip and David, appropriate the prerogatives of the father and attempt to author herself in and through narrative,[3] because she is a daughter in patriarchy, hers is an "autobiography by default," a narrative warped by strategies of repression and displacement. Nevertheless, whenever she can, Esther moves away from the impotence and ambivalence suggested by her rhetorical strategies to a position of retrospective strength, constructing a strategically shaped and selectively "re-presented" version of events which she controls, and which works recuperatively in the *"now"* of writing to tell her side of the story.[4]

As a retrospective narrator, Esther must present the events of her narrative so that they move, if obliquely, not only toward her marriage to Allan Woodcourt, but toward Richard's demise and the "re-placing" of Ada at Bleak House with John Jarndyce as well. The "endings" of Esther, Ada, and Richard's stories adumbrate the spectrum of possible endings figured in "the heroine's text."[5] That spectrum is neither large nor various: the heroine may either remain in her [surrogate] father's house or marry, both of which implicitly limit female freedom of movement and expression; the only other alternative is death. Thus Esther uses Ada and Richard in her narrative as surrogates for herself who enact, and thereby exorcize, those less desirable endings, death or remaining daughter-like at home, ensuring her of the ending she could not have been sure of the first time around—marriage to Allan. Esther's relation to the male characters in her narrative crystallizes for her both the issue of marriage, particularly as the venue of placement and legitimation, and by extension the more fraught issue of power and power relations embedded in the marital configuration. If Esther's task is to marry, those male characters present a spectrum of possible choices. Perhaps, then, it is no coincidence that so many of them may be characterized as either fathers or suitors, in particular John Jarndyce, who is both fatherly guardian and covert suitor. Surrounded by unacknowledged desire, Esther too must be covert. Though the omissions and contortions of her text obliquely call attention to her desire for Allan Woodcourt, she suppresses that desire and refuses to include him as her lover in her narrative. Rather than look too closely at her own suitors, Jarndyce, Guppy, and Allan, Esther displaces her interest in them by making Richard the focal suitor in her narrative. In what follows I will consider the interrelated configuration of these male characters as they are presented in Esther's narrative.

Esther's richest and most complex relationship is not with her future husband Allan Woodcourt, but with John Jarndyce, the father/seducer she presents as desiring to be everything to her: guardian, lover, providential benefactor. Two fundamental paradoxes structure Esther's presentation of John Jarndyce. First of all, Esther needs and wants Jarndyce to be the considerate, generous, sympathetic, asexual, good father she did not have as a child. At the same time she is aware of the coerciveness of his benevolence, and the negative aspects of his surrogate fatherhood, and includes them obliquely in her narrative. More insidiously, though Esther seems to present Jarndyce as powerful and herself as the passive recipient of his good intentions, the shape of her narrative suggests that it is really she who is strong and desirous of power. In order to be good Esther cannot own her own strength. Thus she uses Jarndyce as a surrogate to express the desire for agency she cannot own in herself and attributes to him her own strength, resolution, and desire for responsibility, order, and control.

In addition to "de-fusing" her own dangerous desires, this strategy of displacement, which shapes Esther's presentation of Jarndyce, allows her to give play to a powerful fantasy with regard to him. Just as Esther details her vicarious participation in the romantic love relationship of Ada and Richard early in her narrative as a means of channelling and indirectly experiencing her own romantic yearnings, so she presents Jarndyce as strong, protective, competent, generous, sympathetic, fatherly not because he *is* good, but because she needs him to be that way. In doing so, Esther gives herself the fantasy father she has always wanted, but in addition, she defuses and recuperates in the "now" of writing the latent threat of Jarndyce's sexuality which his transgression of the boundaries of fatherhood has allowed to taint their relationship.[6]

This is not to say that Jarndyce does not have power in relation to Esther. Just before turning her over to Allan as "a willing gift," his greatest act of generosity, and consequently of obligation and control in relation to Esther, Jarndyce lets her know that in proposing to her when she was most vulnerable just after her illness, he had "renewed the old dream I sometimes dreamed when you were *very young* of making you my wife one day" (751–752, emphasis added). What Esther knows retrospectively (and, as I will argue, suspected all along) is that Jarndyce's interest in her was never totally disinterested; that if he is not, in Skimpole's words, the "Incarnation of Selfishness," he is not as selfless and benevolent as her overt text makes him either. Esther certainly does not wish to condemn Jarndyce outright: their relationship is too complex and ambiguous for easy judgments. But though Esther has particular stakes in presenting Jarndyce as a benevolent agent and father figure, she nevertheless embeds her critique of Jarndyce in her narrative, adumbrating the cost of his patronage, benevolence, and desire to sexualize their relationship through strategic juxtapositions, inclusions, omissions, repetitions, and the use of surrogates, particularly Richard, to express the underside of "guardianship" as well.

Esther's description of her first, if incognito, encounter with John Jarndyce in the coach on the way to Greenleaf School is a carefully constructed representation of their relationship though on a first reading we, like Esther the first time around, cannot know it is Jarndyce she describes:

> There was a gentleman in the coach who sat on the opposite seat and looked very large in a quantity of wrappings; but he sat gazing out of the other window, and took no notice of me. . . . I thought he was very strange; or at least that what I could see of him was very strange, for he was wrapped up to the chin, and his face was almost hidden in a fur cap, with broad fur straps at the side of his head, fastened under his chin. . . .
>
> (24)

The image of a "strange" man so wrapped up that no real description of his face is possible gazing out the window, hints at Jarndyce's tendency to aloofness and detachment, and at his need to insulate himself from the world around him. Furthermore, Esther does not say he is "large;" rather, he only "looked very large," an observation which undercuts him even as it voices her sense of his capacity for taking up space in relation to her. Thus what appears to be description is really critique. Jarndyce then begins his first "seduction" of Esther by tempting her with "a piece of the best plum-cake that can be got for money—" (25). As we shall see, Esther quickly learns just how much (or how little) Jarndyce's money can buy, and she shows him relying on the power of money to buy his way out of difficulties. After Esther refuses Jarndyce's "gift," (the only time she ever does so), he does not attempt to engage her again. At this early date he has no language other than that of the father/seducer with which to speak to her, and when it fails he withdraws, effectively cutting Esther off, rather than face a delicate situation he himself has created.

Throughout her narrative, Esther continues to hint at hidden aspects of Jarndyce's character she never overtly discusses. For instance, in her detailing of the layout of Bleak House, she describes Jarndyce's chambers:

> [from Richard's room], you went straight, with a little interval of passage, to the plain room where Mr. Jarndyce slept all the year round with his window open, his bedstead without any furniture standing in the middle of the floor for more air, and his cold-bath gaping for him in a smaller room adjoining.
>
> (63)

Ostensibly, Esther means to suggest that Jarndyce does not indulge in luxuries, nor lavish on himself what others cannot afford. But her "monkish" description points to willful renunciation, the repression of sexuality. Of course, in order to renounce, one must first have desired, something it is not easy for Esther to acknowledge with reference to Jarndyce.

Esther then describes her visit with Richard and Ada to Mrs. Jellyby's as a way of hinting that Jarndyce has difficulty forseeing the consequences of his actions:

> "We rather thought," said I, glancing at Richard and Ada, who entreated me with their eyes to speak, "that she was a little unmindful of her home."
> "Floored!" cried Mr. Jarndyce.
> I was rather alarmed again.
> "Well! I want to know your real thoughts, my dear. I may have sent you there on purpose"
>
> (60–61)

Jarndyce is apparently astonished, and the final line rings false, as if it had been improvised at the moment to cover up his real ignorance of conditions at the Jellybys', a messy situation to which he has contributed through his indiscriminate funding of Mrs. Jellyby. Despite what he has just heard, Jarndyce attempts to cover for Mrs. Jellyby, and, incidentally, for himself:

> "She means well," said Mr. Jarndyce, hastily. "The wind's in the east. . . ."
> "Those little Jellybys. Couldn't you—didn't you—now, if it had rained sugar-plums, or three-cornered raspberry tarts, or anything of that sort!"
>
> (61)

As in his attempt to assuage Esther's anxiety on the way to Greenleaf School, Jarndyce wants to redeem himself with the Jellyby children by showering them with sweets, as if cake will actually help solve the problems of a household in which meals are never thoroughly cooked, envelopes turn up in the gravy, and the children's clothes are worn to tatters. Esther here implicitly criticizes Jarndyce's tactics, for if buying her off did not work, it will not work for the Jellyby children either; and she then juxtaposes this passage with Ada's praise of her own measures for dealing with the Jellyby children: what did begin to make a difference at the Jellybys' was not that it rained sweets, but that "It did better than that. It rained Esther."(61)

Jarndyce's difficulty in coming to grips with things as they are is further underscored in his close association with Harold Skimpole. On the level of plot Skimpole is a minor figure, but he is an important voice in Esther's narrative because he expresses a range of dangerous opinions, which those around him, including Esther, secretly think but are afraid to acknowledge, and because he is the voice of rampant self-interest. In addition, he is used by Jarndyce and Esther to embody a fantasy of irresponsibility and ease that reveals the underside of benevolence and responsibility. Although Skimpole is seemingly very different from the Esther he himself celebrates as the "centre" of a "whole little orderly system" (468), they share a penchant for poetic flights of fancy, which Esther gives play to in herself by recording him at length. More importantly, both possess an accurate and disenchanted eye which comprehends the motives and stakes, subterfuges and euphemisms of those around them.

Esther's first impression of Skimpole is revealing. A complex and richly realized portrait, it is eloquent, precise, and, from the beginning, outdoes Skimpole himself in its ability to comprehend the motives and circumstances of others:

> He was a little bright creature, with a rather large head; but a delicate face, and a sweet voice, and there was a perfect charm in him. All he said was so free from effort and spontaneous, and was said with such a captivating gaiety, that it was fascinating to hear him talk. Being of a more slender figure than Mr. Jarndyce, and having a richer complexion, with browner hair, he looked younger. Indeed, he had more the appearance, in all respects, of a damaged young man, than a well-preserved elder one. There was an easy negligence in his manner, and even in his dress (his hair carelessly disposed, and his neck-kerchief loose and flowing, as I have seen artists paint their own portraits), which I could not separate from the idea of a romantic youth who had undergone some unique process of depreciation. It struck me as being not at all like the manner or appearance of a man who had advanced in life by the usual road of years, cares, and experiences.
>
> (65)

Esther here includes, without particularly calling attention to them, two crucial perceptions of Skimpole. First her language hints at Skimpole's "feminine" seductiveness, his ability to "charm," "fascinate," "captivate" and its dangerous power to deflect attention from underlying or difficult truths. In keeping with this insight, her description of Skimpole's manner of dress suggests an attention to style and effect equally superficial, misleading, and effeminate. Thus Esther's description implies that in accepting from Jarndyce the "cake" she herself has refused, Skimpole in effect seduces the seducer, a powerful role reversal she perhaps envies him but is unwilling to try out.

In addition, for Esther, Skimpole's disenchanted "philosophy of generosity" accurately anatomizes not simply the benefit to the receiver but the gratification of the giver/seducer as well, a subject apparently on her mind:

> "I envy you [generous creatures] your power of doing what you do. It is what I should revel in, myself. I don't feel any vulgar gratitude to you. I almost feel as if you ought to be grateful to me, for giving you the opportunity of enjoying the luxury of generosity. I know you like it. For anything I can tell, I may have come into the world expressly for the purpose of increasing your stock of happiness. I may have been born to be a benefactor to you, by sometimes giving you an opportunity of assisting me in my little perplexities. Why should I regret my incapacity for details and worldly affairs, when it leads to such pleasant consequences? I don't regret it therefore."
>
> (67)

Esther says nothing directly about her own response to Skimpole's "upside-down" philosophy. Rather, she records her evaluation of Jarndyce's reaction:

> Of all his playful speeches (playful, yet always fully meaning what they expressed) none seemed to be more to the taste of Mr. Jarndyce than this. I had often new temptations, afterwards, to wonder whether it was really singular, or only singular to me, that he, who was probably the most grateful of mankind upon the least occasion, should so desire to escape the gratitude of others.
>
> (67)

Esther's parenthetical remark about Skimpole shows they both understand Jarndyce's stakes in his own benevolence. Whereas Skimpole will let everyone be generous and reap the benefit of their need to give, Jarndyce prefers to reserve the luxury of generosity to himself.[7] The involutions of Esther's second sentence implicate a "most grateful" Jarndyce in the enjoyment of that "luxury" without acknowledging the gratitude of his beneficiaries or his own pleasure, and in the enjoyment of Skimpole's dangerously captivating speech, which deflects attention from the destructive underside of his childish dependency. Thus Skimpole knows not only what to say about each character but for that character as well.

Like Skimpole, Esther, too, comprehends the ruses and euphemisms of others, including Skimpole, but especially John Jarndyce. As Esther notices right away, for Jarndyce, the subject of Skimpole's or Mrs. Jellyby's children, the "innocent victims" of their respective parent's self-indulgence, mysteriously shifts the wind to the East:

> Ada and I agreed, as we talked together for a little while upstairs, that this caprice about the wind was a fiction; and that he used the pretence to account for any disappointment he could not conceal, rather than he would blame the real cause of it, or disparage or depreciate anyone. We thought this very characteristic of his eccentric gentleness; and of the difference between him and those petulant people who make the weather and the winds (particularly that unlucky wind which he had chosen for such a different purpose) the stalking-horse of their splenetic and gloomy humours.
>
> (75)

It is indeed "characteristic" of Jarndyce to cover up the problematic implications of his own and others' actions with euphemistic references to mood change that effectively cut off further discussion of the "easterly," or disturbing, aspect of things. Esther indulges him in this because she has a stake in Jarndyce's "eccentric gentleness," and can only hint at his "inconsistencies" and evasions, deprecating her own powers of comprehension, rather than openly questioning his powers of judgment.

Esther also apprehends the more subtle forms of Jarndyce's mechanisms of rationalization, and reminds him of them when he temporarily forgets his own systems of defense. For instance, when Jarndyce finds out that Skimpole has convinced Richard and Esther to pay his most recent debt, and the east wind is about to "blow a gale," Esther redirects his energy to its usual channels of de-fusion:

> I ventured to take this opportunity of hinting that Mr. Skimpole, being in all such matters, quite a child—
>
> "Eh, my dear?" said Mr. Jarndyce, catching at the word.
>
> "—Being quite a child, sir," said I, "and so different from other people—"
>
> "You are right!" said Mr. Jarndyce, brightening. "Your woman's wit hits the mark. He is a child—an absolute child. I told you he was a child, you know, when I first mentioned him."
>
> Certainly! certainly! we said.
>
> "And he is a child. Now, isn't he?
>
> (74)

As Esther can see, Jarndyce's world is precarious, and he needs her to help him prop it up. The very next morning (in Chapter VIII), as Jarndyce gets carried away explaining the vagaries of Chancery justice in the case of *Jarndyce and Jarndyce*, Esther again pacifies him by reminding him of "the bright side of the picture," the changes he himself has wrought for the better in the place Tom Jarndyce saw fit to call Bleak House. They have this conversation in what Jarndyce calls "The Growlery," as he explains:

> ". . . When I am out of humour, I come and growl here."
> "You must be here very seldom, sir," said I.
> "O, you don't know me!" he returned. "When I am deceived or disappointed in—the wind, and it's Easterly, I take refuge here. The Growlery is the best-used room in the house."
>
> (87)

When the complexities of his entanglements become too much for him, Jarndyce "take[s] refuge" in the Growlery, and his need to compartmentalize and contain anger, frustration, and disappointment makes it no surprise that it is the "best-used room" in a renovated Bleak House. In order to deal with the world at all, Jarndyce must have a Growlery, and when the Bleak House household moves to London, he always makes sure to establish a makeshift Growlery wherever they stay.

Up until this point in her narrative, Esther has avoided addressing Jarndyce by name. She is careful to note, however, that when Ada calls him "cousin," he amends it to "Cousin John," but she is aware that her lack of a blood relationship to Jarndyce precludes her use of the same name. When she finally refers to Jarndyce by the overly deferential "sir," Jarndyce suggests that she call him "Guardian" (90). The name, which is also a legal term, is a revealing choice. According to Miss Donny [at Greenleaf School] the mysterious and unknown benefactor who pays Esther's bills is her "guardian;" and he is so, Jarndyce tells Esther during this first morning together in The Growlery, because he "heard of a good little orphan girl without a protector, and . . . t[ook] it into my head to be that protector" (87). But by the time Esther arrives at Bleak House, she is twenty-one (Richard and Ada are nineteen and seventeen respectively) and no longer in need of a guardian legally entitled to custody of her and her affairs. Moreover, a guardian is someone who not only "protects," but *"preserves*; a *keeper"* (*Oxford English Dictionary*, emphasis added) and it is precisely Jarndyce's urge to "keep" and "preserve" Esther that is disturbing to her. As soon as Jarndyce names himself "Guardian," he names Esther:

This was the beginning of my being called Old Woman, and Little Old Woman, and Cobweb, and Mrs. Shipton, and Mother Hubbard, and Dame Durden, and so many names of that sort, that my own name soon became quite lost among them.

(90)

As Axton and others have pointed out, Jarndyce's use of these nicknames for old women "de-sexualizes" Esther, and makes her a fit companion for a "keeper" who is "nearer to sixty than fifty."[8] More insidiously, if the task of a female protagonist is to marry the suitor who can best house her, Esther is "preserved," stuck, because she is already suitably housed in a house not her father's; what's more, in giving her the keys which signal housewifely possession and responsibility, Jarndyce places Esther, as Skimpole puts it, "at the centre of her own little orderly world." In terms of responsibility and control, this is precisely where Esther secretly desires to be, but the displacements of her narrative suggest that if the cost of house-possession is marriage to Jarndyce, or the impossibility of marriage with anyone else, the price is more than she is willing to pay.

Though it is not until very near the end of her narrative that Jarndyce admits he had thought about marrying Esther from very early on her narrative includes instances of his desire, from the beginning of her interactions with him. Esther first openly hints at Jarndyce's desire in a scene sandwiched in between Ada's avowal of her love for Richard, despite his failure to take to the study of medicine, and Allan's departure for India after leaving flowers behind for Esther at Miss Flite's. Esther cannot sleep. Going downstairs, she inadvertantly finds a troubled Jarndyce in the Growlery, and he proceeds to tell her what he knows of her history. In response, Esther " 'blesses the Guardian who is a Father to her!' ":

At the word Father, I saw his former trouble come into his face. He subdued it as before, and it was gone in an instant; but it had been there, and it had come so swiftly upon my words that I felt as if they had given him a shock. I again inwardly repeated, wondering, "That *I* could readily understand. None that *I* could readily understand!" No, it was true I did not understand it. Not for many and many a day.

(214)

Rather than admit the implications of Jarndyce's "trouble," Esther's narrative swerves into gratitude for Jarndyce's benevolence; nevertheless, she includes the broad hint that if Jarndyce is troubled it is because her identification of him as a "Father" figure desexualizes him. The narrative thus hints, even if Esther herself cannot directly acknowledge it, that from the very beginning Jarndyce's looks in her direction have been full of a meaning she has preferred not to see. In the same scene in which Jarndyce suggests that she call him Guardian, Esther notices that when Jarndyce looks at her his mood brightens (91). And, her very first night at Bleak House, when Jarndyce looks at her after contemplating Ada and Richard together, Esther claims that Jarndyce's look is meant to confide to her his hope in Ada and Richard's "dearer relationship" rather than considering that the look may have been meant for her and his hope of *their* dearer relationship (69). Throughout her narrative, Esther redirects her narrative energies rather than come to terms with that which is important enough to her to include obliquely, but too troubling to confront directly.

Rather than look too closely at Jarndyce as a covert suitor, or at her more overt suitors, Guppy and Allan Woodcourt, Esther displaces her interest in them by making Richard the suitor *par excellence* in her narrative. In its most active sense, a suitor is someone who "sues, petitions, or prosecutes at law." Less aggressively, and more like those characters in *Bleak House* whose suits have been embroiled in Chancery for years, a suitor becomes one who brings suit, reifying the action of suing by becoming a "petitioner or plaintiff in a suit." As "suitor" shades off into identity rather than action, it moves back toward its more archaic and passive meaning as "one of a retinue or suite; an adherent, follower, disciple"; and forward to its more recent sense as "one who courts or woos a woman" or "seeks a woman in marriage; a wooer," or lover (*OED*).

Richard is presented in Esther's narrative as a suitor in all senses of the word. First of all, he is a suitor in the case of *Jarndyce and Jarndyce*, which has been under consideration in the Court of Chancery since before he was born. Very early on in Esther's narrative, he becomes Ada's suitor and successfully woos her. Finally, as I shall detail below, Richard, like a cavalier or member of a retinue of old, attempts to live his life according to an archaically determined code of chivalric etiquette not flexible or responsive enough to a newer, more fluid set of circumstances. But "suitor," like so many of the other quasi-legalistic and contractual, quasi-personal and emotional terms of status and endearment in *Bleak House*, works more complexly in the novel than its denotative meanings imply. As "suitor" shades off into its reifed nominatives, it reveals both the passivity and structural imbalance of suing, wooing, and loving. A suitor may choose to sue, or woo, but once he has begun the action, there is always the danger he will "never get out of Chancery:" in initiating a suit, he relinquishes control, ceding power to the arbiter of that suit, whether legal, or marital.

The nexus of Esther's "autobiography by default" and her presentation of Richard is particularly powerful, especially because the connection between the two of them is not immediately apparent. Taylor Stoehr has suggested that Esther is the "heroine" of *Bleak House* and Richard its "hero," but that the "dual point of view keeps the two stories apart in an odd, 'inverted,' way, for Esther's story is largely told not in her own narrative, but in the present tense narrative, while she in turn tells most of Richard's story . . ." (139). Stoehr then goes on to argue that Esther's "sexual-social dilemma and Richard's vocational one are never forced into meaningful contact with each other" (160). Stoehr is right to suggest that there is an important complementarity between Esther and Richard, but his argument loses ground when he reduces Esther to the "heroine" of *Bleak House*, forgetting to emphasize that she is also the narrator of half the novel. As narrator, Esther, as Stoehr points out, is responsible for presenting Richard's story, but what Stoehr does not take into account is that Esther thus shapes and controls that story.

Esther's presentation of Richard, like that of Jarndyce, is multi-layered; and Richard, too, is an important fantasy figure for her. Just as Esther presents Jarndyce as the good father she needs him to be, so she begins by presenting Richard as the young hero of romance she needs him to be. But whereas Jarndyce's failure to live up to Esther's fantasy version of him is covered up and alluded to only obliquely, Esther presents Richard's failure as a hero in detail, as a means of displacing her sense of her own failure as a perfect, silent, still, [Victorian] heroine. Precisely the opposite of Stoehr's final claim is true. It is not that Esther's "sexual-social dilemma and Richard's vocational one are never forced into meaningful contact with each other," but that Esther's narrative makes them opposite sides of the same coin. Just as Esther's "autobiography by default" figures her as a casualty of a sex-gender system which defines female goodness in terms of a renunciation and constraint which her narrative reveals is impossible, so it figures Richard in terms of a gentlemanly code of conduct which her narrative again reveals is no longer viable in a bleak, industrialized, non-heroic world.

For Esther, Richard as hero begins by embodying the privileges and prerogatives of the son in relation to the father: as a "son" Richard has the freedom to move, to leave Bleak House, even to rebel or defy the father. But in defying the father he reveals that the father had been de[i]fied, or put in a position of power which makes defiance necessary in the first place. Esther thus uses Richard and his relationship to John Jarndyce to express both the covert tyranny of fatherhood and her own need to defy the father-Guardian, making Richard's vocational dilemma analogous to her own sexual-social dilemma. Furthermore, her use of a male surrogate, who is free to say and do what she cannot express or enact, makes her apprehension of oppression and entrapment doubly powerful. What Esther's narrative reveals through Richard, who is also herself, is the structural power of the father and its cost to the next generation: if to be a daughter is to be caught and desired, to be a son is to be free to destroy, or be destroyed.

The presentation of Richard in Esther's narrative is structured on the one hand by her early investment in him as a hero of romance, her subsequent (though retrospectively already known) disappointment in him, and his demise, and on the other hand by her narrative use of him to express her repressed and displaced sense of the oppressive underside of guardianship. Thus while Esther begins by presenting Richard as fresh, young, charming, cavalier, she also immediately associates him with Miss Flite, which signals the parameters of possibility for Richard: a kind of heroism no longer possible in a "bleak house" world, or madness, a kind of death. Within these limits there is very little latitude for Richard to work out an alternative to his own obsolescence.[9]

Very early in her narrative Esther presents Richard as the fantasy young man she needs him to be: young, handsome, charming, yet quietly in control. And from the first, she uses her narrative to bring them together. For instance, early on she uses Richard to voice her poetic and her sardonic thoughts. At the same time she suppresses his direct utterance, thus tightly controlling her presentation of him and associating his remarks with herself, then mentioning almost as an after-thought, "I am quoting Richard again," "as Richard said," etc. (37,31). Not wishing overtly to appropriate the male prerogatives of social interaction, however, Esther attributes policy to Richard, "relying on his protection" and deferring to his decision-making and logistical powers, even though, as she soon discovers, she herself is infinitely more decisive.

Esther also remembers on their first night together on the way to Bleak House, Richard "wrapped up with great care" both Ada and herself, but that when they all stood up to get a better glimpse of Bleak House, it was Ada alone whom Richard held "lest she should be jolted down." Richard's choice of Ada over Esther is both self-interested, since she, too, is a party to the Chancery suit, and a class choice which prefers Ada to someone who must work for a living, and does not know who her parents are. Yet Esther had briefly considered that Richard could be interested in her;[10] and what she resents is not so much that Richard prefers Ada, but that he participates in the "conspiracy" to make her a "little old woman" and "Dame Durden." She gets her narrative revenge by infantalizing him, often referring to him as a young "boy," in addition to calling him "careless," "heedless," "off-hand," etc.

A complex and contradictory image of Richard as "cavalier" begins to emerge which highlights the word's most positive senses: "gay," "sprightly," "gallant," "courteous," "protective," but soon shades off into its more ambiguous or double-edged meanings, where "gay" becomes "free and easy," and moves toward "offhand," "haughty" and "disdainful;" and "generous" becomes prodigal, or "careless" (*OED*). Thus while Esther builds Richard up early on, she also hints at his carelessness, irresponsibility, and his tendency to mistake surface for substance. For instance, Esther twice notes that Richard takes Jarndyce's allusions to the East Wind literally. More crucially, Richard lives "by the book" of gentlemanly conduct. When Jarndyce wishes to recompense Richard and Esther for paying Skimpole's debt to "Coavinses," Richard, as a gentleman, refuses to reveal the amount borrowed even though Skimpole's own conduct has hardly been gentlemanly.

Richard's tendency toward literalness and bookish conceptions of conduct is compounded by a lack of tact and subtlety in his perceptions and interactions. For instance, he cannot appreciate Jarndyce's ways of dealing with the world or his reticence with regard to Chancery. Rather, Richard is presented as impulsive, as one who rarely considers the subtleties of perception and judgment involved in successfully interacting with others. His decision about a career is both impulsive, and more aware of the end than the means of achieving that end. After much discussion, Jarndyce mentions "Surgeon":

> "That's the thing, sir!" cried Richard.
> I doubt if he had ever once thought of it before.
> "That's the thing, sir!" repeated Richard, with the greatest enthusiasm. "We have got it at last M.R.C.S."
> He was not to be laughed out of it, though he laughed at it heartily. He said he had chosen his profession, and the more he thought of it, the more he felt that his destiny was clear; the art of healing was the art of all others for him. Mistrusting that he only came to this conclusion, because, having never had much chance of finding out for himself what his was fitted for, and having never been guided to the discovery, he was taken by the newest idea, and was glad to get rid of the trouble of consideration, I wondered whether the Latin Verses often ended in this, or whether Richard's was a solitary case.
>
> (152)

Several things are important here: first, Richard would like to *be* something, a Member of the Royal College of Surgeons, for instance, without the discipline and sustained effort of working towards it. Richard corroborates this notion himself: when Sir Leicester Dedlock, a distant relation by marriage, writes to say he can do nothing "to advance [Richard's] prospects," Richard says, regretfully, " '. . . I apprehend it's pretty clear . . . that I shall have to work my own way' " (104). More disturbingly, and contrary to what Esther says in her commentary on the incident, it seems as if Richard needed to make a decision because of the constant pressure on him to choose; and that Esther has not been as helpful as she might have been. Indeed, she is rather hard on him. Nor does she really seem to understand his situation. Although she has been shaping her audience's perception of Richard all along, it is from this point on that her direct presentation of him begins to favor one dominant interpretation of his attitudes and actions, not particularly sympathetic to him, over other possible readings.

Yet Esther's presentation of Richard remains double-edged. Though she presents Richard as careless and impulsive, she obliquely condemns Jarndyce's tactics. According to Esther, Jarndyce makes himself and Esther the active agents, while Richard becomes the passive, plastic "material" upon which they act: " 'Here's Rick, a fine young fellow full of promise. What's to be done with him?' " (90) Jarndyce says as they tackle household affairs their very first day together in the Growlery. Jarndyce's interest in Richard's choosing a career is tinged with benevolent paternalism, and his rhetoric enlists Esther on his side, the side of the status quo against that of the younger generation, as if to suggest that it is in her best interest, as well as his own, that she see things from his point of view. Implicitly choosing sides, rather than confronting the implications of the kind of pressure Jarndyce [and she] have been putting on Richard, Esther posits two possible explanations of Richard's difficulty in settling on a career. The first is voiced by Jarndyce, who attributes Richard's "indecision of character" to the legacy of Chancery, "that incomprehensible heap of uncertainty and procrastination on which he has been thrown from his birth," as if to say that the influence of Chancery is as powerful as that of parenting, and like a bad parent, "has engendered" bad habits in Richard (151).[11] Esther agrees with this prognosis and offers one of her own which blames an educational system which does nothing more than teach young gentlemen how to "make Latin Verses of several sorts" (151).

This is not to say that neither of these factors figures in Richard's "dilemma." But neither Jarndyce's nor Esther's explanation on its own, or both together, takes into consideration the immediate situation in which Richard finds himself, with all its attendant pressures. Nor do they consider that the kind of education Esther claims Richard has received is that of a gentleman: he has not, like Esther, been brought up to think of himself as having to make his way in the world; rather, he has been educated as befits a man of wealth and leisure. There is no indication who decided Richard's education should take this course, but what is clear is that he is the victim of a class system that posits a certain kind of education for young men of a particular class, regardless of their immediate resources. Whereas Esther has been educated to take her place in the world as someone who must "make her own way" (as has Allan Woodcourt, which is why his mother clings so tenaciously to the former glory inscribed in her family's "illustrious" ancestry), Richard (and Ada, and John Jarndyce) are of a different class: neither Jarndyce or Boythorn, for instance, works for a living, nor are the professions of Richard or Ada's fathers ever mentioned. In insisting that Richard decide upon a career, Jarndyce implicitly asks him to acknowledge a change in class status he is unprepared for; Richard's subsequent interest in *Jarndyce and Jarndyce* can then in part be explained by his desire not simply to avoid working but to recuperate his class status as well.

The question of who or what to "blame" for Richard's predicament contributes to the shaping of Esther's presentation of him. Her language often suggests that Richard's character is, in some fundamental sense, flawed. She describes him as "careless," and refers to his "offhand manner" of agreeing to work hard at his medical studies. Interestingly, from the point of view of responsibility or blame, it is Esther who notes Richard's manner at this point, rather than Jarndyce or Mr. Kenge, with whom Richard is conferring about his choice of career. Esther thus narratively implies that she, anyway, is astute enough to note Richard's lack of commitment, even if they are not. Again, after Richard has left for the Badgers', she notes not simply that he ceased to write, but that he "soon *failed* in his letter writing" (204, emphasis added). Finally, as Esther's narrative works to shape Richard's "fate," she associates him more and more frequently both with the "fascinations" of the Court, and with those who have seemingly been seduced by its charm.

Because Richard speaks from a place of increasing desperation and loss of power and control, Esther uses him more and more frequently to voice what she cannot openly articulate about her own sense of pressure and constraint. For both, Richard overtly and Esther covertly through him, it is primarily Jarndyce, whose problematically benevolent paternalism pressures them either vocationally or sexually, against whom they rebel. Esther first indicates Richard's sense of Jarndyce's power at the moment when she informs her Guardian that Richard and Ada are in love. Jarndyce, rather than expressing pleasure or joy, hints that perhaps they are too young to make such an important commitment, and lets them know that if they should change their minds, he'd be there to help them extricate themselves from their youthful mistake. He concludes:

> "I am only your friend and distant kinsman. I have no power over you whatever. But I wish and hope to retain your confidence, if I do nothing to forfeit it."
>
> (162)

Esther includes both Richard's and Ada's responses because they speak for her as well:

> "I am very sure, sir," returned Richard, "that I speak for Ada, too, when I say that *you have the strongest power over us both*—rooted in respect, gratitude, and affection—strengthening every day."
> "Dear cousin John," said Ada, on his shoulder, "my father's place can never be empty again. All the love and duty I could have rendered to him, is transferred to you."
>
> (162)

The next day Richard leaves to begin his medical studies at the Badgers'. From here on, as Esther's narrative takes shape and allegiances are sorted out, Esther becomes more and more closely allied with John Jarndyce and his interests, while Ada and Richard's romance focuses their interactions. Yet Esther's uneasiness with this set of allegiances is manifested throughout her narrative; and the more pressured she feels, the more she uses Richard as a surrogate who expresses what she herself cannot voice with regard to her relationship with Jarndyce.

Esther feels pressured not simply by Jarndyce's covert suitorship but by the marital attentions of Guppy and Allan Woodcourt as well. Esther's ambivalence about marriage is embedded in and worked out both through the difficulty she has including her future husband, Allan Woodcourt, in her narrative, and through her presentation of Guppy. Although Guppy makes only a few "cameo" appearances, he is, like Skimpole, an important figure because his presence signals Esther's dis-ease about suitors; lovers; relations and obligations between the sexes; sexual knowledge, attention, and intention; and the necessity of participating in a system of barter and exchange, ulterior motive and effect, mystified in the rhetoric of devotion. Guppy becomes both a scapegoat figure for Esther's unresolved feelings about marriage and a shadow suitor whose presence signals a comic-ironic dimension to the subject of courtship which undercuts the more serious suitors with whom Esther is concerned. In addition, the presence of Guppy sheds light on the strategic distortions of Esther's narrative technique. Like Lady Dedlock, Hortense, and Bucket, Guppy figures more frequently in the other narrative, and the discrepancies between his appearance there and Esther's presentation of him reveal both her anxieties about what he represents for her and her use of her narrative to de-fuse those anxieties.

Guppy also functions throughout her narrative as a yardstick of Esther's repressed sense of her own power and self-worth. Very early in her narrative, Esther uses a kind of narrative revenge to undercut Guppy's posturing and his unsolicited attentions by having Peepy beat him, for no apparent reason, with a hoop stick. Her next encounter with Guppy occurs at a more complex juncture, when Boythorn, whom Guppy has ostensibly come to see on law-business, is visiting Bleak House soon after its residents have settled in. Esther is at work on "household affairs," while the others are out on an excursion when Guppy arrives. She begins generously enough, by saying she "was glad to see him because he was associated with [her] present happiness" (111). But the more Guppy stares at Esther after his return from his conference with Boythorn, the more droll, "green," and ill-at-ease Esther makes him:

> Mr. Guppy sat down at the table, and began nervously sharpening the carving-knife on the carving-fork; still looking at me (as I felt quite sure without looking at him), in the same unusual manner. The sharpening lasted so long, that at last I felt a kind of obligation on me to raise my eyes, in order that I might break the spell under which he seemed to labour, of not being able to leave off.
> He immediately looked at the dish, and began to carve. . . .
> "Is there anything I can order for you?"
> "No, I am much obliged to you, miss, I'm sure. I've got everything I can require to make me comfortable—at least I—not comfortable—I'm never that": he drank off two more glasses of wine, one after another.
>
> (112)

Although the dandified Guppy is presented as painfully nervous and awkward, certain details of Esther's story suggest that her control of the situation is more a function of the "now" of her recounting of the incident than her real ease at the time. For instance, although Esther tells us that "all this time Mr. Guppy was either planing his forehead with his handkerchief, or tightly rubbing the palm of his left hand with the palm of his right" and that he requests a fourth glass of wine to help him get through what he wants to say to her "without a continual choke that cannot fail to be mutually unpleasant," Esther finds it necessary to move "well behind" her table to emphasize the barrier between them (113). Guppy then declares himself. Esther's reaction is complex and contradictory: she again notes the barrier between them, as if Guppy's going "down on his knees" were physically threatening to her, and makes a point of saying she was "not much frightened," as if fright were the reaction her audience would expect from a young woman who receives an unwanted proposal. But what she says, so she claims, at least, suggests not fright but strength and assurance, especially when juxtaposed with Guppy's comical parody of a proposal in a cheap romance:

> "Miss Summerson! In the mildest language, I adore you. Would you be so kind as to allow me (as I may say) to file a declaration—to make an offer!"
> Mr. Guppy went down on his knees . . . "Get up from that ridiculous position immediately, sir, or you will oblige me to break my implied promise and ring the bell!"
>
> (113)

Esther is adamant (not unlike her mother and aunt, Lady Dedlock and Miss Barbary). Indeed, throughout the remainder of the scene she is almost ruthless in her deflation of Guppy's pretensions. Guppy himself seems to sense the absurdity of his position *vis à vis* Esther when she orders him to sit back down to the meal she has served him, yet he manages to suggest a certain dignity and delicacy in himself Esther refuses to see: "Yet what a mockery it is, miss . . . to be stationed behind food at such a moment. The soul recoils from food at such a moment, miss" (114). Yet whether he pleads the advancement of her "interests, and pushing of [her] fortunes," his "respectful wretchedness," or "Love," Esther does not relent, not even to ask him what he means by her "interests."

Guppy, as his name suggests, is a rather absurd figure, even without Esther's annihilation of his suit. But his appearance and manners, his relation to the languages of chivalry and law, even his pretensions, while absurd, are also endearingly comic. Yet from Esther's perspective, there is no latitude for an appreciation of his "better" qualities or sympathy for him as a rejected suitor. The concluding paragraph of the chapter, which follows immediately upon Esther's final dismissal of Guppy, hints at Esther's lack of ease without direct commentary by her. As if to insist that Guppy's proposal has not disturbed her, Esther says she "g[o]t through plenty of business" after he left and was "so composed and cheerful that I thought I had quite dismissed this unexpected incident." "But," she goes on:

> . . . I surprised myself by beginning to laugh about it, and then surprised myself still more by beginning to cry about it. In short, I was in a flutter for a

little while; and felt that an old chord had been more coarsely touched than it
ever had been since the days of the dear old doll, long buried in the garden.

(115)

Esther is reminded of her doll because it is to that doll that she had vowed "to
be industrious, contented, and kind-hearted, and to do some good to someone
and win some love to myself if I could," a vow which points to her
apprehension of not being able, despite her efforts, to "win some love to
[her]self." As Alex Zwerdling suggests, despite her self-deprecation, and in
keeping with her strength in this scene, Esther really thinks too well of herself
to like the idea of Guppy as an acceptable suitor (434).

The next chapter of Esther's narrative after the "proposal scene" details her
sense of persecution by Guppy. The Jarndyce household has moved to
London. At night, they often go to the theater where, Esther claims, Guppy
continually stares at her, rather than at the performance. But Esther never
mentions it to Ada, Richard, or Jarndyce; they, in fact, seem to be unaware
of his persistent attention. As Esther presents no corroboration of Guppy's
"haunting" of her, it is impossible to gauge the reliability of her account. But
I would note that Guppy appears in Esther's narrative only at moments
concerned with marriage suits (both his own, and Jarndyce's and Allan's), and
it is perhaps no coincidence that he seems ubiquitous to Esther only in the
same chapter in which she obliquely introduces Allan Woodcourt.

Esther rarely presents Allan Woodcourt directly in her narrative. Rather,
she either conspicuously omits mentioning him; includes him only in his
professional capacity; or relegates him to the final paragraph of a chapter,
including what she has to say about him almost as an afterthought, and
without naming him. When Allan is present, he is (like Ada) made into an
idealized figure, who is silenced and only very rarely permitted to speak
directly. Psychological critics have noted Esther's inability, or refusal, to
include Allan in her narrative and have attributed it primarily to her anxious
concern about successfully securing him as her husband.[12] But this view fails
to explain why Esther is so palpably flustered in the "now" of writing, seven
years after she *has* married Allan. Esther was undoubtedly aware of the
difficulty of her position with regard to Allan at the time, not only because she
is illegitimate but because she is portionless as well: though "pedigree" is
what concerns Allan's mother, Esther reports that Allan's decision to leave for
the East as a ship's surgeon is pecuniary. Nevertheless, since she writes as
"the doctor's wife" her syntactic "dis-ease" becomes harder to comprehend.
It would seem that what troubles Esther has as much to do with her

ambivalence about marriage and power relations both then and in the "now" of writing, as it does with her uncertainty at the time.

Esther first obliquely mentions Allan when she notes at the end of Chapter XII that "a young surgeon" was present when the Jarndyce household dined with the Badgers. Then Miss Flite, who though negatively associated with Richard, is positively associated with Allan, introduces him as "My physician, Mr. Woodcourt" (178). At the very end of the chapter Esther finally, if uneasily, manages to put two and two together, though she then censors what appears to have been a reference by Ada to herself and Allan:

> I have forgotten to mention—at least I have not mentioned—that Mr. Woodcourt was the same dark young surgeon whom we had met at Mr. Badger's. Or, that Mr. Jarndyce invited him to dinner that day. Or, that he came. Or, that when they were all gone, and I said to Ada, "Now, my darling, let us have a little talk about Richard!" Ada laughed and said—
> But, I don't think it matters what my darling said. She was always merry.
>
> (182)

Allan appears only once more in Esther's narrative before her illness, when he comes to say good-bye just before leaving for the East at the end of Chapter XVII.[13] When she attempts to explain why he is leaving, her narrative virtually collapses: the sentences become short and choppy; they are arranged in no particular order; and they are broken by dashes that call attention to her struggle to say what is proper rather than what she really thinks. She mentions Allan's reasons for going, describes his mother, notes his thanks to John Jarndyce for his "hospitality," but never permits him to speak directly in her narrative or say anything to her in particular, because, finally, the passage is not so much about Allan, as it is about Esther's distress at his leaving on "his long, long voyage!" Allan, too, acts by indirection, leaving flowers behind for Esther at Miss Flite's; and Esther suggests that if she cannot own her own feelings, neither can he, since he did not simply give her the nosegay himself. Thus, much of Esther's narrative anxiety with regard to Allan derives not so much from her apprehension that something will prevent their marrying, as from the difficulty each of them has negotiating their relationship, a difficulty which is crucial after Allan's return from India, and which, as the abrupt termination of her narrative suggests, still concerns Esther as she writes.

As I have argued, Esther's presentation of John Jarndyce in her narrative suggests both an element of coercion in his benevolent paternalism, especially with regard to Richard and herself, and a taint of self-interest in his selflessness and in the nature of his philanthropic pursuits. In keeping with this oblique drift, though Esther often mentions how grateful she is to Jarndyce for all he has done for her, the distortions of her text reveal she is nevertheless aware of Jarndyce's less than disinterested motives and her own crucial relationship to, and influence on, him. In her first meeting with him after her illness, Jarndyce almost immediately broaches the subject uppermost in his mind after her health—Richard's spurning of him and his turning toward Chancery. For Esther, Richard expresses what she represses about Jarndyce's benevolent paternalism; and her juxtaposition of her reunion with Jarndyce with his detailing of Richard's implicit transgressions again marks the inverse parallel of their relationships to that coercion.

Soon after this Richard comes to see her at Boythorn's to air his side of the story. The major issue for Richard is "accountability," which, for him, involves someone "in charge," to whom one is "liable to be called to account. (*Shorter Oxford English Dictionary*). And, it is precisely the necessity of accounting for himself to Jarndyce that comprises the burden of Richard's complaint: "on that subject I am anxious to be understood. By you, mind—you, my dear! I am not accountable to Mr. Jarndyce, or Mr. Anybody" (458). Indeed, Richard's talks with Esther at Boythorn's reveal more clearly than before that his interest in Chancery has, in large part, been stimulated by his interest in separating himself from any "accountability" to John Jarndyce. Ironically, he's also using Chancery as a means of proving something, though it is not really clear what, to that same John Jarndyce.[14]

In addition, the close association of Richard with Skimpole at this juncture is no coincidence. Just as Skimpole has been a shadow figure for Jarndyce, so now he becomes a shadow figure for Richard, whose need of a surrogate to give play to his fantasies of irresponsibility and ease is now as great as Jarndyce's. The shift both suggests Richard's need of a fantasy self and slyly compares Richard and the object of his vehemence, implying that at least part of what makes Richard so angry about Jarndyce is that Jarndyce gets away with precisely what he takes Richard to task for: that Jarndyce is able to foster his fantasy of ease and irresponsibility (embodied in Skimpole), while Richard is condemned for his.

The interchanges between Richard and Esther at Boythorn's are revealing in relation to Esther as well. Ostensibly Richard comes to see Esther to vindicate himself. Yet it is Esther who twice introduces the topic of Jarndyce and Richard's relation to him, as well as the topic of Chancery, as if she were prodding him. Indeed, the construction of their conversations suggests both that Esther pushes Richard in a particular direction, and that Esther's stake in their interaction, although assumedly in defending Jarndyce, lies in her own need to work out a defense of Jarndyce. Thus, once again, Esther does not really hear Richard, and his remarking that Esther has her "prepossessions" becomes a double-edged perception. Though Richard means to suggest that Esther has a predilection or bias in favor of Jarndyce as opposed to himself, the expression also points to Esther's own sense in relation to Jarndyce of being "possessed or preoccupied beforehand to the exclusion of later thoughts or feelings." (*Webster's New Universal Unabridged Dictionary*).

Esther's presentation of the scene in Chapter XLIV which is the prelude to Jarndyce's proposal of marriage again underscores the "conspiracy" of benevolence, coercion, self-interest and love that motivates Jarndyce, as it takes advantage of Esther's own feelings of gratitude, and filial love. In it she describes Sir Leicester Dedlock's visit to the Jarndyce household in town, which precipitates her confession to Jarndyce of who her mother and godmother are. Sir Leicester's visit comes at a time when, having returned from her convalescence at Boythorn's after her illness, Esther has again begun to settle into her daily routine, but with the new knowledge of who her mother is and what she looks like now that she has taken stock of her "disfigurement" (both of which, her narrative indicates, weigh heavily on her mind).

Esther constructs her presentation of Jarndyce's proposal of marriage to suggest that though she "believed" she "had never loved him so dearly, never thanked him in [her] heart so fully" (534), the proposal comes at a moment which takes unfair advantage of her excess of "gratitude" as a goad to the desired answer. As Jarndyce offers to help her to the best of his abilities to protect Lady Dedlock, Esther says:

> I thanked him with my whole heart. *What could I ever do but thank him*! I was going out at the door, when he asked me to stay a moment. Quickly turning around, I saw that same expression on his face again; and all at once, I don't know how, it flashed upon me as a new and far off possibility that I understood it.
>
> (535, emphasis added).

The answer to Esther's rhetorical question, an exclamation of desperation she does not even punctuate with a question mark, is provided by the remainder of the paragraph: the only way to get out from under her almost overwhelming sense of gratitude and obligation is to marry him. Indeed, when Jarndyce asks permission to write to her, Esther's double-edged response, "how could I object to your writing anything for me to read" (535) points to the lack of latitude she has in relation to him. Jarndyce then lets Esther know that she has had an influence on him ever since he first saw her in the coach on the way to Greenleaf School, and urges her "to remember now, that nothing can change me as you know me" (536). Esther's inclusion of Jarndyce's generous assurance that regardless of her answer he will not change suggests he is aware on some level that his proposal is liable to pressure Esther, but then pushes further to question why he goes ahead with it if he suspects she may feel pressured. But Esther's hesitancies are included only obliquely; her direct response to Jarndyce encourages him. Yet upon receipt of the letter, Esther does not immediately read it. Instead, she shows herself mentally preparing for its contents by going over in her mind yet again the benefits she has reaped from her association with Jarndyce.

Esther's presentation of the letter is carefully censored and controlled. She does not include it in her narrative; rather, she offers her audience her "interpretation" of what Jarndyce says in it. She claims that the "purport" of the letter was to ask "would [she] be the mistress of Bleak House?" (537). The term "mistress," like "guardian," "ward," "suitor," and other legalistic terms made to do double duty in Bleak House in a personalized capacity, means, quite literally, "a woman who rules others or has control, authority, or power over something; specifically, a woman who is head of a household or institution" (*Webster's*). Esther already is, in effect, the mistress of Bleak House, and whether Jarndyce simply wants to formalize Esther's claim to that title, or asks her in language more direct than she records to be his wife, is not clear. But as Esther assesses it, Jarndyce's proposal "was not a love letter." Underneath the love she claims it expresses, Jarndyce makes two major rational rather than amorous arguments for her accepting his proposal. The first is that once Esther had told him the "secret" of her birth:

> he had considered this step [of proposing] anew . . . and had decided on taking it; if it only served to show me, through one poor instance, that the whole world would really unite to falsify the stern prediction of my childhood.
>
> (537)

The second is that looking ahead, he foresees the time when Ada, coming of age, will leave Bleak House, and "our present mode of life must be broken up" since should Ada leave, Esther, as her companion, would have no ostensible reason for remaining at Bleak House. Thus Jarndyce desires, according to Esther, to continue to be her "Guardian" and to have her "become the dear companion of his remaining life" (537). What is not clear is whether the rhetoric of care and protection, and the absence of more precise terms, such as "wife," is Jarndyce's omission or Esther's editorializing.

Esther claims she was "often blinded" by the letter's "love," "unselfish caution," and "consideration" for her. Though ostensibly she means that she could read no further at times because her eyes were "blinded" by tears, the phrase can also mean that Jarndyce's professions of "love," "consideration," etc., blinded her to the full import of what he is saying. Esther's narrative favors this second reading and redirects her readers' attention to Jarndyce's rationalized reasons for proposing. She then points to what Jarndyce did not say but which was implicitly present:

> But he did not hint to me, that when I had been better looking, he had had this same proceeding in his thoughts, and had refrained from it. That when my old face was gone from me, and I had no attractions, he could love me just as well as in my fairer days. That the discovery of my birth gave him no shock. That his generosity rose above my disfigurement, and my inheritance of shame. That the more I stood in need of such fidelity, the more firmly I must trust in him to the last.
> But I knew it, I knew it well now. It came upon me as the close of the benigant history I had been pursuing, and I felt that I had but one thing to do. To devote my life to his happiness was to thank him poorly, and what had I wished for only the other night but some new means of thanking him?
>
> (538)

Thus, as many critics have noted, Esther moves to accept Jarndyce's proposal because of her sense of obligation to him. But what those critics do not mention is that, as Esther presents it, Jarndyce chooses not simply the moment when Esther feels most grateful and obligated to him, but the moment of her greatest sense of her own vulnerability, when she is most likely to say yes because of her awareness of the attenuation of her circumstances and possibilities, her lack of resources for independence and strength. Thus Jarndyce's proposal brings up for Esther not simply the disadvantages of her illegitimacy and loss of looks, but the difficulty of her position as a dependent, particularly with regard to her continuing in his household without any "official" status.

Nevertheless, Esther decides to accept Jarndyce's proposal, despite the fact that she "cried very much . . . as if something for which there was no name or distinct idea were definitely lost" to her, and despite telling herself that she is "happy for life," as if it were a prison sentence rather than a marriage to which she has agreed. To do away with any traces of former aspirations, Esther decides to burn the flowers Allan left for her when he went away. Though clearly Esther means to symbolize her relinquishing of any hope of a romantic passion, her presentation of "the letter" scene as a whole suggests not so much that it is her insecurities which lead her to let go of that hope as Jarndyce's skillful playing/preying upon her vulnerability which garners the desired resolution to his proposal. Though Esther accepts Jarndyce's proposal, she does not tell Ada, or any one else, for quite some time. In the meantime, she sets out with Charley for Deal to see Richard, and it is again no coincidence that just as she is more pressured than ever by her circumstances, so too is Richard, who is about to quit the army under duress and "devote" himself to his Chancery interests. Just as Esther does not have the resources to resist Jarndyce's proposal, Richard does not have the resources to resist getting more embroiled in Chancery, or in his resentment for Jarndyce, with whom he continues to be as obsessed as he is with *Jarndyce and Jarndyce.*

Esther's eagerness to go to Deal probably has less to do with Richard, than with the "large Indiaman just come home" (544) she and Charley discover in the harbor upon their arrival. Whether or not Esther knew Allan's ship was due, meeting Allan at Deal gives her the opportunity to see him alone. Unlike Guppy's response to her "new face," which she includes verbatim to further deflate him, Allan's reaction is, as is Esther's pattern with volatile issues, almost entirely suppressed. Instead, we have Esther's version of his response, and her interpretation of their interaction. As she considers contacting him, she notes her own ambivalence, "I untied my bonnet, and put my veil half up—I think I mean half down, but it matters very little—" (549), and hints that she is not quite sure what Allan thought, or even, perhaps, thinks.

To defuse the tension of narrating her encounter with Allan, Esther shifts her focus away from Allan and herself to Allan and Richard. But given the symbolic connection between herself and Richard, her shift in focus can be construed as more apparent than real, and in the conversation that ensues regarding Richard, they might just as well be talking about Esther:

> "Do you think him so changed?"
>   "He is changed," he returned, shaking his head.
>   I felt the blood rush into my face for the first time, but it was only an instantaneous emotion. I turned my head aside, and it was gone.
>
>   (550)

Why Esther should blush because Allan has noticed a change in Richard is not clear; but if Allan's response is read as referring to Esther, it is immediately comprehensible. As Allan promises to befriend Richard, Esther thanks him, her "eyes filling fast; but I thought they might when it was not for myself" (550). Though ostensibly the tears Esther is about to shed are for Allan's anticipated generosity toward Richard despite the fact that he has "changed," they are also for herself, who, too, has "changed." Esther concludes:

> And in his last look as we drove away, I saw that he was very sorry for me. I was glad to see it. I felt for my old self as the dead may feel if they ever revisit these scenes. I was glad to be tenderly remembered, to be gently pitied, not to be quite forgotten.
>
> (551)

As Esther plays with a doubly retrospective perspective, writing now that she felt then about her "old self as the dead may feel if they ever revisit," she struggles to name what she read as Allan's feelings with regard to her. Yet what she claims he felt is both ambiguous and projective, a refusal to look at what was really going on either then or now as she writes.

Soon after this Jarndyce broaches the subject of a kind of philanthropic endeavor whereby Woodcourt would be set up to be "Rich enough to have his own happy home, and his own household gods—and household goddess, too, perhaps" (605). As Jarndyce goes on to say to Esther:

> "Do you know I have fancied that he sometimes feels some particular disappointment, or misfortune, encountered in [the old world]. You never heard anything of that sort?"
> I shook my head.
>
> (605)

Esther here ignores Jarndyce's offer of an opportunity to speak about what's on her mind, though he may well have suspected it, and may even have been in Woodcourt's confidence regarding Esther by this time.[15]

The next chapter reveals Ada's secret marriage and Esther's almost traumatized response. Yet, after she returns to the lodging she will now occupy alone with Jarndyce, Esther renews her promise to him. She distances what she says, first by referring to herself as Bleak House's "mistress," and then in the third person, as "she." She then notes that Jarndyce looks at her with "his old bright fatherly look," and concludes:

> I was sorry presently that this was all we said about [Bleak House's thinning fast]. I was rather disappointed. I feared I might not quite have been all I had meant to be, since the letter and the answer.
>
> (616)

The passage points to Esther's guilt; yet, like so much else she says, it can be turned around to suggest that Esther here obliquely blames the "fatherly"

Jarndyce either for not being lover-like enough, or, conversely, for presuming to shift from the "fatherly" place she prefers him in to that of lover.

Indeed, not long after this Esther uses Skimpole's "autobiography" obliquely to condemn Jarndyce's lack of consideration for the difficulty of her position:

> I never read more of [Skimpole's "Life"] myself than the sentence on which I *chanced* to light on opening the book. It was this. "Jarndyce, in common with most other men I have known, is the Incarnation of Selfishness."
>
> (729, emphasis added)

Although Esther's tone implies that she "never read more" because she finds Skimpole's version of Jarndyce outrageous, the very inclusion of it in her narrative works as a covert acknowledgment of her sense of Jarndyce's selfishness. And the juxtaposition of it with her presentation of Allan's proposal, and her necessary rejection of it, works to confirm the sense that Esther has reason enough to endorse Skimpole's point of view.

When Allan proposes, Esther, for once, does not suppress his speech but permits him to speak directly, not simply because it is complimentary to herself, but because what he says is revealing both about him and his love for Esther, and in considering how that love affects her. Most significantly, Allan tells her:

> "Heaven knows, beloved of my life, . . . that my praise is not a lover's praise, but the truth. You do not know what all around you see in Esther Summerson, how many hearts she touches and awakens, what sacred admiration and what love she wins . . . Dear Esther, let me only tell you that the fond idea of you which I took abroad, was exalted to the heavens when I came home."
>
> (731)

Allan literally says that though he liked her well enough before he went away, what really clinches his desire for her is his vision of her "newly risen from a sick bed, yet so inspired by sweet consideration for others, and so free from a selfish thought . . . that [his] fond idea of her was exalted to the Heavens." Esther immediately perceives the implications of what Allan is saying, and although she says nothing to him at the time, in her narrative she remarks, "Something *seemed to pass into my place* that was like the Angel he thought me" (731–732, emphasis added). Esther here points to Allan's limiting version of her and the way it displaces her "self" in favor of an ideal she will have to constrain that self to fulfill. In fact, Esther has already had the "ungrateful" thought, which, of course, she does not communicate to Allan, though she includes it in her narrative, that it is because he has taken so long to make up his mind that she is no longer "free."

Esther then takes the opportunity of Woodcourt's mentioning the "sacred trust" of the new duties Jarndyce has arranged for him to revert to a former sacred trust between them: " 'Ah! Richard!' I exclaimed involuntarily, 'what will he do when you are gone?' " (732). The vehemence and inadvertancy of the remark, as well as the narrative analogue of Esther and Richard, point to its self-referentiality, though Esther says nothing directly of her own loss. Instead, and if Allan can "hear" between the lines, Esther lets him know that she is engaged to John Jarndyce, and that she feels constrained by her almost overwhelming obligations to him:

> "From my childhood I have been, . . . the object of the untiring goodness of the best of human beings; to whom I am so bound by every tie of attachment, gratitude, and love, that nothing I could do in the compass of a life could express the feelings of a single day."
>
> (733)

Oddly enough, as we know, Jarndyce has been in Allan's confidence for some time, yet Allan here registers no surprise at discovering that he has not been in Jarndyce's confidence regarding Esther. Rather, like a dutiful son, he withdraws in favor of "the Father."

Esther's subsequent actions suggest that Allan's proposal has unsettled her because she has to work so hard to present herself as settled. As she slyly has Mrs. Woodcourt (who must know that her son had proposed to Esther only the evening before) note about her, quoting from the Mewlinwillinwodd, she is "like a mountain" (734). But at the same time, Esther shows she is *making* herself steadfast by forcing the marriage issue with Jarndyce to suppress her doubts. What follows is a rather cagey exchange between Esther and Jarndyce during which Esther has to prompt Jarndyce at every turn to set a date for their wedding. Once they agree, Jarndyce says:

> "The day on which I take the happiest and best step of my life—the day on which I shall be a man more exulting and more enviable than any other man in the world—the day on which I give Bleak House its little mistress—shall be next month, then."
>
> (735)

Though Esther can not have known it at the time, she does know retrospectively that Jarndyce has already made up his mind at this point to "give" her to Allan, as her emphasis on his fatherly and "protecting manner" indicates; and the passage obliquely condemns Jarndyce's methods by pointing to his unnecessary and tormenting prolongation of her ignorance.

Meanwhile, Jarndyce goes off to Yorkshire and soon writes to Esther to join him. Once she arrives, he reveals the household arrangements he has made for Woodcourt. Though Esther, of course, knows retrospectively that the arrangements are for herself as well, she reports, faithful to what she felt at the time:

> I am bound to confess that I cried; but I hope it was with pleasure, though I am not quite sure it was with pleasure. I repeated every word of the letter twice over.
>
> (750)

Esther here again points to the torment of Jarndyce's proceedings, which in effect, rub her nose in his power to control both her "fate" and Allan's. Yet rather than say anything about what she really wants, Esther once more buttresses her resolve by repeating "the letter."

The scene that ensues is crucial to an understanding both of why Esther writes her narrative, and the tenor of what she embeds in it. As with Allan's proposal, Esther includes what Jarndyce says verbatim and without comment in her narrative. First of all, Jarndyce admits that he had his own happiness "too much in view" in proposing to Esther. He then obliquely admits both that he had had the "old dream" of making Esther his wife one day since she was "very young," and that he might not have "renewed" it if it had not been for the illness which, he implies, made her less marriagable than ever. Jarndyce then lets on to what he has been up to, but as Esther gives way to tears, he further fuels her covert resentment by confessing that he has fully comprehended both the triangular situation in which he, Esther, and Allan have been embroiled, and his solution "for months and months" while allowing her to labor under the illusion that their own marriage was to proceed as planned. Finally, Jarndyce admits he knew Woodcourt was going to propose, and that he let him do so without telling him Esther was betrothed to himself, as if (since Allan was to report back to him) he wanted to see what Esther would do, i.e., "sacrifice her love [for Allan] to a sense of duty and affection" as he puts it to Mrs. Woodcourt, or try to break the engagement. Apparently, by remaining steadfast, Esther passes some sort of test which allows Jarndyce to bow out and initiate the final transitional stage whereby Bleak House II is established and the rightful husband appears. As Jarndyce himself puts it:

"these surprises were *my great reward*, and I was too miserly to part with a
scrap of it. . . . This day *I give* this house its little mistress; and before God,
it is the brightest day in all my life!
  "Allan . . . *take from me a willing gift*, the best wife that ever a man had."
                                                                    (753, emphasis added)

Thus, though Esther says nothing throughout this whole long scene, her
unmediated presentation of Jarndyce's very Jarndycean actions condemns him
for proceeding as if her obligation to him gives him the proprietary right to
dispose of her when and how he pleases without the proper regard for her, or
how his powerful position might affect her.

The implications of all that has transpired are almost more than Esther can
bear, and she shifts her attention to Mr. Guppy, who awaits her return to
London to renew his proposal of marriage. The return of Guppy in her
narrative is both jarring and unexpected; yet it is symbolically right if Guppy
is a scapegoat figure for Esther's dis-ease about suitors and the necessity of
participating in the barter and exchange of the marriage market. Esther uses
her extended comic presentation of Guppy's second proposal to de-fuse the
tension of, and deflect attention from, the highly problematic scene that she
has only just turned away from.

It is, perhaps, not merely a function of the closing down of Esther's
narrative and of the novel as a whole, but symbolically appropriate that,
immediately after Esther's presentation of the scene in which Jarndyce
"gives" her to Allan, and its parodic counterpart, Guppy's second proposal in
the company of his mother and Tony Jobling, Esther turns to the dissolution
of *Jarndyce and Jarndyce* and the death of Richard. Quite apart from Esther's
stake in Richard, the end of *Jarndyce and Jarndyce* figures the end of
Richard's outlet for his resentment, impotence, and rage, and the loss of his
means for coping with the world. At the same time, the killing off of Richard
is simply the easiest and neatest resolution to a highly problematic and
disturbingly open-ended situation. But from Esther's point of view, Richard,
as a surrogate for her, dies a heroine's death, enacting, and thereby exorcizing
for Esther, one of the two less desirable female scripts, death or remaining
daughter-like in the father's house (which Ada, who moves back to Bleak
House with her child and calls Jarndyce Guardian, fulfills). Yet as Nancy K.
Miller suggests, the death of a heroine may be positively inflected when read
as the heroine's refusal to participate as an object in a sex-gender system of
barter and exchange (36–48). While Esther has just presented herself as
buying into the system by letting Jarndyce, the father-surrogate, give her as

a "gift" to Allan, the son, in keeping with the maintenance of the patriarchal status quo, she uses Richard, as her surrogate who acts out her resentment of Jarndyce's benevolent paternalism, to express her desire to be outside or beyond the reach of patriarchal power by dying, rather than remaining at the mercy of Jarndyce's coercive benevolence. Thus, from Esther's perspective Richard can afford to forgive Jarndyce because he at the same time escapes his influence, whereas Esther, as "gift" and as "doctor's wife," is fully implicated in the marketplace of patriarchal power relations, the conundrum which engenders the writing of her narrative.

Esther now has everything a traditional heroine could want: husband, house, father; is indeed named, placed, and praised as "the doctor's wife." Yet the paradox for Esther is that "she owe[s] it all to him": Allan has simply replaced Jarndyce. Ultimately, then, Esther's narrative is an allegory of the cost and benefits of the daughter's placing of herself in patriarchy. As Esther must be aware as she writes, terminating her narrative with a radically suspended speculation, acceding to male definitions of female goodness, fulfilling gender expectations by becoming "the doctor's wife," fuels female dis-ease yet garners her a certain kind of power from within patriarchy. The work of narrative recuperation is limited, finally, because Esther, working from within the system, must [re]-construct herself out of the very materials which constrain and oppress her. Like all survivors, she is both a victim of structure and circumstance, and a consummate strategist of their manipulation.

NOTES

1. See M.M. Bakhtin, *The Dialogic Imagination*, trans. Caryl Emerson and Michael Holquist, ed. Michael Holquist (Austin: University of Texas Press, 1981), especially "Discourse in the Novel," pp. 259–422. For Bakhtin, the polyphony, or "heteroglossia—" the presence of many "voices"—in the text cannot be reduced to the voice of the author but speaks beyond or around his or her overt intentions.

2. As Wayne Booth puts it in his discussion of Bakhtin in "Freedom of Interpretation: Bakhtin and the Challenge of Feminist Criticism," *Critical Inquiry* 9, #1 (1982), p. 52, "People—and this includes people who inhabit fictions—are essentially, irreducibly subjects,' voices rich beyond anyone's uses, performing in a chorus too grand for any participant's full comprehension."

3. See Diane Sadoff, *Monsters of Affection: Dickens, Eliot, and Brontë on Fatherhood* (Baltimore: The Johns Hopkins University Press, 1982), p. 59 for a further discussion of this notion.

4. Esther's narrative strategies include implicit comparison and contrast through juxtaposing the words or actions of another character with her own; swerving to

avoid narrating something disturbing to her, or to avoid confronting the implications of what she has just narrated; controlling her presentation of character by including their remarks verbatim, or suppressing their direct utterance and re-constructing their dialogue herself; and using the other characters in her narrative to speak for her. See my paper, "Autobiography by Default: Story-Making and Strategy in Esther's Narrative," International Conference on Narrative Literature, Ann Arbor and Ypsilanti, Michigan, April 3, 1987 for a fuller discussion of these strategies.

5. See Nancy K. Miller, *The Heroine's Text* (New York: Columbia University Press, 1980) 1–15. She focuses on eighteenth- and nineteenth-century heroine-centered novels by male authors.

6. A Freudian might argue that Esther's fiction of the perfect father, like that of many incest victims, not only helps the father escape condemnation by denying his desire, but points away from her own latent desire.

7. See R.M. Goldfarb, "John Jarndyce of Bleak House," *Studies in the Novel*, 12 (Summer 1980), pp. 144–152 for further discussion of Jarndyce's less attractive qualities.

8. See William Axton, "Esther's Nicknames: A Study in Relevance," *Dickensian*, 62 (1966), pp. 158–163; and Alex Zwerdling, "Esther Summerson Rehabilitated," *PMLA*, 88 (1973), pp. 429–439.

9. This notion of Richard as obsolete associates him with the Other Narrator's presentation of a large spectrum of male characters from Sir Leicester Dedlock, who, it is implied, is superfluous, and Mr. George, who gives up his Shooting Gallery to become companion to Sir Leicester at the novel's end, to those characters, Mr. Rouncewell, Small, Guppy, etc. who figure the ways and means of the present and future.

10. When Ada, Esther and Richard first meet in the Lord Chancellor's chambers, Esther records in her narrative a slip which suggests that she, at least, can imagine a "plan" by which it is she who is designated by John Jarndyce as Richard's future wife:

> "Mr. Jarndyce of Bleak House, my lord," Mr. Kenge observed in a low voice, "if I may venture to remind your Lordship, provides a suitable companion for—"
> "For Mr. Richard Carstone?" I thought (but I am not quite sure I heard his lordship say, in an equally low voice, and with a smile).
> "For Miss Ada Clare. This is the young lady. Miss Summerson."
> (31–32)

11. D.A. Miller in "Discipline in Different Voices: Bureaucracy, Police, Family, and *Bleak House* (*Representations* I, 1983) discusses the same passage. Miller argues that Richard's "aimlessness internalizes the procedural protractions of the court." But he then goes on to note that George Brimley, one of the first reviewers of *Bleak House* (*Spectator*, September 24, 1853) inflects the passage differently: "Richard 'is not made reckless and unsteady by his interest in the great suit, but simply expends his recklessness and unsteadiness on it, as he would on something else if it were non-existent.'" As Miller then points out, both readings are made possible by the text itself. In the full quote Jarndyce says that Chancery "has engendered or confirmed in him a habit of putting off—" Miller concludes: "Jarndyce kind-heartedly proposes the sociological key to Richard's character in

the same breath as he admits its insufficiency. And what is at stake in his hesitation between 'engendered' and 'confirmed,' between the court as cause and the court as occasion, goes beyond the double view or Richard. Ultimately, the text oscillates between two seemingly incompatible sets of assumptions about the nature of Chancery's power—one deriving from the perception of total domination, the other still attached to the topic of the carceral." (62–63).

12. Zwerdling, pp. 429–439; Valerie Kennedy, "*Bleak House*: More Trouble with Esther?" *Journal of Women's Studies in Literature* I, #4 (Autumn 1979), pp. 330–347.

13. Kennedy, p.339 convincingly argues that Esther obliquely alludes to Allan earlier in this same chapter.

14. See e.g., "Esther . . . you are not to suppose that I have come here to make under-handed charges against John Jarndyce. I have only come to justify myself. What I say is, it was all very well, and we got on very well while I was a boy, utterly regardless of this same suit; but as soon as I began to take an interest in it, and to look into it, then it was quite another thing. Then John Jarndyce discovers that Ada and I must break off, and that if I don't amend that very objectionable course, I am not fit for her. Now, Esther, I don't mean to amend that very objectionable course: I will not hold John Jarndyce's favor on those unfair terms of compromise, which he has no right to dictate. Whether it pleases him, or displeases him, I must maintain my rights and Ada's. I have been thinking about it a good deal, and this is the conclusion I have come to" (463).

15. c.f. p.752, when, as Jarndyce "gives" Esther to Allan he tells her, "I have long been in Allan Woodcourt's confidence, although he was not, until yesterday . . . in mine."

WORKS CITED

Axton, William. "Esther's Nicknames: A Study in Relevance," *Dickensian* 62 (1966): 158–63.

Dickens, Charles. *Bleak House*. Eds. George Ford and Sylvère Monod, New York: W.W. Norton, 1977.

Goldfarb, R.M. "John Jarndyce of Bleak House," *Studies in the Novel* 12 (Summer 1980), 144–152.

Gottfried, Barbara. "Autobiography by Default: Story-Making and Strategy in Esther's Narrative," International Conference on Narrative Literature, Ann Arbor & Ypsilanti, Michigan, April 2–4, 1987.

Kennedy, Valerie. "*Bleak House*: More Trouble with Esther?" *Journal of Women's Studies in Literature* I, #4 (Autumn, 1979): 330–47.

Miller, D.A. "Discipline in Different Voices: Bureaucracy, Police, Family, and *Bleak House*," *Representations* I, (1983): 59–89.

Miller, Nancy. "Emphasis Added: Plots and Plausibilities in Women's Fiction," *PMLA* 96, #1 (January, 1981): 36–48.

Miller, Nancy. *The Heroine's Text*. NY: Columbia UP, 1980, 1–15.

Oxford English Dictionary. 1973 edition.

Sadoff, Diane. *Monsters of Affection: Dickens, Eliot,* and *Brontë on Fatherhood.* Baltimore: The Johns Hopkins UP, 1982.

Shorter Oxford English Dictionary. 1973 edition.

Stoehr, Taylor. *Charles Dickens: The Dreamer's Stance*. Ithaca: Cornell UP, 1965.

Webster's New Universal Unabridged Dictionary. 2nd ed., 1983.

Zwerdling, Alex. "Esther Summerson Rehabilitated," *PMLA* 88 (May, 1973): 429–439.

The Monstrous Actress: Esther Summerson's Spectral Name

Chiara Briganti

It is now generally agreed that Esther is not what Lewes in an early review called "a monstrous failure" (Ford and Lane 61). Alex Zwerdling, in a 1973 essay, was one of the first to rehabilitate her from the accusations of inconsistency and tiresome coyness. He described Dickens' attitude as "essentially clinical," and Esther as "one of the triumphs of [his] art, a subtle psychological portrait clear in its outlines and convincing in its details" (429). Since then Esther has been the subject of a host of psychoanalytic studies, which, however, have produced the questionable results of reducing the novel to a clinical study of neurosis. Zwerdling himself sees *Bleak House* as a study of "the effect of a certain kind of adult violence on the mind of a child" (429). Thus, his reading is the first of a series of traditional psychoanalytic readings of Esther's hallucinatory moments which must fail because they attempt to interpret what these episodes mean rather than *how* they mean, or—more to the point—how they escape signification.[1] These interpretations are all based on the notion of the unconscious as the repository of a seething content which can be sorted out. They all try to find a meaning and often only succeed in killing the literariness of the novel.

The Lacanian approach I propose is more fruitful than a traditional psychoanalytic reading for it is based on the assumption that "the unconscious is not 'within' the subject; it is the third position through which the sender is provided with a receiver . . . all messages, articulated or not, involve us in a dialogue mediated by the code (the unconscious)" (Lacan, *Speech and Language* 264). I believe with Peter Brooks that "[it] is rather the superimposition of the model of functioning of the mental apparatus on the functioning of the text that offers the possibility of a psychoanalytic criticism" ("Freud's Masterplot," 299–300). Therefore, my intention is not to attempt a case study of Esther, but rather to come to terms with Dickens' method of narration from the perspective of text analysis rather than psychocriticism.[2] This will be done by addressing the text as a signifying structure informed by the unconscious, by seeing it not as the product of an individual's imagination but rather as the result of an intersubjective process, and by exploring the ways in which Esther's narrative is inscribed in the novel as a whole.[3]

1. A COLLABORATIONIST'S NARRATIVE

Once one overcomes a certain annoyance at Esther's constant fencing, and places it against the background of the tradition of female writing, one must recognize the necessity of seeing her rhetorical strategies as part of the woman writer's predicament. A quisling, a collaborationist who is faced with the impossible task of articulating her discourse within the boundaries of a structure which denies her very existence, Esther, the woman writer, fears that she will appear monstrous in the eyes of patriarchy, and is aware that only by being duplicitous, only by ostensibly accepting the boundaries of patriarchal discourse, can she become the subject of her text. Duplicity and evasions provide her with the means to achieve narrative authority. As Barbara Johnson has observed in a discussion of Mary Shelley's *Frankenstein*, "in a humanistic tradition in which *man* is the measure of all things, how does an appendage go about telling the story of her life?" (4). By what strategies does the female Other inscribe herself as desiring subject in patriarchal discourse? As Johnson has said of women and autobiography, "What is being repressed [in female autobiography] is the possibility that a woman can write anything that would *not* exhibit 'the amiableness of domestic affection,' the possibility that for women as well as for men the home can be the very site of the *unheimlich*" (10). The female Other inhabits male discourse and redefines it. But in order to install herself in her writing she must accept the necessity of evasiveness, the only strategy that enables her to refuse conforming to "a female ideal which is largely a fantasy of the masculine . . . imagination" (Johnson 10).

While unbridled anger and flamboyant rhetoric explode in the third person narrative, Esther's language is usually subdued, and her rhetoric is carefully restrained. Judith Wilt has observed how Esther's "proper syntactic shape is the parenthetic sentence" (289). In fact, one could argue that her whole narrative is parenthetic. While ostensibly producing a narrative which, in order not to appear monstrous in the eyes of patriarchy, pays attention to linearity, chronology, genealogy, and causality—those structures which have traditionally supported patriarchy—she accommodates whatever appears too subversive to be incorporated in the third person narrative: madness, suicidal impulses, hysteria, incestuous desire. All these find their way into the symbolic structures which at moments disrupt the linearity of Esther's narrative—pockets of meaning which disturb us because they refuse to be determined. Such episodes as the starry circle, the staircases, the ceremony with the flowers, Hortense's walk, Esther's dreams of confused identity, the vision of faraway London have all been explored from various angles, but no thematic reading can account for them. Paul Eggert "explains" their unexplainability by arguing that "Dickens had committed himself to a psychological study deeper, probably, than he had anticipated and more complex, finally, than he could handle" (81). It is true that as a male writer speaking through the consciousness of a woman, and an illegitimate daughter, Dickens faced an enterprise fraught with risks. However, although lacking the vocabulary which would allow him to articulate his psychological concerns, Dickens succeeded in giving them a haunting fictional form. It is precisely through the way they exceed Dickens' *and* Esther's knowledge that those symbolical structures constructed upon the logic of dreams, which disrupt the narrative and signal moments of deep distress, reveal a subtext of madness, illness, and those deep fears which are denied a hearing in the discourse of the third-person narrator. Such moments of aporia in Esther's narrative, which cannot be explained away by a thematic reading that does not take into account the irrational elements that circulate in the text, become the "reserve of silence" of the novel, that which constitutes its very literariness.

2. FINDING A BEGINNING

The distortion of the pattern of Genesis in the first chapter of the novel figures the difficulty of both creating and finding one's origins. Esther, who posits herself as the first speaking subject in the novel, and through whom temporality emerges, echoes it at the outset of her narrative when she claims, "I have a great deal of difficulty in beginning to write my portion of these pages, for I know I am not clever." Her discourse becomes the acting out of her attempt to begin—to find her own origin as well as to "create" her own narrative, an attempt which is complicated by the burden of guilt inherent in her illegitimate birth and by the subversive nature of writing, and particularly of female writing. It is true that, as Boheemen-Saaf has noticed, "orphanhood, a loss of parents, loss of origin and of identity, not only applies to Esther but also summarizes the thematic and structural concern of *Bleak House*" (226). However, a more radical threat than orphanhood lies for Esther in the impossibility of naming her parents without being tainted by their guilt and without being reduced from textual producer to textual product.

Barbara Johnson has recently stated that "three crucial questions can be seen to stand at the forefront of today's preoccupations: the question of mothering, the question of the woman writer, and the question of autobiography" (2). All three converge in *Bleak House* in the figure of Esther and in her troubled relationship with Lady Dedlock. Esther finds some consolation in her disfiguring illness when she realizes that, having lost her looks, she runs no risk of being identified as her mother's daughter:

> I felt, through all my tumult of emotion, a burst of gratitude to the providence of God that I was so changed as that I never could disgrace her by any trace of likeness; as that nobody could ever now look at me, and look at her, and remotely think of any near tie between us.
>
> (449, XXXVI)

Such unbounded selflessness, however, conceals a complex relationship to the mother as the locus of origin, as it is revealed by Esther's thoroughness in destroying her mother's letter. The scars which disfigure her erase her mother's signature from her body in the same way that Esther destroys Lady Dedlock's letter and burns it to ashes to erase this same signature from her text. Esther's concern reflects a larger concern: in an unauthored world, which is the signature that does not transform the text into a forgery? If orphanhood is related to the "transcendental homelessness" that Lukacs has seen reflected in the novel and to the disappearance of God, aberrant parenthood is related to the question of who is the legitimate parent who can claim authority over children and over the text, indeed to the very question of who is speaking and to whom. Esther, the character who is most directly concerned with illegitimacy, is faced with a dilemma: on the one hand, she adheres to the conception of history as "a tracing of origins;"[4] on the other, she deconstructs it by attempting to write her own story while maintaining the secret about her locus of origin—that is, by devising her own myth of self-creation.

Autobiography shares the claim that every narrative makes "to be in a state of repetition," thus suggesting "a movement from passivity to mastery" and "pursuit by a daemonic power" (Brooks, "Freud's Masterplot" 285–87). However, in addition, autobiography reflects the attempt on the part of the writing subject to enact a myth of self-engendering. Mary Shelley's words of introduction to the 1831 edition of *Frankenstein* reiterate the risks involved in any autobiographical endeavor on the part of women:

> I am very averse to bringing myself forward in print, but as my account will only appear as an appendage to a former production, and as it will be confined to such topics as have connection with my authorship alone, I can scarcely accuse myself of a personal intrusion.
>
> (vii)

Such an act is felt as doubly subversive, for it involves placing woman as both subject of the text and writing subject, therefore not only as textual product but as textual producer as well. Like Mary Shelley, Esther too seems well aware of the necessity to justify oneself, to anticipate the charge of intrusion. Thus she begins her narrative by positing her text as only a portion of a larger text, that is, by positing herself as only supplementary, and by disclaiming her ability to deal with language. And, predictably, she is careful not to present her narrative as autobiography. "It seems so curious to me," she says, "to be obliged to write all this about myself! As if this narrative were the narrative of *my* life! But my little body will soon fall into the background now" (27, III, Dickens' emphasis). Her tale, she claims, is not the story of her life, even if,

> I don't know how it is, I seem to be always writing about myself. I mean all the time to be writing about other people . . . but it is all of no use. I hope any one who may read what I write, will understand that if these pages contain a great deal about me, I can only suppose it must be because I have really something to do with them, and can't be kept out.
>
> (103, IX)

Such caution ostensibly shows how well Esther has assimilated patriarchal discourse. She has, in fact, become its mouthpiece. As Jarndyce's protégée, she endeavors to protect the structure that identifies woman with submission and silence. She endeavors to become the Angel in the House. She has internalized the Victorian ideal of femininity so well that she strives toward self-effacement, toward the reduction of her body to a "little body." Literally and metaphorically a housekeeper, she goes around with her basket of keys, busying herself with other people's lives. She desexualizes herself and makes herself a companion, the third term between Ada and Richard, Caddy and Prince.

Always watchful—for as Esther has admitted, she "had always a rather noticing way"—she watches Ada and Richard's affection grow. And yet, try as she may, she cannot quite comply with the Victorian ideal of woman as submissive, sane, and silent. Her behavior betrays yearnings which contradict that ideal and reaffirm the resilience of the Otherness which she tries to efface. So, in spite of her efforts to present herself simply as Ada's companion, she cannot bear to be excluded from Ada's and Richard's lives, and on their first night together she follows them home and spies on them:

> I so longed to be near her, that I determined to go back in the evening, only to look up at her windows.

> It was foolish, I dare say; but it did not then seem at all so to me, and it does not seem quite so even now . . . I listened for a few moments; and in the musty rotting silence of the house, believed that I could hear the murmur of their young voices. I put my lips to the hearse-like panel of the door, as a kiss for my dear, and came quietly down again, thinking that one of these days I would confess to the visit.
>
> (615, LI)

A careful recorder of events in chronological order, she blatantly violates chronology when it comes to relating events that affect her personally. She is silent about Woodcourt's identity and takes her time to reveal it:

> I have omitted to mention in its place, that there was someone else at the family dinner party. It was not a lady. It was a gentleman. It was a gentleman of a dark complexion—a young surgeon. He was rather reserved, but I thought him very sensible and agreeable. At least, Ada asked me if I did not, and I said yes.
>
> (163, XIV)

She has perfectly assimilated the Victorian ideal of industriousness. However, her busy behavior at times becomes frantic and betrays signs of hysteria: "Still I cried very much," she says, after receiving Jarndyce's marriage proposal, "not only in the fulness of my heart . . . but as if something for which there was no name or distinct idea were indefinitely lost to me. I was very happy, very thankful, very hopeful; but I cried very much" (538, XLIV). And the clinking of her basket of keys acquires a sinister ring: they soon cease to be simply the harmless tool of a Dame Durden, and they remind us of their essential function as instruments of power which can be used to penetrate secrets. In a sense, metonymically, they come to stand for Esther herself, the key to the novel, the figure which can make the novel readable, or can hide its secrets, and thus they make her a surreptitious figure of power.

3. HAUNTED HOUSES, HAUNTED NARRATIVES

Esther makes her first appearance in the third-person narrative in the chapter entitled "The Ghost's Walk." "While Esther sleeps, and while Esther wakes," the impersonal narrator says at the beginning of this chapter, "it is still wet weather down at the place in Lincolnshire" (76, VII). Without attempting to draw a psychogram of the novel, one can nevertheless notice the way in which the two narratives are inscribed into each other and the strategic exclusions they operate. One can notice also how they share an unconscious discourse both at the level of the story and at the level of the system generated by the telling of the story. From this perspective, Esther, asleep, becomes the vehicle for the unconscious of the text. The third-person narrative, locked in the timelessness of dreams, becomes her dream, and her narrative becomes the dream of the third-person narrative, its "censored chapter" (Lacan, *Écrits* 50). As Thomas Hanzo has argued, "The objective narrator . . . is Esther's other voice" (40); however it can be equally argued that Esther is the objective narrator's Other.

As the readers of Esther's tale we all are Coleridgean wedding guests, the desire of Esther's narrative being the desire of the Ancient Mariner. Both have confronted taboos and both are compelled to tell their haunting tale. "Haunting" is perhaps the adjective that best describes the novel. And rightly so, considering that "haunting" is an acceptable translation for the German *unheimlich*. *Bleak House*, the novel in which Dickens most explicitly dwells "upon the romantic side of familiar things," provides perhaps the most forceful treatment in all romantic literature of the *unheimlich*.[5] Esther's return to her original home is a return to the lost object of her desire, to her mother, and her narrative becomes her means of partially gratifying her unsatisfiable desire. Esther, still ignorant of her identity, meets Lady Dedlock during her stay at Boythorn's house. She is quite sure, she claims, that she has never seen this lady's face before in all her life. However, she cannot think why the lady's face should conjure up images of her past and why it should affect her so forcefully. She tries to overcome her "unmeaning weakness" by attending to the sermon. But the words reach her "not in the reader's voice, but in the well-remembered voice of my godmother." She wonders whether the reason for this strange occurrence may lie in a certain resemblance between Miss Barbary and Lady Dedlock, but must finally discount such an explanation for the expression of the two women is so totally different. And yet, in spite of her inability to account for it,

> I, little Esther Summerson, the child who lived a life apart, and on whose birthday there was no rejoicing—seemed to arise before my own eyes, evoked out of the past by some power in this fashionable lady, whom I not only entertained no fancy that I had ever seen, but whom I perfectly well knew I had never seen until that hour.
>
> (225, XVIII)

Lady Dedlock's face is inseparable from the memory of Esther's unhappy childhood, and even her voice affects Esther in a strange way and evokes pictures of herself as a child. Robert Newsom, drawing on Freud's notion of the home as the mother's womb—which in *Bleak House* is figured in Esther's first confrontation with her mother—has observed how all of the novel's houses "have both 'canny' and 'uncanny' qualities in varying degrees, and all of them are haunted" (59). However, houses in this novel function also on a less metaphorical level. Esther starts her narrative journey in a house haunted by the guilt of an illicit relationship; she then becomes the housekeeper of the "delightfully irregular" Bleak House, full of unexplored corners. Then, finally, at the end of *Bleak House*, Esther settles into domestic bliss in a "rustic cottage of doll's rooms" (751), with which Mr. Jarndyce, who by now has come to occupy the place of the father, has surprised her. In the new Bleak House there are no more secret passages. Yet even this perfectly neat doll's house is haunted, and Esther, now a happy doctor's wife and the mother of two children, feels the urgency to abandon it to go back to a grievous past to tell her story.

4. SPECTRAL NAMES

Dickens wrote three first-person narrative novels. While *David Copperfield* and *Great Expectations* are autobiographies proper with a narrator who is admittedly concerned with coming to an understanding of his present self through an understanding of the past, in *Bleak House* only obliquely does Esther speak about herself. Furthermore, the past is not sought for an understanding of the present. On the contrary, Esther attempts to bury it as she buried her doll, so that glimpses of her past life become accessible only in highly charged contexts, hallucinatory moments which occur at times of crisis, when Esther is unable to control her narrative. Male first-person narrators have no qualms about making themselves the center of discourse. Esther, on the other hand, seems determined to remain at the periphery of her narrative. If for Pip and David orphanhood is a reflection of a larger sense of dispossession and carries with it the sense of having usurped their place in the world, Esther, as female narrator, feels that not only is she "filling a place in [Miss Barbary's] house which ought to have been empty," but also feels that she is usurping her space in the narrative. Esther's discourse posits itself from the very start as a "portion," an appendage, thus showing *Bleak House* to be an allegorization of female exclusion from patriarchal discourse.

As Foucault has observed, "discourse is at once the object of the struggle for domination and the means by which the struggle is waged" (Harari 42). Discourse and power are related, since to speak is to possess the power to speak. And the inescapable condition for a successful seizure of power is, still according to Foucault, secrecy. Secrecy is certainly the condition under which Esther operates. It is, in fact, the very origin of her being, for the centerpiece of the novel is Esther's secret name—on the one hand her illegitimate origin, and on the other her true spectral name, the name which, according to Hartman, determines autobiography ("Psychoanalysis: The French Connection" 109).

The significance of names in Dickens' novels is a well-trodden critical ground.[6] Through her names, Esther, from unwanted and psychologically abused child, becomes an old woman, thus reaffirming that tendency, constant in all Victorian fiction, to preserve the secret about girlhood and to present women as gendered but not sexual. She becomes a folklore mother figure and is pointedly excluded from a sexual life. "Dame Durden" in particular, as the name of the heroine of a song about a country woman who employed five men servants who mated with her five maid servants on St. Valentine's Day, marks Esther's position as an outsider, while at the same time casting an ambiguous shadow on her role as observer, and certainly contributing to establish the ground for the dismissal of Esther as a tiresome and at times sinister little woman.

One of the first readers to take exception to the tone of this ambiguous Dame Durden was Charlotte Brontë, who in a letter of 1852 to George Smith observed,

I liked the Chancery part, but when it passes into the autobiographic form, and the young woman who announces that she is not "bright" begins her history, it seems to me too often weak and twaddling; an amiable nature is caricatured, not faithfully rendered, in Miss Esther Summerson.

(Wise and Symington III, 322)

However, in spite of her objections, Charlotte Brontë, who in the preface to *The Professor* had stated that one of her ambitions was to integrate the "wild, wonderful and thrilling" with the "plain and homely," was not immune to the fascination of *Bleak House*, the work in which most explicitly Dickens declares a similar purpose. Jean Blackall has observed how the reading of *Bleak House* exerted a seminal influence on *Villette*, and has pointed out also the similarities in the function of nicknames in both novels.[7] Although Blackall does not comment on Esther's "proper" name, given both Brontë's and Dickens' self-consciousness about names, one cannot dismiss as merely coincidental the fact that Esther is the name of the woman who succeeded to Vashti as wife of King Xerxes. In *Villette*, readers will remember, Vashti is the epitome of untrammeled and destructive desire. Charlotte Brontë herself has reacted strongly to a performance of Vashti by the actress Rachel: "Rachel's acting transfixed me with wonder, enchained me with interest and thrilled me with horror" (The Brontës, 3:290). And Lucy Snowe echoes her ambiguous response: "It was a marvellous sight: a mighty revelation. It was a spectacle low, horrible, immoral" (*Villette* 339). The biblical Vashti was repudiated because she refused to perform before the king's men and officials. Brontë's Vashti, like her namesake, while ostensibly offering herself to the eyes of the public, actually offers yet another version of invisibility. If Lucy is a shadow, Vashti has no definable shape. She is not what Lucy had expected, "something large, sallow," but "chaos—hollow, half-consumed: an orb perished or perishing—half lava, half glow" (339). Like Lucy, she can only be perceived through the role she plays, and, like Lucy, she is one with her performance. The spectacle that Vashti offers is the spectacle of feminine *jouissance*, "that moment of sexuality which is always in excess, something over and above the phallic term which is the mark of phallic sexuality" (Mitchell and Rose 137). When King Xerxes consulted the sages as to what ought to be done to Queen Vashti, Memucan replied that she should be repudiated, for her behavior "will come to the ears of every woman, and they will look down upon their husbands . . . This very day the ladies of Persia and Media who have heard of the Queen's conduct are talking proudly and petulantly enough to all the King's officials!" (The Book of Esther 16–18). So

King Xerxes issued a decree ordering that every man should be master in his own house. Esther, one of the women among whom the new bride was to be chosen, was an orphan who had been adopted by the Jew Mordecai. Faithful to the recommendations of her adoptive father, she maintained the secret about her people and her descent, she respected the King's orders, never went to him unless she was summoned, and asked for nothing except what the King's eunuch advised. So she won King Xerxes' favor and grace and became queen. Even as the King's wife she still complied with Mordecai's orders and kept silent, and thus she eventually succeeded in unveiling Haman's plot and in revenging Mordecai and his people. A writer like Dickens' Esther, she "wrote with full authority." Letters fixing the days of Purim and their date "were sent by her to all the Jews." An obedient wife and daughter, she replaced Vashti's subversive behavior with submission and succeeded through the careful manipulation of secrets in saving her people from slaughter.

Esther's story reveals how not only the nicknames, but also the "proper name" of Dickens' heroine reflects a personality so deeply imbued with the values of patriarchal authority that it literally becomes its voice. As in the Bible, Esther's success stands to reaffirm the necessity of obedience and silence for women, Dickens' Esther's belief in her role, the role of the Old Woman who sweeps the cobwebs off the sky, implicitly underwrites patriarchal power. However, it is in the nature of the nickname to point to its function as a substitute, and if one thinks of Esther's namesake, and of Vashti, the spectral name of which the name Esther is a revision and an erasure, it is not surprising that she would accept a series of nicknames which ostensibly alienate her, but also protect her. Thus, while the numerous nicknames given to Esther testify to the difficulty of defining who she is, they also function as a protective device. They protect Esther from an identity which she must find in order to exist but which also entails accepting a burden of guilt and the subversive power of untrammeled desire. In primitive traditions, "the change of a name sometimes serves to protect [a person] against impending danger; [she] escapes by taking on a different self, whose form makes [her] unrecognizable." Thus, "the name of a [person] laboring under disease or bloodguilt is sometimes changed, on the same principle, that Death may not find him" (Cassirer 52).

While Brontë uses names consistently, in *Bleak House* Dickens seems to use them purposefully in different ways in order to maintain better the secrecy about the implications of Esther's spectral name. Repetition, which informs the novel starting with the very choice of a double narrative, is nowhere as conspicuous as in the proliferation of names. Nowhere else does Dickens provide his characters with so many alternative names, thus making them no more than provisional labels which emphasize the uncertainty of identity already suggested by the uncertainty of paternity. Moreover, while in Brontë's *Villette* names contain "the ontological secret of a thing" (4), in *Bleak House* they deny it (Lady Dedlock's "proper" name is Honoria). However, here as well as in *Villette*, to bear a name means to exist. Esther's gesture of consuming the ashes of her mother's letter is better understood once one realizes that the letter, by conjuring up a time during which for her mother she did not exist and was nameless, poses for her the threat of non-existence. Esther herself so expresses her existential *angst*: "So strangely did I hold my place in this world that, until a short time back, I had never, to my own mother's knowledge, breathed—had been buried—had never been endowed with life—had never borne a name" (452). But the name is also a signature. Esther censors Lady Dedlock's letter: she does not give its content, but only relates the effect it produces on her. Furthermore, by destroying it, she erases her mother's signature, that is, denies her mother's right to sign her narrative.

Esther, as a woman writer struggling to impose her own discourse, becomes a sort of collarborationist as well, for by writing, while impeding other discourses, she also underwrites the discourse of patriarchy. She becomes, in fact, its text, and attempts to occupy a position in it. In order to do so she needs a name, for to bear a name implies of course to belong, to occupy a legitimate place. Miss Barbary is aware of this when she asks John Jarndyce to take charge of Esther, lest she should "be left entirely friendless, nameless, and unknown" (213, XVII). It is better still if the names are many and illustrious. Thus Mrs. Woodcourt expatiates on her Welsh pedigree in order to discourage Esther's matrimonial plans. However, in Esther's case finding one's own name also implies confronting sexual guilt. Thus, like the Biblical Esther, Dickens' Esther must choose a strategy of double-crossing by having her discourse become the locus of all that patriarchy excludes. She must assume and shed names to acquire that fluidity which will undermine the acceptance of patriarchy implied by her role as a writer of a safe narrative. Through such fluidity she can be Dame Durden, the child usurping a place in her godmother's house, but also mad Hortense and the woman who has committed a sexual sin. The connection with Lady Dedlock and Hortense indicates the possibility—an ever present possibility in the nineteenth-century novel—that sexual indulgence, madness, and illness for women may be closely related.

5. THE MADWOMEN

Illness and madness are at the center of *Bleak House*. The lucid madness of Miss Flite and the angry madness of Gridley stand to indict the destructive influence of the Court of Chancery. But a more disquieting example of madness is Hortense's, as exemplified by that which Esther describes as "the most singular [retaliation] I could have imagined" (231, XVIII). A most intriguing scene concludes the chapter of Esther's first confrontation with her mother and of her unknowing first confrontation with sexual guilt. Hortense (and it is telling that most male critics fail to comment on this episode), having been slighted by Lady Dedlock's preference for Rosa, "without the least discomposure of countenance, slipped off her shoes, left them on the ground, and walked deliberately . . . through the wettest of the wet grass" (231, XVIII). Hortense's singular retaliation is indeed unaccountable on any rational ground. The lodge-keeper provides perhaps the best explanation when she notices that the French maid "has as good a head-piece as the best. But she's mortal high and passionate" and "She'd soon walk through [blood] as anything else . . . when her own's up" (231, XVIII). Mademoiselle Hortense's rebellious gesture is perceptibly related to her passionate nature and suggests interesting possibilities once one recalls Jo's confusion about the mysterious identity of the woman who approached him, thus linking together Hortense, Lady Dedlock and Esther: " 'If she ain't the t'other one, she ain't the forrenner. Is there *three* of 'em then?' " (383, XXXI). Hortense's madness, related as it is with passion, casts a shadow on Lady Dedlock. Their two faces have already merged in the mirror, when Lady Dedlock, in the chapter entitled "On the Watch," surprised "a pair of black eyes curiously observing her."

> "Be so good as to attend," says my Lady then, addressing the reflection of Hortense, "to your business. You can contemplate your beauty at another time."
> "Pardon! It was your Ladyship's beauty."
>
> (147, XIII)

Later, threatened by Tulkinghorn, Lady Dedlock abandons her composure in the privacy of her room and "lies with her hair all wildly scattered, and her face buried in the cushions of a couch. She rises up, hurries to and fro, flings herself down again, and rocks and moans. The horror that is upon her, is unutterable. If she really were the murderess, it could hardly be, for the moment, more intense" (666, LV).

But Hortense reminds Jo also of Esther, and her madness casts a shadow also on Esther's occasional hysterical behavior. Hortense's madness is checked by a figure of the law. Significantly, while Mr. Bucket "seems imperceptibly to establish a dreadful right of property in Mademoiselle," Hortense loses her human qualities: "something in her dark cheek [beats] like a clock" (647, LIV), she pants "tigress-like" (652, LIV), and "she snaps her teeth together, as if her mouth closed with a spring" (653, LIV). Half-machine, half-wild animal, she has ceased to be a woman, for "woman is 'madness,' while at the same time 'madness' is the 'very absence of womanhood' " (Felman, "Women and Madness" 8), what makes a woman not a woman. Hortense is Catherine Clément's madwoman, who dances her tarantella but whose madness is ultimately ineffectual because it renounces all disguises and exhausts its own subversive energy in a ritual which, like all rituals, provides a safe outlet for that Otherness which patriarchy fears. Esther's madness is not so explicit as the foreign woman's, nor is it channeled into a specific gesture. However, its threatening presence is felt during Esther's hallucinatory moments, brought about by an illness which is metaphoric, since it replaces a sexual meaning with a non-sexual one:

> Dare I hint at that worse time when, strung together somewhere in great black space, there was a flaming necklace, or ring, or starry circle of some kind, of which *I* was one of the beads! And when my only prayer was to be taken off from the rest, and when it was such inexplicable agony and misery to be a part of the dreadful thing?
>
> (432, XXXV)

Characteristically, in Esther's narrative Hortense is not simply a somewhat grotesque figure driven by murderous impulses, trapped in the web that Inspector Bucket has spun for her; she appears rather as a maddened woman, who becomes a prey to seduction. At the end of *Bleak House* the French maid is safely disposed of. Mr. Bucket, like a "homely Jupiter," takes her away, "enfolding and pervading her like a cloud" (653, LIV), and it is perhaps significant that, while at the level of the plot there can exist no doubt that Hortense is a murderer who is fortunately apprehended by a representative of the law, Dickens should metaphorically identify her with the maiden Io, whom Zeus seduced disguised as a cloud. Comparing Inspector Bucket to Zeus creates a semantic field in which is inscribed the possibility that order may be insured by male domination, through a seduction that is dangerously close to a rape. Even if Esther's madness seems well defined by the boundaries of her illness, thus not requiring such a drastic intervention as

Hortense's, she must face a perhaps more unsettling fate. Unlike Hortense, Esther cannot be safely disposed of by the community. Unlike Clément's madwoman, she cannot stop dancing and be again embraced by the village folk. She must keep her place within that flaming necklace. She must continue to be part of a succession of ghosts haunting a ghost.

6. MORE ON SPECTRES

Esther's childhood, she tells us, has been haunted by the ghost of a sinful mother to whom she owes a life inextricably bound with guilt:

> Your mother, Esther, was your disgrace, and you are hers. The time will come—and soon enough—when you will understand this better, and will feel it too, as no one save a woman can.
>
> (453, XXXVI)

Miss Barbary's words acquire an even stronger accusatory ring when Esther becomes acquainted with the story of her parents' illicit relationship: " 'Pray daily that the sins of others be not visited upon your head.' I could not disentangle all that was about me; and I felt as if the blame and the shame were all in me, and the visitation had come down" (453, XXXVI). However, Esther is not the only one to find herself compelled to face a tale of subversive desire, to confront the visitation of the past. Lady Dedlock, alias Honoria Barbary, with no family, by marrying Lord Leicester has inscribed herself in a patriarchal genealogy which is haunted by the ghost of a woman who has been punished for favoring the wrong side in a patricidal civil war. Lady Dedlock, as it is whispered, "had not even a family" (12) when Sir Leicester married her. Through her marriage, while ostensibly acquiring wealth and station, she seals her exclusion from patriarchy by aligning herself with subversive desire. By becoming Lady Dedlock, she becomes the true successor of the woman who haunts Chesney Wold—Sir Leicester's Vashti. As Mrs. Rouncewell tells Watt, the previous Lady Dedlock "had none of the family blood in her veins." Like Honoria, a "lady of a haughty temper," "of a handsome figure and a noble carriage," not well suited to her husband in age and character, the previous Lady Dedlock had been punished for favoring "the bad cause." Lamed by her husband, she nevertheless continued to pace the terrace of Chesney Wold and "went up and down, up and down," until she died swearing to haunt Chesney Wold "until the pride of this house is humbled" (84, VII). The ghost's walk haunts Chesney Wold and is the "discourse of the Other," the unconscious discourse which "*must be heard*" (85, VII), and which permeates the narrative. As Mrs. Rouncewell tells her grandson, "My Lady, who is afraid of nothing, admits that when it is there, it must be heard. You cannot shut it out" (85, VII). The Ghost's Walk bespeaks that which according to Peter Brooks is the "motor of the narrative": "the desire to be heard, recognized, understood, which, never wholly satisfied or indeed satisfiable, continues to generate the desire to tell, the effort to enunciate a significant version of the life story in order to captivate a possible listener" (*Reading for the Plot* 54). That the footsteps are heard again when the past catches up with Lady Dedlock suggests that Lady Dedlock's story is a repetition in difference. And that they were heard for the first time in the chapter in which Esther first appears in the third person narrative suggests that the risk of repetition is present also in Esther's story.

As the Ghost's Walk, the discourse of a woman who has pitted private desire against the social order, echoes to announce disgrace, so Esther realizes that while she is looking at the balustrades of Chesney Wold and at the lighted window which might be Lady Dedlock's, her own footsteps "made an echoing sound upon the flags" and "brought it suddenly into my mind that there was a dreadful truth in the legend of the Ghost's Walk; that it was I, who was to bring calamity upon the stately house, and that my warning feet were haunting it even then" (454, XXXVI). The previous Lady Dedlock initiates a process of feminine filiation, ghosts haunting a ghost, of which Esther too is part. The weight of guilt is inscribed both in the past and in the future, for "no one save a woman" can understand how strangely she holds a place in this world (453, XXXVI). Repetition, which is reflected spatially in the proliferation of names and doubles, is present temporally in the fate of the two Lady Dedlocks, in Esther's confrontation with the guilt of her mother, and in her compulsive return to memories of her unhappy childhood.[8]

Past and future cease to be two separate categories. They converge and become the present which combines the story of three women: both past and present haunt Chesney Wold and thus assert the perennial nature of female desire. Esther can haunt Chesney Wold, and can announce calamity like the previous Lady Dedlocks. So her past, try as she may to repress it, will not be forgotten and returns to haunt her narrative. It returns in dreams, strangely revealing a distress caused by events which have not yet taken place. Thus even before Guppy offers to conduct some research which may push her fortunes, a dream of the days spent at her godmother's anticipates the anguish

Guppy's proposal will cause. Immediately before her conversation with her suitor, Esther falls asleep and dreams of the time when she lived at her godmother's. She dismisses her dream wondering casually whether "it is at all remarkable that I almost always dreamed of that period of my life" (111, IX). However, when Guppy phrases his offer to conduct some research on her behalf—"What might I not get to know, nearly concerning you? I know nothing now, certainly; but what *might* I not, if I had your confidence, and you set me on?"—she becomes almost incoherent in her eagerness to discourage him: " 'I have very little reason to be proud, and I am not proud. I hope,' I think I added, without very well knowing what I said, 'that you will now go away as if you had never been so exceedingly foolish' " (115, X). She then withdraws to her room, where, she says,

> I surprised myself by beginning to laugh about it, and then surprised myself by beginning to cry about it. In short, I was in a flutter for a little while; and felt as if an old chord had been more coarsely touched than it ever had been since the days of the dear old doll, long buried in the garden.
>
> (115, X)

With the doll Esther has buried the substitute for her mother, her lost object of desire. Her loss, unwittingly incurred at birth, will have to be faced again, and this time perhaps less innocently. In *Le Corps-à-corps avec la mère*, Luce Irigaray has suggested that in postulating the founding of human culture on the murder of the father by his sons, Freud forgets a more ancient murder, that of the woman-mother, "a murder necessary to the establishment of civilization" (15–16).[9] After a night-long pursuit, Esther and Inspector Bucket finally succeed in catching up with Honoria Barbary at the burial ground where she has joined her dead lover. The relentless character of Esther and Inspector Bucket's pursuit, even though steeped in loving concern, is reminiscent of Esther's thoroughness in destroying Lady Dedlock's letter and suggests that Hanzo may very well be right in indicating that "structurally . . . Esther is guilty of wishing the mother's death (with Bucket, does she hound her mother to her doom?), just as on a more apprehensible level, she desires the father" (46).[10] During her flight, Esther's mother has ceased to be Lady Dedlock, has shed the identity which marriage with Sir Leicester had conferred upon her, and has become both the drowned prostitute and "the mother of the dead child." Her death is also Esther's death as her mother's child.

After putting "the long dank hair aside," she sees a face that she had not expected to see, as when after her illness, standing for the first time in front

of the mirror and having drawn the curtain and put her hair aside, she had
confronted a strange face, an unexpected face:

> I was very much changed—O very, very much. At first, my face was so strange
> to me, that I think I should have put my hands before it and started
> back . . . Very soon it became more familiar . . . It was not like I had
> expected; but I had expected nothing definite, and I dare say anything definite
> would have surprised me.
>
> (445, XXXVI)

What Esther sees, Boheemen-Saaf has noticed, "is the image of Medusa's
head . . . the usual representation of castrated female sexuality that turns
the beholder into stone" (246). But the Medusa's head is also the figuration
of that which is absolutely Other, the unsayable and the unthinkable.[11] Thus
the image in the mirror, which at first appears unrecognizable and which
gradually Esther accepts as the reflection of her own self, appears as a figure
of the uncanny, that which was once familiar and which has become estranged
through repression.

Esther has felt the urgency of her own sexuality and has lived it vicariously,
through Ada. She has faced madness and has been visited by dreams which
have spoken of self-estrangement and of that death impulse which, according
to Freud, lies beyond the pleasure principle.

This is how Esther recollects the time of her illness:

> In falling ill, I seemed to have crossed a dark lake, and to have left all
> my experiences, mingled together by the great distance, on the healthy
> shore . . . At once a child, an elder girl, and the little woman I had been so
> happy as, I was not only oppressed by cares and difficulties adapted to each
> station, but by the great perplexity of endlessly trying to reconcile them.
>
> (430, XXXV)

Such states of mind, which lie beyond the limits of a domesticated
consciousness, suggest the possibility of a mental disorder which cannot be
accounted for by the immediate causes of the disease. Thus Esther eschews
the patriarchal category of causality and is determined not to attempt to
interpret it by relating the nature of her troubled dreams to her physical illness.
In fact, it is our very ignorance about the causes of this type of mental
disorder, she claims, that makes us impotent to confront it adequately: "It may
be," she suggests, almost echoing Lucy Snowe's words in *Villette*, "that if we
knew more of such strange afflictions, we might be better able to alleviate
their intensity" (432, XXXV). Esther finds a soothing place for recovery in

Mr. Boythorn's house: "If a good fairy had built the house for me with a wave of her wand, and I had been a princess and her favoured godchild, I could not have been more considered in it" (444, XXXVI). However, she cannot indulge in her family romance for long. She is not the favorite child of a fairy godmother and she does not belong in *heimlich* places. She cannot rest forever, but must set out on a journey which will take her to the burial ground from where infection spreads, and from there to her new Bleak House.

Esther's awakening from her journey in pursuit of her mother partakes of the nature of the uncanny, with its "over-accentuation of psychical reality in comparison with physical reality" (Freud, "The 'Uncanny'" 398); for, as Esther says, "the unreal things were more substantial than the real" (713, LIX). And her journey uncannily ends in her confrontation with her dead self. Significantly, in the following chapter, Esther compulsively returns to the time of her illness, even if only to quickly dismiss it: "I had an illness, but it was not a long one; and I would avoid even this mention of it, if I could quite keep down the recollection of [the sympathy of all about me]" (714, LX). However, with her illness, madness has entered her narrative, and madness, as Foucault would argue, "provides a breach without reconciliation where the world is forced to question itself" (*Madness and Civilization* 288).

7. FINDING AN ENDING

> "And how delightful it would be—" But no matter what I thought. I began this book with the intention of concealing nothing . . . but we have *some* thoughts.
>
> (Anne Brontë, *Agnes Grey*)

The language of women, whether authors or characters, is a language traversed by silence and punctuated by pauses. As the female voice in the epigraph from *Agnes Grey* breaks off, so does Esther's, as though attempting to refuse mastery while redefining it. However, while Agnes Grey resumes her narrative and quickly covers up the gap, Esther explicitly refuses to conclude. Her last two words, "even supposing—" become the site of uncertainty, where coherence, plausibility, and knowability are overtly questioned.

While a number of critics still read the ending of *Bleak House* as the somewhat sentimental statement of a writer who believes that generosity, self-denial and goodness of heart can prevail over corruption and disorder, one cannot fail to notice that this ending is only a fragment. And while Lowry Pei has argued that Esther's "discovery of parentage is completed for her, her actual father conveniently replaced with one much more pleasant to contemplate," one cannot but notice that the father has almost married the daughter. By violating the incest taboo, the prototype of all social conventions, Jarndyce has forfeited his role as figure of the Law and thus has aligned himself with all the ineffectual fathers who inhabit this novel.

It is not the death of the father, but a more primordial crime that allows the narrative to unfold. By killing her mother, Esther ceases to be the child and can occupy the mother's place (she does, quite literally, become a mother) Like Lucy Snowe, she too chooses indeterminacy and eschews integration into the Symbolic order. Her language is not the language of male imperatives and does not exclude madness. Esther does not quite remain outside the Symbolic order in the same way as Jo, who is set apart by "physical and emotional loneliness" stemming from lack of education (Boheemen-Saaf 235). While Jo does not possess the key to interpret the network of symbols which makes up society, Esther possesses all the keys, and, in the failure of parental relations, she exposes from within the shortcomings of phallocentrism. Through duplicity and evasions, her Otherness, even if repressed at the level of the plot and encapsulated in a well-ordered little cottage, makes itself heard through the fragmentary character of the ending, through the refusal to impose closure on her text. Having renounced to find its own beginning, it ceases to voice a claim to find its own end. Esther's narrative, as the Discourse of the Other, cannot end. If desire is the "motor of the narrative" and is constitutively unsatisfiable, the narrative cannot end. The text has become yet another veil, the means of partial gratification, a fetish which, as Flieger has said apropos of writing as "perverse" activity, "veils the gaping abyss of the subject" (67). Vashti has hidden herself under the safe mask of a doctor's wife, and Death, the end of the novel and the end of life, will not find her.

8. FINDING A MONSTER

Gilbert and Gubar have written an important account of the relationship between male authors and female characters in Western literary history. Showing how Western tradition favors male authors as the sole generators of

discourse, as fathers, godlike figures who exert patriarchal rights of owner-
ship over literary texts, they suggest that it is through " 'inconstancy'—her
refusal, that is, to be fixed or 'killed' by an author/owner" that woman can
acquire the power to constitute herself as character (16). From the perspective
of Gilbert and Gubar's feminist poetics, Esther is yet another daughter
captured in the mirror of male imagination. To liberate herself, to escape from
the mirror in which she has been imprisoned, they would argue, she must
"replace the 'copy' with the 'individuality.' " However, the status of this
"individuality" is precisely what is problematic in this otherwise attractive
approach. To argue the necessity of operating such substitution implies a
belief in the unity of the subject and an unquestioning acceptance of its role
in the creation of the literary text. If, however, the subject is posited as
illusory construct and the text is seen not as the product of an individual's
imagination, but rather as intersubjective process, the substitution of female
individuality for male-authored copy becomes yet another attempt at establishing the self-sameness of the subject and its primacy over language. It
becomes, that is, an impossible attempt to find an owner for the unconscious.
From a Lacanian perspective, the unconscious is unauthored, and it is
language, a language which can never be mastered, that speaks the subject.
As at the conclusion of the chancery trial it is discovered that no one is the
inheritor of the Jarndyce estate, so at the end of *Bleak House* we discover with
Esther that not even she can author her text, that, in fact, by writing she
unmakes herself.[12] Esther has no need to strive to substitute her individuality
for Dickens' copy. As the unconscious of the text, its Other, her voice has
been heard all along, camouflaged in those dreams and symptoms through
which the unconscious, which can never be imaged for itself, makes itself
heard. And, perhaps, the subdued first-person narrative has not been its only
locus.

The dreamlike quality which shapes Esther's hallucinatory moments also
shapes the present-tense narrative, and thus establishes a disquieting connection between the two, especially when it is corroborated by the way in which
time is figured in the novel, which leads to that which is perhaps the most
daring aspect of *Bleak House*. What is left out at the end is her signature—
an omission which situates her narrative in the unauthored universe of the
first chapter. The indeterminate ending of *Bleak House* reflects the ever-
provisional identity that Esther reaches. As throughout the novel she is
repeatedly threatened by fragmentation, so the ending of the novel can only
be provisional, and its last sentence can only be a fragment. Structurally, such
an ending also establishes a connection with the third-person narrative, in

which the very first paragraphs open on a scenario pervaded by that sense of fragmentation which we have come to recognize as one of the unmistakable traits of modern and post-modern fiction. [13] Fragmentation, a sense of a lack of boundaries between the various elements of reality, and, most importantly, the lack of a sense of origin, are all elements which contribute to create the unsettling appeal of the first chapter by figuring in it a reversal of the pattern of Genesis.

Both in the first paragraph of the first chapter of *Bleak House* and in the first paragraph of Esther's narrative, the desire is the desire to overcome the difficulty of beginning. The first chapter, as Boheemen-Saaf has noticed, opens on "the absence of a beginning."[14] Instead of the waters being separated from the land, there is mud everywhere. Instead of man having dominion over the animals of the earth, we see dogs "undistinguishable in mire," horses splashed in mud, and men all slipping and sliding and "losing their foothold." Instead of the beginning of time, we confront past and present made indistinguishable by the floating of relics from all ages. Instead of the dawning of the day, we witness the death of the sun. The earth, rather than newly created, appears suspended in timelessness. Even the existence of time, in fact, is discounted, for it is doubtful whether "the day ever broke" (5, I). If Esther has striven all along to observe the rules of patriarchal discourse and has shown a preoccupation with genealogy, chronology, and causality, in moments of crisis these categories have broken down, thereby tearing her carefully wrought fabric. Past, present, and future have collapsed, creating that palimpsestic quality which also characterizes the third-person narrative, where time is equally problematic. Chronology, hierarchy, and causality are defied here in a manner that is analogous to the disruption of these categories in Esther's narrative. Esther cannot conclude her tale for, as Lacan puts it, "The unconscious, it is said, . . . needs time to reveal itself. I quite agree, but I ask: how is this time to be measured?" (*Écrits* 77). Quite similarly, locked in the present tense, the third-person narrative can make no claim to beginning nor end, and the scenario it presents is the vision of a nightmare, a nightmare which may very well be Esther's dream of a narrative free from the fetters imposed by patriarchy. Thus it is perhaps significant that although the monster must acquire the disguise of a French mademoiselle or of a ghost in Esther's discourse, in this dream "it would not be wonderful to meet a Megalosaurus, forty feet long or so" (5, I), an image which is strongly suggestive of that "filthy mass of moving flesh," Victor Frankenstein's version of the monstrous. Esther's narrative becomes her attempt to introduce time and thus eliminate this monster, which, as Gilbert and Gubar have suggested, is female within a patriarchal tradition. Of course Esther, as a Victorian female writer, must do her best to eliminate the monster from her narrative by displacing it into a portion which she refuses to inhabit. For it is only recently that women writers have been able to defy patriarchy openly, to see that the Medusa is laughing, and to say with Cixous,

> J'ai une animale . . . Elle m'habite . . . Elle est folle, elle est nerveuse. J'ai le chagrin de le dire. J'en ai le plus grand plaisir. . . . Le vieux Loup veut nous séparer. . . . Il se penche sur le berceau, il nous jette une malédiction: "Si tu l'élèves tu deviendras de plus en plus bête. Tu deviendras folle à la fin. Les hommes ne voudront plus de toi. Tu ne deviendras pas une femme." . . . Chasse-la! Elle revient. Elle se faufile entre mes cuisses. Son souffle est irrésistible. Folle ou femme?
>
> (Cixous Gagnon and Leclerc, 40)

However, even in Esther's Victorian narrative, the monster cannot be eliminated, because the first Lady Dedlock and Hortense are Esther herself, Vashti and Rachel, the monstrous actress, capable of assuming so many disguises.

NOTES

1. Thus, Lawrence Frank, although stating that "Esther's 'case' remains . . . in Chancery" (91), confidently interprets her dream about the staircases as the sign of "frustrated yearnings for rebirth" (100). The starry circle represents for Wilt the "nightmare of solipsism" (307), while for Eggert it represents the desire "to be beautiful, passionate and connected" (79).
2. The most exhaustive discussion of textanalysis as opposed to psychobiography and psychocriticism can be found in Jean Béllemin-Noel.
3. While many studies have been devoted to Dickens' problematic choice of a double voice and to the relationship between the two narratives, rarely have critics commented upon Esther's awareness that her narrative is only a portion of a larger text, her voice only one of a number which insist to be heard—namely the objective narrator's, but also the voice of other writers such as Nemo and Lady Dedlock. Neary, one of the few to notice it, only observes how such awareness "is very mysterious indeed" (24). It may be interesting to notice that although the objective narrator seems well aware of Esther's relevant role, he (she?) mentions her only *in passim*, whereas all the important characters traverse freely the boundary between the two narratives and are conspicuously present in both.
4. I borrow this phrase from Brooks, "Fictions of the Wolfman" 77.
5. For a different analysis of the "uncanny" in *Bleak House*, see Newsom.
6. Concerning the importance of names in *Bleak House*, see William Axton, Lawrence Frank, Karen Chase, and Michael Ragussis.
7. Lucy's nicknames, Jean Blackall argues, ironically fix Lucy in the roles of misanthrope, blue-stocking, and aged crone, while she perceives herself as having

limited intellectual attributes . . . Is it coincidental that with both Esther and Lucy not only the surnames but also the nicknames are used to characterize the heroine, and that they function in a similar way? The nicknames, like the surnames, represent an aspect of the truth: they characterize the heroine as a social creature, as she behaves and is perceived in the world's eyes. Simultaneously, however, they are ironic, because they create an image that belies her inward impulse and condition, her sense of her own identity. (373–74)

8. For the terms "spatial repetition" and "temporal repetition," I am indebted to John T. Irwin's concepts of "spatial" and "temporal doubling," 55.

9. Cited in Margaret Homans, *Bearing the Word*, p. 2.

10. Boheemen-Saaf finds an interesting link between the first chapter of *Bleak House* and Lady Dedlock's flight: "the narrator uses the image of flooding water—a traditional symbol of the female, the other, the unconscious—to denote the breakdown of the hierarchical order" (233). However, in Boheemen-Saaf's view, the narrative refuses to recognize otherness: "A full recognition and acceptance of Lady Dedlock's otherness," this critic argues, "would have destroyed the hierarchical order in which the binary pair 'Father-M(other)' is positioned in the *Scala Naturae*" (249).

11. For a discussion of the Medusa's head as the figure of Otherness, see Jean-Pierre Vernant, *La morte negli occhi: Figure dell'Altro nell'antica Grecia*. Trans. Cristina Saletti. Bologna: Il Mulino, 1987.

12. As Roland Barthes says, "Writing is the destruction of every voice, of every point of origin . . . that neutral . . . space where our subject slips away, the negative where all identity is lost" (Barthes, "The Death of the Author" 142).

13. In *Mimesis*, Auerbach, for instance, has described the modern novel as presenting "fragmentation of the exterior action . . . reflection of consciousness, and . . . stratification of time" (488).

14. For an analysis of *Bleak House* from the point of view of the "interest in origins and beginnings" in positivist thought, see Boheemen-Saaf.

WORKS CITED

Auerbach, Erich. *Mimesis: The Representation of Reality in Western Literature.* Trans. Willard Trask. Garden City, N.Y.: Doubleday, 1953.

Axton, William. "The Trouble with Esther." *Modern Language Quarterly* 26 (1965): 545–77.

Barthes, Roland. "The Death of the Author." *Image/Text/Music*. Trans. Stephen Heath. New York: Hill and Wang, 1977: 142–148.

Bèllemin-Noel, Jean. *Vers l'inconscient du texte*. Paris: Presses Universitaires de France, 1979.

Blackall, Jean Frantz. "A Suggestive Book for Charlotte Brontë." *Journal of English and Germanic Philology* 76 (July 1977): 363–83.

Boheemen-Saaf, Christine van. " 'The Universe Makes an Indifferent Parent': *Bleak House* and the Victorian Family Romance." In *Interpreting Lacan* (Psychiatry and the Humanities 6). Eds. Joseph H. Smith and William Kerrigan. New Haven: Yale UP, 1983.

Brontë, Charlotte. *Villette*. Harmondsworth: Penguin, 1984.

Brooks, Peter, "Freud's Masterplot: Questions of Narrative." *Yale French Studies* 55/56 (1977): 280–300.

———. Reading for the Plot. Design and Intention in Narrative. New York: Knopf, 1984.

Cassirer, Ernst. *Language and Myth*. Trans. Susanne K. Langer. New York: Dover, 1953.

Chase, Karen. *Eros and Psyche: the Representation of Personality in Charlotte Brontë, Charles Dickens and George Eliot*. Methuen: New York and London, 1984.

Cixous, Hélène and Catherine Clément. *The Newly Born Woman*. Trans. Betsy Wing. (Theory and History of Literature, 24). Minneapolis: U of Minnesota P, 1986.

Cixous, Hélène, Gagnon, Madeleine and Annie Leclerc. *La Venue à L'écriture*. Union Generale d'Éditions: Paris: 1977.

Dickens, Charles. *Bleak House*. Norton: New York and London, 1977.

Eggert, Paul. "The Real Esther Summerson." *Dickens Studies Newsletter* 11 (Sept. 1980): 74–81.

Felman, Shoshana. "Women and Madness: The Critical Phallacy." *Diacritics* 5 (Winter 1975): 2–10.

Flieger, Jerry Aline. "Trial and Error: The Case of the Textual Unconscious." *Diacritics* 11 (1981): 56–67.

Ford, George H. and Lauriat Lane, eds. *The Dickens Critics*. Ithaca, N.Y.: Cornell UP, 1961.

Foucault, Michel. *Madness and Civilization: A History of Insanity in the Age of Reason*. Trans. Richard Howard. New York: Random House, 1973.

Frank, Lawrence. "'Through a Glass Darkly.' Esther Summerson and *Bleak House*." *Dickens Studies Annual*, vol. 4. Ed. Robert B. Partlow, Jr. Carbondale: Southern Illinois UP, 1974: 91–112.

Freud, Sigmund. "The 'Uncanny'." *Collected Papers*. Trans. under the supervision of Joan Rivière. New York: Basic Books, Inc., 1959: 368–407.

Gilbert, Sandra M. and Susan Gubar. *Madwoman in the Attic: The Woman Writer and the Nineteenth-Century Literary Imagination*. New Haven: Yale UP, 1979.

Hanzo, Thomas A. "Paternity and the Subject in *Bleak House*." In *The Fictional Father: Lacanian Readings of the Text*. Ed. Robert Con Davis. Amherst: The U of Massachusetts P. 1981: 27–39.

Harari, Josué V. "Critical Factions/Critical Fictions." *Textual Strategies*, Ed. Josué V. Harari. Ithaca: Cornell UP, 1979: 11–72.

Hartman, Geoffrey. "Psychoanalysis: The French Connection." In *Psychoanalysis and the Question of the Text*. Ed. Geoffrey Hartman. Baltimore and London: The Johns Hopkins UP, 1978: 86–113.

The Holy Bible. Trans. James Moffatt. New York: Doran, 1926.

Homans, Margaret. *Bearing the Word: Language and Female Experience in Nineteenth-Century Women's Writing*. Chicago: U of Chicago P, 1986.

Irwin, John T. *Doubling and Incest/Repetition: A Speculative reading of Faulkner*. Baltimore: The Johns Hopkins UP, 1975.

Johnson, Barbara. "My Monster/My Self." *Diacritics* 12 (Summer 1982): 2–10.

Lacan, Jacques. *Écrits: A Selection*. Trans. Alan Sheridan. New York: Norton, 1978.

―――. *Speech and Language in Psychoanalysis*. Trans., Notes and Commentary by Anthony G. Wilden. Baltimore: Johns Hopkins UP, 1981.

Mitchell, Juliet and Jacqueline Rose, eds. *Feminine Sexuality: Jacques Lacan and the école freudienne*. Trans. Jacqueline Rose. New York and London: Norton, 1982.

Neary, John M. "*Bleak House:* From Phenomena to Story." *Massachusetts Studies in English* 9 (1984): 13–31.

Newsom, Robert. *Dickens on the Romantic Side of Familiar Things: Bleak House and the Novel Tradition*. New York: Columbia UP, 1977.

Pei, Lowry. "Mirrors, the Dead Child, Snagsby Secret, and Esther." *English Language Notes* 16 (1978): 144–56.

Ragussis, Michael. "The Ghostly Signs of *Bleak House*." *Nineteenth-Century Fiction* 34 (1979): 253–80.

Shelley, Mary Wollstonecraft. *Frankenstein: Or, The Modern Prometheus*. [1831 ed.] New York: Signet, 1965.

Vernant, Jean-Pierre. *La Morte negli Occhi: Figure dell'Altro nell'Antica Grecia*. Trans. Caterina Saletti. Bologna: Il Mulino, 1987.

Wilt, Judith. "Confusion and Consciousness in Dickens' Esther." *Nineteenth-Century Fiction* 32 (1977): 285–309.

Wise, Thomas James and John Alexander Symington, Eds. *The Brontës: Their Lives, Friendships and Correspondence in Four Volumes*, The Shakespeare Head Brontë. Oxford: Shakespeare Head Press, 1932, III.

Zwerdling, Alex. "Esther Summerson Rehabilitated." *PMLA* 88 (May 1973): 429–39.

Prospecting for Meaning in *Our Mutual Friend*

Richard T. Gaughan

So many of Dickens' characters in *Our Mutual Friend* are so entrapped and mutilated by the roles they are forced to play and by the rules and values of their society that meaningful action seems all but impossible. Characters like Lizzie Hexam and John Harmon are forced to live stories they did not author and cannot rewrite. Jenny Wren, the attenuated and battered symbol of imagination in the novel and a parody of childhood and all that childhood means to Dickens, is a reminder of the irreversible damage the social world has already done to the hopes of any escape from that world through innocence or imagination. The only characters who seem to have any freedom at all are those who, like Fascination Fledgby and Lammle, manipulate and dominate others through the secret exercise of their will behind the mask of social propriety. But, even this freedom is illusory. Lammle and Fledgeby are so bound to each other and so completely defined by the version of the social game that they play that their schemes amount to little more than the rearrangement of players in a closed and zero-sum game.

The reason meaningful action seems impossible in this novel is because the narrative world is so closed and self-sufficient that it is, or pretends to be, a complete and impenetrable reality independent of the characters who comprise it. All the apparent divisions within the social world, like the division between the world of Podsnap and the world of the waterfront, are only superficial. The waterfront community's values, its tolerance of the robbing of dead men but intolerance of even the hint of scandal, perfectly parallel Podsnap's tolerance of political corruption and his peremptory dismissal of everything that does not conform to his narrow morality. Gaffer Hexam disinherits his son as impetuously as old man Harmon disinherits his and tries to impose his own ideas on his family as rigorously as "My Respectable Father" does on Eugene Wrayburn. There are, ultimately, only the values and rules of the social world endlessly repeated, sometimes unintentionally parodied, but almost always embraced even by those characters, like Charley Hexam and Bradley Headstone, who are partly or wholly excluded from respectable society. The apparent social mobility of characters, though it may seem vertical—a climbing or descending the social ladder—is always lateral and cyclical. There is no up or down in this world,[1] no winners or losers, only the relentless repetition of a fixed set of social roles. Movement and change are only the occasional exchange of roles by actors who are individually dispensable.

There seems to be no alternative to the dehumanized world presented in the novel except the alternative of what Adorno calls negation. Adorno claims that art and thought realize themselves most fully not in what they can assert as positive and systematic but in what is discovered through the negation and decomposition of what can be positively thought or systematically expressed.[2] Whatever is positive and can be formalized is, by virtue of that fact alone, antithetical to the critical dialectic of thought and is, to some extent, oppressive and dehumanizing. Similarly, in *Our Mutual Friend* Dickens presents a social world that is both positive and dehumanized and must enact the decomposition of thematic and formal coherence to find in negation what is denied or perverted by both the social and narrative systems.

Since the triumph of the human will, especially the will to subdue everything to a coherent order, seems to be at the root of the problem[3] (hence the elaborate pun on Harmon's will), Dickens uses passivity in the character most centrally involved in the novel's plots, John Harmon, to find in the negation of will the human qualities that have been lost in its exercise. The suspension of Harmon's will frees him from his narrowly defined social identity so that he can create an identity based on his relationship with others. This is not to say that Harmon is free to create an identity *sui generis*. The identity he can create will be social but in a broader sense than the identity prescribed by the closed system of social conventions and values. This identity will be social in the sense that it is based on the relationships Harmon can establish with other characters, but these relationships must develop outside socially prescribed roles. To establish these relationships, Harmon uses temporary and symbolic versions of himself—his disguises—to test the responsiveness of others.

Harmon's use of symbolic versions of himself to discover his identity, however, is perilously close to society's use of masks to manipulate and dominate others and, in particular, to Bradley Headstone's use of disguise to stalk Lizzie Hexam and Eugene Wrayburn. The only difference between Harmon's and Headstone's use and understanding of symbolic disguises is the fine but significant distinction between using symbolic forms as a way of responding to and understanding a world that is not defined entirely by the social will and imposing symbolic forms as realities in and of themselves. As slight as this distinction may seem, it is one that frees Harmon to search for an authentic identity and condemns Headstone to live out to the death the spiritual sterility of the society whose values he has so completely embraced.

The way John Harmon escapes from the tyranny of social conventions and the fatal repetition of his family's history sets the pattern for how the novel will proceed. Harmon's presumed death places him outside the social world and the influence of his father's will, but he is not free of the effects of the values that control the social world. He can create and sustain a new identity only through deception and duplicity—the very methods society thrives on. John Harmon cannot successfully escape the tyranny of the past unless he conceals the fact that he is still alive and finds a way back into the world that is not already controlled by social values. This forced concealment and Harmon's need to find out the truth about his world make him act in ways that are reminiscent of the way society functions. There is, however, a difference in purpose. Like Jenny Wren, Harmon is aware that his deceptions and disguises are a self-conscious means of protecting himself in a hostile world. His disguises are at once decoys to draw off the predators, or even the predator in any given character, and a filter through which he can clarify possible relations between himself and others. They are questions he asks of others so that he can define himself in terms of a response and not a fixed social role. By using his disguises to sift through his world to find something authentic, Harmon reverses and redeems his father's greedy sifting through the mounds of dust for lost and discarded valuables.

Although both Harmon's disguises and the conventions and values of society are artificial and self-conscious, there is an important difference in the way each is self-conscious. Harmon's disguises are self-conscious not only because he is aware that he is not, or is not entirely, the person he pretends to be, but also because he is aware that these symbolic versions of himself alter the way others can be seen as well as the way others see him. In his disguise as John Rokesmith, Harmon gives up the social power he could have by laying claim to his father's legacy so that he can learn how others will act towards him in the position of relative powerlessness. Only by circumventing the power relationships on which society thrives in ways such as this can Harmon make his relationships to others authentic.

The self-consciousness of social values and conventions, on the other hand, is little more than the awareness of the arbitrariness of those values and conventions—the awareness, in other words, of the need to exclude everything that is not defined by the closed system of those values and conventions. Paradoxically, because social roles and identities are understood as arbitrary they must be imposed on others as absolutely true to conceal their arbitrariness. The only trick is making others recognize and accept any given social persona: the outward appearance of wealth, success, or power. Since there is no provision in the collective mind of society for the possibility that the ways society orders and understands the world might not be entirely true, surface appearances that conform to social values must be accepted as true. This is why masks and social positions are exchanged and circulated with the same rapidity and ease as currency and with the same uncritical belief in an assumed and usually inflated value. Nevertheless, as Lammle and Fledgby understand, the complacency and self-satisfaction of the guardians of society in their splendid and shining structure is neither the whole of the social reality nor even its most crucial part.

The self-reflective nature of conventionalized social life, in fact, indicates the troubling leap of faith made by society to conceal the grave discrepancy between its elaborate displays of power and luxury and the precarious resources on which those displays rest. Implied in self-reflection is a sense of limited resources which must be expanded through increasingly elaborate interpretive structures. The more elaborately resources are circulated, the longer it takes for the exhausted system to crash. Because Harmon's use of disguise eventually produces something new—an identity that is based on relationships that are outside the system—it is a resource for establishing a relationship to the world and not, as are social masks, a shell game to protect dangerously depleted resources.[4]

Although Harmon's disguises do help keep him safe from society, he must also somehow use the advantage of disguise to reenter that world. This advantage, the ability to change identities, however, is based on his own lack of identity. After Harmon, in disguise, revisits the scene of his betrayal, he quite literally becomes the Man from Nowhere (an ironic fulfillment of the role assigned him by Mortimer Lightwood during his narration of the Veneerings) but only once his disguise is off:

"It is a sensation not experienced by many mortals," said he, "to be looking into a churchyard on a wild windy night, and to feel that I no more hold a place among the living than these dead do, and even to know that I lie buried somewhere else, as they lie buried here. Nothing uses me to it. A spirit that was once a man could hardly feel stranger or lonelier, going unrecognized among mankind, than I feel."[5]

Immediately after this reflection Harmon admits, " 'But this is the fanciful side of the situation. It has a real side, so difficult that, though I think of it every day, I never thoroughly think it out' " (422). Harmon's recollection of his drugging and near death, the events which have made him the man from nowhere, leads him to an even more radical confusion of identity and more total alienation from the world:

"I could not have said that my name was John Harmon—I could not have thought it—I didn't know it—but when I heard the blows, I thought of the wood-cutter and his axe, and had some dead idea that I was lying in a forest.
"This is still correct? Still correct, with the exception that I cannot possibly express it to myself without using the word I. But it was not I. There was no such thing as I, within my knowledge."

(426)

Disguise serves many purposes, but, because it is self-conscious, it cannot alleviate Harmon's alienation from the world. He must use disguises to rediscover his "I" and not as substitutes for that identity. Harmon needs to find a way to reintegrate himself among the living without submitting to his father's legacy. This is the "real" side of his dilemma, the side which involves losing the security and power of disguise. The only way available to him is to accept a suspended or interrupted identity, to be a stranger even to himself, so that his identity can be a process of responding to the world and not a submission to predetermined social roles.

A version of this necessary passivity in the face of a predetermined social world is the phenomenon of near-death. Miller has commented on the baptismal character of the river and the rebirth signified by near-death (Miller, "*Our Mutual Friend*," p. 177). Near-death, however, is also the suspension of the human will. It is the state in which human life itself exists only as pure potential. As such, it escapes the tyranny of social conventions and any definition as simply materiality. A conscious desire to live in the world does not have much to do with this suspension of life or its subsequent recovery, as this description of Riderhood suggests:

Now he is struggling harder to get back. And yet—like us all, when we swoon—like us all, every day of our lives when we wake—he is instinctively unwilling to be restored to the consciousness of this existence, and would be left dormant, if he could.

(505)

It is the suspension itself that is important because it undermines the assumption that things have to be the way they are. Even in the case of the incorrigible Riderhood, the witnesses, to his revival instinctively hope that he will return from his state of suspended animation a changed and better man. The very fact that he has fallen between the cracks of the ordinary conceptual categories that both he and his society use to order and define the world means that those categories might not entirely define the way things are and that a radical change in the way the world is imagined is possible.

To bring about such change, however, whether through near-death or disguise, requires not only the relinquishing of power over others but also the surrender of certainty about personal identity. For Riderhood to have a new life means he must surrender his old habit of thinking solely in terms of calculated self-interest. He must, as Harmon does, accept an identity that is open and responsive to others. When this opportunity to relinquish certainty about identity is refused, as it is in the case of Riderhood, the values of society, especially the power relations that underlie society, take over as the source of personal identity. This is what happens to the unfortunate Bradley Headstone whose refusal to be responsive to the reality of himself and others perverts the depths of his character and turns the respectable schoolmaster into a psychotic killer.

In many important respects Bradley Headstone is the character who best personifies the thematic forces at work in the novel. Like Lizzie and Charley Hexam, Headstone comes from a socially disreputable class. He aspires to and attains a measure of respectability by accepting respectability as an end in itself and by repressing himself into the appropriate shape for his role in respectable society. When he meets Lizzie, however, the mechanisms of this repression fail him and he is forced to come to terms with that part of himself which exceeds the conventions of respectability, and he must do this without the aid of those conventions and his veneer of respectability.

This division in Bradley Headstone is more than just a conflict between good and evil or between the emotional and the rational (Wilson, p. 82). Headstone embodies the conflict that pervades the novel between what is real and what is accepted as real. His passion for Lizzie alienates him from the conventionalized social world and forces him to find a new relationship to himself and his world that can better accommodate that part of him that cannot be reduced to respectability. For this reason, Headstone is a genuinely tragic character. He is forced to confront, on an isolated and intensely personal level, a conflict of values which is characteristic of the world in which he lives. All that is admitted by society as real and all that is not converge in Bradley Headstone when he has lost the safety of his respectable life. He is the logical consequence of the values of the world in *Our Mutual Friend* and must face the consequences of these values in a way no other character does. The novel is, in many ways, the story of Bradley Headstone writ large.

The tragedy of Bradley Headstone is so powerful that it threatens to dominate the novel and overshadow Harmon's redemptive mission. Headstone's tragedy, however, is compromised by his unwillingness to forego the values dictated by society. Even in the midst of his suffering Headstone never surrenders his subservience to the idea of respectability. He refuses to see Lizzie in any way other than as a lower class women who can be recuperated to respectability under his tutelage. In spite of his passion, Headstone never acknowledges Lizzie's reality as an independent character. Lizzie is, at first, a symbol of his repressed past (perhaps even a symbol of his mother), and later, she becomes a symbol of the passions he can no longer repress for the sake of respectability.

Headstone's use of Lizzie as a symbol betrays the relationship between symbol and reality. Symbolic apprehension of reality, as it is practiced by Jenny Wren and Harmon, attempts to interpret possible relationships between self and world without pretending to appropriate the world in the symbol.[6] Jenny and Harmon try to build a relationship between themselves and the world that can then be adjusted and that is responsive to others. Headstone's passion for Lizzie, too, can put him in a new and more adequate relation to the reality of his own feelings but he forfeits this opportunity by turning Lizzie into an object to be possessed.

Just as society mediates everything through its conventions, Bradley Headstone, ultimately, mediates his love for Lizzie through his personal mythology. Similarly, he makes Wrayburn and Rogue Riderhood into symbolic characters in his private psychodrama. Wrayburn comes to represent the easy respectability that must always elude Headstone because of his class origins and Riderhood comes to represent the class that Headstone has left but from which he can never escape. By forcing these characters into symbolic roles which are themselves defined by society's values, Headstone translates the depths of his inner self into terms commensurate with the values and conventions of society. Instead of apprehending his own inner reality and the reality of others outside the conventions of society, Headstone turns himself into a character in a conventional and fairly trite social and literary melodrama and becomes a victim and villain rather than a tragic figure.

Headstone's inability to free himself from the values of society makes his use of disguises a way to impose his will, that is, the will of society, on others. Harmon's disguises, on the other hand, are intended as ways to allow a relationship between himself and others to develop. Harmon's identity depends entirely on the way others respond to him not on what he can make other do my concealing himself. Headstone's identity depends on denying relationships to others and on restraining and concealing himself. Headstone, in other words, fails to use his disguises symbolically, as the medium of an encounter with the world. As a result, Headstone repeats Harmon's experience of lost identity with a chillingly ironic twist. Headstone becomes literally and permanently the Man from Nowhere: he loses his personal identity entirely, because he clings so tenaciously to the phantom identity assigned him by society. Not surprisingly, then, it is Headstone, and not Harmon, who loses all control over his disguises. By the end of the novel it is virtually impossible to say whether the role of schoolmaster fits Headstone any better than the role of bargeman.

Because Headstone stakes so much on his disguise, because he identifies symbol and reality, any frustration of his will locks him into a spiraling need for more fictions, all of which serve to justify the image of respectability. Even when he is frustrated in his pursuit of respectability, he erects perverse justifications for his frustration:

> The state of the man was murderous, and he knew it. More; he irritated it, with a kind of perverse pleasure akin to that which a sick man sometimes has in irritating a wound upon his body.
>
> (609)

Headstone imposes a contrived and self-serving structure on events which then becomes his only reality. However perverse Headstone's behavior, he is consistent in seeking to support the *image* he has of himself and is forced constantly to substitute one fictitious version of himself after another once his passion for Lizzie obliterates his fiction of respectability and leaves him with nothing but his conflicting desires.

Like the society of Lady Tippins, the Veneerings, and Podsnap, Headstone gets lost among his own constructs. From the start society is immersed in mutually supporting fictions, but Bradley Headstone shows that the origins of such self-enclosed and self-generating systems lie in the choices an individual makes in the attempt to define a self and a world. Headstone, stripped of his veneer of respectability, is the embodiment of the conflict between the conventional and all that exceeds the conventional and can, like John Harmon, defy society by making this conflict the basis of his identity. Instead, he denies this conflict, thereby effectively denying himself, and locks Wrayburn, Riderhood, Lizzie, and himself in a personal and nightmarish version of society's more dressed-up dance of death. His selection of the bargeman's disguise only reflects his loss of himself and completes his regression into fixed social and conventional patterns that have long since splintered his character and condemned him to destruction.

This is the darker and more individual relationship to the personal and social values that are the origin of the larger self-enclosed and self-generating social systems. In Headstone's decision to force his deeper nature into the confines of the conventional are the origins of Chancery, the Circumlocution Office, and Podsnappery. Bradley Headstone is a Pip whose expectations are exposed more savagely and more honestly. If Bradley Headstone is an evil character, he is evil for very specific and very familiar reasons. He is evil because he chooses to make his life into a fiction and because he denies anything outside that fiction. He refuses to establish a relationship between himself and his own inner reality and the reality of others. Instead, he chooses the grim struggle for power that has always lurked just beneath the surface of respectable restraint.

When Headstone drowns Riderhood in a fatal embrace, he is doing more than killing a past he has worked so hard to deny. He is killing that part of himself that rejected a more authentic approach to the depths of himself and the complexities of his world. The man who rejects a new life and the man who rejects a new sense of what is real fall into the lock, the mechanism designed to alter and control the water's natural flow, and die in the stagnant slime of their refusals.

As important as the contrast between Harmon and Headstone is for the thematic concerns of the novel, it is even more important as a clue about a conflict in formal tendencies and values that Dickens uses to develop an identity for his novel that is independent of the constraints of the world depicted by the novel. Harmon and Headstone are not only characters who represent or embody thematic categories (for example, good and evil, passivity and will, etc.), they are also characters who represent or embody the more purely symbolic and narrative problems in the novel that produce and are reflected by the thematic conflicts. Taken as contraries in Blake's sense, they represent the two tendencies that define the novel as a symbolic form: its tendency to impose formal coherence and its capacity to express multiple and often incongruous perspectives on experience. These more purely narrative concerns are not, like the values of society, arranged in a static and self-reflecting order. Instead, they are set into direct and creative conflict with each other.

Each of these tendencies, through the character who embodies it, asserts itself as preeminent—as a definitive description of the novel as a symbolic form. But, each assertion also calls forth its contrary assertion, in effect, its own negation. The demands of formal coherence, for example, cannot be asserted without exposing the need for a contrary: the multiple and heterogeneous ways the novel symbolically represents and explores the world. There is no resolving the conflict between these contraries since the contraries continually change how each can be understood at any given moment in the novel. As a result, Dickens is not exorcising any artistic, let alone moral, demons in the conflict between Headstone and Harmon but is displaying and using self-consciously the novel as a symbolic form so that a relationship to the world that is obscured by the self-reflecting symbolic systems of the social world on the thematic level can be recaptured on this symbolic and more purely narrative level. These contraries and the ways they define each other become a kind of purely symbolic story about narrative concerns that parallels and, in some ways, redeems the thematic story.

In this narrative about narrative, the novel at times is represented by Bradley Headstone. In many ways, the novel shares Headstone's Pygmalion fantasy and sets about to shape its thematic content into its own chosen coherent image. This is a necessary part of what the novel does and what the novel is, and though it is not the only or, given the values criticized, the most savory part, the novel is always at least a little like Bradley Headstone and can, unless there is a balancing contrary, share his fate. The novel also shares John Harmon's search for a responsive relationship to the world it depicts. It is a symbolic form through which new and inclusive relations to experience can be imagined. To the extent that it is like this, however, the novel, like Harmon, cannot be presented by Dickens as nothing more than a self-sufficient coherent reality. It must be open—a pattern of reciprocally related imaginative responses to experience rather than a coherent system in which symbols and truth are hastily equated. The novel must have, like Harmon, a suspended identity.

That Dickens features both Harmon and Headstone so prominently in the novel is one important way Dickens can escape repeating in his exploration of the novel's symbolic and narrative identity not only Headstone's self-destructive identification with his fictions but also the sterile coherence of the social world. What is at issue here is not just the moral ambiguity of Dickens making symbolic forms that are every bit as tyrannous as the social world that is depicted, it is that the novel as a symbolic form is inherently and formally ambiguous and that Dickens deliberately uses this ambiguity as an alternative to the dehumanizing certainties of the social world.[7]

Nor are Harmon and Headstone the only characters who represent such purely narrative concerns about the novel. Silas Wegg, for example, expresses, in comic form, his society's values and parodies the stories of other characters. Wegg's extortion scheme and his prospecting for treasure are a pointed parody of Harmon's relationship to Bella and Headstone's relationship to Lizzie and a less direct parody of both the narrator's and Harmon's attempts to sift and pan the social world for authenticity. But, because he knows, or thinks he knows, what he is looking for he simply repeats the errors of the social world and, like Headstone, ends up chasing a phantom of his own making.

Wegg's habit of chasing his own phantoms also serves another important purpose in the novel. Wegg, together with Venus, represents the potential failure of the novel to achieve a balance between responsiveness to the world and the demands of coherence. Wegg, who mimics the values of the social world, and Venus, who articulates creatures out of their remains, represent what the novel would be if it limited itself simply to reproducing the values of the social world. For this reason, Wegg and Venus haunt the novel like a comic bad conscience. That Venus is eventually saved may have less to do with any redeeming moral qualities he may have than with the fact that he never fully believes in Wegg's schemes. This gives Venus the self-consciousness he needs to save himself, a self-consciousness that resembles in its saving purpose Harmon's self-consciousness. Wegg, on the other hand, is adept at creating fictions, like the one about "Our House," which he then accepts as true. This disastrous habit of believing in his own fictions not only parodies society's and Headstone's belief in their own fictions, it serves as a constant reminder of what the novel must not do.

If Wegg and Venus illustrate some traps the novel must avoid, Jenny Wren illustrates the kind of complex relationship the novel can establish to its world. As the dolls' dressmaker, Jenny, like Dickens, reproduces in miniature the world of the glamorous and captures it in its most characteristic costumes. But, this reproduction of the social world, like the novel's own, only serves to highlight the terrible price that society exacts for the sake of its carefully controlled show. That Jenny is physically crippled and emotionally hurt by the very world she reproduces so faithfully indicates the very real effects the narrow and self-serving symbol system of society has on those it excludes and ignores.

Jenny responds to this oppressive world with a sadly precocious cynicism that makes what should be her fairytale dreams of romance into fantasies of defensive and retaliatory violence. But Jenny also acts in a way that is directly contrary to the values of the world that has hurt her. She uses her hands and her quick observation not only to reproduce the world of the glamorous but to find and make contact with her own world. Unlike the hands that grasp for power and money or the clenched fist Bradley Headstone slams down on the burial-ground enclosure, Jenny's hands search for a responsive contact with those she loves and trusts. This kind of touching implies a relationship to another who has not been already appropriated and digested by the demands of a system, either personal or social. The touch is the only real alternative on the thematic level to a social system that thrives on sameness and dominance. It is a moment of contact between characters who regard each other as independent fellow creatures, not as objects to be possessed or controlled. Even the most extreme version of touching, violent blows, is a way Harmon and Wrayburn are freed from their imprisoning social roles and are able to reconstitute their relationship to the world.

For Dickens to reenact on the symbolic level of the novel Jenny's touching of others on the thematic level, he must minimize the violent imposition of symbolic forms that produces moral and physical deformity, transform this violence into a form of human response to the world and not simply an act of aggression against it, and delineate the way the social world is made by those who seem to be nothing more than its mirrors. He needs to attack that world at its core, and this core is its certainty about its wholeness. To mount such an attack, Dickens decomposes the social world into the many symbolic perspectives and assertions that go into its making, thereby making the apparently complete social whole a multiform set of assertions about the world that then creates the need for other assertions, no one of which predominates over any other.

The many characters who make these symbolic assertions together form what Bakhtin calls a dialogue about the novel and its relationship to its world.[8] The characters wrangle with each other over how and what their world means and in so doing wrangle with each other over how and what the novel itself means. Such a dynamic arrangement is decidedly contrary to the neat arrangement of the representatives of society around the Veneerings' dining-room table where the characters act like so many Leibnizian monads, each reflecting, from his own particular angle, the totality of the social world. This static arrangement of monads, however, is an ideological sleight-of-hand used to conceal the underlying struggle for power.[9] Once this illusion is exposed and dispelled and the characters are understood as incarnations of symbolic assertions about the world, their arrangement becomes something more akin to the structure of an atom. The characters are related as symbolic force fields which determine and shape each other through their energy and momentary configuration rather than through their reflective powers. The coherence they have is the result of these momentary configurations and not of a settled system mirroring itself in all its details. By operating on both levels simultaneously, Dickens can decompose into a search for meaning, on the narrative and symbolic level, the story he is composing into a coherent system of meaning on the thematic level.

On this level of decomposed form, the story about how the novel means, Dickens works out his alternative to the otherwise monolithic social world he creates. For it is on this symbolic level that Dickens can do what the social world he depicts cannot: make not only explicit symbolic assertions about the world but also show the way each assertion, once made, changes the world it seeks to define, thereby changing what the assertion itself can mean. The social world, like its representative, Podsnap, flourishes away whatever does not conform or cannot be reduced to its norms. Characters like Riah and Betty Higden who, because of religion or class, do not fit the mold are relegated to the margins of the social world. Such characters, of course, cannot escape and are not freed from the effects of the society that neglects and ostracizes them. Riah must play the odious role of the Jewish usurer to protect his respectable Christian master and Betty Higden is hounded by the specter of the poor house up until her death. But, such characters are effectively excluded from the way society conceives of itself, from the identity the society develops for itself.

Dickens, on the other hand, not only includes characters like these in his story, he makes the marginalized world they inhabit, a world of symbolic values that is created by the dominance of the social world but that is also a response to all that is ignored by it, an integral part of the novel's identity as a narrative and symbolic form. The novel, in other words, unlike the social world, is about not only what it can assert directly and explicitly about its world and about itself, but also about the effects of all assertions on what the world can mean and, therefore, on how the world is. The world the novel represents, then, is not some truer and fully developed world that has been buried or submerged by society and can be excavated. It is the world that has been obscured by certainty but that is always being revealed through the conflict among the characters' various attempts to define and live in it. This is one reason why the characters never seem to find what they are looking for or find only what they don't expect. The treasure they are looking for is never what it seems because, by searching for the treasure, the characters have changed everything, including the role they play and what the treasure is.

Similarly, for Dickens, the meaning of his novel cannot be simply a nugget sifted out from meaningless dirt. What happens to the dirt and the change that takes place in the landscape and in the prospector, are as important as any nugget that might be found. Like his many failed prospectors but with more foresight and skill, Dickens sets out to sift and pan this curious and dead world to find out what, if anything, is still alive. But, as certainty and system fail, as meaning slips, like so much dirt, through the fingers grasping for power or money, Dickens makes it increasingly clear that the search for meaning itself, the act of sifting and panning, and not any fixed center of meaning, is the only real treasure to be found.

NOTES

1. The only real exception to the moral geometry of the novel is Jenny Wren's invitation to Riah to "Come up and be dead!" (335). The paradoxical nature of this invitation already suggests that the formal coherence characteristic of the novel's world will not give the characters the authenticity they seek.
2. Theodor Adorno, *Minima Moralia,* trans. E. F. N. Jephcott (London: Veso, 1974), 126–127, 144, 227.
3. J. Hillis Miller says of the world in *Our Mutual Friend:* "Man has absorbed the world into himself, and the transformed world has absorbed him into itself, in an endless multiplication of nothing by nothing." *Charles Dickens: The World of his Novels* (Cambridge: Harvard UP, 1959), 298. Here, Miller extends the discussion of the ambiguity of will in Dickens, especially the tendency of will, however well motivated, to become just one more form of aggression, to the collective human determination to subdue the world to definite human ends. The results, though entirely human in one sense, are also entirely dehumanizing.
4. I have in mind here Ruskin's idea that labor is an act of creation, similar to the labor of birth, and that profit is based on the production or discovery of something new. In contrast to Ruskin's ideas about labor is Marx's idea that labor is the basis of value in a closed economic system and that profit is the surplus value derived from unpaid labor. The social world of *Our Mutual Friend* seems to operate according to Marx's ideas, especially the idea of deriving profit from deprivation, while Harmon and, I believe, the novel as a whole operate according to Ruskin's. See John Ruskin, *Unto This Last and Other Writings,* ed. Clive Wilmer (New York: Penguin Books, 1985), 213, 217 and Karl Marx, *Wages, Price and Profits* (Peking: Foreign Languages Press, 1975) 48–49, 54.
5. Charles Dickens, *Our Mutual Friend* (New York: Penguin Books, 1971) 422. All future quotations will be from this edition and will be cited in parentheses.

6. The conception of symbolism I am using here is based on Cassirer's ideas. Cassirer claims that symbols, especially language and art, are not mental creations affixed to the world or separate realities derived from or imposed on the world but are ways of objectifying knowledge of and responses to it and therefore are instruments of discovery, rather than simple definitions. See Ernst Cassirer, "Language and Art I," in *Symbol, Myth, and Culture: Essays and Lectures of Ernst Cassirer 1935–1945,* ed. Donald Philip Verene (New Haven: Yale UP, 1979) 148, and *An Essay on Man* (New Haven: Yale UP, 1944) 143. I take Cassirer's use of the term objective to mean shared knowledge or perception rather than the more usual meaning of a reification of the living world.

7. My ideas about the formal conflicts that go into the identity of the novel are based in part on Adorno's ideas about the dialectical nature of art. Adorno conceives of autonomous art, art freed from serving any purpose other than its own self-defined purposes (for example, religious art), as locked in a struggle, perhaps a losing struggle, with its own contradictions. Foremost among these contradictions is form's relationship to content. Content is assimilated to and integrated with the internal demands of form, but, since content comes from the world outside the art work, this assimilation and integration must always be incomplete. Form, then, at least according to its own laws of integration, must fail if it is to succeed at all. If it were to succeed completely, it would fail even more seriously since it would then produce a kind of art completely divorced from the human world or a kind of art completely divorced from the human world or a kind of art that is fundamentally dishonest. Theodor Adorno, *Aesthetic Theory,* trans, C. Lenhardt, eds. Gretel Adorno and Rolf Tiedermann (London: Routledge & Kegan Paul, 1984). Adorno's ideas about the dialectical nature of art, both in relation to its autonomous concerns and in relation to the world art seems to withdraw from, are scattered throughout the work, but pages 6–11, 201, 207, 255, and 266–267 seem to be fairly representative.

8. M. M. Bakhtin, "Discourse in the Novel," in *The Dialogic Imagination: Four Essays,* trans, Caryl Emerson and Michael Holquist, ed. Michael Holquist (Austin: U of Texas P, 1981) 259–422. Bakhtin makes this comment that seems directly applicable to *Our Mutual Friend:*

> Languages of heteroglossia, like mirrors that face each other, each reflecting in its own way a piece, a tiny corner of the world, force us to guess at and grasp for a world behind their mutually reflecting aspects that is broader, more multi-leveled, containing more and varied horizons than would be available to a single language or a single mirror.
>
> (414–415)

See also "The Problem of Speech Genres," in *Speech Genres & Other Late Essays,* trans, Vern W. McGee, eds., Caryl Emerson and Michael Holquist (Austin: U. of Texas P, 1986) for a more general treatment of the way language necessarily becomes a dialogue about the world.

9. Miller, *Charles Dickens: The World of his Novels,* p. 291. Here Miller says:

> The proper model of the universe of *Our Mutual Friend* is not that of a non-Euclidean space filled with incommensurate local monads entirely isolated from one another. It is rather that of a large number of interlocking

perspectives on the world, each what Whitehead would call a special *prehension* of the same totality. But Dickens can never present the totality as it is in itself. Indeed, there is no such thing as the world in itself.

I would agree that the model of isolated monads is inadequate and that Dickens cannot present the totality directly and explicitly, but I believe that the totality is always changed by the characters' attempts to define it and that Dickens does present the totality indirectly on the symbolic level of the novel as the open totality of all the attempts to define and live in the world.

WORKS CITED

Adorno, Theodor. *Aesthetic Theory*. Trans. C. Lenhardt. Eds. Gretel Adorno and Rolf Tiedermann (London: Routledge & Kegan Paul, 1984).

———. *Minima Moralia*. Trans. E. F. N. Jephcott (London: Veso, 1974).

Bakhtin, M. M. "Discourse in the Novel." In *The Dialogic Imagination: Four Essays*. Trans. Caryl Emerson and Michael Holquist. Ed. Michael Holquist (Austin: U. of Texas P, 1981).

———. "The Problem of Speech Genres." In *Speech Genres & Other Late Essays*. Trans. Vern W. McGee. Eds. Caryl Emerson and Michael Holquist (Austin: U. of Texas P, 1986).

Cassirer, Ernst, *An Essay on Man* (New Haven: Yale UP, 1944).

———. "Language and Art I," in *Symbol, Myth, and Culture: Essays and Lectures of Ernst Cassirer 1935–1945*. Ed. Donald Philip Verene (New Haven: Yale UP, 1979).

Dickens, Charles. *Our Mutual Friend* (New York: Penguin Books, 1971).

Marx, Karl. *Wages, Price and Profits* (Peking: Foreign Languages Press, 1975).

Miller, J. Hillis. *Charles Dickens: The World of His Novels* (Cambridge: Harvard UP, 1959).

———. "*Our Mutual Friend*," in *Dickens: A Collection of Critical Essays*. Ed. Martin Price (Englewood Cliffs: Prentice-Hall, Inc., 1967).

Ruskin, John. *Unto This Last and Other Writings*. Ed. Clive Wilmer (New York: Penguin Books, 1985).

Wilson, Edmund. "Dickens: The Two Scrooges." In *The Wound and the Bow*. (New York: Farrar, Straus, Giroux, 1970).

"A Speeches of Chaff":
Ventriloquy and Expression
in *Our Mutual Friend*

Patrick O'Donnell

In an age of public spectacle for which P.T. Barnum serves as the ultimate
exemplar, Dickens' novels provide a succession of forays into the spectacular.
The spectacle can be viewed as a displacement of "private" anxieties and
fantasies onto the public stage. The authorial dream of omnipotence, for
example, is represented in spectacle via the guise of the master of entertainments or the entrepreneur. This dream is countered by the illusory heterogeneity of the entertainment itself which, fractured into the diversionary
activities of clowns, mimes, freaks, and the vertiginous confusion of the
"three-ring" circus or sequential "side-shows," threatens to slip out of the
ringmaster's control. As the carnivalesque accoutrements of the spectacle
indicate, it is transgressive, often blurring the line between "public" and
"private," or "outside" and "inside." In this way, the authority which ordains
a fictive world and fills it with "identities" is questioned by the very spectacle
that theatricalizes authorial projections and ordinations.

In Dickens' novels, the spectacle or story unfolds as a profusion of voices;
the author is at odds to maintain control over this cacophony for the sake of
his identity as the origin *of this work*. As Alexander Welsh's recent
reconstruction of Dickens' biography argues, commencing with the writing of
Martin Chuzzlewit, Dickens became markedly, at times, obsessively, concerned with issues of copyright and control over his work—and, by extension,
with the nature of his authorial identity as a form of writing (cf. especially
104–22). Dickens, no doubt, delighted himself and his readers with the early
discovery that he was capable of ventriloquizing a capacious assortment of

247

"typical voices." Even more, he found that he was able to create such convincing new characters as to provide a readership with a growing body of work that was more recognizably "Dickensian" with each new installment of "the Dickens world." Yet the incorporation of this world carries with it a price in the form of an authorial self-recognition. Founded upon the very "stuff" of Dickens' art—his ability to consume and recast fictions, plots, characters and voices, re-presenting them as part of a spectacle—the whole production, made public and jettisoned from the authorial self, has the capacity to alter radically the consistency and homogeneity of authorial identity in its separation from its "source." The "publication" of identity which, paradoxically, necessitates a questioning of the origins of identity as other than itself, might be said to characterize the crucial project of Dickens' major novels.[1]

To focus upon the specific representation of identity that I wish to discuss in this essay, particularly in the later fictions (but observable throughout his work), Dickens "throws" or scripts the tumultuous voices of his many characters with an increasing sense that, the more successful or spectacular the act of ventriloquy, the more self-questioned is the singular identity who is the source of those voices. The problematic endings of such novels as *Bleak House*, *Great Expectations*, and *Our Mutual Friend* are symptomatic of what might be termed Dickens' "modernization," where, increasingly, the constraints of plot become more self-consciously artificial in the effort, if not to control, then at least to remark ironically upon the relation between the created "world" and the authoring identity which serves as the foundation of that world. The "double-voiced" discourse of *Bleak House*, wherein Esther and a parodic echo of the classic omniscient narrator alternate chapters, the doubled-back commentary on narrative identity formulated by *Great Expectations*'s skeptical revision of *David Copperfield*, the sheer lack of vocal singularity in any aspect of *Our Mutual Friend*—all speak to Dickens' growing sense that identity is a linguistic effect or a figure of speech, a represented form of indeterminacy that reveals its foundations in the "unrepresentable."

In Dickens' last-completed novel, identity has become (to use Bakhtin's terminology) "pluralized" to the extent that Dickens' most successful ventriloquistic spectacle is a most public abandonment of the private, coherent "self," though the novel retains skeletal traces of the attempt to preserve an older, more masterful version of identity.[2] In *Our Mutual Friend*, Dickens is compelled to give up for good the "private" self—that idealized and narcissistic embodiment of knowledge, control, and desire—for a version of the "public" self, split up or spread amongst the novel's characters. These

PROGRAMME.

MR. LOVE

WILL PRESENT AN ENTERTAINMENT, ENTITLED

LOVE'S MIRROR

OF MANNERS, CUSTOMS, AND ECCENTRICITIES;

OR, GLIMPSES OF LIFE & CHARACTER AT HOME & ABROAD.

With entirely New and effective Mutative Costumes and Appointments throughout.

"To hold as 'twere THE MIRROR up to Nature."—SHAKSPEARE.

Prefatory Observations—Occasional Memorandums—An Old-fashioned Authority—Ridicule or Censure—An Amusing Way of correcting Faulty Habits—Cracking Jokes—A Thrifty Dutchman—His Peculiarities described—His Amusements and Literary Pursuits—His curious Conversions.

ILLUSTRATION . . . . . Mynheer VANSOURCROUTENHAUZEN.
(With a Story about a Hare.)

His Acquaintances—A Rush of Ideas to the Head—A Contributor to the Magazines.

ILLUSTRATION . . . . Miss SALMAGUNDI.
(A Literary Lady.)

Enigmas, Acrostics, and Charades—Ladies' Belle Assemblée—Miss Measureverse—Her Extraordinary Genius for Poetry —Twenty different Topics at Once.

BILOQUIAL ILLUSION AND VOCAL SKETCH :—" CELLAR COLLOQUY."
Mr. Multiple—His Peculiarities—Treacherous Memory—Advice Gratis.

ILLUSTRATION . . . . Mr. MULTIPLE.
(An Amateur Physician, Optician, Mathematician, and Musician.)

You don't look Well—Mr. ——, I forget his Name—His Case described—Voyage to America—Biddy O'Callaghan— Her Misfortunes.

ILLUSTRATION . . . . BIDDY O'CALLAGHAN.
(An Irish Nurse.)

A confirmed Gossip—Modern Innovations—Fielding's Little Benjamin—Smollett's Strap—Cervantes Nicholas.

ILLUSTRATION . . . . AMOS POPPIN.

(The Anglo-French-Canadian Village Barber, a Hybrid Animal; in Language, English; in Dress and Manner, French; in Shrewdness, Yankee.)

With a Scene in a Barber's Shop.

A Barber-*ous* Operation—The Heads of the People—Timothy Tricksey, Esq.—A Determined Gamester—Sent to Coventry—A Lac of Rupees—Long Tails.

SONG, "COME, SHOW ME THE MAN."
ORIGINAL MUSIC, COMPOSED FOR MR. LOVE, BY BLEWITT.

AFTER WHICH, MR. LOVE WILL PRESENT A VOCAL SKETCH,

Written for him by CHARLES FORRESTER, Esq., and delivered by Mr. LOVE, with great applause, in New York and New Orleans, also in Paris and London, entitled

A TRAVELLER'S REMINISCENCE,

OR, MINE HOST'S DILEMMAS AT THE NAG'S HEAD ON THE HEATH.

IN WHICH MR. LOVE WILL REPRESENT A CONFUSION AT THE HOTEL BETWEEN THE FOLLOWING PERSONS CONNECTED WITH THE SKETCH :

FIDGET BUTTS—A ready-witted fellow, *Landlord of a diminutive rustic Road-side Public-house, called the Nag's Head on the Heath (with an empty Larder.)*
JERRY—A stupid fellow from Somersetshire, *Boots and Knife-Cleaner at the Nag's Head.*
GREGORY }
HUMPHREY } *Active fellows, Waiters at the Nag's Head.*
Mr. O'GRADY—From Tipperary, *a Gentleman fond of whisky and " something substantial."* }
ALDERMAN GRIFFIN—From London, *a Gentleman who " don't like to give any trouble."* } *Hungry Travellers, just arrived at the Nag's Head.*
DOLLY—*Chambermaid at the Nag's Head.*
SNIFFLE—*Gardener at the Nag's Head.*
SNUFFLE—*Stable Boy at the Nag's Head.*

MR. LOVE.

AT THE END OF THE PIECE, MR. LOVE WILL INTRODUCE

AN ECCENTRIC FINALE BY ALL THE CHARACTERS (NINE) AT ONCE,

AN EFFECT NEVER BEFORE ACCOMPLISHED BY ANY OTHER ARTIST.

garner representation as a multitude of fragmentary voices whose origin is an "overhearing," a recapitulation and reformation of acculturated linguistic expressions that bear the marks of passage from privacy to "publication." In the most characteristic expression of the novel, Sloppy, that paragon of disorder, "do the Police," those paragons of order and authority, "in many voices" as he reads to Betty Higden from a newspaper. The phrase neatly summarizes the master trope of the novel—that of ventriloquy. Throughout *Our Mutual Friend* ventriloquy serves as a figure for Dickens' historic revision of the power and uses of voice in a novel which reflects the anxious recognition that the representation of "voice," in reading and writing, signifies the conversion of identity into a public spectacle. It is what this spectacle both represses and reflects—even as it formulates a commentary on this double movement—that is the subject of my analysis.

One of Dickens' lesser-known contemporaries, an historian of ventriloquy and a publicist who "spoke for" a popular impersonator, provides some interesting conceptions of the figure of ventriloquy that illuminate the dramatization of voice in *Our Mutual Friend*. Dickens may not have read George Smith's *Programme of the Entertainment: Preceded by Memoirs of Mr. Love, the Dramatic Polyphanist* upon its publication in 1856, but he may well have had occasion to view Mr. Love's act during one of the impersonator's two thousand performances in the City of London between 1836 and 1856.[3] The Dickens fascinated by the glossolalia experienced by the subjects of mesmeric trances, the stage performer who "did" the voices of his own characters to the point of exhaustion in public (and before his daughter and a mirror in private) would surely have found the activities of the "polyphanist" pertinent to his own attempts at ordaining and controlling the vocalizations of his novels.[4] Smith's pamphlet describes Mr. Love as, literally, a man of many parts: not only are his programs largely comprised of dramatic sketches in which he plays all the roles and throws all the voices, but they also occasionally include the performer's lecture on "The Difference Between True and Spurious Ventriloquy" or, perhaps, "A Zoological Concert, Consisting of Imitations and the Voices and Cries of Animated Nature" (32; 35).[5] Such characters as "Mr. Sparkle" and "Mr. Multiple" fill Love's programs and offer interesting, if coincidental prefigurations of the glittering Veneerings, the "Sparkler" of *Little Dorrit*, or the multiple Harmon-Handford-Rokesmith of Dickens most ventriloquistic narrative [see figure]. Smith argues that the genuine ventriloquist (i.e., anyone who projects different voices and breathes life into either an impersonated character or a dummy) "can summon up innumerable spirits" and must possess "a natural flexibility of features, so as to be able to destroy, to all outward appearance, his own identity, and to assume instantaneously any expression of countenance which the character to be sustained . . . may require" (20–21). For Smith, as I will argue, for Dickens, ventriloquy and impersonation are conflated activities which create the illusion of simultaneity between the actor and the personality he assumes (or the ventriloquist and the dummy he manipulates). At the same time, in the act of ventriloquy the illusion of simultaneity is shown up for its pretense as the erasure of an identity which is really imposed upon the simulated "other," even as it is disguised *as* "other." The success of the spectacle depends entirely upon the controlled suppression of the authorial "self" and an equally controlled sublimation or multiplication of the self as "characters."

The ventriloquist speaks *for* another *through* the impersonated other. In the illusory abolition of his own identity, he generates the fiction that he is merely standing in for the other who is controlling the disclosure while, all the while, the impresario dictates what is said.[6] For the spectacle to work, its metonymical underpinnings must be disguised by the author and "suspended" by the third party in the act, the audience, who knows that the "spontaneous" dialogue between the dummy and the ventriloquist is a pre-scripted monologue. Similarly, in the case of the "polyphanist," who Smith describes as speaking in several languages and "throwing his voice" into the various characters he impersonates, the audience must be willing to ignore the fact that one person is playing all of the roles even while it delights in the virtuosity of the single performer. Smith quotes an unidentified "modern writer" in suggesting that control over distance is the crucial factor in successfully creating this proper, contradictory relation with the audience:

> It would seem to follow, that the closer the person to be deceived is to the ventriloquist, the illusion must be more complete, seeing that the sound imitated, is the sound that strikes the performer's own ear, which it is obvious may not suit the variously arranged auditors in a larger theater. As the sound which reaches our ears must necessarily vary with the distance it has come—and as each variation is a specific imitable sound—so the ventriloquist has only (but assuredly it requires exquisite skill and ingenuity to do this artistically and effectively) to vary his imitation progressively, in either direction, to give a perfect illusion of advance and retreat.
>
> (14)

In this example, the distance between the ventriloquist and the audience is measured and closed, while it is exactly this distance (similar to the "concavity" that Hollander notes must be present, literally and figuratively, for an echo to occur [1–2]) that allows for the successful completion of the illusion. The fictions of ventriloquy and impersonation operate by means of several paradoxical effects that must be accepted, then ignored by the audience. These include maintaining control over the gaps between the performer and the spectators which must be disguised to simulate identification and proximity; establishing the singular omniscience of the ventriloquist or impersonator who must be pluralized, as voice is "thrown," into multiple roles; and concealing the identity of the ventriloquist who must go under the guise of the public "other" to the absconded author of these illusions.

So stand the conditions of Smith's ventriloquistic aesthetic, and they are illuminating for the discussion of "voice" in a novel made of simulated voices—mediatory and authorial, silent and domineering, spontaneous and prescribed. Sloppy may "do the Police in different voices" (243), but he is hardly an exceptional "polyphanist" in *Our Mutual Friend*. If the ventriloquist or impersonator is viewed as one who dominates the discourse while disguising that domination as an impersonation, then the Lammles, Fledgeby, Boffin, Podsnap, Jenny Wren, and even John Harmon are all ventriloquists pursuing various ends. Dickens' impersonation of his own characters in public and private "impersonates" the doubled, ventriloquistic relations between author and characters in the novels, especially in the case of those who, like Podsnap, see themselves as officially dispersed in others: "it was a trait in Mr. Podsnap's character . . . that he could not endure a hint of disparagement of any friend or acquaintance of his. 'How dare you,' he would seem to say, in such a case. 'What do you mean? I have licensed this person. This person has taken out *my* certificate. Through this person you strike at me, Podsnap the Great' " (307). As Dickens licenses Podsnap to say these things (significantly, in the mode of indirect discourse), so Podsnap certifies or prohibits the voices and actions, indeed the very being, of others—he speaks through them; they are his agents. Podsnap's gestures are authoritative and orchestral as he waves pieces of unpleasant reality out of existence; he dominates the mind of his daughter as an author might feel the necessity of "speaking for" a particularly passive, "weak" character.

Though he is admonished in the novel, Podsnap bears some faint resemblances to his maker who, in George Henry Lewes's recollection, "once declared to me that every word said by his characters was distinctly *heard* by him; I was at first not a little puzzled to account for the fact that he could hear language so utterly unlike the language of real feeling, and not be aware of its preposterousness; but the surprise vanished when I thought of the phenomena of hallucination" (101–2). Lewes notes that while evidence of "the phenomena of hallucination" (that is, speaking or hearing in different voices) is a sign of insanity in most instances, for the artist it is a mark of creativity. For Lewes, the difference between the schizophrenic and the sane artist is a matter of belief: "The characteristic point in the hallucinations of the insane, that which distinguishes them from hallucinations equally vivid in the sane, is the coercion of the image in *suppressing comparison* and all control of the experience. Belief always accompanies a vivid image, for a time; but in the sane this belief will not persist against rational control" (95–96). Thus, Lewes would say Dickens is sane and brilliant (despite some artistic faults such as lack of true ideas) because he had mastery over the voices he hears, does not ultimately believe in their reality, and can successfully channel them into the rationally patterned work of art. Unlike Sloppy who merely reads the voices he imitates, and who, with his "polysyllabic bellow" (250) can barely manage his own apparel ("he stood . . . a perfect Argus in the way of buttons" [390]; his hat is a patchwork conglomeration "from which the imagination shrunk discomfited and the reason revolted" [391]), Lewes's Dickens originates and orchestrates the voices he overhears. More like Podsnap effectually, if not intentionally, this version of Dickens is that of the successful impersonator: he not only "does the Police" but, as an artist who employs and contains the dichotomies of reason and the imagination, he polices well the momentary illusion of being overwhelmed by the public projections of his own voice. For Lewes, as for Smith, the maintenance of distance within the illusion of similitude is the crucial factor in determining the successful projection of voice. In Lewes's rationalization of "hallucination," and in an exhibition of authorial domination that becomes fascistic under the iron hand of Podsnappery, Dickens is both "medium" and "control," author and impersonated character, keeping his own lips buttoned while intonating and harmonizing the voices of the spectacle's assembled cast.

Lewes hints at the possibility, however momentary, of an "insane" Dickens gone out of control, unable to transform the many voices he projects into the designs of art because he has forgotten whose singular identity originates those voices. To control the discourse, in this sense, is to remember who (like "Podsnap the Great") lies behind authored expressions, and "who" is their point of reference. Yet, in *Our Mutual Friend*, the portrayal of unsuccessful attempts to control speech and thought, paired with interwoven cases of mistaken or forgotten identity, create an "authorial crisis" of such magnitude that Dickens must ironically cast the conclusion of the novel in the form of a precocious magical realism complete with an Edenic arbor, a golden bower, and even a floating infant bearing the maker's mark ("By a master stroke of secret arrangement, the inexhautible baby here appeared at the door, suspended in mid-air by invisible agency" [841]). The harmonic, fairy-tale ending of the novel has called for a good many causal readings. As a conclusion that evidently configures a new society founded upon charity rather than greed, or rather, a beneficent rather than stingy patrimony, it closes off one of Dickens' most resolute plots. Still, there survives the sense, represented by the ceaseless wails of "the inexhaustible," that the raised voices and spirits of *Our Mutual Friend*, while abruptly silenced by the contingencies of plot and closure, have hardly been brought under control.[7] Indeed, what might be called the theatricalizations of voice in the novel—the cries of the infant, the unstilled babble of the Veneerings and "The Voice of Society," the pastoral echoes of the Upper Thames which commemorate the death of Betty Higden—variously serve as ironic commentary upon the inefficacy of plot and its containments when countered by the noisy, "sloppy," unharmonious supplements of voice and impression.

Henry James's famous complaint in his negative review of *Our Mutual Friend* was just this: that Dickens had lost control over his artistry, that he had failed to administer his own fancies properly, and that, as an author, he was "exhausted."[8] Yet we may regard this exhaustion as a recognition that there is something in "voice" that floods the confines of narrative architecture, a residue that can not be wholly contained, or only represented as a sign of that which precedes and escapes "narration." This vocal residue may be seen as a kind of negativity marking the distance (that element of ventriloquy which, again according to Smith, *must* remain under the artist's control) between voice as projected, or written down, and its origins. Such distance is an absence that both contravenes and necessitates the fiction of an authorial "presence" behind the voice, just as there must be distance between the ventriloquist and his dummy so that a voice can be thrown, or concavity so that echo can be heard. The conception of voice which, Michael Beaujour suggests, links sounds and presence within the Judeo-Christian tradition is challenged by the increasingly conflicted recognitions of impersonation in Dickens' novels:

> Indeed, until very recently, voice implied presence, a spatial and temporal coincidence between a speaker and at least one hearer. . . . In the context of myth and poetry, in . . . certain heightened mutual states, people would hearken to the voices of deities, angels, saints, and spirits of the dead. Even animals and inanimate things would be expected to speak under the proper circumstances. Although "hearing voices" remained an uncanny experience, it was not exclusively a pathological one. Witness Abraham, or Moses. "God

called unto him out of the midst of a bush, and said: 'Moses, Moses.' And he said: 'Here I am.' " Such a call could lead to a *vocation*. . . . A person might also feel *possessed* by a supernatural being, who would substitute its own voice for that of its human *medium*. Voice manifested presence. A voice-event was an epiphany. Even simulation, the actor's, for instance, or that of the rhapsodist and the ventriloquist, indicated that someone was sufficiently present to confer presence upon a fictitious, alien voice.

(273)

Lewes wanted to portray Dickens ordaining and "overhearing" the voices of his own characters—the author playing both God and Moses—as a vocational, rather than a pathological event, but for Dickens himself, the distinction may not have been so easy to make. This is particularly so in *Our Mutual Friend* where "alien voices" seem to possess their originator and threaten, rather than ensure the self-sustaining epiphanic moment. As Beaujour argues, the simulation and mimicry of other voices for which Dickens is so well known suggests the presence of the author behind the roles. But in *Our Mutual Friend*, the fragmentation of the complex relation between represented speech (the only way voice may be "thrown" in writing) and authorial presence posits a crucial revision of "voice" as the public expression of the self which undermines what that expression formerly guaranteed: the locating and representing of identity ("Here I am") and its authoritative sources.[9] In short, the novel portrays a crisis of representation; it is most self-revelatory when, beneath its harmonies, the residual, parasitical "noise" of speech is heard.[10]

In the most general sense, acts of ventriloquy or impersonation constitute an attempt to create a fictive "other," then to control the other's speech while representing it as issuing forth from the "individual." If the illusion is successfully conveyed, the "author" has accomplished the double task of making himself and his "characters" present at once. Such acts abound in *Our Mutual Friend*: they run the gamut from instances where one, simply, speaks for another to the employment of catechisms, highly artificial frames of reference, dictated speeches, and soliloquies disguised as "duets," all imposed upon potentially dialogic situations for the purpose of mastering the discourse. Acts of ventriloquy are employed by villains, like the Lammles, or heroes, like Boffin and Harmon; their apparent success in the novel varies with the manifest moral worth of the scheme the impersonator perpetrates.

Yet, especially in the most successful ventriloquizations, such as the one where the Boffins and Harmon co-author the script of Bella's transformation from greedy rags to beneficent riches, the "act" seems excessive, the threat of

failure ever-present, and the balance between good intentions and domineering method tenuously maintained. In cases of failed ventriloquy, of course,
the moral point is strongly made ("one should not try to control the speech and
actions of others *if* the ends are self-serving"). In these instances, wrongdo-
ers, like the Lammles, are exiled from Eden to the hell of "the Continent," or
like Fledgeby, meted out a physical punishment fitting the crime. But
decidedly in those acts of ventriloquy supposedly motivated by good
intentions, after the rewards have been distributed, there still remains the
sense that the crucial distance between origin and medium has broken down,
and that the "ventriloquist" is made to wear the emperor's new clothes—a
sense that may help explain the response, continuous since the novel was first
published, that the Golden Dustman's conversion into philanthropist from
miser is unconvincing and fraudulent. Somehow, the transference of identity
has been *too* successful, and the "polyphanist" playing the part of the miser
begins to receive dictation from the persona he has created and directed:

> "Never thought of it afore the moment, my dear!" Boffin observed to Bella.
> "When John said, if he had been so happy as to win your affections and possess
> your heart, it comes into my head to turn around upon him with 'Win her
> affections and possess her heart! Mew says the cat, Quack quack says the duck,
> and Bow-wow-wow says the dog.' I couldn't tell you how it came into my head
> or where from, but it had so much the sound of a rasper that I astonished myself.
> I was awful nigh bursting out a laughing though, when it made John stare!"
>
> (848)

In this scene of comic recognition, Boffin's "rasper" seems harmless enough,
but recalling the moment itself, he admits loss of control over the origins of
his speech as he sinks to an animalistic level in an imitation of the cat's meow
and the dog's bark. The comic framing of this admission allows the narrator
and the reader to pass it all off as part of the good design—perhaps, even, the
coup de grâce—that will bring Bella into harmony with the mind of Harmon.
But in this condoned speech act there is some interference, a rasping that
surpasses design and intention while revealing the anxiety that accompanies
all speech acts in *Our Mutual Friend* as they negotiate the extremes of failure
and overdetermination.

To focus on Boffin's "rasper" or any of the many other instances where
expression is excessive or noisy in *Our Mutual Friend* is to notice a slippage
in the connection between "voice" and "identity" which the presence of voice
naturally assumes, and which the figures of ventriloquy and impersonation
serve to complicate. The artificiality of the connection is most notable when
those who have tenuous identities attempt to speak. George Sampson, the

pale, wan suitor of Bella, then her sister, Lavinia, is thoroughly dominated by the many-voiced Mrs. Wilfer (herself a compilation of roles) to the extent that even when he is full of feeling, he cannot speak: "The friend of the family was in that stage of tender passion which bound him to regard everybody else as the foe of the family. He put the round head of his cane in his mouth, like a stopper, when he sat down. As if he felt himself full to the throat with affronting sentiments" (155). Lady Tippins, whose identity is composed of fictions about non-existent lovers, is known "by a certain yellow play in her throat, like the legs of scratching poultry" (54). Rogue Riderhood, who plays Lightwood to Heastone's Wrayburn, can be heard to "throw his words . . . for his voice was as if the head of his boat's mop were down his throat" (109). Headstone himself, when he plays the role of teacher, is a master of language, but when he is confronted by the object of passion whom he wishes to teach, his voice becomes a parodic representation of repressed desire: " 'I should like to ask you,' said Bradley Headstone, grinding his words slowly out, as though they came from a rusty mill; 'I should like to ask you, if I may without offence, whether you would have objected—no; rather, I should like to say, if I may without offence, that I wish I had the opportunity of coming here with your brother and devoting my poor abilities and experience to your service' " (401). To a cab driver, Old Harmon is "a speeches of chaff" (98), as if voice conveyed the husk of personality rather than any internal presence of being. Rokesmith's voice is "agreeable in tone, albeit constrained" (141); Jenny Wren's voice crazily alternates between the angelic and the demonic as she speaks of visiting seraphim one moment, then talks of the punishment she would confer upon a fictive husband ("Him") should he turn out to be, like her father, a drunkard: " 'When he was asleep, I'd make a spoon red hot, and I'd have some boiling liquor bubbling in the saucepan, and I'd take it out hissing, and I'd open his mouth with the other hand—or perhaps he'd sleep with his mouth ready open—and I'd pour it down his throat, and blister and choke him' " (294). This seems a particularly fitting punishment for a potential wastrel in a novel where "voice" is often the conveyance of will, and "harmoney" a kind of moral reward.

Figuratively, the intensity of these examples resides less with the content of the communication and more with the faulty instruments of mouths and throats often envisioned as stopped up, unhinged, or in some way mutilated. Speech is often *disfigured* in *Our Mutual Friend*: what we "hear" in each of these cases is the noisy interference of the linguistic medium itself. Something stands between the "self" who wishes to speak and what gets said; this "something" signifies a partial loss of control over the speech act both for those who act as ventriloquists or impersonators as they attempt to script the discourse (like Boffin), and those who are the subjects of ventriloquy (like Bella or Georgiana Podsnap). These are instances of parasitical speech in Michael Serres's sense of the "parasite" as the element in communication that generates static, feeding off the relation between speaker and hearer, both complicating and, paradoxically, nurturing that relation (3–47; 94–97; see also Wilden 395–412). The "speech defects" of the novel thus work to question the efficacy and origins of speech in the individual speaker, and the ability of the speaker to transmit "self-presence" to another.

More revealing examples of such "interference" occur when a certain kind of speech act, intended to promote and control discourse going under the illusion of "communication," actually thwarts that effort—a failed ventriloquy in the literal sense. When the Lammles attempt to open up lines of communication between an uncooperative Fledgeby and Georgiana Podsnap, or when they try to convince the Boffins to take them as stand-ins for Rokesmith and Bella, they assume the role of ventriloquists who cannot get the dummy to speak. In the former instance, the "conversation" begins with Alfred Lammle trying to force Fledgeby to pay Georgiana a false compliment:

> "Georgiana," said Mr. Lammle, low and smiling, sparkling all over, like a harlequin; "you are not in your usual spirits. Why are you not in your usual spirits, Georgiana?"
>
> Georgiana faltered that she was much the same as she was in general; she was not aware of being difficult.
>
> "Not aware of being different!" retorted Mr. Alfred Lammle. "You, my dear Georgiana! who are always so natural and unconstrained with us? who are such a relief from the crowd that are all alike! who are the embodiment of gentleness, simplicity, and reality!"
>
> Miss Podsnap looked at the door, as if she entertained confused thoughts of taking refuge from these compliments in flight.
>
> "Now I will be judged," said Mr. Lammle, raising his voice a little, "by my friend Fledgeby."
>
> "OH DON'T!" Miss Podsnap fairly ejaculated: when Mrs. Lammle took the prompt-book.
>
> "I beg your pardon, Alfred, my dear, but I cannot part with Mr. Fledgeby quite yet; you must wait for him a moment. Mr. Fledgeby and I are engaged in a personal discussion."
>
> Fledgeby must have conducted it on his side with immense art, for no appearance of uttering one syllable had escaped him.
>
> (315)

The painful discussion goes on in this vein for several pages, with the Lammles taking both their own parts and those of Fledgeby and Georgiana, who remain nearly silent throughout. The Lammles' attempts to "raise the spirits" of their guests are fruitless, but their purpose—which is merely to produce speech between two silent parties and, thus, initiate a deeper relation—is clearly frustrated in the ventriloquistic effort to originate and dominate the substance of speech. Instead, the silent parties inadvertently control the speech of the sparkling "harlequin" and his wife by virtue of their refusal to talk: each new tack in the discussion becomes increasingly predictable and more easily subverted by those who wish to avoid communication. Eventually, the Lammles' discourse, with its false starts, repetitions, and clichés appears to be scripted by those playing the dummy hand. The failure of these parasites is both communicative and economic: they succeed in generating only noise where they would create a relation between dominated identities; appropriately, in the end, they are exiled from the master's table where they sought to feed. Their scheming begins on a honeymoon when the celebration of their own new relation is revealed to be a case of reciprocal mistaken identity; since they cannot leech off each other, they attempt to construct a system of communication that will allow them to "parasite" others. Here, the inability to articulate a social identity—the harlequinade as airy as the illusory perfect house which the Lammles have never seen and will never buy, but which all their friends are convinced is "made for them"—is projected as vain speech.

The Lammles, of course, are castigated, and the Boffins and Harmons elevated according to the worth of their intentions, but as I have suggested, the means by which all achieve these ends are similar. Just as the Lammles try to "script" Georgiana and Fledgeby, so is Bella scripted by her husband and adopted parents. The novel authorizes the latter activity through the concordances of plot, but in both cases, there is a contamination of expression—whether a "rasping" or the furious intonations of a frustrated harlequin—which interferes with the "clarity" of a speech act portending the desire for the creation of "proper" relations. Indeed, contamination, mutilation, and disarticulation of expressions, bodies, voices, and rivers abound to such an extent in *Our Mutual Friend* that, to take one of these elements alone, the disfigured vocal embodiments of problematic identities threaten to drown out any celestial strains issuing forth from the golden bower of the Harmons' domestic paradise. Before he dies, Gaffer Hexam fearfully asks Lizzie, " 'Have we got a pest in the house? Is summ'at deadly sticking to my clothes? What's let loose upon us? Who loosed it?' " (121). His questions express a general anxiety regarding the pest that contaminates the house of this novel, typified by all of the parasites who live off the waste and death of others. Venus's decomposed skeletons, Jenny Wren's mutilated dolls, and Boffin's dust heaps may be seen as physical analogues to the disfigurations and "waste" of speech in the novel, from Wrayburn's pointless riddles to Wegg's mutilation of the classics. The incremental effect of the novel's literal and figural parasitical relations suggests that the "world" of *Our Mutual Friend*, while highly organized, is also entropic, and that such a world sustains its orders and hierarchies at the expense, and in fear of, that within it—death, alterity, heterogeneity—which it would silence. The systems of communication which authorize this suppression are, thus, inherently ironic, in that the suppression, like the attempts to ventriloquize speech, actually *produces* the interferences of the novel.

So fragile and tenuously maintained are the communicative systems of *Our Mutual Friend* that many of its speakers feel compelled to create unnecessary fictions in order to frame speech, as if it needed to be, literally, shored up. Similarly, the speakers of the novel often talk too much, as if the generation of a linguistic excess ensures the continuance of a speech act verging on insignificance even as it is more elaborately framed and compounded. Between Mary Ann and Miss Peecher there must be the fiction of a catechetical "exam" in order to enable a discussion about Headstone's relationship to Lizzie; between the Inspector, Lightwood, and Wrayburn there emerges the sheer linguistic waste of an elaborate fiction about lime barges and lime salesmen which outruns its initial use as a cover for their investigation of Gaffer's disappearance long before the talk of lime is ended. Perhaps the most egregious example of this kind of linguistic excess is devised within a scene apparently concerned with the portrayal of an act of clerical benevolence, but an act that almost disastrously interferes with the progress of the novel at a climactic point. Near the end, Lightwood, the Milveys, and Jenny Wren are hurrying to Eugene, who is close to death. The Milveys are delayed from a timely arrival at the train station by one Mrs. Sprodgkin, an annoying parishioner who inevitably demands their attention at moments when they can least afford to return it. Mrs. Sprodgkin is portrayed as having "an infection of absurdity about her, that communicated itself to everything with which, and everybody with whom, she came into contact" (817). Mrs. Milvey refers to this parasite as " 'such a marplot,' " a fair and accurate label considering that Mrs. Sprodgkin threatens to bring the advancement of the climax to a screeching halt by keeping the Milveys from their appointed time and place in the text. A more visible pest like Silas Wegg is simply a Mrs.

Sprodgkin writ large, for the only useful purpose the wrecker of ballads and syntax serves is to foul up Boffin's schemes for restricting Harmons' identity and reuniting him with his pre-destined bride; like Mrs. Sprodgkin, Wegg is all noise and marplot. To be sure, the Milveys get to the station on time, just as the dust heaps and Wegg are carted away in the conclusion of the novel: the contamination of the discourse is partially absolved through the highly contrived concordance of plot. But in between the initiation of the mystery of mistaken identity and its resolution, Dickens has generated a good many plots and characters who resemble the "no thoroughfare" down which Wrayburn leads Headstone. These, figuratively, are blind alleys where the only "self-discovery" comes in the form of mirroring or doubling that reflects an "identity" borne of the excesses and repetitions of desire, either unsuccessfully repressed or allowed expression in the excesses of language: thus, after a nightlong chase, Wrayburn faces his alter ego while speaking casual nonsense to Lightwood. From the old pensioner who appears at Bella's wedding (and who, with two wooden legs, doubles Wegg) to Old Riah, whose lengthy complicity with Fledgeby simply *interferes* with all attempts to see him as the good Jew counterpart to Fagin, Dickens "contaminates" his own novel with apparent and real parasites, and with parasitical plots and relations that unnecessarily complicate the narrative communications and exchanges of *Our Mutual Friend*.

In a large sense, such contaminations are what fiction is made of: fiction can be viewed as a conglomeration of voices, or entanglements, or unnecessary complications that separate beginning from end, intention from act.[11] But this conception of fiction is countered by that ventriloquistic desire which comes under the name of "authorial intention." To recall Smith's discourse on ventriloquy, the successful polyphanist must control the distance between the real and apparent origins of voice so that the audience can indulge in the paradoxical illusion that the actor simultaneously is and is not the voice he projects, or that the dummy is a separate identity containing the displaced "presence" of the ventriloquist. The contaminations of speech in *Our Mutual Friend* undermine the assumed or intended connections between voice and presence and dispel the illusion of simultaneity between speaker, medium, and represented speech. In its very constitution, the act of ventriloquy puts its own illusory processes into question as it theatricalizes the re-presentation of identity. In similar ways, *Our Mutual Friend* stages the disarticulation and reconstitution of the "I" who speaks, but within this process it necessarily produces something else—a supplement or noise—that precedes the formation of any articulated identity.

* * *

John Harmon's story originates in the tale of "The Man from Somewhere," told by the laconic Mortimer Lightwood within view of "the great looking-glass above the sideboard" of Veneering's table. In this scene, J. Hillis Miller remarks, "Veneering gradually manifests himself like an ectoplasmic vision at a seance, hovering in the space behind the mirror, a space which is both the imaginary space of the novel and the inner space of the reader's mind" (*Form*, 41). While Dickens summons forth Veneering's substanceless spirit at the novel's inception, he cancels Harmon and displaces his identity onto, successively, Julius Handford and John Rokesmith. The "original" Harmon is reconstituted in the end not as an "ectoplasm," but as the reincarnation of the "real" John Harmon nicely juxtaposed to the vanquished Veneerings.

But Dickens does not stop there. In the "Postscript, in Lieu of a Preface" to the novel, he recounts the salvation of his own text from the Staplehurst railway accident of 1865. Of his own potential conversion into an ectoplasm, Dickens writes: "I remember with devout thankfulness that I can never be much nearer parting company with my readers for ever, than I was then, until there be written against my life the two words with which I have this day closed this book—THE END" (894). In sealing his narrative with the temporary deliverance of his own identity, Dickens openly declares one of the conscious purposes of his writing: to establish a "company" of "kept" readers. This readerly company is analogous to the new community assembled in the Golden Bower at the novel's redemptive conclusion—a resurrected society established in direct contrast to the "Society" of noisy Veneerings and Podsnaps, who are reduced to so much hot air in the end.

Thus, the plot of this novel of mistaken and found identities appears to fulfill the discovered intentions of the postface, save that Dickens brings up the "writing against life" which presently closes the novel and will serve as the monumental inscription marking the passing of the author. In this retrospective supplement to the novel (which displaces a non-existent "preface," or a more proper introduction, and which can also be seen as an instance of the author stepping from behind the mask to "face" the audience) Dickens offers a revealing commentary upon those artifices of *Our Mutual Friend*— especially the constraints of plot—which he has contrived in order to establish an ironic "authority" over the novel's unruly spirits. Here, Dickens both commemorates the saving of the self and the text while foreshadowing the disappearances of the authorial self as something recorded *by* a text, a "writing against life." In so doing, he reforges the conception of identity as "the subject in process," a continuous evolving of the "self" in language as both the expression and repression of what comes "outside" language—what Julia Kristeva calls "the chora" or "the modality of significance in which the linguistic sign is not yet articulated as the absence of an object" (28). For Kristeva, the "semiotic" is that aspect of language which cuts across its "symbolic," formalistic, syntactically "correct," "logical" dimensions. The semiotic ruptures of discourse—its "noise," lyric and prosaic excesses, rhythmic resonances, and play—faintly echo what she conceives to be the "preface" of discourse, society, and identity, which is the absence of these as separable from the negated subject, the maternal body, *become* an object in the realm of the symbolic. In the "Postface," Dickens appears to turn away from the negated subject of Ellen Ternan. She accompanied him on the journey and was rescued by the author, but her presence on the scene was unrecorded for fear that her being identified as Dickens' fellow traveller would result in bad publicity—he, thus, records her absence in the epitaph.[12] In bringing up, as it were, both the death of the author and the negation of the subject, the "Postface" reflects back on the novel proper to suggest that the disfigurations of voice and body in *Our Mutual Friend* counterbalance its postings of identity even as the fiction of identity attempts to frame, silence, or symbolize the linguistic traces of "the absent object" which precedes it. In scrutinizing the novel's "semiotic" dimension, those places where the representations of speech, like the bodies which speak, are partial, cut up, discontinuous, we can shadow that absent object of *Our Mutual Friend*, which is, indeed, its hidden subject—what stands behind its author and the profusion of characters and voices he projects.

I have previously suggested how ventriloquy can stand as a figure for the complex process of identity formation Kristeva describes, and what that process reveals and represses. Surrounded by those who would make her speak words she cannot say and who cut her short when she begins to voice her own desires, Georgiana Podsnap typifies all of the novel's subjects who are silenced or whose voices and fates seem to be pre-scripted by the dominating, authorial discourse of fathers, avuncular stand-ins, would-be husbands, domineering hostesses, shrewish wives. To a lesser extent, Bella, Lizzie Hexam, Twemlow, Mr. Wilfer, even Jenny Wren (who is a ventriloquist herself) find themselves the subjects of attempted acts of ventriloquy which would confer upon the ventriloquized subject an identity, but one that is not his or her "own." Perhaps the most comic portrayal of this state of affairs can be seen in the case of Pleasant Riderhood, who is pressed by the articulator of bodies, Mr. Venus, to say the right word to his proposal of marriage, but who successfully refuses the subjection to him in declaring that she "will not be seen in that bony light." In *Our Mutual Friend*, while the Georgianas and the Lizzies may often stay silent before the onslaught of a louder, more domineering voice, the speaking subject—because it is plural, multivocal—cannot be so easily disposed of. With its huge cast of characters, each with his or her own idom and idiosyncrasy, the novel pursues the notion of a "collective subject" which in its more disruptive moments speaks against the vacuous "voice of Society" and the sentimentalized homogeneity of the charmed circle of the Golden Bower. In this way, the idea of a single voice, an authorized speaker, a ventriloquistic presence, is challenged by the sheer "partiality" of voice and character in the novel. Indeed, even in those speakers who most effectively seek to ventriloquize others, there is a civil war between "authorized" or "articulated" speech and those rebellious intonations which exceed or refuse the rigidities of official discourse: an hysterical tone can be heard in Harmon's midnight soliloquies as well as Headstone's passionate outbursts; Boffin can complete with Wegg or the Lammles or Podsnap in the art of double-talk, though, of course, he is "just playing."

Eruptions of what Kristeva refers to as the "semiotic" into speech acts occur, of course, in all of Dickens' novels, but they are often located within the confines of the habitual speech patterns of particular (usually eccentric) characters such as a Sam Weller, or a Sarah Gamp, or a Flora Finching. As a counterweight to these, there is the controlling voice of authority—that of the omniscient narrator of many early novels; or the older, world-weary self reflecting back on youth in *Great Expectations*; or the dry, jaded voice of the quasi-omniscient narrator of *Bleak House* acting as an ironic corrective to Esther's presumed sentimentality and egotism. *Our Mutual Friend* might be seen as the result of the intensification of the semiotic in Dickens' corpus; here, there is no normative "center" of speech, not even that of the furtive narrator who, when he speaks, does so in the voice of the mock-parliamentarian or mock-historian. The type of "speech defect" exhibited in the more concentrated medium of Flora Finching in *Little Dorrit* becomes, in *Our Mutual Friend*, what might be termed a "communication disorder" to be observed in many aspects of the novel. Flora introduces herself to Mr. Dorrit, who does not know her, in this manner:

> "I beg Mr. Dorrit to offer a thousand apologies and indeed they would be far too few for such an intrusion which I know must appear extremely bold in a lady and alone too, but I thought it best upon the whole however difficult and even apparently improper though Mr. F.'s aunt would have willingly accompanied me and as a character of great force and spirit would probably have struck one possessed of such a knowledge of life as no doubt with so many changes must

have been acquired, for Mr. F. himself said frequently that although well educated in the neighbourhood of Blackheath at as high as eighty guineas which is a good deal for parents and the plate kept back too on going away but that is more a meanness than its value that he had learnt more in his first years as a commercial traveller with a large commission on the sale of an article that nobody would hear of much less buy which preceded the wine trade a long time than in the whole six years in that academy conducted by a college Bachelor, though why a Bachelor more clever than a married man I do not see and never did but pray excuse me that is not the point"

(680).

Naturally, Mr. Dorrit is speechless before this onslaught, the subject of which is deferred beyond the point of logic and reason. Even if one were to regard Flora's speech as having the potential to "make sense," working back through it in order to determine its original point of reference would involve laborious and improbable speculations whose yield, in terms of knowledge of "what she is talking about," would be small. Flora's speech is both rhapsodic and dissociative, and it functions as a kind of jamming device in *Little Dorrit*. Such speech undermines "relationality" in several senses; within it, syntactical chains are broken, patterns of significance are skewed, and information is converted into pure sound as Flora's narcissistic relation to the world of persons and objects around her is rendered as a linguistic meandering, all echo and repetition. This severing of language from a referential ground signifies the intrusion of the semiotic into the discourse of Dickens' novels.

Linguistic disorders of this kind are dispersed throughout *Our Mutual Friend*. Eugene, for example, interrupts the Veneerings' dinner-table conversation with this piece of nonsense about "the man from Tobago," the introduction to the story of "the man from Somewhere," John Harmon: "'Except . . . our friend who long lived on rice-pudding and isinglass, till at length to his something or other, his physician said something else, and a leg of mutton somehow ended in daygo'" (54). Eugene's statement is a parody of reference, a riddle which confounds the relation between answers and clues while providing a groundless "context" for Harmon's story. Later in the novel, Eugene will mystify Boffin by confusing the literal and metaphorical implications of the parable of the bees, as he will madden Headstone by taking pieces of his figurative speech literally, out of context, in order to drive the schoolmaster from the room. After Headstone has gone, Eugene remarks to Mortimer that "one would think the schoolmaster had left behind him a catcechizing infection" (348), though whether the communicative breakdown has begun in Headstone's strained questions or Eugene's punning answers is unclear—this "infection," analogous to Mrs. Sprodgkin's spreading "contamination" of speech, defines the "no thoroughfare" of their relation to each other.

In his own realm of influence, Headstone participates in an education system where "the adult pupils were taught to read (if they could learn) out of the New Testament; and by dint of stumbling over the syllables and keeping their bewildered eyes on the particular syllables coming round to their turn, were absolutely ignorant of the sublime history, as if they had never heard of it" (264). Here and elsewhere, in the fragmentation of discourse, the distance between linguistic sign and point of reference is so great that elaborate fictions of reference and cohesion (like that of the lime salesman) must be produced so that the threatened loss of connection between sign and signified can be reconstituted and sustained. Frequently, the difference between the literal and figurative levels of language are collapsed in an effort to articulate and embody "selfhood" amidst the "disarticulation" of the novel. A "non-reader" like Rogue Riderhood believes nothing exists until it is "took" down and "spelled out," that is, until his oral lies are converted into inscribed truths by "the binding powers of pen and ink" (196), never mind that the unreadable syllables of inscription bear no relation to the reality they supposedly describe. For Wegg, every far-fetched rhyme can be transformed into occasional verse; for Podsnap, a single "no" and a gesture can sweep away whole worlds and their contexts; for Mrs. Wilfer, every stray piece of conversation is transformed into a reference concerning her undeserved fate as Mrs. Wilfer. Even Harmon (in the role of Rokesmith) both "figures" and disfigures language as he vows to bury "John Harmon additional fathoms deep" and to heap "mounds and mounds of earth over John Harmon's grave" (425), as if he could sever his relation to the past merely through the employment of a figure of speech which metaphorically entombs its speaker while bearing literal reference to the most tangible element of his past, his inheritance of the dust mounds.

As is the case with those instances where ventriloquy fails in its efforts to control speech, these forced connections, while intended to reforge syntactic relations and to represent identity, actually work to undermine them. The collapsing of the distance between, for example, the literal and figurative senses of a phrase inevitably result in a parody of sense, just as Eugene's nonsense, or Jenny Wren's demonic rhapsodies, or the fragmented remembrances of Headstone's pupils abjure the cohesion of "normal" speech. These relational breakdowns are, again, evidence of the semiotic, which is "artic-ulated by flow and marks: facilitation, energy transfers, the cutting up of the corporeal and social continuum as well as that of the signifying material"

(40). In Kristeva's view, this form of "articulation" is in counterpoint to "the realm of signification . . . a realm of *positions*" and of the "*identification* of the subject" (43). In a novel of mistaken identity, it is "identity" seen as a linguistic positioning or form of signification that is questioned in the disfigurations of language, even as identities, represented as characters, are contained by the form of plot. Analogously, as Kristeva suggests, the "social continuum" and the "corporal" are "cut up" in the novel, and in the representation of bodies in *Our Mutual Friend*, Dickens gives fullest expression to the semiotic "origins" of identity in the inarticulate.

The "social continuum" can be defined as a network of class and kinship relations which contribute to the formation of the "self" as a body and being related to others through economic and linguistic systems of exchange. In Lévi-Strauss's classic formulation, the objects or signs of these exchanges are women, and the subjects, men, both of whose social identities depend upon the continuance of a totemic, partriarchal economic system.[13] In *Our Mutual Friend*, the skewing of familial and genealogical relations occurs alongside the exploding of linguistic relations, and in these disfigurations, the connection between "the semiotic" and "the social" is forged. Bella, Jenny, and Lizzie are all daughters of non-existent or spurious mothers: with the exception of Betty Higden, a Mother Hubbard figure who disappears, significantly, into the pastoral landscape of the novel less than half-way through, the "proper" maternal bodies of the novel are absent. As if to compensate, the relations of the three major female characters to their fathers are defined in terms of a mother to her child. Metaphorically, Bella, Lizzie, and Jenny are orphans (like Harmon) biologically born of their parents, but in fact, socially responsible for mothering their own fathers in an overdetermined manner: as Roger Henkle argues, the portrayal of Jenny and her relation to her father is a parody of all those Dickensian "little women" in whom the good mother and the "daughterly" woman are combined.[14] Women are, thus, "positioned" in their nominative common roles as mothers, but the social continuum which depends on their acceptance of these positions is made vulnerable to a collapse of the relational differences which "normally" exist between fathers and daughters when the daughters become mothers or wives. When this takes place in a novel where the collapsing of the distance between the literal and figural levels of language is a common occurrence, then the "incest threat" takes on a doubled, and more than faintly symbolic quality. These displaced manifestations of the maternal body in the relations between fathers and daughters in *Our Mutual Friend* signify disruptions of "the normal order," as if to say that what lies behind the order for

Kristeva—the mother, the female subject—*will* exhibit herself. But within the dominant masculine order that Dickens represents as assuming control with "the happy ending" of the novel, the representation of the female subject must appear as hysterical (Jenny), cloyingly sentimental and, paradoxically, greedy (Bella), or rhapsodic (Lizzie).

One, indeed, senses a irreparable breakdown of the social continuum when analogous reversals of father-daughter relations are seen to extend elsewhere to other gender and class relations. In *Our Mutual Friend*, where fathers become infants, an heir to a fabulous fortune becomes a secretary (for the purpose of seeing how a poor girl will do if *she* crosses class lines) while his servants become his masters. Heterosexual relations are thoroughly skewed when one regards the broken affair between Venus and Pleasant Riderhood as a disagreement over stuffed parrots, or the promised intimacy between Sloppy and Jenny Wren an the culmination of a fiction about "the coming of Him" in a striking deflation of Lizzie's salvatory relation to Wrayburn. A poor Jew is made to play the role of a rich usurer, and poor Twemlow is continually at odds to explain the difference between acquaintance and friendship. In short, relations and identities of all kinds are in a constant state of flux and crisis in the novel; this is most evident in the rivalries between symbolic brothers or "partners" (Headstone/Wrayburn, Riderhood/Gaffer, Harmon/Handford/Rokesmith). Everything, of course, appears to be set right at last, but the positioning of characters into "proper" relations in the novel's conclusion requires a kind of authorial force that explodes into violence (the sadism of Fledgeby's beating, the "well-deserved" junking of Wegg, Wrayburn's drowning, Headstone's and Riderhood's double-murder) all expended for the sole purpose, in terms of plot, of getting Bella and Harmon and Lizzie and Wrayburn together. In a sense, the "victory" is Pyrrhic, and the damage has been done. Despite Twemlow's admirable, but impotent rejoinders, not only is the vacuous "Voice of Society" the last chord struck in the novel, not only does Dickens feel it necessary to tack on a postface which connects his authorship with acts of textual and corporeal redemption while repressing the female subject, but even with the closing act—Harmon's accession to fortune and the death and rebirth of Eugene Wrayburn—there is the sense that the "reward," the confirmation and renewal of identity, is a socially capricious act of providence undertaken by an ironic author through the vehicles of Lizzie and the Boffins.[15] As the language and vocalizations of the novel are fragmented, so its social fabric is still torn even after authorial recuperation. The attempt to mend it, beyond the level of plot, results in a self-referential, authorial "salvation" that leaves its marks upon the text, as well as upon the bodies of its characters.

Eugene Wrayburn is a crucial representation in *Our Mutual Friend* of what Kristeva refers to as "the corporeal," and he is one of Dickens' most complex creations: much like Charles Freeman of John Fowles's *The French Lieutenant's Woman*, he can be viewed as either the last Victorian or the first Modern.[16] Wrayburn has all the symptoms of a peculiarly modern disease— urban anomie—yet he also stands as Dickens' satriric comment on the leisurely Victorian gentleman: well-educated and bored, typically in pursuit of a lower-class woman whom he is willing to bed but whom he will not marry against a paternal injunction. If Henry James thought that *Our Mutual Friend* bore the strain of authorial exhaustion, then surely that malady is most readily located in Wrayburn. Through much of the first half of the novel, Wrayburn possesses no "self" in the usual senses of the word: he has no work, no project, no relationships save his thoroughly laconic friendship with Mortimer and his distanced, parasitical relation with his father. Up to a point, his one legitimate function in the novel seems to be that of the *eiron*, a voice who mocks the pretensions of those of his own class. Then he meets Lizzie and Headstone, and the pursuit of both not only gives him something to do, but confers upon him a personality and a body—those of the lover and the revenger.

Eugene thereby becomes the focal point of one of the novel's double plots, and upon his living or dying (as the elaborate passages describing his "rising" and "sinking" would lead us to believe) hinges much of the general pathetic effect of the novel. The resurrection of his body from the waters above Henley bears enormous symbolic weight, for it seems it would not have been enough just to "save" Bella alone: that salvation is "spiritual," a change of heart about the importance of money. Wrayburn's revival, on the other hand, gives "body" to the salvatory scheme of the novel, as if there is the necessity of a physical exchange for the corpse (George Radfoot's) which floats up out of the Thames at the beginning of the novel. Wrayburn's rising body potentially "redeems" all the dead who have sunk, unnoticed, into the river and who have floated up to the surface again, their identities erased by the work of time and nature, their bodies resurrected in pieces as contributions to the likes of Venus's miscellanies. Risen and reborn, Eugene is the anti-parasite, a metaphorical response to the overwhelming social "world" of the novel where life is a matter of feeding off the wastes or riches of another. Like Bella, Wrayburn undergoes a personality change in the end, but this is only the final result of the ordeal his body endures after it has been beaten and drowned, and after this distended recovery where he resembles a corpse lacking speech. His body, like Esther Summerson's, is permanently mutilated by what has happened to it: "Sadly wan and worn was the once gallant Eugene, and walked resting on his wife's arm, and leaning heavily upon a stick. But, he was daily growing stronger and better, and it was declared by the medical attendants that he might not be much disfigured by-and-by" (883). While the disclaimer (like the one stating that true love can ignore Esther's scars in *Bleak House*) is recuperative, Eugene's body, salvaged from the river, is his old body; it bears the marks, as a figure for the body of the text, of what has passed; it is disfigured, though "not much," by symbolic orderings of plot.

Eugene's body is one of the tropes for the semiotic in *Our Mutual Friend*, one of the places where signification—here, the representation of corporeal identity—is "cut up." His voice is low and serious, robbed of its ironic gaiety, and now conveying the diminished presence of a sober, fully-initiated Wrayburn; but his face, which impassively has stared down an enraged Headstone in an alley, is a kind of slate upon which is written the partially erased marks recalling the passionate violence he has suffered. Even his name suggests this paradox: "Eugene" comes from the Greek, meaning "well-born," but "Wrayburn" suggests one who has been scarred by the sun. Fathers, whether biological (Eugene refers to his father as M.R.F. or My Reverend Father) and authorial have not been kind to Eugene, and their distance from him is scored as an intimacy of relation in other ways, whether it is in M.R.F.'s attempt to control genealogy by dictating who his wife will be, or Dickens' need to mark Wrayburn, as he does Esther with the "summer son," with the signs of passage. Eugene eventually gets his way with his father, who will accept his marriage to Lizzie, a "will" which is part of the larger incorporation of his salvaged and renewed identity into the redemptive social scheme of the novel: he vows to Mortimer that he will work at his vocation and proudly parade Lizzie about town as his wife in defiance of the older, unregenerate, "Society" of the novel. In so doing, he has joined that smaller, utopian society which includes the Harmons, the Boffins, Lizzie, Sloppy, Jenny Wren, and by extension, Twemlow.

Eugene's identity has been formed and his "voice" socialized, but his body, like the other disarticulations and disfigurations of *Our Mutual Friend*, reminds us that the presence bearing the nominative language of the well-born has been preceded by *and is founded upon* separation, non-identity, the "sinking" of the speaking subject before it rises to speech and the whispered word that will convert the "other" (Lizzie) into an object ("wife"). Eugene's scars heal over what Kristeva calls "the scissions of matter" (160) that mark

the return in language of what has been rejected, or re-thrown (like voice) by
the subject in the process of transformation into an identity proper. What has
been rejected in *Our Mutual Friend* may be viewed as the form of
self-negation represented in the character of Headstone, Wrayburn's rival and
double, whose erotic energies are translated into the suicidal impulses that
result in his embracing of a muddy grave with Rogue Riderhood. Eugene's
body registers this rejected negation, as surely as it retains it. Similarly, Jenny
Wren's dolls stand in for that rejected part of her make-up, her befuddled
father ("Mr. Dolls") and her own crippled body, which she would transcend:
even as she speaks through her dolls, they act as displacements and retentions
of her own dwarfish corporeality, as well as representing the "high lady" she
is not.

This form of negation is pervasive, and it seems that the characters of the
novel are either in the process of succumbing to it or "controlling" and
displacing it through acts of impersonation and ventriloquy. Thus, Podsnap
"negates" a daughter and, in so doing, represses the threat to his own identity
as father and author of this child—a threat temporarily embodied in the
ambivalent positions of other daughters-cum-mothers in the novel before they
are reincorporated back into the masterful familial harmony of the plot. Thus,
in "The Feast of the Three Hobgoblins," where Mr. Wilfer is "revived" with
the news that Bella and John are engaged, Bella is soon to engage in a series
of "mysterious disappearances" as she is enfolded in Harmon's arms:
" 'Well,' " replied "the cherub" (Mr. Wilfer), " 'when you—when you come
back from retirement, my love, and reappear on the surface, I think it will be
time to lock up and go' " (674). Here, Bella's identity—her *will*, which has
been represented throughout the novel as motivated by greed—is doubly-
sunk, almost as if to parody Eugene's "surfacing" from the Thames as an
identity with a will at last. Before her father, who has, here, resumed his
authoritative role (he will "lock up" shop at this point, his daughter now
properly disposed of), Bella "sinks into" the breast of her husband, a
"disappearing" which is the sign of romantic love and the final vanquishing
of her old willful, acquisitive "self." These disappearances are the parodic
echoes and final suppressions of the foundations of "identity" in *Our Mutual
Friend* represented as, precisely, a negation ("sinking") which precedes its
formation.

In a larger sense, corporeality, the visible sign of this negation, is what is
"abjected" in the novel, to use the term Kristeva develops in *Powers of
Horror*. For Kristeva, the abject is everything that the body casts off from
itself (excrement, filth, skin, food) in the continuous reformation of a

"clean," "proper" identity; this process, and the abjected material itself, signifies a recollection of sorts: "Abjection preserves what existed in the archaism of pre-objectal relationship, in the immemorial violence with which a body becomes separated from another body in order to be" (10). That "other body" is, as I mentioned earlier, the maternal body, which for Kristeva is *not* the biological mother but the name for the subject *before* it becomes a subject—an authorized, singular, sexual and social being in submission to the paternal laws and orders of existence. So great is the fear wrought by the recognition that all of these orders rest on their own negation—for by definition, "order" is the maintenance of a hierarchy of differences, whether syntactic, sexual, or social—that all traces of the pre-subjectival "past," the heterogeneous "before" of identity's nonfiguration under the rules of signification, must be repressed, though these traces are retained in the semiotic representations of the body, politic and corporeal. What is "abjected" or thrown off, then, and what reappears piecemeal as the semiotic in *Our Mutual Friend* is the noise, subjectival displacements, linguistic and bodily contaminations and disarticulations, excremental waste of the dust heaps and muddy flats of the river, drowned bodies and skeletons, and drowned out, disfigured voices that fill the novel. These signify the "horror" of the maternal body "viewed as an engendering, hollow and vaginated, expelling and rejected boy" (*Revolution*, 153). This cast-off body is a form of absence, but it is also the "place" where identity begins, just as echo, the repetition of sound, "begins" in a hollow. Physical and textual bodies, always on the verge of disarticulation and abjecting their "wastes" even as they retain traces of their origin, serve as commemorations of identity and its foundations in the absent maternal body—an "identity" which voice and body make "present" in the form of a meditation between origins and ends.

Derrida suggests that speech is a kind of theft, an expulsion of breath and voice "spirited away" from the body that recalls to the "speaking subject . . . his irreducible secondarity, his origin that is . . . eluded; for the origin is always . . . eluded on the basis of an organized field of speech in which the speaking subject vainly seeks a place that is always missing" ("La parole soufflée" 175; 178). As I have been suggesting, Dickens constructs the "organized field of speech" in *Our Mutual Friend* nostalgically, through the concordances of plot and voices at the end of the novel, or parodically, through the "Voice of Society" heard in the conversations at Veneering's dinner table. But what "eludes" the organization of the novel, the semiotic element, remains as that which has been "thrown" or abjected. The anxiety aroused by the recognition of the abject which implicates the abysmal foundation of all signifying orders and proffers "the horror" of non-identity represented in Western culture as the maternal, the feminine, the contaminated, is to some extent "managed" in the novel by the appropriations of voice and plot, most often in those instances where daughters are spoken for by fathers and husbands. But the controlling act, as the figure of ventriloquy suggests, resurrects this *anagnorisis* even as it seeks to suppress it. The throwing of voice, Dickens' multiplication of identity into a heterogeneous assortment of "many voices," recalls the abject, that which escapes objectification, just as the recasting of Eugene's identity recalls, fadingly, his immersion into the maternal, excremental element of the river as the climactic event in the deadly rivalry with his brother/double, Headstone.

For the author who seeks to order the identities of his many characters into being, to give them inimitable forms of speech and personality, then to plot their destinies, such recognitions necessarily must be as disturbing as they are unavoidable. *Our Mutual Friend* is "about" this recognition and its discontents. Dickens' "intention" in this regard is a complicated matter, for on the one hand, as Lewes's testimony, the Postface, and the figure of ventriloquy all suggest, he viewed himself as "the inimitable" origin of all his characters and voices, and their savior. Identity, in this authorial view, is not a matter of social, historical, or biological relations, but a gift benevolently conferred by the maker of his stand-ins. Bella's sense that new identities (babies) come floating down the Thames when they will (like the corpses with which the novel beings its fluctuations), compounded with Eugene's death and rebirth by water, confirm the notion that the articulation of selfhood within this authorial vision is symbolic and transcendental. Finding one's true self in this equation would be equivalent to finding one's true voice (that is, the "one" which is determined to be true by the author): thus, Eugene whispers the magic word to Jenny ("Wife") that initiates recovery; Harmon and Boffin speak in their "own" sincere voices to Bella in the recognition scene, while Mrs. Boffin, silenced throughout the third and fourth books because her voice would give her away, can speak again at last. Accordingly, the novel, in its symbolic aspect, reflects a strong sense of identity as having its origins in a providential author; this symbolic order is sustained by the renewed society of the novel's ending, and by the laws of marriage and the redistribution of wealth—as Boffin "gives back" Harmon his own inheritance—amongst men.

On the other hand, countering this sense of authorship, is what must be seen as the novel's center of gravity: its disfigurations and multiple voices, its rhapsodies and hysterical outbursts, its labyrinths, doublings, and dead ends. Focusing as we have on the semiotic aspects of the novel, we can see a different version of authorship and identity emerging—one which Dickens "recognized" even as he suppressed it, and even then, ironically, if one regards the artificialities of closure in this novel as parodic. Here, Dickens countering "intention" may be seen as an irrepressible consciousness of the limitations of his power as an authorial identity who wholly originates and controls all that he has conjured up. For if, as the novel seems to tell us in so many ways, "identity" can be seen as a "voice" constituted by the fictions of law, genealogy, and paternal economy, but ever-recalling (abjecting) its "dissolute," maternal origins, then the identity of the author, brought under question as "the identity of identities," is subject to the same paradoxical definition. In this view, the author is the "origin" of the characters and voices he creates, but if that origin is *represented* in writing as a form of negation, then "who" is Charles Dickens, and what is his vocation? The intensity with which both questions about authorship and identity are implicitly asked in the novel suggests the modernity of Dickens' vision in which his own sense of identity is clearly conflicted and unresolved.

Perhaps Henry James was right, after all, that the author had been exhausted by his "labors" (the maternal body, again, resurfaces), but the exhaustion suggests less a lack of inspiration than a revelation that writing cannot fully contain or figure forth the authorial inspiration of character with life and speech. Notably, the attempts to "write down" identity in the novel are nearly always portrayed parodically, from Riderhood's swearing "himself" in the form of an "Alfred David," to Eugene's thought that he can "organize himself" with the purchase of a "secretary" containing a pigeonhole for every letter of the alphabet, to Harmon's notion that he can hide his former self and be reborn in the form of a scretary who takes dictation from Boffin. The inscription of identity into nominative and narrative orders becomes, in these examples, a form of deciphering that simply repeats the arbitrary signs of the name imposed upon a body and the nominal subject. As an author who generates names and identities by the hundreds, Dickens both creates and loses his subject in this novel, which is the recovery and reformation of one's "own" identity. Like Shakespeare's "farewell to the stage," *Our Mutual Friend* might be seen as a work in which authorial identity is at stake—most crucially, in Dickens' case, in terms of its gender, as the authoring father recalls and "throws" off the non-identical origins of identity in the voices of his characters and the scenes of his spectacle. As in *The Tempest*, the crisis of authority in *Our Mutual Friend* may be partially resolved by "magic," but it is hardly expunged by the resolution. And while, unlike Prospero, Dickens does not give up his art in this novel, he does discover that what founds the making of novels and the projection of voice into character is quite different from any version of intention or identity he could possibly authorize. In *Our Mutual Friend*, Dickens discovers that to throw one's voice is a kind of suicide—as Derrida suggests, a separation of the spirit from the body, and more specifically, an unsettling abnegation of the (male) authorial self. He finds that to be an author—a father of identities—is to confront the facelessness of one's own identity, or to face one's own "maternal" aspect, and to acknowledge identity's groundless origins even as writing it down marks its entrance into the world.

NOTES

1. The discussion of self-construction and identity in Dickens' fiction has a long history, beginning with Miller's analysis in *Charles Dickens* where he develops the theme of identity as a representation of "intersubjectivity" always threatened by "bad communication"; in *The Form of Victorian Fiction*, Miller goes on to relate the "theme" of intersubjectivity to the form of the novel itself. My divergence from these early readings of Miller's resides in a more complex notion of the relation between "voice" and "subject." Useful thematic discussions of self-construction in *Our Mutual Friend* are offered by Stewart and Knopflemacher; more recently, compelling discussions of identity in Dickens besides Miller's are those of Weinstein and Welsh (*From Copyright to Copperfield*). Weinstein's readings of *David Copperfield* and *Little Dorrit* a concerned to establish the relation between character and desire as the psychological projection of identity against its social confinement; Welsh is concerned to thematize the relation between writing and identity. In contrast, my reading of *Our Mutual Friend* stresses "identity" as resulting from a semiotic process that is thoroughly "social" and that, in narrative terms, fractures the conventions of theme, character, and figure. My ideas about identity coincide to a large degree with those of van Boheemen, whose insightful work on genre, gender, and identity appeared as I was composing my own views of subjectivity in Dickens. In her Lacanian feminist analysis, van Boheeman writes that "[t]he novel as a family romance, reductively personifying the complexity of experience as the contrastive pair of father and mother, is both the intensified reflection of the implication of gender in signification and the prime object for studying its history and functioning, especially with regard to the constitution of the subject" (30). This succinct formulation leads van Boheeman to conclude that the "plot" of the novel is its exclusion of the "other," or mother, and it will be seen to what extent "she" is the *partially* excluded middle of *Our Mutual Friend*, or rather, how that exclusion can be characterized as the unsuccessfully repressed partial object(s), of the maternal body. But in her reading of *Bleak House*, van Boheeman, in my view, totalizes this plot, thus re-repressing the semiotic element which I claim "survives" such totalization, as well as founding it: the story of the novel can be seen equally as a history of the semiotic rupturing of discourse and as a history of the patriarchal plot of "the family romance."
2. My use of the Bakhtinian vocabulary in this essay suggests the basis of my

argument in his understanding of "heteroglossia" in the novel as induced by generic and historical circumstances; however, I also intend to modify the sense of "heteroglossia" by my reading of subjectivity in Dickens. See *The Dialogic Imagination*, 84–259, 262–63, for the development of this concept. Bakhtinian readings of *Our Mutual Friend* include Garrett (89–94), who is primarily concerned with the relation between form and rhetoric, and who unproblematically accepts Bakhtih's "totalization" of the novel, and Larson (281–312), who interestingly discusses the relation between verbal fragmentation, allusion, and indeterminacy in the novel but who still insists upon the sporadic orchestration of multiple voices in Dickens which serves, occasionally, to "stabilize" the discourse. Prow uses Bakhtin to discuss "register" in *Little Dorrit*, i.e., the presence of different ideologically grounded linguistic modes by which "the reality-effects and fiction-effects of the literary text are generated" (269).

3. The full title of George Smith's *Programme* is *Programme of the Entertainment: Preceded by Memoirs of Mr. Love, the Dramatic Polyphonist; Remarks on Single-Handed Entertainments, Anecdotes of Eminent By-Gone Professors; An Explanation of the Phenomena of Polyphony, & c.; Being Mr. Love's Improvement in Point of Distance, Power, Number of Voices, and Variety of Expression, on the Art of the Ventriloquist; in Which the Errors of Writers on the Subject, and the Impositions Practised on the Public by Pretended Teachers and Lecturers on the Talent, are Clearly Pointed Out*. Smith writes that Mr. Love "has been enabled to appear with almost uninterrupted success, for more than TWO THOUSAND NIGHTS in the metropolis; a circumstance entirely without parallel in the history of public amusements really, or professedly, sustained by individual talent" (29). The Pilgrim Edition of the *Letters of Charles Dickens* indicates a letter from Dickens of 10 March 1843 addressed to a Mr. Love: the letter itself, mentioned in the *Samuel T. Freeman & Co. Catalogue* of April, 1917 is not reprinted in the Pilgrim Edition (III, 461). The editors of the *Letters* note that Mr. Love is "unidentified"; the Mr. Love of George Smith's pamphlet had many London engagements in 1843, so it seems likely that Dickens wrote the ventriloquist, perhaps to express appreciation for one of his performances.

4. See Kaplan for a description of John Elliotson's Svengaliesque mesmerizing of the O'kee sisters during 1838: the sisters often passed into "a state of harmless but vocal delirium" under Elliotson's influence, or spoke in many tongues (41). Kapian meticulously details Dickens' longstanding involvement with Elliotson and the psuedoscience of mesmerism beginning in the late 1830s. Mamie Dickens' oft-noted description of her father acting out his characters before a mirror occurs in her *My Father As I Recall Him*, quoted in Page (144).

5. Lambert briefly discusses the practice of the "monopolylogue" in the Victorian popular arts which featured a single actor taking on several different roles (91). For Lambert, the "monopolylogist" can stand as a figure for Dickens' authorship, particularly in his early novels where, Lambert argues, he is particularly concerned to represent and impose his authorial singularity through his several characters. Quite problematically, in my view, Lambert declares that Dickens' later fiction (because it contains, statistically, fewer "suspended quotations") shows Dickens' waning anxiety concerning authorial control and self-reference in his mature work, particularly because he could gain the adulation and attention he sought in increasingly numerous public performances. Control and the maintenance of authorial identity, I will argue, remain problems for Dickens in *Our Mutual Friend*, and their figurations cannot be reduced merely to matters of

syntax. Strictly speaking, however, Mr. Love is a "monopolylogist" or "poly-phanist" rather than a ventriloquist proper, though the relations between the actor and the character he throws himself into, and the ventriloquist and his dummy, are clearly analogous "speech acts"; or, rather, the latter is a heightened parody of the former. Smith argues that any act of throwing one's voice, or casting oneself in the voice of another, is ventriloquistic, and distinct from acts of "imitation" or mimicry involving animal sounds, miming of idiolects, etc.

6. Interestingly, Smith insists that the "entertainment" of the good ventriloquist must be carefully constructed and written down. The "natural" imitator who fails to adhere to the discipline of the dramatic principles which arise when the act is "written down" and when its forms of delivery are prescribed will both bore the audience and antiquate himself: "The mere ventriloquist who appears before his auditors, without having previously provided himself with a set entertainment, or, having done so, without knowing how to deliver it, necessarily finds himself under the awkward necessity of uttering what comes uppermost in his mind, or nearly so; and is a character belonging to a by-gone age; one whose stock in trade bears about the same proportion to the effects belonging to a successful modern piece within this department, as the street fiddler to a Paganini, a street-post painter to a Landseer, the tragedian of the booth in a village fair, to an Edmund Kean, or a Macready; or the dismal lamps and ill-made ways of mud, characteristic of olden time, to the brilliant lights and well-constructed iron-roads of the present day" (24). Thus, the sequence of "proper" impersonation for Smith would be, first, authoring the script, then, erasing the identity of the author/impersonator as the voice is "thrown" into another character or a dummy whose identity is, thereby, created in the act. Smith seems to have misunderstood the implications of his pedagogy here when, earlier in the tract, he scolds false ventriloquists for plagiarizing Mr. Love's material!

7. The most interesting explanations of closure in *Our Mutual Friend* are offered by Knopflemacher and Stewart, who argue for the work of the redemptive imagination in the novel's ending, by Hutter, who suggests the novel is balanced between fragmentation and threatening or beneficent forms of "articulation," and by Simpson and Arac, who suggest in quite different ways that the novel negotiates between the tropes of synecdoche and metaphor, with the novel's ending reinforcing metaphor as the figure of social or personal integration.

8. James further notes that in *Our Mutual Friend* Dickens falls to properly "represent" society: "What a World were this world if the world of *Our Mutual Friend* were an honest reflection of it! But a community of eccentrics is impossible. Rules alone are consistent with each other; exceptions are inconsistent. Society is maintained by a natural sense and natural feeling. We cannot conceive a society in which these principles are not in some manner represented" (471). Again, James seems to recognize that *Our Mutual Friend* works against "representation," but this is exactly the nature of the young novelist's complaint. Carroll's discussion of James is revealing in this regard: he describes the Jamesian conception of the subject as centered, framed, and thus represented by the artist (55), though he points out that the relation between the author and the subject or "central consciousness" is made especially problematic in the Prefaces.

9. See Derrida, *Speech and Phenomena* 48–59; 70 87 for the critique of the assumed, semiotic relation between "voice" and "presence." My discussion of voice in *Our Mutual Friend* is indebted to Derrida's understanding of the history of that relation.

10. In his reading of Dickens through Georges Bataille, Kucich describes as "excess" the particular forms of erotic energy which defy representation in language and which motor identity as a kind of negative transcendence. Kucich's work is illuminating in this regard, and my sense of "residue" bears some resemblance to his concept of "excess," but I part company with him when "excess" is coupled with a mystified sense of authorial self-abandonment, contrasted to evidences of Dickensian "self-restraint" in his closed forms and stylistic repressions. My understanding of the problematic of identity in *Our Mutual Friend* relies more upon conceiving identity as a construct of repetition founded upon the negation of its own origins and presencing in voice; it is acculturated and, as something represented in language (the discontents of this representation being part of the problematic), inescapable. See Kucich, *Excess and Restraint* and "Dickens and Fantastic Rhetoric."

11. Different views of "entanglement" as the substance of fiction are offered by Miller, *Fiction and Repetition*, and Brooks, who formulates a psychoanlytic view of repetition and complexity in narrative as forestallments of the "death" or end of the text. Luckacher reads the "no thoroughfares" of *Our Mutual Friend* as blockages by which Dickens both remembers and represses the "primal scene" which lies at the source of his fiction.

12. The biographical details of the Staplehurst railway accident and Dickens' heroic efforts there can be found in Johnson, 1018–21.

13. See Lévi-Strauss, 75–108; see also Rubin for commentary on the contents of Lévi-Strauss's structural anthropology and "the traffic in women."

14. See Kosofsky Sedgwick and Sadoff for divergent views of sexual and familial relations in *Our Mutual Friend*. Zwinger offers the most illuminating discussion I know of father-daughter relations in Dickens' fiction.

15. Welsh (*City*) comments at length on the possible connections between "Dickens" and Providence.

16. In addition to Kristeva, I am indebted to Cameron and Scarry for my understanding of "corporeality" in Dickens.

WORKS CITED

Arac, Jonathan. *Commissioned Spirits: The Shaping of Social Motion in Dickens, Carlyle, Melville, and Hawthorne*. New Brunswick: Rutgers UP, 1979.

Bakhtin, M.H. *The Dialogic Imagination: Four Essays*. Ed. Michael Holquist. Trans. Caryl Emerson and Michael Holquist. Austin: U of Texas P, 1981.

Beaujour, Michael. "Phonograms and Delivery: The Poetics of Voice," in *Notebooks for Cultural Analysis, Vol. 3: 'Voice'*. Ed. Norman F. Cantor and Nathalia King. Durham: Duke UP, 1986: 266–79.

Brooks, Peter. "Freud's Masterplot: Questions of Narrative." *Yale French Studies*, 55/56 (1977): 280–300.

Cameron, Sharon. *The Corporeal Self: Allegories of the Body in Melville and Hawthorne*. Baltimore: Johns Hopkins UP, 1981.

Carroll, David. *The Subject in Question: The Languages of Theory and the Strategies of Fiction*. Chicago: U of Chicago P, 1982.

Derrida, Jacques. "La parole soufflée." In *Writing and Difference*. Trans. Alan Bass. Chicago: U of Chicago P, 1978: 169–95.

———. *Speech and Phenomena and Other Essays on Husserl's Theory of Signs*. Trans. David B. Allison. Evanston: Northwestern UP, 1973.

Dickens, Charles. The Pilgrim Edition of *The Letters of Charles Dickens, Volume III: 1842–43*. Ed. Madeline House, Graham Storey, and Kathleen Tillotson. Oxford: Clarendon, 1974.

———. *Little Dorrit,.* 1857. Rpt. New York: Penguin, 1967.

———. *Our Mutual Friend.* 1865. Rpt. New York: Penguin, 1971.

Frow, John. "Voice and Register in *Little Dorrit.*" *Comparative Literature*, 33 (1981): 258–70.

Garrett, Peter K. *The Victorian Multiplot Novel: Studies in Dialogical Form.* New Haven: Yale UP, 1980.

Henkle, Roger B. *Comedy and Culture: England 1820–1900.* Princeton: Princeton UP, 1980.

Hollander, John. *The Figure of Echo: A Mode of Allusion in Milton and After.* Berkeley: U of California P, 1981.

Hutter, Albert D. "Dismemberment and Articulation in *Our Mutual Friend.*" *Dickens Studies Annual*, 11 (1983): 135–75.

James, Henry. "Review" of *Our Mutual Friend. The Nation*, 21 December 1865. Rpt. *Dickens: The Critical Heritage.* Ed. Philip Collins. New York: Barnes & Noble, 1971.

Edgar Johnson. *Charles Dickens: His Tragedy and Triumph.* New York: Simon and Schuster, 1952.

Kaplan, Fred. *Dickens and Mesmerism: The Hidden Springs of Fiction.* Princeton: Princeton UP, 1975.

Knoepflmacher, U.C. *Laughter and Despair: Readings in Ten Novels of the Victorian Era.* Berkeley: U of California P, 1971.

Kristeva, Julia. *Powers of Horror: An Essay on Abjection.* Trans. Leon S. Roudiez. New York: Columbia UP, 1981.

———. *Revolution in Poetic Language.* Trans. Margaret Waller. New York: Columbia UP, 1984.

Kucich, John. "Dickens' Fantastic Rhetoric: The Semiotics of Reality and Unreality in *Our Mutual Friend.*" *Dickens Studies Annual*, 14 (1985): 167–89.

———. *Excess and Restraint in the Novels of Charles Dickens.* Athens: U of Georgia P, 1981.

Lambert, Mark. *Dickens and the Suspended Quotation.* New Haven: Yale UP, 1981.

Larson, Janet L. *Dickens and the Broken Scripture.* Athens: U of Georgia P, 1985.

Lévi Strauss, Claude. *The Savage Mind*. Chicago: U of Chicago P, 1966.

Lewes, George Henry. "Dickens in Relation to Criticism," in *Literary Criticism of George Henry Lewes*. Ed. Alice Kaminsky. Lincoln: U of Nebraska P, 1964: 94–105.

Lukacher, Ned. *Primal Scenes: Literature, Philosophy, Psychoanalysis*. Ithaca: Cornell UP, 1986.

Miller, J. Hillis. *Charles Dickens: The World of His Novels*. Cambridge: Harvard UP, 1958.

―――. *Fiction and Repetition: Seven English Novels*. Cambridge: Harvard UP, 1982.

―――. *The Form of Victorian Fiction*. Notre Dame: U of Notre Dame P, 1968.

Page, Norman. *Speech in the English Novel*. London: Longmans, 1973.

Rubin, Gayle. "The Traffic in Women," in *Toward an Anthropology of Women*. Ed. Rayna R. Roiter. New York: Monthly Review P, 1975: 157–210.

Sadoff, Diane. *Monsters of Affection: Dickens, Eliot, and Brontë on Fatherhood*. Baltimore: Johns Hopkins UP, 1982.

Scarry, Elaine. *The Body in Pain: The Making and Unmaking of the World*. New York: Oxford UP, 1985.

Sedgwick, Eve Kosofsky. "Homophobia, Misogyny, and Capital: The Example of *Our Mutual Friend*." *Raritan*, 2 (1983); 126–51.

Serres, Michel. *The Parasite*. Trans. Lawrence R. Schehr. Baltimore: Johns Hopkins UP, 1982.

Smith, George. *Programme of the Entertainment: Preceded by Memoirs of Mr. Love, the Dramatic Polyphonist*. London: W. Kenneth, 1856.

Stewart, Garrett. *Dickens and the Trials of the Imagination*. Cambridge: Harvard UP, 1974.

van Boheeman, Christine. *The Novel as Family Romance: Language, Gender, and Authority from Fielding to Joyce*. Ithaca: Cornell UP, 1987.

Weinstein, Phillip. *The Semantics of Desire: Changing Models of Identity from Dickens to Joyce*. Princeton: Princton UP, 1984.

Welsh, Alexander. *The City of Dickens*. New York: Oxford UP, 1971.

―――. *From Copyright to Copperfield: The Identity of Dickens*. Cambridge: Harvard UP, 1987.

Wilden, Anthony. *System and Structure: Essays on Communication and Exchange*. 2nd Ed. London: Tavistock, 1980.

Zwinger, Lynda. "The Fear of the Father: Dombey and Daughter." *Nineteenth Century Fiction*, 30 (1985): 420–40.

Sympathetic Criminality in
the Mid-Victorian Novel

Alexander Pettit

Unlike its eighteenth- and early nineteenth-century predecessors, the mid-Victorian novel is marked by the authorial assumption of the once-sovereign right to judge and to punish criminal behavior in a manner not strictly answerable to the existing legal code. Neither Defoe nor Fielding, in spite of the charges of subversion leveled against their novels by their contemporaries, were given to punishing their characters in a manner that in any way contradicted the dominant punitive ideology of early Hanoverian England; and the success of the Newgate novels of the 1830s depended on the graphic exploitation of officially-sanctioned public execution (Hollingsworth 13). The mid-Victorian novel, by way of contrast, occupies an historical position in which the roles of criminal, society, and legal system are in a state of interactive redefinition that allows the novelist considerable interpretive flexibility.

By the middle of the nineteenth century, the active collaboration of novelist and reader becomes essential to the successful portrayal of that character whom I will call the "sympathetic criminal": he or she who commits an offense clearly beyond the pale of both legal sanction and conventional authorial indulgence, yet who is ultimately the recipient of an authorial lenity that the reader must endorse if the novel is to cohere. The effective presentation of such a character is facilitated by what Janice Carlisle identifies as the essentially symbiotic relationship of the mid-century author and his or her reader. Carlisle argues that the major novelists of the period "adopted" Carlyle's radical aesthetic belief that "[t]he creative role of the writer is . . . only part of a more extensive process in which the audience's imagination is an equally indispensable agent" (15); she adds that "[t]he lesson of sympathy and common humanity that the [mid-century] novelist professed . . . can be a goal only if it is also the process by which the reader apprehends and actually experiences its validity" (16).[1] The emergence and the acceptance of a relaxed standard of punishment in the novel offers a compelling test of this shared "sympathy."

The genesis and development of the sympathetic criminal is best understood in terms of the alteration of the dominant assumptions of the English juridical ethos from the eighteenth to the nineteenth centuries. The eighteenth-century conception of the criminal as marginally human property upon whose body punishment was routinely enacted yielded to the Victorian infatuation with the "psychology" of the offender, the social causality of crime, and the comparative ethical value of various penal systems.[2] The criminal thus became a social being—a statistic, if we are to accord proper credit to the burgeoning social sciences—whose crime was inseparable from the environment in which, or by which, it was produced. The reader of the mid-Victorian novel is required to accommodate this movement through the recognition of a didactic realignment of criminal character, criminal deed, and criminal environment: the commission of crime is now presented as antithetical, rather than endemic, to the dramatic world shared by criminal and other characters. A corollary both in juridical reform and in the novel concerns the notable revision—the abstraction—of the way in which the "victim" of crime is designated.

Young Tom Gradgrind, the whelpish thief in *Hard Times*, and Hetty Sorrel, the foolish and narcissistic infanticide in *Adam Bede*, illustrate a tendency in the characterization of the criminal that is additionally evident elsewhere in the novel of the period. Tom is designed to be disagreeable; and yet, as F. R. Leavis points out, "[his] escape is contrived, successfully in every sense, by means belonging to Dickensian high-fantastic comedy" (243–44). Zelda Austen, in her response to feminist dissatisfaction with Eliot, concedes that Hetty "is a girl with whom a George Eliot could have little in common," but adds that "Eliot, even while she reveals [Hetty's] limitations mercilessly, makes one's heart bleed for her" (559).[3] Hetty, significantly, is accorded the eleventh-hour reprieve that was denied her eighteenth-century prototype. While the unconventional abandonment of the legalistic interpretation of behavior establishes the treatment of these criminal characters as congruent with broader trends in Victorian punitive ideology, it is in fact the very conventionality of these novels that ultimately serves as the agency through which the sympathetic interpretation of criminality is justified to the reader. In *Hard Times* and *Adam Bede* the commission of crime facilitates the teleologically necessary progression towards the reinforced vitality of the family; an evaluation of the tiny corpses and broken safes that the reader encounters along the way is thereby discouraged. The achievement of much the same goal devolves from the somewhat adumbrated criminality of Frederick Hale in Mrs. Gaskell's *North and South*; in each of these cases, the novel uses its own familiar language to justify the inclusion of a new and radically different sort of character.

The moral configuration described by this juxtaposition of characterization and closure would be less remarkable if it were presented by novelists of a more uniformly radical stripe or a less morally precise era. It will not do, however, to make of Tom or Hetty a Falkland, who (in *Caleb Williams*) generates sympathy as a vehicle for Godwin's "idealistic notions as to the futility and even the injustice of legal punishments for crime" (Sherburn ix): the Dickens of the 1850s was becoming increasingly conservative in his opinions about the punishment of crime and the treatment of the criminal (Collins 17, 190, 236; E. Johnson 2: 672), and few would ascribe to Eliot a concordance with the license suggested by Godwin's tarnished radicalism. We should have still less cause for concern if the crimes committed bore the familiar and unmistakable stamp of moral—soon to be "Millite"— justification found, for example, in much popular balladry. That no such qualifications apply in the present instance, and that Dickens and Eliot nonetheless absolve their criminals so readily, suggest the presence of a challenging phenomenon, the study of which should enhance our understanding of the complex relationship of crime, punishment, morality, and literature in the nineteenth century.

Tom's and Hetty's crimes are similar in substance to those that had long provided the novel with its sensational element. The mitigated mid-Victorian presentation of both the criminal deed and its punishment is evident if we recall the popular literature of the eighteenth century, wherein we find the birth and the early development of the sympathetic criminal in the novel.

The roughly one hundred years between the publication of Fielding's *Jonathan Wild* and Dickens' *Hard Times* saw the rise and fall in England of what Michael Ignatieff justly calls "the severest criminal code in Europe" (18). Traces of the feudal conception of crime as an affront to the person and property of the sovereign are evident in a profusion of restrictive eighteenth-century land and game laws, and the ease with which one could acquire the capacious designation of "criminal" had not yet been called into question by the sustained efforts of the reformers. Such a volatile configuration of ruling and subject classes encourages a political interpretation of the criminal act, and, thus, tends to render the criminal legitimate in the eyes of the populace: the eighteenth-century criminal, according to Michel Foucault, "[was] almost entirely transformed into a positive hero" through the agency of "broadsheets, pamphlets, almanacs and adventure stories" (67). The idea of criminality as political representation here emerges. Writing of the "fourth estate" or "mobility" in 1752, Fielding noted that "tho' this Estate have not AS YET claimed that Right which was insisted on by the People or Mob in old Rome, of giving a negative Voice in the enacting Laws, they have clearly exercised this Power in controlling their Execution" (*Covent Garden* 31). Some popular novels, Lennard J. Davis argues, endorsed the notion of the criminal as a symbolic point of resistance to the evils allegedly inflicted upon the lower social strata. Davis believes that

> [t]he felonious act committed by the criminal was frequently associated with the political aspirations of the poor and the lower classes. These facts lead to an understanding of the way in which novels themselves were so fascinated by the criminal. It is clear that this interest comes from more than mere prurience and lechery and seems to amount to a definite political interest and ideological stance.
>
> (129–30)

Davis adds that "such literature served the needs of the upper classes too, since the moralizing of the repentant felon amounted to a form of social control" (130). Davis (as well as Fielding) describes what is clearly an unstable relationship between ruler and ruled; further, it must be acknowledged that the transposition of this relationship onto the novel insists upon an intercourse between novelist and various pockets of readership that is necessarily fragmented and imprecise, and thus not conducive to the acceptance of literary criminality on any common moral ground. The inception of the broadly didactic criminal in the novel (insofar as that didacticism was to operate through the diffusion of sympathy rather than through unmitigated and politically interpretable admonition) depended on the ability of the criminal character to embody a sort of compromise among conflicting political or moral ideologies; he or she needed to become more successfully identified with a common moral currency and less so with the frequently sensational and variously explicable particulars of crime and punishment.

This was not to be the bequest of the eighteenth-century novelist, who (perhaps hampered by the inapplicability of the idea of moral consensus to an age addicted to opposition) gradually came to favor a narrative strategy "between" that of the turgid broadside and that of the muted mid-Victorian novel. The novelists of the eighteenth century relied upon the flexible social interpretation of criminality and upon the ready acceptance of comic violence in the novel that their period, as if in defiance of the severity of its penal code, sanctioned. Ian Watt aptly notes the concern in *Moll Flanders* "with areas of individual morality where the last two centuries have taught us to make careful distinctions, but where the early eighteenth century tended to be a good deal less sensitive" (128–29). The significant shades of "individual morality" assume a greater complexity by the middle of the eighteenth century as the reader is introduced to a host of characters who demonstrate an increasing degree of disrespect towards the conventional boundaries between criminality and moral impropriety. Humor and irony here become the novelist's allies in his improbable solicitation of the reader's sympathy. The gambit is an effective one: when we read the novels of that period outside of the constraints of an imported system of morality, it becomes difficult to condemn Parson Adams and his hyperactive crabstick, and a burlesque like *Roderick Random* does not so much elicit disapprobation as tickle the funny bone. Morally emphatic criticism acknowledges this popular response, even while inveighing against the bloated naturalism of the novel. Dr. Johnson apparently had Fielding and Smollett in mind (Paulson and Lockwood 230) when he wrote that

> MANY Writers for the sake of following Nature, so mingle good and bad Qualities in their principal Personages, that they are both equally conspicuous; and as we accompany them through their Adventures with Delight, and are led by Degrees to interest ourselves in their Favour, we lose the Abhorrence of their Faults, because they do not hinder our Pleasure, or, perhaps, regard them with some Kindness for being united with so much Merit.
>
> (233)

The reader, then, is tricked into accepting a potentially objectionable character through a literary sleight of hand: the misdeeds of a Roderick Random are presented in a manner that explicitly discourages any imputation of criminality. While this sort of subterfuge is vile effluvium to the sensitive nose of the neo-classicist, it does identify an important juncture in the development of the sympathetically-portrayed criminal: the reader, by the middle of the eighteenth century, is being called upon to exercise a greater moral discrimination of character, to employ, as Fielding said, "a very accurate Judgement and elaborate Inquiry to determine which Side the Ballance turns" (*Jonathan* 10). What Johnson may well have imagined as an adversarial relationship between the increasingly sophisticated novelist and a morally culpable public represents the emergence of a dialogue in which the reader's moral and critical response becomes necessary to the thematic success of the novel. The unwary reader, insensitive, or merely unaccustomed, to the power of irony, may interpret Fielding's Jonathan Wild as a genuinely "great man," and the reader who wears his collar a bit too high and tight will doubtless overlook the good-humored dignity of a Parson Adams.

The mid-Victorian sympathetic criminal distances himself or herself from the preeminently comic and invariably fleeting moral tergiversations of the likes of Roderick Random, Parson Adams, and Tom Jones through the acknowledged severity of his or her offense; additionally, he or she is distinct from such as Moll Flanders and Jonathan Wild in his or her non-affiliation with what Watt describes as "one of the characteristic institutions of modern urban civilization [which] had come into existence by the early eighteenth century: a well-defined criminal class . . ." (95). The criminal as a component of a thriving subculture had become too familiar a figure to amuse or to instruct the reader of the 1850s. Tom and Hetty, although their crimes represent more extreme legal transgressions than does Moll's prostitution,[4] pointedly lack the appeal to social vicariousness upon which the success of such "histories" as Moll's to a certain extent depends.

It would be remarkable if a Victorian character could maintain an habitually criminal affiliation while recommending himself or herself to our sympathy. The sympathetically-portrayed Victorian prostitute, for example, is routinely presented as a by-product of the criminal class rather than a willing member of it: consider the distance between an enterprising businesswoman like Moll and a miserable casualty like Gaskell's Lizzie Leigh or Dickens' Nancy. Eliot's chapter on "The Harvest Supper" leaves no doubt that Hetty was suitably distant from the social world of even a petty criminal like Ben Tholoway, the thresher at the Hall Farm who had been "detected more than once in carrying away his master's corn in his pockets" (563). Similarly, if young Tom Gradgrind had been a thriving professional thief rather than, as Edward Alexander points out, preeminently an illustration of "the failure of Utilitarian . . . ethical doctrine" (166), he would resign his claim on the sympathy of the Victorian reader along with his specific didactic and teleological function and his potency as a vehicle for social criticism.

In contrast to the legally-extraneous (i.e., not to be allowed as "evidence") relationship between setting and deed seen in the case of Moll Flanders, the mid-Victorian environment explicitly accepted the imputation of responsibility for its criminal element. The blossoming of various and at times contradictory efforts of earlier theorists and reformers such as Blackstone, Howard, and Bentham was in part responsible for a Victorian interpretation of crime that would scarcely have been recognized by Fielding: Ignatieff notes that "[i]n place of a traditional view of crime as merely an immemorial form of human wickedness and sin, the reformers succeeded in popularizing a new vocabulary of alarmism that interpreted crime as an indictment of a society in crisis" (210). Crime in the mid-Victorian novel, reflectively, is frequently an "inside job." The offender is often selected from the respectable social mainstream, his or her disruptive and frequently ambiguous act presented as the culmination of a behavioral process open to analysis on psychological and social grounds: consider Tom, Hetty, Ralph Nickleby, Merdle, Bulstrode, Frederick Hale, and, perhaps, Veneering and Melmotte. The focus of the novel has shifted from the "dastardly deed" to the circumstances of its development. It is no coincidence, certainly, that crime in the mid-Victorian novel is often performed "offstage."

Dickens and Eliot downplay the particulars of crime both by placing their narrative emphases on events antecedent to the commission of crime and by offering only retrospective descriptions of the crimes. That these descriptions are somewhat pitifully tendered by the criminals themselves encourages the reader to sort through the considerable data that he or she has accumulated on the now-confessed criminal before offering judgment. The authors thus facilitate what we may imagine as a movement from the rather severe "letter" of the law to its decidedly reformist "spirit"; this movement must be regarded vis-à-vis the contemporary legal status of larceny and infanticide.

Young Tom steals the sum of " '[a] hundred and fifty-four, seven, one' " (Dickens, *Hard Times* 139) from his eminent employer and brother-in-law, Josiah Bounderby of Coketown. His crime is commonplace in an increasingly urban culture: David Jones notes that along with assault and disorderly conduct, the "dominant characteristic of urban crime rates over the eighteenth and nineteenth centuries was the high proportion of property offences, notably larceny, which accounted for up to a third of summary proceedings and two-thirds or more of indictable" (5). Ruskin's condemnation of theft as "the most complete and excuseless of human crimes" (17:392) notwithstanding, the mid-Victorian tendency was toward lenient punishment of its legion thieves. Doubtless due as much to the abundance of such offenders as to clamoring for further reform, transportation for seven years—or the combination of "not more than two years" imprisonment and, for male offenders, discretionary public whipping—replaced capital punishment for larceny under the provisions of Peel's 1827 revision of the criminal code (Radzinowicz 1:579–80). By the 1850s (which period the backdrop of the Preston strike allows us to assign to the action of *Hard Times*) Tom's punishment most likely would have been imprisonment only: the whipping of civilians had declined and the convict ship, which had sailed but infrequently in the '40s, had all but given way to the refurbished prison system by 1853.[5]

Tom's family position would have ensured that he enjoy all of the comforts available to the more privileged residents of the Victorian prison. Given this certainty, it is not strange that Dickens rather parcels Tom across the sea: the reformed Gradgrind the Elder is less tainted by this criminal complicity than he would have been by any association with the pampered prisoner against whom Dickens had been waging war since *Pickwick Papers* and whose alleged indulgence by the authorities had become a lively topic in *Household Words*.[6] The surrogate "transportation" which Dickens accords Tom links that youth's voyage more to the hopeful emigration of Micawber (and, after 1849, to the emigrations of searchers after Australian and American gold) than to earlier convict passages such as that endured by Hetty Sorrel.

R. W. Malcolmson's and Lionel Rose's recent studies prove that infanticide was a common crime in both the eighteenth and the nineteenth centuries. Rose notes that "the story of infanticide is primarily an account of the fate of illegitimate babies" (10; see also Malcolmson 206) and of babies killed in the first year—frequently the first week—of their lives (7 ff.). The appalling statistics which Malcolmson and Rose offer gain valuable perspective when we consider that bastardy, but not fornication, was illegal in Hetty's England, and that, therefore, a grim legal pressure encouraged covert methods of postpartum population control among women in her situation. Until 1861 the charge of concealment of birth (i.e., by "secreting [the] corpse" [Rose 1], and so in fact concealing the child's *death*) could not be made independently of the charge of murder (Rose 70). In Hetty's time concealment and murder were in fact legally coequal. An excerpt from a curiously-framed document known as "An Act to prevent the Destroying and Murthering of Bastard Children" (21 Jac. 1, c. 27) deserves our attention:

> ". . . if any Woman . . . be delivered of any Issue of her Body, . . . which being born alive, should by the Laws of this Realm be a Bastard, and that she endeavour privately, either by drowning or secret burying thereof, or any other Way, either by herself or the procuring of others, so to conceal the Death thereof, as that it may not come to Light whether it were born alive or not, but

be concealed: In every such Case the said Mother so offending shall suffer Death as in Case of Murther. . . ."

(Radzinowicz 1:431)

This Act, extant from 1623 to 1803 (and we must recall that the main action of *Adam Bede* takes place from 1799–1801), is, according to Leon Radzinowicz, "one of the few in English criminal law which were framed contrary to the principle of presumption of innocence" (1:431). The identification of the criminal deed is thrown into confusion by this juridical inversion: a de facto proof of the equation of murder and concealment being difficult or impossible to establish, it rather appears that the concealment of demonstrable sexual intercourse was being punished. The alteration of traditional standards of innocence and guilt rendered the Act unpalatable even to those who were to enforce it: Radzinowicz notes that the Act "was hardly ever put into operation although at that time the English Legislature was not alone in considering the crime to which it related a very serious one" (1:433).

Hetty's sentence is exceptional, all the more so when one considers that the child's premature birth (Haight 277) and the fact that another adult was present at the birth (Eliot 478) could have been expected to exempt the accused from the charge of murder (Radzinowicz 1: 434). It is doubtful, however, that Eliot was familiar with all of the intricacies of and exceptions to the Act; more pertinent to the present argument is that Eliot in fact metes out a lighter penalty than that received by Hetty's original: the executed child murderer Mary Voce.[7] One senses that the rusty old Act was employed only reluctantly, and more in response to Hetty's persistent refusal to confess than to her actual criminal deed. Hetty's obduracy at her trial sways the court as much as does the evidence of her guilt: after the verdict had been announced, "[s]till the sympathy of the court was not with the prisoner: the unnaturalness of her crime stood out the more harshly by the side of her hard immovability and obstinate silence" (482). It seems likely that the slightest show of remorse or maternal affection would have elicited a sentence more in keeping with prevalent judicial interpretations of the bastardy law.

The reprieve which Eliot appended to the Mary Voce story represents the usual course of eighteenth-century punishment: J. J. Tobias notes that "[i]t does not seem that at any time in the eighteenth century, in any part of the country, more than sixty per cent of those sentenced to death were actually executed" (140), and Malcolmson leaves no doubt that the figure was considerably lower in infanticide cases (197 ff.). Foucault's identification of the sovereign "as the power that could suspend both law and vengeance" (53) is here represented as the power of the gentry to direct a social drama alternately redemptive and condemnatory: Hetty's life ultimately rests in the hands of her aristocratic seducer.

Hetty is also guilty of vagrancy, an increasingly evident offense throughout the eighteenth and nineteenth centuries, and one, it should be added, irreconcilable with the Victorian emphasis on the salutary value of work to which Murray Krieger assigns an important role in *Adam Bede* (206). Hetty violates the Vagrancy Act of 1744, which, Ignatieff notes, "empowered magistrates to imprison wandering lunatics and 'all persons wand'ring abroad and lodging in alehouses, barns and houses or in the open air, not giving a good account of themselves' " (25).[8] Mayhew's characterization of vagrants as generally young and as "first the beggars, then the thieves, and, finally, the convicts of the country" (3:398) represents a common perspective, and one evident in a remark by the Windsor landlord about the earrings and the locket that Hetty is trying to sell: " 'And they might think the things were stolen, as you wanted to sell 'em . . . for it isn't usual for a young woman like you to have fine jew'llery like that' " (428). Taken together, the criminal designation of vagrancy ("moving on" as crime; consider Jo in *Bleak House*), and the punishment of transportation (punishment as expulsion from the motherland), illustrate inverse aspects of a regional chauvinism not greatly at odds with Eliot's own regionalism, outlined in "The Natural History of German Life" and evident in her frequent punishment of characters who, like Hetty, David Faux (in "Brother Jacob"), and Maggie Tulliver, stray too far from home. Donald Stone's provocative remark that "Hetty's most unforgivable offense is her refusal to submit to the idyllic way of life Eliot celebrates in the novel" (208) has a foundation in law as well as in (as Stone argues) the poetry of Wordsworth.

The portrayal of the sympathetic criminal, as I have argued, requires the reader to reappraise the relationship between environment and criminal deed in a manner that is compatible with the tenets of juridical reform. Tom and Hetty—the thief and the murderess—are sympathetically cast as symptoms of a world gone wrong; to present them as natively or incorrigibly deviant would be to undermine the basic premises of reformist society. This conceptual alteration makes these criminals in a significant sense "victims," and thereby allies them more closely with the protagonists of the "industrial novels" with which *Hard Times* is sometimes grouped[9] than with their predecessors in earlier criminal literature. In transposing the object of criminality, *Hard Times* and *Adam Bede* again assume what is fundamentally a reformist posture. Tom and Hetty become incorporated into a delineation of the victim which, no longer describing either the awful monarch or the Job-like Heartfree or Dr. Primrose, becomes tripartite: it now includes not only the increasingly impatient "immediate victim" (Foucault 47), but also, paradoxically, the criminal himself or herself, as well as the offended sensibility of the dominant middle class.

Bounderby is of course the immediate victim of Tom's crime, and yet that Tom is himself the victim of the over-assertion of a specific social doctrine—the extrapolation of which is both Tom's crime and Bitzer's detection of it—is far more important to our understanding of *Hard Times*. Tom partakes of the editorial voice in *Hard Times* no less than do Sleary and Stephen Blackpool: his hatreds are, at the outset in any case, Dickens' hatreds; his subjection at their hands is Dickens' most forceful indictment of them. The Tom who tells his sister that " 'I wish I could collect all the Facts we hear so much about . . . and all the Figures, and all the people who found them out . . . and blow them all up together' " (40) sounds quite like the Dickens who defined the scope of his attack in an 1855 letter: "My satire is against those who see figures and averages, and nothing else—the representatives of the wickedest and most enormous vice of this time . . ." ("To Charles Knight" 263–64).[10] It is unlikely that Dickens intended his reader to regard Tom with the contempt with which we are to regard, for example, corrupt and unquestioning ideologists like Slackbridge and Bitzer.

Tom—and in this sense he is a rarity in the Dickens canon—is very much the Victorian "social" or "environmental" criminal: he is not evil, he has been crushed.[11] Tom's behavior, with the notable exception of the planning and execution of the robbery, is disconcertingly passive: he "[gives] himself up to be taken home like a machine" when caught peeking at the circus (10); he waits for trains that never deliver their promised passengers (159). That Tom does not "do," but is rather "done to," confirms him as a "victim" of the debilitating ideological "crime" that the novel attempts to unmask. Dickens advises us in the heading of his second chapter that "Murdering the Innocents" (2) is the crime with which he is concerned; larceny is venial indeed next to such grand fare. Consider the use of the passive voice in the following passage:

It was very remarkable that a young gentleman who had been brought up under one continuous system of unnatural restraint, should be a hypocrite; but it was certainly the case with Tom. It was very strange that a young gentleman who had never been left to his own guidance for five consecutive minutes, should be incapable at last of governing himself; but so it was with Tom. It was altogether unaccountable that a young gentleman whose imagination had been strangled in his cradle, should be still inconvenienced by its ghost in the form of grovelling sensualities; but such a monster, beyond all doubt, was Tom.

(101)

The cause and effect here need no elaboration. The crime that "strangles" Tom is the same crime that claims as its victims the bulk of the characters in *Hard Times*; and those who adjust to its strictures are invariably presented in a worse light than are those who, by however questionable a means, rebel against them.

A retrospective consideration of an identifiable pattern of sympathy in Dickens' novels offers a further clue about the reasons for the author's portrayal of Tom. Edgar Johnson comments that "the novels that follow *David Copperfield* continue the theme of orphaned, unfortunate, or neglected childhood," and adds that "Sissy Jupe and the Gradgrind children" are part of a tradition that includes Esther Summerson and Jo, Arthur Clennam and Amy Dorrit, Pip and Magwitch, and John Harmon and Jenny Wren" (2: 685). At first glance Tom may appear unsuited to a company of characters the sympathetic reception of whom is either assumed, or whose development of a claim to such status constitutes a fundamental movement in the novel. Tom's (albeit understated) inclusion in the list is in fact thoroughly justifiable: Dickens, himself of course carrying such colorful and confused baggage from his own childhood, goes to some pains to present Tom as a particularly abused member of a group towards which he was by nature unswervingly sympathetic. Gradgrind's blunt remark that " 'Louisa . . . has always been my favorite child' " (183) is indicative of Tom's short shrift of paternal affection; Loo's selfless love for her brother thus assumes a somewhat conspiratorial flavor that invites the reader to view Tom with sympathetic indulgence. More telling still is that Tom's logical attribution of his crime to his education draws from Gradgrind a reference to his son as a "deplorable object" (216), and inspires in Gradgrind the hope that " 'may God forgive you [Tom] as I do' " (217)! That . . . Gradgrind's catharsis is here being accented is well and good; it is difficult, however, to reconcile his reaction to young Tom's exposure of his system with his earlier, indulgent response to Louisa's remarkably similar, and every bit as condemnatory, exposure of the same (167 ff.). This is hardly a just turn of events when we consider that Tom, to his great detriment, has been far the better pupil. Tom is handled as roughly by his father as Amy Dorrit is by hers; he is denied not only the pathetic paternal reconciliation tendered to Louisa, but even the grotesque reconciliation allowed to Amy.

Bounderby, only the most visible representative of those whose conformist social philosophy has been assaulted by Tom's individualistic eruption, expresses the pervasive belief in crime as an attack on dominant social values when he endeavors to explain the nature of Tom's crime: " '. . . it's not the sum; it's the fact. It's the fact of the bank being robbed, that's the important circumstance' " (138). The presentation of crime by Dickens and the interpretation of crime by Bounderby express equally significant boundaries of nineteenth-century legal philosophy; taken together, these models describe the criminal as both victim, or social product, and criminal, or social offender. It is the uneasy fluctuation between these two poles that defines both the debate between reformers and juridical conservatives, and, in part, the course to be negotiated for the sympathetic criminal in the mid-Victorian novel.

The modern conception of infanticide as a crime against another person had no legal accommodation until the repeal of 21 Jac. 1, c. 27, after which time the prosecution "had first to establish that the infant victim was an independent human being" in order "to prove murder" (Rose 70). While the law would struggle with the intricacies of this delineation throughout the nineteenth century (Rose 70–78), the frequent association of infanticide with illicit pregnancy continued to encourage an interpretation of infanticide as a crime against society, much as the living (although legally ambiguous) bastard was regarded more as an emblematic punishment for the mother than as a human being (Chesney 349). Hester Prynne's scarlet letter represents a metaphoric enactment of this ethic, and the deaths of both Hetty's and Tess Durbeyfield's children are testimonies to the illegitimate child's prescribed role as inhuman social scourge.

The offended social body is well represented at Hetty's trial: Bartle Massey's misogynistic recounting of the morning session and the reappearance of the rather sinister John Olding complement a trial before counsellors " 'who [Bartle says] look as hard as nails' " (474). Martin Poyser, in one of the novel's most jarring moments, becomes the personification of society at the trial. A polarity is created between him and Hetty: he elicits the sympathy of " '[e]verybody in court' " merely by having " 'to look at the prisoner at the bar' " (473). The reader, privy to Hetty's tortured journey and well aware of the display of sympathy that it has ardently if suddenly inspired in Eliot, struggles against the censoriousness of a man whose "sense of family dishonour" had been described as "too keen . . . to leave room for any compassion towards Hetty" (459). As the trial progresses, the reader inclines towards the hope for leniency cherished by Dinah and Adam, and ultimately fulfilled by Eliot.[12]

That the "seduced woman"—unwed mother and infanticide—was herself a victim was a common liberal refrain. An anonymous 1876 review of *Daniel Deronda* casts a retrospective glance at Hetty as a "helpless victim" whose destruction by machine-like social forces generates more "pang and shiver of feeling" than do the deaths of either Desdemona or Juliet (23).[13] Although such a character could draw tears from the eyes of many a Victorian reader, and although a patronizing eagerness to cast the "fallen woman" as victim was apparently prevalent among the middle class (Rose 20), the law codified this sentiment at a decidedly cautious pace. The early nineteenth-century reformer George Onesiphorus Paul's remark to a female offender against the bastardy law that she, and not her lover, was legally accountable for the crime " '[b]ecause women were not legislators and men were parish officers' " (qtd. in Ignatieff 109) anticipates the failure in Parliament of the 1840 Seduction Bill that aimed to aid the " 'betrayed' victims" (Rose 30) of seduction. Adam's broken pre-trial discourse about the " 'justice' " he wants meted out to Arthur Donnithorne has as its basis an insistence upon Arthur as a criminal and Hetty as his victim (466–70); Arthur ensures Hetty's status as victim when he repents of the " 'horrible wrong' " that has resulted in his lover's undoing, and adds that " 'God knows, I'd give my life if I could undo it' " (515).

Tom's theft is the guarantor of Dickens' theme: it confirms as irrevocable the sequence of events that will enable the "broken and chastened" Gradgrind (Collins 194) to end his days in a family marked more by the presence of bittersweet love than by the pursuit of "ologies." Gradgrind's cathartic journey from the "large, far-flung, austere and impersonal [structures]" of the typical Dickensian "Society," to the "intimate, secure circles" of the Dickensian "Community" (Korg 85)[14] leads him to a mock trial before the ghosts of his past and the angels of his future; the theft that occasions Gradgrind's humiliation before Tom and Bitzer assures his benign acceptance of the fairy-tale ideology of Sleary and the subsequent coherence of his remaining family. Equally significant is that the parodic union of Bounderby and Mrs. Sparsit, the false family constructed in accordance with the social tenets that Dickens argues *preclude* family, dissolves in the aftermath of the events that have united the Gradgrinds. A sentence, a punishment, is exacted that this order may be enforced: the course of Dickens' novel tends equally towards the resurrection of the family bond from the rubble of Tom's delinquency and towards the expulsion of the revitalized family from the social mainstream."[15]

So it is as well in *Adam Bede*: " 'Trouble's made us kin,' " says Adam to Martin as he prepares to follow the Poysers from Hayslope (508),[16] and thus, as Krieger notes, to "[uproot] the most soundly rooted of the communal elements that gave Loamshire its meaning" (213–14). The expulsion of the Poysers and the Bedes is prevented only by Arthur's interested intervention, itself a reprieve of sorts, and as such a sobering reminder of who controls the punitive power in Eliot's earthy hamlet.

As Tom's crime makes a father of one whom (like Adam Bede and Felix Holt) convention would have shorn of his debilitating pride in the principles that have separated him from his family, so does Hetty's crime make a wife of one whom convention would have us want wed. Hetty's crime allows the pairing of Adam and Dinah and thus brings them into harmony with the meliorist propagative community of *Adam Bede*. Teleology is thus served: the important designation of being Adam's romantic interest is transferred from Hetty to Dinah in proportion as Dinah's move from transience to the acceptance of family and mundane geographic community is inverted in Hetty's rejection of community and commencement of vagrancy.[17] Hetty's crimes assure Adam and Dinah's status as propagators of the community.

It should come as no surprise that Dickens' and Eliot's presentations of crime and punishment posed a formidable ethical challenge to some mid-Victorian readers. Mrs. Oliphant, for example, took Dickens to task for forging a seemingly insoluble link between the lad deprived of "imagination, fancy, [and] poetry" and the young man who "will rob the bank and become a dissipated little provincial scoundrel" (454); she scoffed at this "lame and impotent conclusion" that she believed "[was] the end and aim of Mr Dickens in writing *Hard Times*" (454). One Reverend J. C. Robertson, claiming that "of all the characters for whom our authoress has been pleased to bespeak our interest, Hetty Sorrel is the most remarkable for unamiable qualities" (477), unfavorably compared the "influence" of a "class of books" which includes *Adam Bede* to that of "the 'Jack Sheppard' school of literature" (498). Such assaults, however, miss their mark for precisely the same reason that Dr. Johnson's critique of Fielding and Smollett does so:[18] they refuse to regard as legitimate the disjunctive relationship between author and law; they refuse, that is, to extend to the novelist privileges of legal and moral judgment traditionally reserved for the State and her Church. The success of the sympathetic criminal in the novel—and in a sense the success of the broader concept of "fiction"—rests on the acceptance or the rejection of this abstruse and presumptuous demand. *Hard Times* and *Adam Bede* construct alternate dramatic worlds on the fringe of the law; a willingness to accept the irregular tenets of these worlds anticipates the relative moral and legal generosity of the modern era, and a reluctance to do so recalls the closer cooperation of law and literature of the eighteenth century. In the mid-Victorian collision of these interpretive tendencies we may detect a fundamental and propulsive tension among literature and law and morality.

The eighteenth-century criminal novel in which "[p]ublic execution, or the threat of execution, is a required element . . . as is the repentance that results from the gallows encounter" (Davis 126) gives way, in the nineteenth century, to a novel in which the roles of society and, specifically, of family assume a greater significance than do the mitigated criminal act and the punishment therefor. That this system has its own beauty must be granted as a matter of course by the admiring reader of the Victorian novel. It also, let it be noted, has its own utility. The dynamic of sympathetic criminality offered by the novel, unlike the punishment exacted by the Fatal Tree, carries the implication of communal and individual rehabilitation, the stuff of final chapters and epilogues. The Gradgrinds, the Poysers, and the Bedes learn strength, humility, and cohesiveness; and neither Tom nor Hetty proves unregenerate: they ultimately do nothing to discredit those who have eased the burden of their punishment. Tom's repentance is backed by the rehabilitative force of protracted reflection; both he and Hetty die returning to the bosom of community. The most ardent reformer could have imagined no better system.[19]

NOTES

1. Carlisle lists Dickens, Thackeray, Eliot, Trollope, Gaskell, Kingsley, and Charlotte Brontë in this connection (15).
2. This "alteration" is thematic to bibliographic entries by Foucault and Ignatieff; Foucault notes that since the eighteenth century "judges have gradually . . . taken to judging something other than crimes, namely, the 'soul' of the criminal" (19).
3. See also Carlisle, who argues that "George Eliot's [narrator] pleads for a comprehension that will embrace sympathy. [Eliot] asks a good deal of both her art and her readers. The challenge that Hetty posed was, I think, greater and more profoundly personal than George Eliot at first realized. Sometimes, for instance in the pathetic appeals at the end of chapter 37, she betrays her uncertainty. Yet only a novelist who trusts her powers would choose child-murder, an uncompromisingly repulsive crime, to test her readers' acceptance of her perspectives" (193).

Austen (and Carlisle) by no means represent a consensus among critics: Beer notes that "[m]any critics have found fault with George Eliot's presentation of Hetty, seeing it as ungenerous and rebuffing in its insistence on her small scope, her paucity of love, her vanity" (69). Auerbach, for example, maintains that "Eliot endows [Hetty] with no spiritual or physical gifts that will draw the reader's sympathy" and that "the novel's rhetoric forbids the reader to like Hetty . . ." (174).

4. It was not until the passage of the Criminal Law Amendment Act of 1885 that "the professional bawd had to operate under cover, and became as unquestionably criminal as the thief or forger" (Chesney 364).

5. Collins notes "the virtual end of transportation by 1852" (7). Stephen explains that "[t]he punishment of transportation was gradually abolished between 1853 and 1864 . . . and penal servitude or imprisonment and hard labour on public works was substituted for it" (1: 482).

6. Korg notes that the prison in *Pickwick* "has some admirable qualities lacking in the outside world" (91); references to the coddled prisoner are legion elsewhere in Dickens' novels. Collins repeatedly cites "Pet Prisoners" (*Household Words* 27 Apr. 1850: 97–103), to which he attributes representative "attitudes" on this subject (155); see also "In and Out of Jail," by Dickens, Morley, and Wills.

7. Haight reprints Eliot's "History of 'Adam Bede'" (*Letters* 197–99); Taft's pamphlet places Eliot's aunt, Elizabeth Tomlinson, at the execution (591).

8. Ignatieff quotes from the Act (17 Geo. II, c. 5).

9. Raymond Williams's durable category also includes *Sybil, Mary Barton, North and South, Alton Locke,* and *Felix Holt*; see Williams 87–109.

10. Cf. Forster, who, in a rare laudatory Victorian review of *Hard Times*, defended the novel against the aspersions of "any man, who . . . should accuse Mr Dickens of attacking this good movement and the other, or of opposing the search after statistical and other information by which only real light can be thrown on social questions" (302). Forster exonerates the novel only by removing its thematic basis.

11. Tom, unlike Stephen Blackpool's wife, is therefore "reclaimable." Cf. Collins, who argues successfully that Dickens was generally disinclined to believe in "character-change" and in, specifically, the "reclaimable" prisoner (82). Dickens could apparently relax his contempt for the corrupt, or corrupted, character in deference to his broader thesis.

12. See also Carlisle: "When [Adam] stands by Hetty during her trial, the reader is asked to take the same stand" (212).

13. Holmstrom and Lerner attribute this review to the October 1876 issue of the *Westminster Review* (Holmstrom and Lerner 22); it does not in fact appear in that issue. Fulmer lists no *Westminster Review* articles on *Deronda* for 1876, although she says that "[e]ach review [in Holmstrom and Lerner] is annotated separately in [her] bibliography" (155).

14. Korg is discussing Raymond Williams's *The English Novel from Dickens to Lawrence*; his remark is not made specifically in reference to *Hard Times*.

15. Catherine Gallagher has made a similar point; see Gallagher 155.

16. Consider also Adam's "growing tenderness [towards Seth] which came from the sorrow at work within him" (531), and his increased patience with his mother (508).

17. Auerbach notes that Hetty and Dinah gradually exchange physical characteristics as the novel moves towards Adam's and Dinah's betrothal (175).

18. Theodore Martin wrote in 1879 that Robertson was already "old-fashioned" when he published his article on Eliot (24).
19. I am indebted to Cindy Kelly for her generous assistance in the preparation of this article.

WORKS CITED

Alexander, Edward, "Disinterested Virtue: Dickens and Mill in Agreement." *The Dickensian* 65 (1969): 163–70.

Auerbach, Nina. *Woman and the Demon: The Life of a Victorian Myth*. Cambridge, MA: Harvard UP, 1982.

Austen, Zelda. "Why Feminist Critics Are Angry with George Eliot." *College English* 37 (1976): 549–61.

Beer, Gillian. *George Eliot*. Bloomington: Indiana UP, 1986.

Carlisle, Janice. *The Sense of an Audience: Dickens, Thackeray, and George Eliot at Mid-Century*. Athens, GA: U of Georgia P, 1981.

Chesney, Kellow. *The Victorian Underworld*. London: Temple, 1970.

Collins, Philip. *Dickens and Crime*. London: Macmillan; New York: St. Martin's, 1962.

Davis, Lennard J. *Factual Fictions: The Origins of the English Novel*. New York: Columbia UP, 1983.

Rev. of *Daniel Deronda*, by George Eliot. *The Westminster Review* (1876 [?]). Rpt. in Holmstrom and Lerner 22–23.

Dickens, Charles. *Hard Times*. Ed. George Ford and Sylvère Monod. New York: Norton, 1966.

———. "To Charles Knight." 30 Jan. 1855. *Selected Letters of Charles Dickens*. Ed. David Paroissien. Boston: Twayne, 1985. 263–64.

[———, Henry Morley, and W. H. Wills.] "In and Out of Jail." *Household Words* 14 May 1853: 241–45.

Eliot, George. *Adam Bede*. Ed. Stephen Gill. Harmondsworth: Penguin, 1980.

Fielding, Henry. *The Life of Jonathan Wild*. London: Oxford UP, 1932.

———. *Covent Garden Journal* 20 June 1752. Rpt. in *The Covent Garden Journal* ed. Gerard Edward Jensen. Vol. 2. New York: Russell, 1964. 2 vols. 31–35.

[Forster, John.] Rev. of *Hard Times*, by Charles Dickens. *Examiner* 9 Sept. 1854: 568–69. Rpt. in *Dickens: The Critical Heritage*. Ed. Philip Collins. New York: Barnes & Noble, 1971. 301–3.

Foucault, Michel. *Discipline and Punish: The Birth of the Prison*. Trans. Alan Sheridan. New York: Vintage-Random, 1979.

Fulmer, Constance Marie. *George Eliot: A Reference Guide*. Boston: Hall, 1977.

Gallagher, Catherine. *The Industrial Reformation of English Fiction*. Chicago: U of Chicago P, 1985.

Haight, Gordon S. *George Eliot: A Biography*. New York: Penguin, 1985.

————, ed. *Selections from George Eliot's Letters*. New Haven: Yale UP, 1985.

Hollingsworth, Keith. *The Newgate Novel 1830–1847*. Detroit: Wayne State UP, 1963.

Holmstrom, John, and Laurence Lerner, eds. *George Eliot and Her Readers: A Selection of Contemporary Reviews*. London: The Bodley Head, 1966.

Ignatieff, Michael. *A Just Measure of Pain: The Penitentiary in the Industrial Revolution 1750–1850*. London: Macmillan, 1978.

Johnson, Edgar. *Charles Dickens: His Tragedy and Triumph*. 2 vols. New York: Simon, 1952.

Johnson, Samuel. *The Rambler* 31 Mar. 1750: 18–24. Rpt. in Paulson and Lockwood 230–34.

Jones, David. *Crime, Protest, Community and Police in Nineteenth-Century Britain*. London: Routledge, 1982.

Korg, Jacob. "Society and Community in Dickens." *Politics in Literature in the Nineteenth Century*. Lille: Centre d'Etudes Victoriennes, 1974. 85–111.

Krieger, Murray. *The Classic Vision: The Retreat from Extremity in Modern Literature*. Baltimore: Johns Hopkins UP, 1971.

Leavis, F. R. *The Great Tradition*. New York: New York UP, 1963.

Malcolmson, R. W. "Infanticide in the Eighteenth Century." *Crime in England 1550–1800*. Ed. J. S. Cockburn. Princeton: Princeton UP, 1977. 187–209.

Martin, Theodore. "From *The Life of H. R. H. The Prince Consort*." Holmstrom and Lerner 23–24.

Mayhew, Henry. *London Labour and the London Poor*. 4 vols. London: Griffin, 1861.

[Oliphant, Margaret.] "Charles Dickens." *Blackwood's Edinburgh Magazine* 77 (1855): 451–66.

Paulson, Ronald, and Thomas Lockwood, eds. *Henry Fielding: The Critical Heritage*. London: Routledge; New York: Barnes and Noble, 1969.

Radzinowicz, Leon. *A History of English Criminal Law and its Administration from 1750*. 4 vols. London: Stevens, 1948–68.

[Robertson, Reverend J. C.] Rev. of *Scenes of Clerical Life, Adam Bede,* and *The Mill on the Floss*, by George Eliot. *Quarterly Review* 108 (1860): 469–99.

Rose, Lionel. *The Massacre of the Innocents: Infanticide in Britain 1800–1939*. London: Routledge, 1986.

Ruskin, John. *Works*. Ed. E. T. Cook and Alexander Wedderburn. 39 vols. London: George Allen, 1903–12.

Sherburn, George. Introduction. *Caleb Williams*. By William Godwin. New York: Rinehart, 1960. vii–xiv.

Stephen, Sir James Fitzjames. *History of the Criminal Law of England*. 3 vols. London: Macmillan, 1883.

Stone, Donald. *The Romantic Impulse in Victorian Fiction*. Cambridge, MA: Harvard UP, 1980.

Taft, Henry. "An account of the Experience and Happy Death of *Mary Voce*. . . ." *Adam Bede*. By George Eliot. Ed. Stephen Gill. Harmondsworth: Penguin, 1980. 589–92.

Tobias, J. J. *Crime and Police in England 1700–1900*. Dublin: Gill, 1979.

Watt, Ian. *The Rise of the Novel: Studies in Defoe, Richardson and Fielding*. Berkeley: U of California P, 1957.

Williams, Raymond. *Culture and Society 1780–1950*. New York: Harper, 1958.

Recent Dickens Studies: 1988[1]

Susan R. Horton

For the most part the richest contributions to Dickens studies in 1988 appeared in works without the word *Dickens* in their titles: in studies of the rise of advertising and its role in producing the mass audience which in turn produced the writers like Dickens who served it; in studies of the rise of domestic fiction and its role in generating certain visions of the female and displacing Victorian discomfort with female sexuality. Some of the most engaging works actively resist our temptations to periodicize literature neatly. Keeping one eye on the Romantics and another on the Victorians, they succeed in uncovering and analyzing the profoundly participatory role fiction played in transforming versions of subjectivity produced by the works of the Romantics into the very different post-Romantic version of subjectivity required by the new age of urban industrial capitalism. At the heart of all these studies is the question, "How did the novel get to *be* that way in the nineteenth century, and what does its form tell us about the people and the age that spawned it, and that it in turn spawned." Thirty book-length studies are in this first tier, seven of which are distinct because of what I have elsewhere called "brokering":[2] that is, they use the methods and vocabulary of New Historicism or post-structuralist theories to address students as well as established scholars and to demonstrate how certain kinds of contextual readings not only enrich our understandings of Dickens and his age, but allow Dickens' works to comment proleptically on our own historical moment at the same time. Lest this appear to be a special pleading for new method over old, let it be noted that Harold Bloom's two recently-appearing edited collections of essays, one on *Bleak*

House and another on *David Copperfield*, the latter beginning with a reprinting of a piece of Barbara Hardy's 1970 book *The Moral Art of Dickens* and ending with a piece of Ned Lukacher's 1986 psychoanalytic study *Primal Scenes*, because of Bloom's shrewd selection and juxtaposition of essays, prove once again not only that the best readings can comfortably cohabit no matter when they were written and what their approach, but that *all* the best critical readings have always told us about something more than their ostensible subject.

Remaining works appearing in 1988 fall into one of the five more traditional categories: thematic close readings of particular novels or groups of novels; additions to our fund of sources and influences; biographical material (in which category I include discussions of new information about Dickens' writing process); discussions of film or dramatic adaptations of Dickens; or new editions of Dickens' works, which by and large I have not included since they are readily available in Alan Cohn's bibiographies in issues of *The Dickens Quarterly*. With a few exceptions, writings falling into these last five groups are addressed by way of fairly lavish annotated summations in the bibliography, where, given my audience of adept close readers, little will be lost: if I hum a few bars, readers can fill in the rest. At times I discuss works appearing in 1986 or 1987 that may not have been sufficiently applauded in these pages;[3] occasionally I have been unable to resist nodding in the direction of work appearing in 1989.

Among the works that fold Dickens and his works into a general discussion of how mid-to-late nineteenth-century notions of "subjectivity" determined both authorship and forms of authority is Paul Coates's *The Double and the Other: Identity and Ideology in Post-Romantic Fiction*. Works of fiction exist in that space between the Double and the Other, and to enter the work of fiction as either reader or writer is to engage in an attempt to transform the Other into a Double: the unlike into the "like me." The author's writing can be interpreted as a constant struggle to replace the image of that recalcitrant Other with that of the Self, "in a process of projection probably bound in with the mechanisms of colonialisation made available by the age of rapid transport" (2). Paradoxically, the Double enhances the ideology of individualism: it puts the self in the place of the Other who resembles it as an identical twin, thus denying an identity to the Double/Other. Realist novelists fight shy of the Double to protect the illusion of the actual existence of character; that is, they seek to deny characters are their projections. "Fear of the Double is fear of self-knowledge: the Romantic's fear of the feasibility of the self's total reification by science"(3). The Romantic's attitude toward the Double is contradictory: oppos[ing] it because it mechanically presents the body as soul-less mechanism; yet embrac[ing] it because it is the unconscious" (4). As self becomes more dependent on Other in an increasingly mediated world, rearguard actions are launched to re-divide them" (4). "Hence the compensatory emergence of nationalism that accompanies the growth of the world economy. The attempt to expel the foreign element fails however: the implication of self and other is already too deep. Hence the foreign appears in the form of the self: outside it perhaps, but its Double" (4). In this context Coates provides a useful definition of ideology, the essence of which lies in its being "the institutionalized bipartisanship of the imperative to 'see the other side of the question,' which transforms the potential for change inherent in contradiction into a steady state of balance. Ideology socializes the individual by bringing him or her to internalize the dividedness of a class society in the form of the structure of 'objective value-free judgment'— thereby enabling the system to rule the subject, by dividing it. The antithesis between the 'here' of the individual and the 'there' of others is translated into internal space." Gary Day's essay, "Figuring out the Signalman: Dickens and the Ghost Story," identifies Dickens' narrator's uncertainty about the ghost in that story as a function of a similar "split self," wanting to be "both spectator and actor," wanting both to move towards and away from knowledge, desiring a "paradoxical abolition and retention of difference" (40).

Coates's play with "out there" and "in here," with Freud's *Fort/Da* and with its deigetical form in fiction, "here"/"there" or "then"/"now," produces some shrewd readings of Dickens' canon. It explains in new ways, for instance, some of the effect of *Bleak House* on readers. There the present tense "seems pointless, for it lacks the sense of inevitability, authority and teleology implicit in the preterite, which has patently *led to something* it now chronicles from a distance. . . . The absence of the preterite indicates Dickens' inability to *put behind him* what he sees; the nut of the law proves hard to crack, and its practitioners sit there on the page, refractory and intractable, as the author strives with all his rhetorical might to move them; make them go somewhere"(25).

Nancy Armstrong in *Desire and Domestic Fiction: A Political History of the Novel* also draws on such "formal" matters as the rhetorical strategies in the Brontës, Austen, Gaskell, Eliot and Dickens to explore how those "became techniques of social control." Her general thesis is that "the social difference between male and female depend on a form of subjectivity that in turn depends on gender difference," (41) and that those things in turn were produced in part in fiction. Earlier nineteenth-century writers such as Fredric

Rowton believed in an essential difference between the minds of men and the minds of women, and insisted that women were to write by nature "as partners" rather than "as rivals" to men, thus ensuring that women's writing could complement—but never engage critically—with that of men. Lack of access to economic and political power authorized certain forms of writing while barring certain other forms: women could write about the home, but not about the marketplace. This would not be news, but for the fact that Armstrong emphasizes at every point the fact that these conditions for writing (and for writing's reception) were not only an extension of the themes organizing the novel as a form, but themselves testimony to the power of those organizing themes to transform a readerships' understanding of social roles available to them. "Respectable fiction . . . was that which replayed political conflict in terms of sexual differences that upheld a peculiarly middle-class notion of love. It is no accident, then, that novels by such major authors as Dickens and Thackeray move toward fulfillment of the sexual contract with all the consistency of novels by Austen, the Brontës, and Gaskell. "The division and balance of authority described by Rowton was obviously understood as the only way to resolve a conventional plot. Successful conclusion could be none other than a life free of physical labor and secured by the patronage of a benevolent man" (42). The idea that women gained their "authority" through the benevolent protection of a man served as an effective justification for excluding women from business and politics, and Armstrong explores this "social contract" and how it regulated actual social relationships in the nineteenth century. She explores the form and consequences of the authority women *gained* through this "social contract" as well as what men *lost*. What men lost, among other things, was access to the kind of improvisational power found in bricolage and "making do" (to invoke Michel deCerteau) which women represent (and which, parenthetically, I would say is the way to read Mary Shelley's *Frankenstein*, "the monster" himself being a most resourceful version of quilt-making, the efficacious and imaginative use of leftovers which is quintessentially female,) but which Armstrong points out exists in Dickens only in the "fetishized" worlds of Wemmick's castle, Venus's bottle and bone shop, and other such places where males gather, but do not know how to use, the "detritus" out of which women build lives.

My own analysis here does not quite resemble that of Chris Baldick in his *In Frankenstein's Shadow: Myth, Monstrosity, and Nineteenth Century Writing*, where he explains the popularity of Frankenstein and other monsters in nineteenth-century writing as deriving "from images of political monstrosity brought vividly before the attention of the British public by the early debates over the French Revolution" (92), or from a vision, first of course offered by Carlyle, of an artificially galvanized mass of a society governed by scientific rationality and the cash nexus alone. Dickens Baldick calls "the Dantean poet of this galvanic wasteland" (106), from *Pickwick Papers*'s "gallows humor" to Dickens' constant scattering and dismembering and focusing on body parts, to the obverse, the "artificial assemblages which unite their parts in a human patchwork" (110) as well. Included is the Dickensian concern with the "fabrication of identity" so obvious in *Martin Chuzzlewit*, in *Hard Times* in Bitzer and Tom, and par excellence in the figure of Pip, who exhibits not only anxieties about his artificiality, but a sensitivity to being exhibited and a propensity to turn on his "makers," as do all "monsters."

Like Coates and Baldick, Armstrong's conceptual structure for understanding the nineteenth century and the writing it produced generates new and enriching readings of Dickens' novels. Her assessment of the Victorian audience's fascination with Nancy's death scene, that it "had everything to do with the fact that Nancy is the representative of another class's sexuality (not middle class and repressed) while *at the same time* she represents a very positive middle-class virtue as the nurturant, forgiving mother to Sikes, Oliver, and most other males, is persuasive. "One could say [her] body provided a field where two notions of the family confronted one another and the old gave way to the new" (183). Victorians could not deal with the notion of "combination" or collaboration: they viewed all forms of social organization as sexual violation; nor could they deal with the forms of authority or social power—permeable, collaborative—that the female represented. It is no accident then that domestic fiction which "contained disorder within the household" should dramatically rise in popularity in the 1840s. It is also no accident that audiences should thrill not simply to the death of Nancy, who embodied discomfitting apparent contradictions like those between sexuality and maternity; independence and collaboration, but that they should need to see her reduced to a pool of gore on the floor.

Like the rest of the best writers on Dickens this year, Armstrong sees the novel in the nineteenth century as marking the birth of sociology, "represent[ing] the disruption of domestic order in terms of combination; the destruction of boundaries between nature and culture reveal[ing] itself in a mixture of genders and generations and associat[ing] such dissolution with filth and disease, (as in *Bleak House* or *Our Mutual Friend*,) whereas an earlier novel such as *Oliver Twist* is the most revealing display of social redemption through the domestication of desire" (185).

Another writer who sees *Oliver Twist* and the other early novels as "anticipat[ing] a social science" is David Trotter, whose *Circulation: Defoe, Dickens, and the Economy of the Novel*, I would be inclined to name as my personal favorite for 1988. The "social state" of a city depends on its "moral state," which in turn depends on its physical state, its supply of food, water, housing. "Dangerous zones" of the city disrupt the economy of trade: they constitute a "blockage or obliteration of channels" (77). In what then becomes a Foucauldian and DeLeuzian and Guattarian analysis, Trotter places Dickens in his times: the economy of trade generated a "medical police" whose job it was to identify zones and classes, map and analyze them, "to produce them as objects of knowledge" (77). "To do so was not to disperse them, but to keep them in play as reminders of the necessity and beauty of circulation." Dickens encountered the rhetoric of sanitary reform in the 1840s. At the same time . . . in his novels is "an economy of conversion which represents the city as hell. The efforts of Social Science to produce the zones and classes of the city as an object of knowledge are themselves circumscribed by an economy of conversion which directs both life and narrative away from any form of worldliness" (77). But *Oliver Twist* is a novel of "the converted," not of conversion (77–78). Like Defoe's Colonel Jack, Oliver Twist is subject to extrinsic forces—the workhouse, and so on. Defoe allows this subjection to forces to construct identity for Jack. But Dickens represses the extrinsic. He discusses in events that took place before the start of the novel a source of identity even stronger than social or criminal classification. In doing so, he removes his novel from an economy which makes it possible to conceive of the exchange and circulation of identities. *The Old Curiosity Shop* retains this pattern: extrinsic forces have no effect on character: do not "circulate through" it. But Trotter identifies one crucial scene in which characters circulate through one another, the scene in which Nell and her grandfather share a barge with some drunken travellers. "She happened, while she was thus engaged, to encounter the face of the man on deck, in whom the sentimental stage of drunkenness had now succeeded to the boisterous, and who, taking from his mouth a short pipe, requested that she would oblige him with a song." Says Trotter, "This sentence begins in Nell's mind and ends in extrinsic engagement. In return for transport and a place to sleep, Nell sings" (82–83). Here, then, Dickens reflects an economy of exchange, which results in among other things a less paranoid attitude towards the city. Immediately thereafter, in fact, Dickens' narrator says, "it was like being in the confidence of all these people to stand quietly there, looking into their faces as they flitted past." "Dickens' recognition that exchange can quite legitimately constitute identity and relationship has disciplined his writing, removed its hysterical edge" (83).

Trotter's use of the image of circulation allows for wonderful re-readings of the entire Dickens world and canon. In slums like Saffron Hill, "circulation is threatened by overflow as much as by blockage. Epidemic, rumour, and riot obscure the act of exchange—nobody knows how they are transmitted" (89). Subjectivity and identity is a product of the circulation of energies and other subjectivities through the self. "Bad" characters in Dickens' novels are those who are "closed up": through whom neither information (Carker, Nadgett, Jaggers), nor fellow-feeling (Miss Havisham, Mrs. Clennam, the Murdstones), nor money (the Deadlocks, the Podsnaps) is allowed free passage or flow. All those Dickensian reticules decorated with rivets and closing with a snap take on new significance here. Even Dickens' journalistic pieces in *Household Words* take on new richness read through Trotter. "It would not reduce Dickens' politics absurdly to say he was for circulation and against stoppage and that he wasn't at all afraid of the literal application of the metaphor to everyday existence. . . . the lives of the poor could be made tolerable by proper circulation of air and water through their houses" (103). The 1829 Metropolitan Police Act instituted Foucauldian surveillance, and is reflected in Dickens' portrayals of what Trotter calls "official hermeneuts" like Nadgett (116). Dickens' interest in physiognomy, too, arises because the "body becomes the medium of that circulation of signs which sustains and enlivens the social body" (118). In this context, immovable and unreadable faces like Mrs. Clennam's take on even more significance, as do the various "signings" of the body which characters themselves undertake in order to be read, as Edith Dombey's scoring her body with her jewelry. Dickens' works, as his world, become epistemologically readable as a play on an economy of signs and money—circulating or not circulating, with good or ill consequences.

Both D.A. Miller's "Secret Subjects, Open Secrets," and his *The Novel and the Police* offer an even more complex survey of the same terrain, pointing out there is no difference between the "self-concealment" of the good characters and that of the "bad," and noting that in a capitalist economy, something removed from circulation and exchange or hoarded is worth nothing. The epistemological question, then, becomes what value can be put upon an innerness that is never recognized in intersubjectivity. The nineteenth-century novel is itself a kind of answer: it is a kind of "box," or "little room" that confines both writer and reader, producing "open secrets." David Copperfield succeeds by disciplining himself, which is in fact what writing is all about. For Miller, then, *David Copperfield* is not about the constraints imposed by a Murdstone so much as about "the ways in which two modes of discipline are played off against one another in a single system of social control" (108). "The difference between the liberal and carceral camps is not substantive, but only effective, has thus the status of a secret—that is to say, inevitably, an open secret. Accordingly, the novel must both keep this secret and give it away. Keep it, because the liberal/carceral opposition is the foundation of the liberal subject as well as the basis of the novel's own role in producing him. Give it away, because this opposition is effectively maintained by seeming always in need of maintenance" (109). One can see here again the ways in which such analyses offer explanations not just of Dickens, or of the nineteenth century, but of how subjectivity and state produce one another to the present day, and not surprisingly Miller, like Trotter and Armstrong, also sees the novel form as itself contributing to the continuation of the "individual" isolated "subject": "Every novel reading subject is constituted . . . within the categories of the individual, the inward, the domestic" (82), in which even the length of a novel requires withdrawal to a private sphere in which to read it, producing "a subject habituated to psychic displacements, evacuations, reinvestments, in a social order whose totalizing power circulates all the more easily for being pulverized" (xii–xiii).

The difference between Trotter's and Miller's readings and more traditional historical readings produced in 1988 is that the latter presume that the social conditions in which Dickens was writing serve only as more or less conscious "sources" for Dickens' writings rather than as conceptual and emotional raw materials which circulate through Dickens himself. Such could be said for instance of Laurence Lerner's *The Frontiers of Literature*, which sets out to explore "the adjacent territories to literature . . . history, crying, persuading, and play" (3). Dickens appears entirely in his first chapter on "History," where, by comparing Dickens' "historical narrative" of his stay at Warren's Blacking Factory with the "fictitious narrative" as it appears in *David Copperfield* and Dickens' descriptions in novels, he attempts to "explore the emotional involvement" which will enable us to notice "elements in the fiction that seem to be there for some private reason which the uninformed reader would have to guess at" (22). "The natural next step," according to Lerner, would be "to look for explanation of artistic success and failure, asking whether such involvement is an advantage or disadvantage aesthetically" (22). Lerner's conclusion—that Dickens' style "drops into cliché writing about class conflict, and crackles with life when he writes of the delights of machinery and progress" (58)—of course follow "naturally" and inevitably from his method, which presumes the possibility of detaching Dickens as individual from the currents of ideas/fears/emotions which circulated through him. Graham Daldry's *Charles Dickens and the Form of the Novel* suffers from the same divisions. So also does Jeremy Hawthorn's *Bleak House*, which aspires to be a book for students, but which by dividing its chapters as it does, and introducing snippets of earlier criticism into the work as well, ends up doubly decontextualizing or taking Dickens "out of circulation": Dickens from the ideas circulating through both him and his times, and the earlier critics cited in the book from the texture of the exposition which give life to those separate "points."

A similar attempt to "broker" theory for students is in Kenneth James Hughes's *Signs of Literature: Language, Ideology and the Literary Text*, one chapter of which focuses on "Diegesis, Mimesis, Realism and Charles Dickens' *Hard Times*." I applaud the effort, which might help us get past the kind of schizophrenia that results when we talk to students about literature in one way in the classroom and then retreat to our studies to write about it in quite different ways. But the six pages devoted to *Hard Times* hardly allow for much sophisticated analysis, though Hughes does manage to raise the question of the issue of "realism" as a convention, and to suggest how we might see Dickens' opening paragraphs in *Hard Times* as a critique of nineteenth-century notions of empiricism.

Much more successful in the attempt to "broker" newer ways of reading and newer vocabularies is David Musselwhite's extremely quirky and fun to read *Partings Welded Together: Politics and Desire in the Nineteenth-Century English Novel*, which with a light hand introduces what he says are lectures originally written to introduce undergraduates to the uses of Derrida, Foucault, Lacan, Deleuze and Guattari, Macherey, Renee Balibar and Ernesto Leclau. His every page shows how these ways of seeing inspire new readings of Jane Austen, Mary Shelley, Thackeray, and Dickens. Like Trotter, Armstrong, and Weissman, his basic thesis is that the nineteenth-century novel was "the most important agency for the process of internalization, or subjectivization, of the 'idea of the state.' " (8). One of the ways in which novel reading itself *works* is in working out "one of the fundamental contradictions of the bourgeois order . . . its social schizophrenia—that paradoxical determination to both homogenize and individualize the occupants of a social space—especially the masses" (3). His object, then, becomes the exploration of the question, "How . . . from Austen to Dickens, the exuberance and the threat of the forces let loose by the development of industrialism and the French Revolution—I have in mind the creation of a new urban populace on the one hand and the affording of new human possibilities on the other—are steadily but ineluctibly worked within a new axiomatic, a new set of rules and constraints, of prescribed places and possibilities that made them both manageable and self-monitoring" (9). The nineteenth-century novel helped to do that by deploying notions of "class," by determining the nature of knowledge, the role of women, "representative democracy," by perpetuating and deepening the distinction between "public" and "private."

These same words are given a slightly different spin in Judith Weissman's *Half Savage and Hardy and Free: Women and Rural Radicalism in the Nineteenth-Century Novel.* If the Romantic heroine was the free spirit, roaming the rural countryside, subject to Wordsworth's voyeuristic gaze, perhaps, but all the same in equal part with men contributing her physical labor to the economic welfare of that rural society, the heroines of Victorian fiction are deformations of those earlier Romantic heroines, and a product of identifiable, historically specific conditions. Belonging to the city and not the country, to men who produce money and not food, they live on, but transformed by film, fiction, and advertising. Instead of doing the work that belonged to them in an agricultural economy, they now "have been given a formidable new job, taking care of their perpetually endangered men" (142). It is, of course, the myth Dickens perpetuates as well. The Romantic fascination and sympathy with the mad undergoes a transformation in which Victorian heroines "go mad in the service of men," and Romantic heroines "float down from Shelley's empyrean sphere, first to the isolated home of Jane and Rochester and then to the urban homes of Victorian businessmen in the fictions of Thackeray and Dickens. In the process of descent, sensibility and love and imagination become masochism and madness—and all the better for men who look for their wives in schools like Miss Pinkerton's or the mental hospitals where they would have learned humility . . . They have their source in Romanticism, but they serve what the romantic poets saw as their enemy—the economy processes of industrial capitalism" (163).

Mary Poovey's *Uneven Developments: The Ideological Work of Gender in Mid-Victorian England* also sees the nineteenth-century subject as being constituted in the discourses of law, medicine, and literature; like Weissman she sees Dickens as part of the symbolic work necessary to manage nineteenth-century anxieties about women and their aggressiveness: "through a series of substitutions, [to] neutralize the sexuality he associates with some women, only to betray its imaginative persistence by the very labor with which he writes it out" (12). Dickens' works translate the deep structural relation into a psychological narrative of individual development, in which both provided individual readers with an image of what identity was, and created a subject position that reproduced the kind of identity in the individual reader" (89). Implicit in the "literacy" in this period, she says, was the textual construction of an individual psychology. Explicitly, "this process was part of the legitimazation and depoliticization of capitalist and market and class relations, that the definition (and defense) of the English writer's social role was intimately involved in both and that stabilizing and mobilizing a particular image of woman and the domestic sphere, and woman's work were critical to all" (89).

Rosemarie Bodenheimer's *The Politics of Story in Victorian Social Fiction* identifies three kinds of plots in nineteenth-century fiction: Romantic plots with middle-class heroines, appearing in industrial novels by women, which "are fictional conduits for imagining the nature of social government and the possible directions of social change." These explore the struggle for social power between landed gentry and the newly ascendant industrial entrepreneurs of the north. There is then the turn from Romantic plots to Romantic rhetoric, and in this second kind of plot there are two sub-categories: novels with pastoral realms and mythic histories functioning as alternatives or correctives to courses of thought and action in the social order (i.e., "fictional appeals to nature or to a value-laden past [that are] open to dismissal as escapist or nostalgic fantasy" (9). These can also be seen as dialectic, as genuine alternatives to the social order. There are also "novels where creating a pastoral "place" is a chief strategy of social argument (such as in *Oliver Twist*, *Alton Locke*, or Elizabeth Gaskell's *Ruth*). In these novels, "post-Wordsworthian pastoral writing emerges as a complex arena of resistance to the environmentalist view of character rather than as a univocal gesture toward a utopian place" (9). Finally, there are novels that grapple with the idea of history itself, such as Disraeli's *Sybil*, Eliot's *Felix Holt*, or *Hard Times*, all of which create a continuum from a valued past to an imagined future which excludes the fragmented or forgetful politics of the present. There is despair in all of them about progress: instead, they "implicitly revise the status of social-problem fiction as instruments of social intervention: in these works the novel form itself becomes a recuperation and a repository of history" (10). While it is obvious that Bodenheimer's study is mining some of the same veins as those of Armstrong, Weissman, and others, hers adds much. Among other things, it offers a reassessment of what we consider "bad" or "good" fiction. Some fictions "erase or deny what they transform," and some "articulate in the very act of fantasy the pressures of an ineradicable social predicament" (10).

Dirk DenHartog's *Dickens and Romantic Psychology: The Self in Time in Nineteenth-Century Literature* in yet other ways reads Victorian fiction as a struggle to re-fashion Romantic versions of self and society. With Rousseau's *Confessions*, and a bit later with Wordsworth, *memory* came into its own "not just as a literary topic but as a desired mode of awareness." Dickens' novels he sees as perhaps the most persistent and full attempts to explore the ambiguities and dilemmas generated by this new emphasis on memory, and he explores the degree to which this concern with the self and its memory (which by definition translates into a concern for the self's continuity) translated into both thematic material for the novelist, and into a medium for the investigation of other themes. The unleashing of the forces of individualism, capitalism, urbanization, secularization and technological progress in post-French Revolutionary culture produced a phenomenological effect on consciousness which came to be also a "cause" within the circumstances that produced it. This effect/cause DenHartog calls "the experience of modernity," and it is recognizable in such things as a simultaneous and ambivalent delight and fear in equal intensity to "the possibility of freedom and expansion." In this context he considers the continuities and the tensions between Wordsworth's *Prelude* and Dickens' *Great Expectations* evident among other things in their different senses of the personal past. Most interesting is the question of "authority" that is bound up in this experience of modernity, which reveals itself in the Victorian writer—including Dickens—swinging wildly between "Romantically legitimated freedom [of the individual], and habitually authorized restraint" (7). The fascination in the nineteenth-century novel, for instance, of the subject of adultery is an instance of exactly this alternating desire for individual freedom, and the constraints imposed by religion, law, and conventional morality. The nineteenth-century novel constantly explores this shift in authority from moral law or social law, to the psychic sense of personal "rightness" of conviction—which of course holds within it the implicit Romantic assumption of the "rightness"—let alone the availability to consciousness—of the self's "feelings" about the self. The strain between the integrity of the self and its proper expansion constitutes the post-Romantic dialectic, and is worked out most fully in Dickens' writings: not only in his novels, but in his letters as well. When, for instance, he refers to the letter to Forster in which Dickens describes his "unsettled and wayward feeling which is part (I suppose) of the tenure on which one holds an imaginative life, and which I have . . . often kept down only by riding over it like a dragoon," DenHartog is no doubt right to see in the tone and substance of that letter "a combination of the stern-faced Carlylean relish with which the simile of the dragoon is seized upon . . . [and] simultaneously a positive valuing of the subversive and anarchic and an ennoblement of repression as the necessary cost of survival in the struggle of life" (34). Not surprisingly DenHartog lingers long over the figure of Dombey, who represents in many ways the ideal of Victorian manliness, embodying a "sexual schism . . . not founded in nature, but aris[ing] . . . from the repression that such an ideal ennobles" (40). *Little Dorrit* is in dialogue with the same Wordsworthian psychology present in *Dombey and Son*, with the former novel inconclusively suspended between "a fascination that its conservatism might offer the answer to life's problems after all, and a persistent distrust of such an appeal, in part fidelity to the troublesome expansive impulses that are irreconcilable with self continuity in its wordsworthian definition" (80). Amy Dorrit's father in his problematic relation to his own memory is thrown into exemplary contrast with the Wordsworthian Amy, who has a solid and permanent identity based on her own continuity, which is in turn based on her own memory of who she is and has been through time. The tension between the individual self, and allegiances beyond the self, is the hallmark of modernism, and *Great Expectations* is about finding "room" to negotiate and find a balance between these two. Pip's betrayal and subsequent return to Joe enact a path of estrangement and restoration that stands as a qualified version of the spiritual-cum-psychological autobiography Wordsworth had traced in *The Prelude*.

Although the title does not reveal its affinities with DenHartog's analysis, J. Fisher Solomon's "Realism, Rhetoric, and Reification: Or the Case of the Missing Detective in *Our Mutual Friend*" is, by way of an explanation for the reader's dissatisfaction with the Harmon mystery of that novel, a study of the repercussions of urban capitalism as they are reflected in the historical division between aesthetic realism and aesthetic naturalism. In realism, "social institutions are presented as human relationships." In naturalism, "man and his surroundings are always sharply divided" (38). That is, in the realistic novel there is a dialectic relation between subjective free will, and the social group. In the naturalistic, there is a breakdown of this dialectical equilibrium leading to a breakdown of subjective freedom. Thus, man is portrayed as subordinate to and determined by his background, and "environment displaces its inhabitants in the role of hero" (380). Finance capitalism is responsible for the reifications in novels of such things as death and money. *Our Mutual Friend* is both naturalistic—a tale of urban reification and semantic emptiness—and a realistic one reflecting the more hopeful and productive aspects of nineteenth-century industrialism. In that context, then, the Harmon mystery can best be explained in this way: Harmon's scheme subverts the naturalistic (and semiotic) dictates of the past (as represented by the will) on behalf of a subjective plan to take control of his own life (41).

The same wild swings between a belief that the individual controls his own destiny, and that that destiny is controlled by forces beyond individual control, is explained in very different ways by different writers. George Levine's wonderfully substantial *Darwin and the Novelists: Patterns of Science in Victorian Fiction*, a piece of which appears in his essay "*Little Dorrit* and Three Kinds of Science," is by no means a simple study of how Darwin "influenced" Dickens and other nineteenth-century writers, but an exploration of how the same questions—about the sources of authority (religion, politics, epistemology), about the relation between the personal and the social to the "natural," about origins, progress, endings, organicism (social and biological)—shaped, infused, and produced both the discourse of science and the discourse of literature. (In this respect, his work reminds one of Gillian Beer's.) He describes, for instance, a "sort of gestalt of the Darwinian imagination [that is] detectable in novels as well as in science" (13). Even talk of a "human *subject*," for instance, implies both man as an object of study, and the possibility of identifying material explanations for human behavior. Third-person narration reflects a stance of "detached authority" that pervades both fiction and science writing, as well as a Baconian shift away from traditional authority and towards the authority of experience that can be gained by a "rigorous disinterestedness." At the same time, in characters such as Jaggers or Tulkinghorn, we see played out the possibility of such rigorous disinterested observation while the observer himself escapes observation. Levine's wonderful paralleling of Darwinian-/scientific stances and Dickensian/narrative stances bears repeating: Uniformitarianism, in which "all events can be explained casually, and by causes now in operation" (15). Change, a phenomenon emphasized since Darwin, in which "realist narrative change and development become both subject and moral necessity and tend also to be a condition of plausibility (i.e., of plot) (17). A blurring of boundaries, including the conceiving of time as a continuum, so that characters "tend to be a condition of time and circumstance more than of 'nature' " (17). We find in both Darwin and Dickens an emphasis on connections both ecological and geneological: in Darwin's image of "the tangled bank," and in Dickens' characters' endless interconnectedness. A sense of abundance, in which survival depends on variation, diversification, and multiplicity—a description which of course fits Dickens' peopled fictional world (18). A denial of design and teleology, as narrative unfolds without external intrusion (18). The presence of both mystery and order, with the presence of an "order" not obvious on the surface (19). The necessity for the inclusion of the conception of "chance" as an explanation for change—the equivalent of "sudden, inexplicable mutation" in Darwin (19). There is much more, on *Bleak House* in particular, but I will only refer here to Levine's intriguing discussion of the "three sciences" reflected in *Little Dorrit*. Natural theology suggests a world that is rational, just, divinely inspired, meaningful; thermodynamics, a world fallen from a golden age and in decline; evolutionary biology, a world moving towards a golden age. These three conflicting visions are played out in *Little Dorrit*, in the possibility of harmony amid disintegration; faith in energy and free choice; in the power of love over system; of energy over entropy.

Carla Peterson, in *The Determined Reader: Gender and Culture in the Novel from Napoleon to Victoria* in many ways traces some of the same tensions—such as those in DenHartog, between a Romantically engendered belief in the "rightness" of individual freedom to make moral choices, and a traditional need to rely on external sources (church, state, or the social order) for moral authority—but she grounds and explains these two positions as the result of "two different and antithetical reading traditions" (83). Evangelical literature has stressed humanity's original sin, and therefore need to accept God's judgment and trust in Providence over individual will. Both the advent of Romanticism and secular literature emphasized instead the innocence of the individual, and encouraged self-reliance. Charlotte Brontë's *Jane Eyre* and Dickens' *David Copperfield* reveal the "pull" exerted by these two different traditions. Both Jane Eyre and David Copperfield read books from both traditions, both describe their readings and the conflicts that reading produces in them, but their solutions to the conflict differ greatly. For Brontë/Jane Eyre, both literary traditions must be seen as negative insofar as they depict women as inferior. She has, then, three choices: to move to a world of "culture in the wild," to accept one or another of these existing literary traditions and adopt the vision of woman implied in them, or to accept the traditions and rewrite the texts of those traditions. Brontë, says Peterson, chooses the third option. Dickens attempts to reshape many elements of these two literary traditions, but ultimately he can reach no reconciliation, and his reader/writer protagonist ultimately chooses "the ways of Providence over those of Nature" (85–86). Peterson re-reads in wonderful ways even little Davey's Crocodile Book, which is itself, she says, one of the texts of Victorian culture shaping

Davey—and by extension, Dickens. "Is the dreadful animal capable of being tamed?" asks the book innocently. "Yes . . . all animals can be rendered mild and inoffensive," is the ostensibly "innocent" but thoroughly Murdstonian reply.

While David smarts from Murdstone's blows, he reads Foxe's *Book of Martyrs*, and, says Peterson, internalizes his "guilt," and "his sense of self as alienated subject and his loss of self as subject are induced by the alienating mirror image" (118–19). By contract Jane Eyre never feels that alienation. Consequently, as narrators of their own lives, David and Jane behave very differently. David as writer belittles his own works: "a little something" written "in secret": a "good many trifling pieces" (127). Dickens' narrative choices make David Copperfield, unlike Jane Eyre's autobiography, not his own interpretation of his life, but rather, of his written account of Agnes's "reading" of his life. Agnes's is a Providential perspective, so David never really does become, as Jane Eyre, the hero of his own story. Ultimately, then, Dickens comes to reject the "unitary" solution of *David Copperfield* that could clearly no longer account for the increasing complexity of values in Victorian culture, and his acknowledgment of such complexities is reflected in the increased problematization of narrative genre and authority in such later novels as *Bleak House* and *Great Expectations*.

I can imagine both Peterson and DenHartog in comfortable dialogue with Franco Moretti, whose *The Way of the World: The Bildungsroman in European Culture* distinguishes between the British *bildungs* hero—like Pip or David—and that of other European countries. The British hero had to be "common," (just what Pip is of course chided by Estella for being). Pip plummets because he tries to reject his "commonness." In doing so, however, he alienates himself from the English novelistic hero, which privileges not the more upper class hero, as Goethe does, but the other, socially "neutral" and thus potentially universalistic one (190). The English middle class, says Moretti, has never produced institutions or culture of anything like a comparable distinctiveness and density to those of the "upper," or for that matter, the "working class." Such heroes as Pip or David represent a class in the middle—between Steerforth and Heep—which has neither the galvanizing force of the upper class, nor of the lower. If the English hero wants to have a destiny, then, he has to preserve precisely those "common" qualities— anonymous, ordinary, and widespread—that characterize him from the start. The "common" hero is the structural requisite of the fairy-tale novel and at the same time not coincidentally the representative of a new middle class endowed with little daring and a dim self-consciousness. This hero is "an essential component of a *democratic* culture" (191), and more to the point, "democracy is not interested in the production of good novels. If anything, it aims at limiting the domain of the novelistic, at counter-balancing the destabilizing tendencies of modernity; aims at reducing the rate of 'adventure' in our lives while expanding the jurisdiction—so inert in narrative terms—of 'security' " (192). The more a society perceives itself as a system still unstable and precariously legitimized, the fuller and stronger the image of youth. Youth acts as a sort of "symbolic concentrate" of the uncertainties and tensions of an entire cultural system. The hero's growth becomes the narrative convention that permits the exploration of conflicting values. Since British society was stable, unlike that of other European countries, youth in its novels cannot and does not want to identify with the spirit of adventure of modern youth (185). Thus, says Moretti, we have the "feeble and snobbish behavior of Pip," and novels by Dickens which "keep alive the taxonomical rigidity of the 'traditional-feudal' after the erosion of its material bases" (194).

This central notion that some of the lack of adventurousness in nineteenth-century heroes is a function of a society afraid of and failing to reward daring comes up in several other offerings in 1988 to good point. Robin Gilmour's "Between Two Worlds: Aristocracy and Gentility in *Nicholas Nickleby*" rightly notes that while we recognize the poor in Dickens' novels and often sympathize with them, and recognize the aristocracy as well, we are not often sympathetic to those trying to make their way up in the world, into the middle class. Nicholas Nickleby, in saying "I am a son of a country gentle-man . . . and your equal in birth and education" reveals the "touchiness" of the period to the "assertiveness of the middle class" (111). In *Nicholas Nickleby* there are characters "cramped" by bierarchy and style associated with aristocratic dominance, and characters as young middle class heroes struggling to assert dominance. We could place here too Joyce A. Rowe's discussion of Dickens' Pip in her *Equivocal Endings in Classic American Novels: the Scarlet Letter, The Adventures of Huckleberry Finn, The Ambassadors, and The Great Gatsby*. While Moretti compares the "common" Pip to more aristocratic European heroes of the Bildungsroman, Rowe compares him to the distinctly American pattern of experience exemplified in Huck Finn. The natural anger we might expect in Pip toward those who revile and exploit him, she says, is instead turned inward at his own commonness. "Pip's snobbery thus points up the association between class aspiration and psychic repression, and suggests not only the cost to the self of survival in English society, but also the mechanism by which society defends itself against an awareness of the suffering of its victims" (69).

I leave it to later generations of critical geneaologists to inquire into the reasons why the late 1980s generation of critics exhibits such urgency and fascination in exploring the Victorians' mechanisms for chopping, channeling, and confining individual energy and self-expression.

Since we are here discussing versions of the self constructed in fiction by and in nineteenth-century novels, which are of course in turn interpretations of literary *character* in nineteenth-century fiction, it might be useful here to insert mention of Jonathan Arac's very substantial essay "*Hamlet, Little Dorrit*, and the History of Character" appearing in *South Atlantic Quarterly*, since his subject is in fact how certain notions of "character" have only become available to us as a result of "successive cultural formations" through time. Dickens, says Arac, provides a focus for thinking about the process by which the modern sense of character was brought into existence through—not by—Shakespeare. In an argument and analysis too rich and complex to do justice to here, Arac's essay becomes a demonstration of and a plea for a new kind of literary history that would consider the history of reception of literary works in order to better understand the production of the subject and the process of intertextuality. Focusing on *Little Dorrit*, Arac demonstrates how our present interpretations of Arthur Clennam as a character became possible only through a devising of a conception of character that was historically constructed by criticism of Shakespeare carried on through the centuries after Shakespeare, and constituted of three distinct discursive strands coming together: one from the inward-turned practices of the *Bildung*, one from the externalized theatrical practices that feed into gothic fiction, and a third "intellectual" line from the new literary criticism of Shakespeare that began in the romantic period (321–313). I note this essay here because if the attempt of much writing on and around Dickens in 1988 concerned itself with how the nineteenth century constituted subjectivity, we need to be aware at the same time of how we, in 1988, in seeing and describing nineteenth-century self-constructions in the ways that we do, are inevitably in *our* moment a part of—inside—that same process, which of course is consequently constituting our constitutions of the nineteenth century.

I would say of all the reading done for this survey, I learned most—about the nineteenth century, about Dickens, about readers and reading—from David Musselwhite's discussion of Dickens' career. Musselwhite's analysis turns on its head the by-now critical-canonical assessment that Dickens' early novels are lesser because he portrays only "flat" characters with "no depth," and that Dickens improved as he began to portray the "inner psychological reality" of his characters. "It is the surface," says Musselwhite, that needs to be protected from the morbid fascination with and privileging of the 'deep,' the 'inner,' the 'psychological' which has so often been taken to be the 'mark' of the 'great' novelist" (14). His argument is that "Boz" was a better writer than "Dickens" precisely because "Boz" was fascinated by the surface of things, the variegated play and heterogeneity of the world about him which to a large extent Dickens abandons in the process of constituting himself as a "great" novelist. Dickens' "greatness" maybe lies in the fact that he was *the* great Pied Piper of the nineteenth-century bourgeoisie in that in his work he piped out and drowned the swarming energies of the heroic period—though, like the Pied Piper, too, the price of destroying the rats was the tragic immolation of childhood as well" (14–15). What Musselwhite means by all this provocative stuff is that the State is quite happy to have us privilege the "inner": "You don't hate Mrs. Thatcher, you hate your mother." What Musselwhite's analysis also explains is Dickens' increasing restlessness and frustration almost in direct proportion as his success as a "great" novelist grew. In his chapter "The Commodification of the Novelist" he recounts the history we all know, but with a new twist: Since *Martin Chuzzlewit* and *American Notes* were not the successes Dickens had hoped for, *Dombey and Son* had to be. So, with that book Dickens undertook a "massive act of self-management and self-promotion—of self-control even," in which the death of little Paul becomes the death of Dickens' *own* childhood innocence and the death of Boz, and Dickens' endless headaches and heroic pedestrianism bespeak a profound questioning of his own identity as player. Permanence and transience play themselves out both personally and in *Dombey and Son* in those pairs of "permanancies" and "temporaries" like Nipper/Toodles. In a deLeuzian/Guattarian analysis slipping in and out of *Anti-Oedipus* and *Mille Plateaux*, Musselwhite sees the later Dickens suffering from the loss of his multitudinous, "excessive," fluid self which he has "sold" in order to purchase a "greatness" requiring that he chop and crop himself in order to be the "serious" novelist. In this context Musselwhite re-reads Dickens' autobiographical fragment describing his time in Warren's Blacking Factory in an intriguing and entirely new way. No longer primarily the pitiful story of the child Dickens' Oedipal betrayal, an interpretation that only interiorizes and privatizes the energies of the self, it becomes instead what is in a way an even more pitiful story: "What the fragment offers us is a *relation*—that is, a narrative which constructs a relation: Dickens' relation to his parents. Thus what Dickens achieves in the relation that is the 'Fragment' is the production of a fitting childhood for the man who is to be Dickens the author. . . . It is the appropriation of the myth of the boyhood trials of the unrecognized genius . . . a retrospective construction of an eminently marketable identity" (163). What got lost between "Boz" and "Dickens" was that communal, combinatory, participatory self that was Dickens, or, to use Trotter's conceptual framework, Dickens "stopped himself up" in the interest of "greatness," in an act of economic exchange which his novels themselves explore, as for instance, in the figure of Dombey, "caught between his fantastical consolations that only become a prison—and a state of being that is molecular, fluid, migratory: a state that is both a nightmare and a terrible hope" (153).

While this new reading of Dickens' childhood and of the autobiographical fragment is different from that of Lukacher's *Primal Scenes*, I would be sorry to have to reject either one. Lukacher's general attempt is to "situate the prehistory of psychoanalysis in the Dickensian text—to construct—a Dickensian intertext that forces us to regard Dickens' relation to the history of psychoanalysis in a new light" (276). Lukacher's thesis is that working at the blacking factory, and thinking about the troubles in his childhood home, with its own sets of embarrassments and problems, led Dickens to find a "home away from home" in the streets, and he associates this with the "over-productivity" Dickens needed to do at Warren's. Into adulthood, then, the place Dickens went to encourage his productivity and deal with what he thought was a necessary over-productivity as a writer and to find solace was *at the same time* the place that called up his early painful memories. Using both Freud and Benjamin, Lukacher reads the streets Dickens walked by night as his "primal scene," at the same time soothing and exacerbating his artistic dilemma. "Dickens recalls in the 1847 fragment that Warren's Blacking was not far from the Lowther Arcade in the Strand. Inspired by Benjamin's *Passage Work*, Johann Geist has catalogued all the nineteenth century arcades. He cites a history of London toy shops that describes the Lowther Arcade . . . as 'an Aladdin fairy palace crowded with all the glories and wonders a child's fancy can conceive.' Between Warren's Blacking and Lowther Arcade, the twelve-year-old Dickens must have suffered exquisitely indeed. The 'secret passage' of Dickens' primal scene runs from the workhouse to a child's fairyland. The task of reading Dickens is the task of locating that 'secret passage' in each of his texts, and of rewriting the history that history always forgets" (296). For Lukacher, then, Dickens' novels become various attempts to master the memory of that early pain. In *The Old Curiosity Shop* and *Barnaby Rudge* "Dickens could doubtless hear . . . the remorseless voice of his own memories" (305). In *Martin Chuzzlewit, Dombey and Son,* and *David Copperfield* "the inability to forget is the great theme" (318). *Little Dorrit*, like all the other novels, is full of "no thoroughfares," or no ways out of memory. In the final figure of John Jasper, Lukacher assumes a particular ending to the novel in order to say that Dickens has constructed the split personality whose normal self cannot recollect the acts committed by its psychotic double.

Another 1988 book that opens up new readings of Dickens' canon is Jennifer Wicke's *Advertising Fictions: Literature, Advertisement, and Social Reading* which studies Dickens along with Henry James, James Joyce, and of course P.T. Barnum to construct an archaeology of the cateclysms wrought by the advent and growth of advertisement. Dickens' career is concomitant with the institutional formation of advertising, and the economic crises of overproduction that engendered it. Defining advertising as "a social writing that presupposes a particular form of social reading," (20) Wicke proposes we see the nineteenth century as a time in which the "textuality" of advertising increasingly "saturate[d] mid-nineteenth century culture, and, as the public is taught to read it, the text/image nexus of advertising is able, by virtue of its universal dissemination, to shape social narrative and provide the sense of proffering social reality" (20). Dickens' novels provide both "a reading of advertising and [are] a harbinger of it;" are "a palimpsest of advertising practices" (20). They become attempts to make society visible to itself, with visibility itself often being a function of classes or people manipulating advertising on their own behalf. Her analyses are witty and rich as they trace Dickens' progress from *Sketches by Boz*, in which Dickens "reads the city" like a text, focusing often on signs, window-lettering, shop-window displays, to *The Old Curiosity Shop*, in which he "develops explicit theories of advertising" (36)—one thinks of Vuffin's wonderful exposition on his giants' new career as walking advertisements and Mrs. Jarley as sophisticated advertising genius—to *Martin Chuzzlewit*, where Montague Tigg is a master of self-advertisement, and Martin himself experiences in Eden the dangers of believing advertisements, to *Bleak House* and *Our Mutual Friend*, which demonstrate an ongoing textual investment in advertising, both illuminating "features of advertising that take finance capitalism into the precincts of language and narrative" (46). Behind the Deadlocks, "Blaze and Sparkle" the jewelers and "Sheen and Gloss" the mercers "is the mediated voice of bourgeois society . . . transmogrified by an advertising discourse" (47). Mrs. Jellyby's campaign for Borrioboola-Gha might be seen as the first successful direct mail campaign—at Caddie's expense, and the Veneering's private party is a triumph of direct mail as well.

There would be several ways to "place" N.N. Feltes's *Modes of Production of Victorian Novels*, but the context of advertising will do as well as any. Devoting a chapter on the publication of *Pickwick Papers* because it "marks the transition . . . from the petty-commodity of the production of books to the capitalist production of texts," (3) Feltes sees encoded in that novel an ideology of how, by whom and for whom it was produced. All of us have heard endlessly about that "novel-reading public" which Dickens served, but rarely does one think about the fact that that novel-reading public was *itself* a product of advertising efforts on the part of the publishing industry, which then went about finding writers who could turn out products for that newly-produced audience of readers. The writer, like Marx's weaver, presented his product (it's interesting to think about the word "text" in this context) to the bookseller. He is, like that weaver, the owner of nothing but his labor power, and the literary text, his product, was "newly defined as a commodity, newly available as the locus of surplus value" (6–7). Feltes's discussion of the copyright struggles of Dickens takes on new meaning here. Up until the nineteenth century, authors were thought to own their productions as "privilege" rather than as "right." But in order for the publisher to make money from a writer's writings, he had to have the rights to an author's work as a commodity. That in turn meant the writer had to be able to see his labor (writing) as a commodity he owned—in order to sell it over to the publisher. Thus, the "commodity text" was born. Not just the fact of that written production, but its *form* as well was determined by its mode of production. The series writer had to produce or discover in each successive book or installment or part that "virtually limitless multiplication of ideological inventions, and combinations, and configurations which interpellate by constituting the bourgeois subject" (9). So, for someone like Dickens, his labor must produce a new, improved, giant economy size or never-before-seen product each month or week. Borrowing heavily on Eagleton's work on the professionalization of writing, Feltes's study is useful, though one would wish his language were a bit less repetitive.

A few studies appearing in 1988 fold Dickens into a discussion of perhaps more discomfitting characteristics of the nineteenth century. One such is Patrick Brantlinger's *Rule of Darkness: British Literature and Imperialism, 1830–1914*, the fourth chapter of which concentrates on Dickens' and other writers' fascination with the transportation of criminals to Australia, and with Australasia as "an ideal standard against which to measure life at home," (28) as well as, of course, a place where 'ne'er do wells' could see a land of promise and social rehabilitation. Brantlinger also sets Dickens' writings in *Household Words* alongside of writings of Bulwer-Lytton and Samuel Sidney to indicate how all exhibit unfortunate signs of a racism that cannot be denied. "Dickens thought savages so far beneath Europeans on the great chain of being that only fools expected to 'railroad' them into civilization" (178) is Brantlinger's assessment, and in his chapter "Black Swans; or Botany Bay Eclogues," he pushes us to confront the "undeniable and virulent racism" evidenced in the essay Dickens co-authored with Wilkie Collins, "The Perils of Certain English Prisoners," in the Christmas 1857 issue of *Household Words*, as well as in his letter to Angela Burdett-Coutts in which he expresses the wish, after hearing about the purported "mutiny" at Cawnpore, India, that he could "strike that Oriental race with amazement . . . [by] proclaim[ing] to them that I should do my utmost to exterminate the race upon whom a stain of the late cruelties rested." Brantlinger's guess that *A Tale of Two Cities* may have had the mutiny of 1857–58 as one of its inspirations is a plausible one.

If Brantlinger folds Dickens into his discussion of Victorian imperialism and racism, the collection of essays edited by Michael Cotsell, *Creditable Warriors*, the third volume in a series devoted to the exploration of English literary responses to foreign cultures and countries from the Restoration to World War I, explores various writers' relations to British expansion and the alternative of a growing "Europeanism." In the process, these essays explore and revaluate Romantic responses to foreign travel, consider the search abroad for "civic images" to oppose to industrialism, fiction and expansion, the Europeanness of mid-Victorian poetry, the rise of tourism, the fascination with Italy and the Levant, and British relations with America and Ireland. This collection was unavailable to me at the time of this writing, but its list of subjects and contributors suggests it to be a rich addition to the literature on British literary responses to imperialist expansion.

Barbara Gates in *Victorian Suicide: Mad Crimes and Sad Histories* uses Dickens' novels as part of the evidence to be studied in coming to understand Victorian attitudes towards suicide. In the nineteenth century, folklore regarding suicide flourished alongside legal verdicts and medical knowledge. In Carlyle, Mill, and Florence Nightingale, we can see that "will power" was by and large seen in the nineteenth century as the number one defense against self-destruction. Close on its heels was "displacement": suicide was something that happened to other people, otherwheres. To Dickensians, the most interesting parts of her work will be those in which she discusses Ralph Nickleby as an instance of haunted suicide . . . plagued by phantoms of the self [which] appear to the self as an "other." Such phantoms are "aspects of the self displaced and imagined as things or people outside the self" (109). Along the way she discusses also the procession of poor or "fallen" women

Dickens portrays as "always a headerin' down here to the water to drown out of desperation" ["Wapping Workhouse," from *The Uncommercial Traveller*], and pairs sentimental and suicidal deaths like Little Paul's and Carker's in *Dombey and Son*.

If Gates's book offers us a way to contextualize Dickens' references to suicide, A. Susan Williams's *The Rich Man and the Diseased Poor in Early Victorian England* similarly contextualizes both Dickens' speeches (like that of 1851 to the Metropolitan Sanitary Association), and his other involvements with sanitary reform, as well as his use of disease as metaphor within his novels, so that we can better recognize both the "typicality" and source for his novelistic descriptions of "swarms" of working class people, or such references to the poor as that in *Little Dorrit* to "fifty thousand lairs" (68).

At the top of the list of biographical works appearing in 1988 one must of course put Fred Kaplan's *Dickens: A Biography*. This regular reader of both John Forster's and Edgar Johnson's biographies confesses, in what is perhaps her own failure, some difficulty finding much that significantly adds to or alters our existing perceptions of Dickens, but the writing in this new biography is surely clear, graceful, straightforward, and the judgments temperate. The discussions of Ellen Ternan are probably especially temperate and fair; they are surely liberally sprinkled with the cautious tone of which phrases such as "given that, . . . it seems likely that . . ." are the hallmark. Given the critical temper of our times it's not surprising to find the word "culture" sprinkled into this biography as it was not in earlier ones. I must confess, however, to some small distress at readings of Catherine that may be insufficiently sensitized by the work of feminist theorists and critics. Spending many hours in the British Museum poring over love letters written to Catherine during their courtship and experiencing rather intense exasperaion at what I took to be Dickens' often manipulative and patronizing admonitions to her to stop being "a coss [cross] pig," I wonder whether we might benefit soon from a fairer reading of Catherine's life as much as from another of Charles's. At the least one might hope for fewer references to Catherine's "obese insensitivity," (377) even if or when such descriptions are somewhat mitigated by recognitions that Dickens himself may have been equally "insensitive," or exasperating: "perfectly capable of insisting on managing everything himself and then blaming Catherine for being dependent on him" (378). There may yet be, among Dickens biographers, too much uncritical adoption of Charles's own perspective: his blame of Catherine for his many children and his premature oldness, "the unwanted assumption of middle age while inwardly feeling young, romantic, and unfulfilled" (222), a few too many uncritical sentences such as "In being fettered to Catherine, he was still victimized by his mother" (376). In the end, one is still left wondering what *Catherine's* inward feelings at no longer being "young, romantic, and unfulfilled" may have been.

One biographical study that proved an unexpected pleasure in 1988 was Michael Allen's *Charles Dickens' Childhood*. Allen painstakingly checked church records, rental records, local Public Records Offices in London and beyond to discover such things as exactly where Dickens' family houses were and when occupied, what the neighborhoods and neighbors were like, what rent was paid, how lavish or confined the accommodations. Among the unexpected discoveries for me was that, based on the period of tenancy of the Dickens family in one particular house, it is possible to deduce that Dickens spent longer at Warren's Blacking than we had thought, "until March or April, 1825." Allen thinks he's tracked down the house where Dickens lodged while working at Warren's—on Lant Street, near the Marshalsea. We also learn somewhat more of John Dickens from Allen's research, and more of the formative years. Dickens' "aiming high" we know came from his father, but what deepens our understanding is that during the Chatham period "the genteel way of life in an otherwise violent and bawdy town formed Charles' view of his family's position in the community and his own expectations from life. It was the sharp contrast, the depth of the fall, that proved so bitter" (9). Among the joys provided by this book are the telescopings of time in which Allen gives us a view of certain sites before Dickens' time, during, and up to the present day, as in this representative sentence: "Number 18 St. Mary's Place deteriorated badly during the early part of this century and then suffered bomb damage during the second world war. It was left derelict for some time and finally demolished in the 1950s. William Giles' [Dickens' teacher] survived a little longer, being pulled down in the 1960s. The sites of both houses are now covered by car parks. A nearby block of flats has been named Copperfield House" (69).

Arguably, one might learn something about the life of the later Dickens by reading Fred Busch's novel *The Mutual Friend*, which imagines a fictional-ized, cynical, gout-ridden, self-absorbed and tormented Dickens as described through the novel's narrator, Dickens' tour manager, George Dolby. Donald Greiner's study of the novels of Fred Busch, *Domestic Particulars*, devotes a chapter to *The Mutual Friend* and pronounces Busch's novel, that is structured through a series of voices—Dolby's, Dickens', and a thoroughly fictional "Moon's" among them—one that "struggles against Dickens' words even as they admire them" (72). Purists might be offended by this fictional use of

Dickens, but I found it great fun, and a fine way to humanize a Dickens who may tend paradoxically to become ever more distant and abstract precisely in proportion as one tries to bring him close by "studying" him.

NOTES

1. I want to acknowledge here the late Professor Alan M. Cohen of Southern Illinois University, who faithfully provided me each month a copy of the bibliographies he compiled for *The Dickens Quarterly*. I want also to thank George Worth of the University of Kansas, who without being asked thoughtfully provided me with an advance copy of the bibliography he had compiled for his survey of 1987 Dickens studies. In addition, the staff of the New York Public Library deserves a special vote of thanks. Their well-oiled efficiency and gracious cooperation in producing, usually within five minutes, all the materials I needed was invaluable. The same can be said for the unerring intellect and good sense of David M. Harmon, whose collaboration and conversation, as always, was beyond evaluation.
2. See my "The Institution of Literature and the Cultural Community," in *Literary Theory's Future(s)*, ed. Joseph Natoli. Urbana: U of Illinois P, 1989, pp. 267–320.
3. At times I have referred to works covered by George Worth in his 1987 survey, or by David Paroissien in his survey of 1986. In such cases, my inclusions should be taken as evidence of my perhaps excessive enthusiasm for these works rather than as of their failures to cover them adequately.

BIBLIOGRAPHY

Abbott, H. Porter. "Tyranny and Theatricality: The Example of Samuel Beckett," *Theatre Journal* 40, i (March 1988): 77–87. Dickens' Rigaud/John Baptiste and Beckett's Lucky/Pozzo. Latter of each pair is "tyrannized by the former's theatricality," theatricality being itself a mode of power, as Shakespeare and Genet's work also reveals.

Ackroyd, Peter. *Dickens's London: An Imaginative Vision*. London: Headline, 1987. Includes long excerpts from Dickens' works with Ackroyd's introductions and commentary. Profusely illustrated with contemporary photos.

Allen, Michael. *Charles Dickens' Childhood*. New York: St. Martin's, 1988.

———. "The Dickens/Crewe Connection," *Dickens Quarterly* 5, iv (December 1988): 175–85. William Dickens, Charles grandfather, was butler to the Crewe family, which had houses in London, Staffordshire and Cheshire, where Charles' grandmother Elizabeth was a servant. Dickens' father thus grew up with the Crewe family until the age of 19. That genteel existence was formative.

Altman, Rick. "Dickens, Griffith, and Film Theory Today," *South Atlantic Quarterly* 88, xii (Spring 1989): 321–59. "Griffith learned important aspects of his craft by paying close attention to the techniques of Dickens, who "sits astride two opposed 19th century conceptions of novel writing: one has become, through the influence of such figures as Flaubert and James, a central tradition of our high culture; the other has had difficulty surviving. Much popular fiction of the last century is as hard to locate today as the popular melodramas of the same period. Dickens retains his importance because he is a pivotal figure—accepted by scholars of the novel, yet shot through with the themes and structures of the popular serial." (330)

Andrade, Mary Anne. "Pollution of an Honest Home," *Dickens Quarterly* 5, ii (June 1988): 65–74. In *David Copperfield*, every villain is one who invades and "pollutes" a domestic group; oedipal overtones of an intrusive male gaining ascendency over an existing mother/child pair.

Arac, Jonathan. "Hamlet, *Little Dorrit*, and the History of Character," *South Atlantic Quarterly* 87, ii (Spring 1988): 311–28.

Armstrong, Nancy. *Desire and Domestic Fiction: A Political History of the Novel.* New York: Oxford UP, 1987.

Bailin, Miriam Lynn. "The Consummation of Debility: Illness and Convalescence in Victorian Fiction." *Dissertation Abstracts International* 49 (December 1988): 1459A [California.] Includes one chapter on Dickens.

Baldick, Chris. *In Frankenstein's Shadow: Myth, Monstrosity and Nineteenth Century Writing.* New York: Oxford UP, 1987.

Basch, Françoise. "Reflexions sur le sentimental et le 'genre' dans *David Copperfield* et *The Mill on the Floss*." *Cue* 28 (October 1988): 112. Abstract of a conference paper.

Baughman, Linda Y. "Echoes of *Oliver Twist* in *Great Expectations*" MA thesis; University of Louisville, 1987. Strongest precedents for *Great Expectations* in structure, characters, and motifs are borrowed from *Oliver Twist* rather than from *David Copperfield*, and its autobiographical themes from *Oliver Twist* rather than from *David Copperfield*.

Baumgarten, Murray, ed. *Reading Great Expectations: Resource Materials for Teaching and Study.* Santa Cruz, Cal.: The Dickens Project, 1988. Includes 329 pages plus 37 minutes of video tape of the Dickens Players in "reader's theatre" performance of selections from *Great Expectations*; audio tape of the same; 51 slides of Victorian London from contemporary illustrations; a software program for Apple II; selections from Fred Kaplan's and John Forster's biographies; Richard Altick chapter from *Victorian People and Ideas*.

Bentley, Nicolas, Michael Slater, and Nina Burgis, eds. *The Dickens Index.* Oxford: Oxford UP, 1988. A 5,000-entry dictionary of allusions, unfamiliar quotations, obsolete words and slang, topical, historical, and topographical references.

Bentson, Alice N. "The Smallweeds and Trooper George: The Autochthony Theme in *Bleak House*." *Mosaic* 21, iv (Fall 1988): 99–110. The Smallweed's "willlessness" is an indication of a deep, mythic fear concerning indepen-

dence and self-definition (or autochthony) which is played out in the contest
between them and Trooper George. Connections made between Oedipus/le-
glessness/lack of self-determination.

Bielecka, Daniela. "Dickens in Poland." *Dickens Studies Annual* 17 (1988): 195–223.
Early Polish translators of Dickens created an image of Dickens as
storyteller, not novelist. Dickens was for a time wildly plagiarized in Poland.
Survey goes up to World War II, includes discussions of theatrical and film
adaptations in Poland.

Blamires, Harry. "Charles Dickens." *The Victorian Age of Literature*. York Hand-
books (Harlow, UK, 1988): 23–32. Background materials: The Reform Bill,
the railroads, comedy, Dickens' childhood, brief thematic summaries of
major works.

Bloom, Harold, ed. *Charles Dickens's David Copperfield*. New York: Chelsea, 1987.
Reprints essays by Barbara Hardy to D.A. Miller and Ned Lukacher in
useful ways to revalue Dickens.

————. ed. *Charles Dickens's Bleak House*. New York: Chelsea, 1987. Reprints
essays from Hillis Miller to John Kucich.

Bodenheimer, Rosemarie. *The Politics of Story in Victorian Social Fiction*. Ithaca:
Cornell UP, 1988.

Bonheim, Helmut. "The Principle of Cyclicity in Charles Dickens' 'The Signalman.'"
Anglia: Zeitschrift fur Englische Philologie. 106, iii–iv (1988): 380–92.
Structuralist analysis of the Signalman narrative, which contains a number of
"recurring partials," elements of language that recur at intervals: word stems
and verb patterns, gestures, plot segments and narrative techniques. Each
story is a triad of three cycles: arrival/descent; recognition/misrecognition;
explanation/denial of supernatural; departure and ascent. All structural
elements suggest the narrative of ghost story or folk tale.

Brantlinger, Patrick. *Rule of Darkness: British Literature and Imperialism, 1830–
1914*. Ithaca: Cornell UP, 1988.

Brisanti, Chiara. "Female Characters and the Vanishing Author in Jane Austen,
Charlotte Brontë and Charles Dickens." *Dissertation Abstracts International*
49 (March 1989): 2664A. [Penn State]

Broyard, Anatole. "All The Comforts of Dickens," *The New York Times Book Review*,
May 1988: 13. Note regarding the Oxford Illustrated Dickens and the appeal
of reading Dickens' works.

Bull, J. A. *The Framework of Fiction: Socio-Cultural Approaches to the Novel*.
London: Macmillan Education, 1988. Despite a negative review in the
Dickensian, a solid materialist approach to the novel; discussion of how
ideological pressures of modes of publishing, marketing and consumption
affected the production and reception of novels.

Caramagno, Thomas Carmelo. "The Dickens Revival at the Bijou: Critical Reassessment, Film Theory, and Popular Culture." *North Queensland Register* 15

(Fall 1988): 88–96. Dickens films of the '30s and '40s, and post-Wilson criticism.

Carter, Ronald and Walter Nash. *Discourse Stylistics*. London: Basil Blackwell, 1988. Introduction to linguistic stylistics and the study of discourse. Models and techniques for analysis, covering levels of discourse, syntax, phonology, social context in relation to literary conventions. uses Hemingway, Auden, Wordsworth, Hopkins, and Dickens.

Chaudhuri, Brahma. "Dickens and *The Critic*: 1852–53," *Victorian Periodicals Review* 21, iv (Winter 1988): 139–44. *The Critic* was a monthly literary journal appearing fortnightly beginning November 1843. The gossip columns in *The Critic* reveal how literary London was talking about *Bleak House* as it was appearing in serial. The 'Skimpole/Hunt controversy was carried on in the pages of *The Critic*.

———. "Dickens and the Women of England at Stratford House." *English Language Notes* 25, iv (June 1988): 54–60. On November 29, 1852, women met to consider giving a memorial to women of the United States on the subject of slavery. The same day, a pamphlet on *Uncle Tom's Cabin, Bleak House*, slavery and the slave trade was published by Lord Denman. Lord Shaftersbury worried about the effects of Mrs. Jellyby portrait as a too-broad-based satire against missionary philanthropy.

Chittick, Kathryn. "Dickens and Parliamentary Reporting in the 1830's," *Victorian Periodicals Review* 21, iv (Winter 1988): 151–60. Dickens sat as a court reporter during the repeal of the Test Acts, the end of the reign of George IV, passage of the Reform Bill, and two general elections in two years. Discussion of the requirements for serving as Court Reporter in Dickens' time, who read newspapers at that time, and how the tendency to serialize came from Dickens' experiences at this time.

Cipar, Sister Mary Cleopha, O.S.U. "Picaresque Characteristics in *Nicholas Nickleby*." *The Dickensian* 84, Pt. 1, # 414 (Spring 1988): 42–46.

Coates, Paul. *The Double and the Other: Identity as Ideology in Post-Romantic Fiction*. Houndmills, Basingstoke: Macmillan: 1988.

Columbus, Claudette Kemper. "The (Un)Lettered Ensemble: What Charley Does Not Learn About Writing in *Bleak House*," *Studies in English Literature* 28 (Autumn 1988): 609–23.

Cotsell, Michael. *Creditable Warriors*, Vol. III (1830–1876). Atlantic Highlands, NJ: Humanities, 1988.

———. "Nicholas Nickleby: Dickens' First Young Man," *Dickens Quarterly* 5, iii (September 1988), 118–28. The Royal Shakespeare Company Production was "on the money" in its production of social life of the 1830s, studying music, government, education, work, wages, newspapers. Earlier novels focused on lowlife villains, comic bumblers. The mature novels were written by an author who belonged to the adult respectable society where one "fires Mrs. Gamp and brings *The Lancet* to investigate Mr. Bumble." From that perspective "some things that were once intensely present become further away."

Cox, Don Richard. "Shaw on *Edwin Drood*: Some Unpublished Letters." *The Dickensian* 84, Pt. 1, # 414 (Spring 1988): 27–29.

Crawford, Iain. "Machinery in Motion: Time in *Little Dorrit*." *The Dickensian* 84, Pt. 1, # 414 (Spring 1988): 30–41.

———. "Pip and the Monster: The Joys of Bondage," *Studies in English Literature* 28 (Autumn 1988): 625–48.

Cummings, Katherine, "*Bleak House*: Remarks on a Daughter's Da." *Style* 21, ii (Summer 1987): 237–58. Through Freud and Derrida, discusses how the narrative faces two directions—past and present; incorporates two worlds (public/private) is told in two voices (serious/parodic), the latter post-modern. Esther represents herself as an orphan who means to be a copy, a (g)hostwriter who erases herself—or tries to. Her loss of identity is doubly related to the name(s) of the father: to Nemo and to John Jarndyce.

Cunningham, Valentine. *In The Reading Gaol*. London: Basil Blackwell, 1988. The punning title gives the game away: much theory, because it "emphasizes closed texts, solipsistic narratives, and the absence of extra-texual references," has imprisoned reading. Examines various literary works including *Hard Times*. This Dickensian survey would seem to suggest critics using theory, far from ignoring extra-textual references, are in fact deeply in debt to historical understandings and cultural backgrounds.

Currie, Richard A. "Dickens and Internalized Aggression," *Dissertation Abstracts International* 49 (November 1988): 1148A–49A [New York]. Aggression in female protagonists.

Curry, George. "Charles Dickens and Annie Fields: The Multi-leveled relationship between the English Novelist and the Wife of his American publisher, James Thomas Fields." *Huntington Library Quarterly*, 51, i (1988): 1–71. A patient accounting of Annie Fields's dairy from 1859 to 1870, revealing her "idealized attachment" to Dickens, and information about Dickens' health during that time, meetings between the Fields and Dickens in England and the United States. Includes evidence that the Fields knew of Ellen Ternan.

Daldry, Graham. *Charles Dickens and the Form of the Novel: Fiction and Narrative in Dickens' Work*. Totowa, New Jersey: Barnes, 1986; London: Croom Helm, 1987.

Darby, Margaret Flanders. "Fault Lines in Dickens." *Dissertation Abstracts International* 49 (October 1988): 825A [SUNY at Binghamton]. A feminist reading of the female characters in Dickens' novels.

Davis, Robert Sawin, Jr. "The Organic Way to Experience: A Theory and Study of Organic Form in 19th Century British Novels." *Dissertation Abstracts International* 48/49: 2342. 1987 [Miami University]. Discusses *Bleak House* and *Hard Times*, Pater's *Marius the Epicurean*, George Moore's *Mike Fletcher* and Conrad's *Heart of Darkness* as "organic novels," because they "abide by Coleridge's aesthetic theory of the imagination's esemplasticity." All "display the five traits of plant development: internality, assimilation, growth, interdependence of parts, and priority of the whole." Romantic symbolism, much of it archetypal, is also present.

Day, Gary. "Figuring Out the Signalman: Dickens and the Ghost Story," in *Nineteenth Century Suspense from Poe to Conan Doyle*, ed. Clive Bloom et. al. Houndmills, Basingstoke: Macmillan, 1988: 26–45.

DenHartog, Dirk. *Dickens and Romantic Psychology: The Self in Time in Nineteenth Century Literature*. New York: St. Martin's, 1987.

Dickens, Cedric. *Drinking with Dickens*. New York: New Amsterdam Books, 1988. Reissue of the 1980 book published by the great-grandson of Dickens.

Donoghue, Denis. "The English Dickens and *Dombey and Son*." Reprinted from *Dickens Centennial Essays*, 1971, in *England, Their England: Commentaries on English Language and Literature*. New York: Knopf, 1988: 177–97.

Eagleton, Terry. Introduction to *Hard Times*, ed. Terry Eagleton. London: Methuen, 1987. Includes the 1854 text together with Eagleton's Introduction, critical commentary, reading list, and notes.

Easson, Angus. "Emotion and Gesture in *Nickolas Nickleby*," *Dickens Quarterly* 5, iii (September 1988): 136–51. Whereas Dickens' characters sometimes use self-conscious or mechanical gestures, in *Nicholas Nickleby* "the sense still predominates that the physicality of gesture helps give emotion value, which value is not in the reader's estimation alone, but is also built into the value systems of the characters themselves."

Eigner, Edwin M. *The Dickens Pantomime*. Berkeley: The U of California P, 1989. Dickens based his characters on the dramatic personae of pantomime and structured his novels according to two patterns of early nineteenth-century pantomime, a pattern based on transformations effected by stage magic. These transformations of character mirror the structural transformation of pantomime itself. Study is based in part on unpublished pantomime manuscripts in the British Library and the Huntington Library as well as collections of programs from the British Theatre Association Library.

Everson, Philip Andrew. "Proof Revisions in Three Novels by Charles Dickens: *Dombey and Son, David Copperfield*, and *Bleak House*." *Dissertation Abstracts International*, Vol. 48/06–A, 1459, 1987 [University of Delaware]. Examines the effects of monthly serial publication. Assumes proof revisions were made to get the right number of pages, more than for aesthetic reasons.

Feltes, N. N. *Modes of Production of Victorian Novels*. Chicago: U of Chicago P, 1986.

———. "Realism, Consensus and 'Exclusion Itself'" Interpellating the Victorian Bourgeoisie," *Textual Practice* 1 (Winter 1987): 297–308.

Ferguson, Kathleen. "'A Very Pleasant, Profitable Little Affair of Private Theatricals?': A Study of the Changing Narrative Voice in the Novels of Charles Dickens." *Dissertation Abstracts International* 49 (Aug. 1988): 257A, 1985 [Ulster].

Fielding, K.J. "The Dickens World Revisited," in *Dickens and Other Victorians: Essays in Honour of Philip Collins*, ed. Joanne Shattock. New York: St.

Martin's, 1988: 53–64. Is there any fruitful relation between Dickens' journalism and his fiction. The novels direct us *outward* to the world where social reform is espoused. Agrees with Raymond Williams that Dickens "deeply and vividly dramatized" situations to bring about an imaginative "regeneration."

————, ed. *Speeches: A Completed Edition*. Hemel Hempstead, Hert.: Harvester, Wheatsheaf, 1988. A reissue of the speeches originally published by the Clarendon Press, 1960.

Fisher, Leona Weaver, ed. *Lemon, Dickens, and Mr. Nightingale's Diary: A Victorian Farce*. English Literary Studies Monograph Series, 41. Victoria, BC: U of Victoria, 1988.

Forsyte, Charles. "How Did Drood Die?" *Dickensian*, 84, Part 2, No. 415 (Summer 1988): 80–95.

Fredricks, Dan. "The Overlooked but Omnivorous Vholes: The Rhetoric of Consumption in *Bleak House*," *Dickensian*, 84, Pt. 3 No. 416 (Autumn 1988): 172–79. Serpent and vampire swallowings.

Friedman, Barton R. *Fabricating History: English Writers on the French Revolution*. Princeton: Princeton UP, 1988, especially "Antihistory: Dickens' *A Tale of Two Cities*," pp. 145–71. How narrative strategies shape and are shaped by events. Dickens' narrators describe not from afar, but immersed in history. Carton/Dickens have a "prospective" version of history, Carton "forecasting a France redeemed within history" (150). The sequence of dates in *A Tale of Two Cities* suggests that two temporal dimensions exist in the novel: the *aevum*, in which duration changes nothing, and history, in which duration changes everything.

Friedman, Stanley. "A Considerate Ghost: George Rouncewell in *Bleak House*," *Dickens Studies Annual* 17 (1988): 111–28. A major motif in *Bleak House* is actual or figurative ghosts. The timing of Rouncewell's appearances and ways in which his responses and actions influence our perception of major events suggest he functions as "ghost."

Gates, Barbara T. *Victorian Suicide: Mad Crimes and Sad Histories*. Princeton: Princeton UP, 1988.

Gibson, Colin, ed. *Art and Society in the Victorian Novel: Essays on Dickens and His Contemporaries*. New York: St. Martin's, 1989.

Gilead, Sarah. "Barmecide Feasts: Ritual, Narrative, and the Victorian Novel." *Dickens Studies Annual* 17 (1988): 225–47. The failed feasts of *Orley Farm, Great Expectation,* and *Adam Bede* generate, complete, or comment adversely on compensatory rites of passage; become structural as well as thematic tensions providing closure but undermining the putative moral or psychological contents of such closure.

Gilmour, Robin. "Between Two Worlds: Aristocracy and Gentility in *Nicholas Nickleby*." *Dickens Quarterly* 5, iii (September 1988): 110–18.

Ginsburg, Michal Peled. "Truth and Persuasion: The Language of Realism and of Ideology in *Oliver Twist*." *Novel* 20 (Spring 1987): 220–236.

Glancy, Ruth. "The Shaping of *The Battle of Life*: Dickens' Manuscript Revisions," *Dickens Studies Annual* 17 (1988): 67–89. Discusses changes made in the story at proof stage, and concludes the time lag so important and powerful in *A Tale of Two Cities* is not mastered well yet in *The Battle of Life*; the former also reworks and improves on the story's theme of heroic sacrifice.

Goodman, Marcia Renee. "Mothering and Authorship: Little Women, Dickens, and the Art of Projection." *Dissertation Abstracts International*, Vol. 48/09–A: 2344, 1987 [University of California, Berkeley]. Dickens' use of maternal heroines as authorial analogues; the relation between the novels' fantasies of mothering, and portrayals of the act of storytelling. Focuses on those Chesterton called "little mothers." Begins with nurse-narrator in "The Holly-Tree Inn" and "Nurse's Stories," and examines heroine's function in *The Old Curiosity Shop, Bleak House,* and *Little Dorrit.* Looks at the metaphor of mothering to describe the act of writing, and observes Dickens' preoedipal fantasy of origins, to establish the mother's position in the discourse of creativity. Adds to other side of the story that Barthes and Said, and Dickens critics like Dianne Sadoff omit in their exclusive concern with writing as a way of telling the oedipal story as an attempt to "father" the text. Attempt to unravel Dickens' ambivalence about the myth of maternal power that he helped to construct. First chapter, *"The Old Curiosity Shop* as Schizophrenic Text: Little Nell as Mother and Child," explores Dickens' identification with his heroine's emotional abuse and description of her partial escape through fantasy, his alternating celebrations and condemnations of her sacrificial deal as saving mother figure. Second Chapter, "At Home with Guilt: Esther Summerson, Charles Dickens, and Autobiography in *Bleak House*" examines the tension between Esther as self-abnegating housekeeper and as self-confrontive writer, and Dickens' personal investment in her fragmentation. " 'Swallowed Alive': The Dangers of Mothers and Stories in *Little Dorrit*," discusses several fantasies of maternal power. Here storytelling is imagined as a maternal and threatening act.

Gordon, Catherine M. "The Great Novel by Many Hands: Charles Dickens: [Catalogue of] Subjects from the Novels of Charles Dickens, 1838–1870." *British Paintings of Subjects from the English Novel, 1740–1870.* New York: Garland, (1988), 197–209; 359–68. Contains parts of the 1981 Courtauld Institute of Art, University of London Dissertation.

Greiner, Donald J. "The Mutual Friend: 'Mouse in the Paws of His Language.'" *Domestic Particulars: The Novels of Frederick Busch.* Columbia: U of South Carolina P, 1988.

Greenstein, Michael. "Between Curtain and Caul: *David Copperfield's* Shining Transparencies," *Dickens Quarterly* 5, ii (June 1988): 75–81. Window imagery, lifting the curtain; the relation of characters to casements.

Harris, Jean. " 'But He Was His Father': The Gothic and the Impostorious in Dickens's *Pickwick Papers.*" *Psychoanalytic Approaches to Literature and Film*, ed. Maurice Charney and Joseph Reppen. Rutherford, NJ: Fairleigh Dickinson UP, 1987: 69–79.

Hawthorn. Jeremy. *Bleak House.* Houndsmill, Basingstoke: Macmillan, 1987.

Herst, Beth F. "*Nicholas Nickleby* and the Idea of the Hero." *Dickens Quarterly* 5, iii (September 1988): 128–36. Nicholas as picaroon, inheritor of eighteenth-century tradition of LeSage, Fielding, and Smollett, but Dickens' commitment to the "natural young man" is ambivalent, "nature" itself tending to evaporate in the face of Dickens' rhetoric.

Herzog, Tobey C. "The Merry Circle of *The Pickwick Papers*: A Dickensian Paradigm," *Studies in the Novel* 20, i, (Spring 1988): 55–63. The structural design of *Pickwick* is that of character interaction guided by the structural and symbolic properties of circles, including the paradigmatic merry circle with its social and familial code of trust and love. Wardle at center of one circle; Weller at center of another.

Higbie, Robert. "*Hard Times* and Dickens' Concept of Imagination," *Dickens Studies Annual* 17 (1988): 91–110. The themes of *Hard Times* include "the limits of the imagination." Discusses also the function of the circus in the novel.

Holloway, John. "Form and Fable in *Hard Times*," in *Art and Society in the Victorian Novel: Essays on Dickens and His Contemporaries*, ed. Colin Gibson: 29–42. Readers' affection for and fascination with Bounderby. He has the Victorian quality of " 'grit' "; is "something of a fable-giant" of Grimm "in his castle." Echoes of language of Biblical parable in the novel. The "duologue," and the "type-act" are two formal aspects combining to depict a world in which society preys on rather than providing for the individual.

Hughes, Kenneth James. "Diegesis, Mimesis, Realism and Charles Dickens' *Hard Times*," *Signs of Literature: Language, Ideology and the Literary Text*. Vancouver: Talon Books, 1986: 151–56.

Hunt, Peter. "Chesterton's Use of Biography in his *Charles Dickens* (1906)," *The Dickensian* 84 Pt. 3, # 416 (Autumn 1988): 130–41.

Irving, John. "Charles Dickens: The King of the Novel." *Brick* 34 (Fall 1988): 6–16.

Kaplan, Fred. *Dickens: A Biography*. New York: Morrow, 1988.

———. "The Real Charles Dickens, or The Old Animosity Shop." *New York Times Book Review*, 2 Oct. 1988: 15–16. Brief observations on the man, including "Dickens' feelings about fatherhood and family ranged from tired tolerance to absolute detestation."

Karl, Frederick R. "Contemporary Biographers of Nineteenth-Century Subjects: The Novelists," *Dickens Studies Annual* 17 (1988): 285–316. Includes discussion of the 1977 edition of Johnson.

Kassman, John. *Introducing Dickens*. London: Unwin Hyman, 1988.

Kellermann, Henryk. " 'Good, Murderous Melodrama': Die Harmonie von Aussage und Erzahltechnik im frohen Dickens-Roman *Oliver Twist*. GRM NF 38, iv (1988): 411–28.

Kettle, Arnold. "Dickens and the Popular Tradition," and "*Our Mutual Friend*." Reprints these Kettle essays in *Literature and Liberation: Selected Essays of Arnold Kettle*, ed. Graham Martin and W. R. Owens. Manchester: Manchester UP, 1988), 140–67; 168–80.

Knoepflmacher, U. C. "From Outrage to Rage: Dickens' Bruised Femininity," in *Dickens and Other Victorians: Essays in Honour of Philip Collins*, ed. Joanne Shattock: 75–96. If Dickens, as his daughter Kate said, didn't understand women, he did understand "the importance of femininity as an indispensible requisite for the well-being of a fully-gendered psyche." Psychic disappointment can turn into anger. *David Copperfield* and *Great Expectations* show "gender imbalance that harks back to childhood loss." "Incompleteness" of Pip and David has to be feminized (by Agnes, etc.)

Lane, Lauriat. "Re-Reading Victorian Fiction: Steven Connor's *Charles Dickens* and James Kavanagh's *Emily Brontë.*" *International Fiction Review* 14, ii (Summer 1987): 92–98. Attempt to discredit any and all post-structuralist readings and a plea for retreat from such things as the metonymy/metaphor distinction of Jakobson and a return to interpretative categories such as "symbolic," "realistic," or "naturalistic," although those of course were also seen as "jargon" in their time as well.

Leech, Geoffrey. "Stylistics and Functionalism," in *The Linguistics of Writing: Arguments Between Language & Literature*, ed. Nigel Fabb, Derek Attridge, Alan Durant, and Colin McCabe. New York: Methuen, 1987. *David Copperfield* as instance of how "attribution of meaning through ideational and interpersonal rhetoric can [like textual rhetoric] manifest ambiguity. David's saying "Agnes was very dear to me . . . but she was not mine, she was never to be mine. She might have been, but that was past." The question is "to whom do we attribute the meanings in the passage? Is it the implied authorial consciousness of the mature Dickens looking back on his youth? Or is it the young Dickens, suffering the pangs of love, whose thoughts are being reported in free indirect speech? If it is the mature biographer's voice anticipating the future, then we find out later, when he does marry Agnes that we have been conned. So retrospectively, to avoid imputing bad faith to the mature David (and by implication Dickens), we should conclude that it *was* free indirect speech."

Lerner, Laurence. "History." *The Frontiers of Literature*. Oxford: Basil Blackwell, 1988.

Leung, Yiu-Nam. "Charles Dickens and Lao She: A Study of Literary Influence and Parallels." *Dissertation Abstracts International* 49 (July 1988): 87A [Illinois].

Levine, George. *Darwin and the Novelists: Patterns of Science in Victorian Fiction*. Cambridge: Harvard UP, 1988.

———. "*Little Dorrit* and Three Kinds of Science," in *Dickens and Other Victorians: Essays in Honour of Philip Collins*, ed. Joanne Shattock: 3–24.

Litvak, J. "Back-to-the-Future: A Review Article on the New Historicism, Deconstruction, and 19th Century Fiction." *Texas Studies in Literature and Language* 30, i (1988): 120–49.

Long, William F. "Dickens and the Adulteration of Food," *The Dickensian* 84 Pt. 3, # 416 (Autumn 1988): 160–70.

LITIR Computerized Project on Victorian Studies. Will process, print, and bind Bibliography of Dickens works appearing in any time span. Price per copy, $40. Order from Access Elite, Inc. Box 840, Sub. P. O. 11, Edmonton, Alberta, Canada T6G 2EO.

Lund, Michael. *Reading Thackeray*. Detroit: Wayne State UP, 1988. Tactics serial writers employ to engage readers. In passing references to Dickens.

Lukacher, Ned. *Primal Scenes: Literature, Philosophy, and Psychoanalysis*. Ithaca: Cornell UP, 1986.

MacKay, Carol Hanbery. "The Melodramatic Impulse in *Nicholas Nickleby*," *Dickens Quarterly* 5, iii (September 1988): 152–63. Prior to the appearance of the Crummles theatrical troupe, Dickens had been teaching us how to read and recognize melodrama at work in his novel by way of his use of soliloquy, feigned surprise, eavesdropping. The experience of melodrama helps us acquire a critical distance from emotion.

Manning, Sylvia. "Dickens' *Nickleby* and Cavalcanti's: Comedy and Fear," *Dickens Studies Annual* 17 (1988): 47–66. The 1947 film version of Nickleby directed by Cavalcanti. The difference between the film experience occurring in those who have read the novel (who find the film funny) and those who have not (who will experience horror). Film constitutes an interpretation of the novel. The medium of film has constraints and powers particular to it. Rendition in story "creates an interpretation with a strong life of its own." The film version aborts the Kronos myth opposition of bad and good fathers and relegates the Crummles to the realm of make believe, away from the "reality" of the central characters.

Marks, Patricia. "Storytelling as Mimesis in *Our Mutual Friend*," *Dickens Quarterly* 5, i (March 1988): 23–30. *Our Mutual Friend* is about storytelling: the Lammles, Podsnaps, Wegg are all monologic; Lizzie and Noddy Boffin dialogic.

Marlow, James E. "Social Harmony and Dickens' Revolutionary Cookery," *Dickens Studies Annual* 17 (1988): 145–57. A "spiritual hunger" hung over England post–1830s and 1840s. Dickens' featuring of food, restaurants, food customs reveals English interest in good food, prevalence of bad across all classes, concern with dyspepsia, digestion. Political economy could improve if the domestic economy did.

Martin, Francoise. "L'image de Londres chez Dickens et Gustave Doré: *Bleak House* et London, à Pilgrimage." CUE 28, (October 1988): 25–38.

Martin, Philip W. *Mad Women in Romantic Writing*. New York: St. Martin's, 1987. Chapter on Dickens.

McCarthy, Patrick. "Designs in Disorder: The Language of Death in *Our Mutual Friend*," *Dickens Studies Annual* 17 (1988): 129–44. Dickens deals with death in terms of myth.

Meckier, Jerome, "Dickens and the Newspaper Conspiracy of 1842," *Dickens Quarterly* 5, i (March 1988): 3–17, and *Dickens Quarterly* 5, ii (June 1988): 51–64. In America Dickens was taken advantage of: by pirates in 1842 and by scalpers in 1867. The relatively modest protests in his speeches about the lack of copyright laws were blown out of proportion (perhaps as part of a conspiracy) by American newspapers, and it is misleading to think of them in the plural, since "in fact, there was only one American press, no matter how many cities Dickens travelled to."

————. *Innocent Abroad: Charles Dickens' American Engagements.* Louisville: U of Kentucky, 1988. Using letters, diaries, and publisher's records, enumerates the reasons for the failure of Dickens' American tours. (See above.) Dickens also grew less equalitarian and more British; saw everything more satirically at home; became a radical pessimist, a dedicated reformer who ruled out a utopian future. His second visit was an ironic second coming. Poor planning and management meant scalpers benefited more than he. His dealings with American publishers were not as smooth or lucrative as they might have been. Health problems and eagerness to bring Ellen Tiernan have been exaggerated.

Meisel, Perry. *The Myth of the Modern: A Study in British Literature and Criticism after 1850.* New Haven: Yale UP, 1987.

Mensel, Ewald. "Das Bild der Eisenbahn in Charles Dickens' *Household Words* und *All the Year Round." Die Neueren Sprachen* 87 (October 1988): 538–53.

Miller, D. A. *The Novel and the Police.* Berkeley: U of California P, 1988.

————. "Secret Subjects, Open Secrets," reprinted in Harold Bloom, ed. *David Copperfield: Modern Critical Interpretations*, New York: Chelsea, 1987: 89–109.

Monod, Sylvère. "Revisiting Sketches by Boz," in *Dickens and Other Victorians: Essays in Honour of Philip Collins*, ed. Joanne Shattock: 25–36. Dickens' theme is that "human gullibility is a consequence of snobbish ambition," but the surprise of the *Sketches* is the attitude towards children in that book. In large numbers, "children are an affliction."

————. "Where There's a Will . . .," *Dickens Studies Annual* 17 (1988): 179–94. Shakespearean allusions in Dickens; includes comparisons with Conrad's use of Shakespearean allusion.

Moretti, Franco. *The Way of the World: The Bildungsroman in European Culture.* London: Verso/Methuen, 1987.

Murphy, Colonel N.T.P. "Around Charing Cross with David Copperfield," *Punch* 295 (9 December 1988): Issue 7718: 24. Dickens' London haunts as they are today. Rule's, halfway down Maiden Lane, is the only restaurant still surviving where Dickens could still recognize his old table. Refers to Dickens working in "Lamert's" Blacking Factory.

Musselwhite, David E. *Partings Welded Together: Politics and Desire in the Nineteenth-Century English Novel.* London: Methuen, 1987.

Myrick, Patricia Lynn. "Gothic Perceptions of the Past in the Nineteenth-Century Novel: Dickens, Hawthorne, Eliot, and James." *Dissertation Abstracts International* 49 October 1988: 812A [Indiana].

Nelson, Harland S. "Shadow and Substance in *A Tale of Two Cities, The Dickensian*, 84, Part 2, No. 415 (Summer 1988): 96–106. J. F. Smith's *the Shadow and the Substance* as source.

Newsom, Robert. *Dickens on the Romantic Side of Familiar Things: Bleak House and the Novel Tradition*. New York: Columbia UP, 1977. Reissued this year in soft-cover by the Dickens Project at Santa Cruz. Detailed discussion of Freud's uncanny. Dickens's comment that he "dwelt purposely upon the romantic side of familiar things" identifies a central imaginative principle in his art, the same interplay being at work in Dickens' own life at time of writing *Bleak House*. The concluding chapter argues that understanding this polarity can help redefine the novel as a literary form. (Originally published in 1977).

Norris, William J. "My Life as Scrooge: Reflections on a Decade of Humbug." *Chicago* 37 (Dec. 1988): 138–39, 172, 174, 176. A long-time Scrooge in Goodman Theatre's production discusses his role.

N.W. "Within Ailing Distance." *Canadian Literature* 117 (Summer 1988): 3–5. Editorial on *Hard Times* as an "indictment of Social Stupidity."

O'Keeffe, Anthony. "*The Old Curiosity Shop*: Fancy, Imagination, and Death." *South Atlantic Review* 53, iv (November 1988): 39–55. The novel's dichotomies (rural/urban) constitute a debate between two ways of seeing the world that can be understood by reference to Coleridge's distinction between fancy and imagination.

Page, Norman. *A Dickens Chronology*. New York: G. K. Hall, 1988. An aid to finding out such things as when Dickens' quarrel with Thackeray began and ended. Includes dinner dates with Macready, requests for contributions to charity, and so on. Each volume presents by year, month, and sometimes day events recorded in dairies, notebooks, journals, and secondary sources.

———. *Speech in the English Novel*. Atlantic Highlands, NJ: Humanities, 1988. Rprt. from 1973. Chapter on the nature and function of fictional dialogue and its relation to real speech in the novels.

Parker, David. "A Phiz Tribute to Cruikshank." *The Dickensian* 84, Pt. 1, # 414 (Spring 1988): 6–7.

Pasto-Crosby, Elizabeth Anne. "Realism in Bleak House and *Las novelas de Torquemada*." *Dissertation Abstracts International* 49 (December 1988): 1452A. [Cornell]. Uses Ingarden and Gadamer to discuss realism.

Pemble, John. *The Mediterranean Passion: Victorians and Edwardians in the South*. Oxford: Clarendon, 1987. Travel between 1830 and 1914 as a significant part of British life. Travel to Italy and beyond. Inter alia references to Dickens' life, to characters who travelled: Little Dorrit returning from the South with "the ripening touch of the Italian sun . . . visible upon her face," making her "something more womanly" i.e., more sexually desirable. The "inoffensive gaiety of the Mediterranean people suggested childhood in its most endearing aspect." "Patriotism" and "discontent" did not need to intermingle in Italy as Dickens thought they did in England.

Dickens liked the "physical symptoms of decay" he found in Italian cities like Parma, Ferrara, and Mantua.

Peterson, Carla. *The Determined Reader: Gender and Culture in the Novel from Napoleon to Victoria.* New Brunswick, NJ: Rutgers UP, 1986.

Poovey, Mary. *Uneven Developments: The Ideological Work of Gender in Mid-Victorian England.* Chicago: of Chicago P, 1988; London: Virago Press, 1989.

Power, Henriette Lazaridis. "Shaharazade's Wake: The Arabian Nights and the Narrative Dynamics of Charles Dickens and James Joyce." *Dissertation Abstracts International* 49 (December 1988): 1465A. [Pennsylvania].

Preston, Edward G. *Hastings in Dickens and Dickens in Hastings.* [N.p.] Literatours, 1988.

Robson, W. W. "The Choir-master and the Single Buffer: An Essay on *The Mystery of Edwin Drood*," in *Art and Society in the Victorian Novel: Essays on Dickens and his Contemporaries*, ed. Colin Gibson, 43–62. Can Forster's account of Dickens' plans for this novel be trusted? Proposes Dickens was going to wrap up the story "with a spectacular final coup not to be equalled in detective fiction until Agatha Christie's *The Murder of Roger Ackroyd*." His reasons: (1) The period of Dickens' life (the end of public readings would lead to Dickens' attempt to "take a final bow" in print); (2) The personal significance Edwin Drood would have for Dickens: a divided character in disguise, like Dickens; (3) Dickens' fascination with the *Arabian Nights*.

Rogers, Philip. "Scrooge on the Neva: Dickens and Tolstoy's Death of Ivan Ilych." *Comparative Literature* 40 (Summer 1988): 193–218.

Rogoff, Gordon. "The Old Virtuosity Shop," in *Theatre is Not Safe: Theatre Criticism, 1962–1986.* Evanston: Northwestern UP, 1987: 212–13. The Royal Shakespeare Company's "Nicholas Nickleby" is perfect because "the flatness in Dickens is perfect for the thin British actors today."

Ronthaler, Jorgen. "Dickens-Kolloquium an der Karl-Marx-Universitat Leipzig am 21, und 22, Oktober 1987." *Zeitschrift fuer Anglistik und Amerikanistik* 36, ii (1988): 149–50. Reprint of conference papers on "Charles Dickens und die Folgen für den modernen englischen Roman."

Rosenberg, B. "Israel Potter: Melville Anti-History." *Studies in American Fiction* 15 ii (1987): 175–86.

Romig, Evelyn M. "Twisted Tale, Silent Teller: Miss Havisham in *Great Expectations*," *Dickens Quarterly* 5, i (March 1988): 18–22. Miss Havisham is emblematic of what each of the storytellers in the story is doing: creating his or her own world in story, each "world" a prison.

Rowe, Joyce A. "Mark Twain's Great Evasion: Adventures of *Huckleberry Finn*." *Equivocal Endings in Classic American Novels: The Scarlet Letter, Adventures of Huckleberry Finn; The Ambassadors; The Great Gatsby.* Cambridge: Cambridge UP, 1988: 46–74.

Rye, Marilyn. "The Fictional Autobiography: First Person Narratives as Narratives of Power in *The Blithdale Romance, Le grand Meaulnes,* and *Great Expectations." Dissertation Abstracts International* 49 (July 1988): 87A [Rutgers].

Sadrin, Anny. *Great Expectations.* London: Unwin, 1988. Backgrounds, critical discussions of the work, discussion of manuscripts and memoranda, chronology, etc.

Sanders, Andrew. " 'Cartloads of Books': Some Sources for *A Tale of Two Cities,*" in *Dickens and Other Victorians: Essays in Honour of Philip Collins,* ed. Joanne Shattock: 37–52. Irish dramatist Watts Phillips's play *The Dead Heart* has a plot like that of *A Tale of Two Cities.* Debt also to Carlyle. Essay title refers to Dickens' borrowings of books on the French Revolution from Carlyle's library, including *Le Tableau de Paris* of Louis-Sebastien Mercier.

———. *The Companion to a Tale of Two Cities.* Dickens Companions 4. London: Unwin Hyman, 1988.

Sawicki, Joseph. "(Un)Twisted: Narrative Strategies in *Oliver Twist." Victorian Newsletter* 73, (Spring 1988): 23–27. Despite the contradictions in *Oliver Twist,* the intent is to show good wins out, but there are some unsettling characteristics in the good characters.

Schatzberg, Walter et. al., compilers. "Charles Dickens (1812–70)." *The Relations of Literature and Science: An Annotated Bibliography of Scholarship, 1880– 1980.* New York: Modern Language Association, 1987): 251–53.

Schaumburger, Nancy E. "Partners in Pathology: David, Dora, and Steerforth." *Dickensian* 84 Pt. 3, # 416 (Autumn 1988): 154–59. Single parent children and their self-realization.

Schlicke, Paul and Priscilla Schlicke. *The Old Curiosity Shop: Annotated Bibliography.* NY: Garland, 1988.

Sealts, Merton. M., Jr. *Melville's Readings,* rev. and enl. ed. Columbia: U of South Carolina P, 1988. In passing, references to Lizzie and Herman's various readings of Dickens' novels at various times in their lives.

Seehase, Georg. "Der Autor und sein Held: Uberlesungen zum Verstandnis des konstlerischen Erbes von Charles Dickens (1812–70)." *Zeitschrift fuer Anglistik und Amerikanistik* 36, ii (1988): 101–11. Paper read at Leipzig colloquium.

Shatto, Susan. *The Companion to Bleak House.* London: Unwin–Hyman, 1988. Profuse factual annotations naming contemporary sources, identifying allusions, information on topography, social customs, costume, furniture. Some discussion of illustrators, manuscripts and number plans.

———. "Lady Dedlock and the Plot of *Bleak House," Dickens Quarterly* 5, iv (December 1988): 185–91. Interpreters have misinterpreted because they have based their readings on an error in Angus Wilson's *The World of Charles Dickens.* In fact Lady Dedlock's liaison with Captain Hawdon *is* connected with her involvement in Chancery.

Shattock, Joanne, ed. *Dickens and Other Victorians: Essays in Honor of Philip Collins*. New York: St. Martin's, 1988.

Slater, Michael. "Dickens in Wonderland," in *The Arabian Nights in English Literature: Studies in the Reception of the Thousand and One Nights into British Culture*, ed. Peter L. Caracciolo. Basingstoke, Hamps.: Macmillan; New York; St. Martin's, 1988: 130–42. George Meredith sent Dickens *The Shaving of Shagpat: An Arabian Entertainment*. This informed *Hard Times*, and stories in *Household Words* for 1859.

Solomon, J. Fisher. "Realism, Rhetoric, and Reification: or, the Case of the Missing Detective in *Our Mutual Friend*." *Modern Philology* 86, i (August 1988): 34–45.

Spencer, Sandra. "The Indispensable Mr. Wills," *Victorian Periodicals Review* 21, iv (Winter 1988): 145–51. The "strong editorial hand" of William Henry Wills. Dickens and Wills balanced one another: Dickens was artistic; Wills practical. Four phase relationship existed ending in Dickens trusting Wills to edit *Household Words* alone during Dickens' second American tour, as well as manage various personal duties.

Squires, Michael. "The Structure of Dickens' Imagination in *Little Dorrit*," *Texas Studies in Literature and Language*, 30, i (Spring 1988): 49–64. Uses Structuralist and Foucauldian analysis to describe "the universal structure of the human mind manifest[ing] itself in paradigms of characterization capable of transfer from one character to another and from parent to child." Fundamental narrative unit of *Little Dorrit* is that of a character positioned between two opposite but equal forces, one of loss and one of support.

Stanton, Michael. "Charles Dickens: *Used Up*," *The Dickensian* 84, Pt. 3 # 416 (Autumn 1988): 142–52. Stage history of the Dion Boucicault farce performed by Dickens and Company.

Stein, Robert A. "Pip's Poisoning Magwitch, Supposedly: The Historical Context and its Implications for Pip's Guilt and Shame." *Philological Quarterly* 67, i (Winter 1988): 103–16. British legal system at the time of writing *Great Expectations* helps in understanding Pip's behavior towards Magwitch. Letter to Home Secretary of State would have been correct avenue of petition. Sentence of Magwitch was the accurate one. Traditionally a speech such as Magwitch's "My Lord, I have received my sentence of death from the Almighty . . ." would have been appropriate, but uttered at the gallows, not at the time of sentencing.

St. Germain, Joan. "Dickens' *Oliver Twist*," *Explicator* 46, iii (Spring 1988): 16–20. Oliver is caught between duality of alternating forces in light and dark.

Stoler, John A. "Libido in *The Old Curiosity Shop*: Dickens in Quilp." *South Carolina Review* 5 (Fall 1988): 65. Little Nell is equivalent to Quilp who is equivalent to Mary Hogarth, who is equivalent to Charles Dickens.

Stone, Harry. Interviewed by Herbert Mitgang. "1857 Story is Attributed to Dickens." *New York Times* 21 June 1988: C19. Attribution of a story purportedly in *Household Words*.

Storey, Graham, "Dickens in His Letters: The Regress of the Radical," in *Dickens and Other Victorians: Essays in honour of Philip Collins*, ed. Joanne Shattock: 65–74. Dickens' letters reveal a radical but increasingly authoritarian (and hence regressive) Dickens. Dickens' radicalism became mixed with comedy and grotesquerie; more personal, less socio-political.

Storey, Graham, Kathleen Tillotson, and Nina Burgess, eds. *The Letters of Charles Dickens: 1850–52.* Oxford: Clarendon P, 1988.

Sutherland, John, "Chips Off the Block: Dickens's Serializing Imitators," in *Dickens and Other Victorians: Essays in Honour of Philip Collins*: 97–119. Discusses Dickens' method of serial writing in context of other serial writers such as Cruikshank and writers for *Punch*. Dickens failed to notice at time of *Our Mutual Friend* that the serial form was "already nostalgic." Suggests Dickens liked the form because he could do it well. "The failure of others certified his success."

Swann, Charles. "Wainewright the Poisoner: A Source for Blandois /Rigaud?" *Notes and Queries* 35 (September 88): 321–22.

Tillotson, Kathleen. *"Bleak House* at a Seance." *The Dickensian* 84, Pt. 1, # 414 (Spring 1988): 2–5. "Who Killed Tulkinghorn?" is a question at a seance in Henry Spicer's *Facts and Fantasies*.

———. *"Bleak House*: Another Look at Jo," in *Art and Society in the Victorian Novel: Essays on Dickens and His Contemporaries*, ed. Colin Gibson: 16–28. Evidence suggests Jo didn't take shape in Dickens' mind as early as Forster's biography suggests.

———. "Henry Spicer, Forster, and Dickens," in *Dickensian* 84, Part 2, No. 415 (Summer 1988), 66–78. Spicer's plays and other works published in *All The Year Round*; a chronology of the friendship of Spicer, Macready, Forster, and Dickens.

Tracy, Robert. " 'The Old Story' and Inside Stories: Modish Fiction and Fictional Modes in *Oliver Twist.*" *Dickens Studies Annual* 17 (1988): 1–33. The novel is full of storytellers and story readers: the physician delivering Oliver remarks, "The old story. No wedding ring, I see."

Trotter, David. *Circulation: Defoe, Dickens, and the Economy Of the Novel.* Houndmills, Basingstoke: Macmillan; New York: St. Martin's, 1988.

VanBoheemen, Christine. *The Novel as Family Romance: Language, Gender, and Authority from Fielding to Joyce.* Ithaca: Cornell UP, 1987. Has chapter on *Bleak House*.

Vesa-Ritter, Max. "Loi, innocence et crime dans *Oliver Twist*: Étude psycho-critique." CUE 28 (October 88): 113–14. abstract of paper read.

Waterhouse, Ruth. "Self-Reflexivity and 'Wraetlic word' in *Bleak House* and *Andreas.*" *Journal of Narrative Technique* 18 (Fall 1988): 211–25.

Waters, Catherine. "Ambiguous Intimacy: Brother and Sister Relationships in *Dombey and Son.*" *The Dickensian* 84 Pt. 1, # 414 (Spring 1988): 8–26.

Watson, John. "Laughter, Imagination and the Cruelty of Life: A View of *Oliver Twist*," in *Art and Society in the Victorian Novel: Essays on Dickens and His Contemporaries*, ed. Colin Gibson. The ways in which comedy tends to overwhelm suffering in *Oliver Twist*, until the end, when "terror quite freezes laughter" (14).

Weissman, Judith. *Half Savage and Hardy and Free: Women and Rural Radicalism in the Nineteenth Century Novel*. Middletown, CT: Wesleyan UP, 1987.

Weber, Jean-Jacques, "Dickens' Social Semiotic: The Model Analysis of Ideological Structure," 95–112 in *Language, Discourse, and Literature: An Introductory Reader in Discourse Stylistics*, ed. Ronald Carter and Paul Simpson. London: Unwin–Hyman, 1989. Uses Dolezel's work in narrative semantics to show how different modals construct different types of narrative worlds. (Turbulence of Boundarby's versus the moral values of Sissy, Stephen and Rachel, etc.)

Welsh, Alexander. *From Copyright to Copperfield*. Cambridge: Harvard UP, 1987.

Wicht, Wolfgang. "Von *David Copperfield* zu Ian McEwans *The Cement Garden*: Veranderungen im Diskurs der Ich Erzahler." *Zeitschrift fuer Anglistik und Amerikaistik 36, iv (1988): 306–17.*

Wicke, Jennifer. "The Dickens Advertiser." *Advertising Fictions: Literature, Advertisement, and Social Reading*. New York: Columbia UP, 1988.

Wiesenfarth, Joseph. "*Great Expectations*: The Gothic Tradition Personalized." *Gothic Manners and the Classic English Novel*. Madison: Wisconsin P, 1988: 83–100.

Williams. A. Susan. *The Rich Man and the Diseased Poor in Early Victorian Literature*. Atlantic Highlands, NJ: Humanities, 1987.

Wilson, A. N. *Tolstoy*. London: Hamish Hamilton; New York: Norton, 1988. Passing references to and comparisons with Dickens as person and as writer.

Woods, Leigh. "'As If I had Been Another Man': Dickens, Transformation and an Alternative Theatre." *Theatre Journal* 40, i (March 1988): 88–100. A study of Dickens' acting reveals a distinctive vision of the possibilities of acting and the stage. Of the 23 roles Dickens played between the ages of 21 and 45, all but 2 are comedy and farce. Dickens favored disguise or transformation. Dickens did old men because his physical capabilities suited him best to play their "stiffness." Affection for multiple roles. "Dickens' compulsion to assume many roles stands as a form of existential escape at certain moments of his life."

Worth, George, "Mr. Wopsle's Hamlet: Something Too Much of This," *Dickens Studies Annual* 17 (1988): 35–46. A study of what the critics over the last thirty-five years have made of the Hamlet/Wopsle episode, how our readings have been enriched, but how common sense readings are still the best.

Yamamoto, Shiro. "*Hard Times*: Forms and Content—Dickens, Leavis, and another Tradition?" *Studies in English Literature (1988): 35–50.*

Elizabeth Gaskell:
A Critical History and
a Critical Revision

Hilary M. Schor

There is a kind of excitement in Gaskell scholarship these days, an energy and pleasure rare even in the already heady circles of Victorian studies, as if individual critics who thought they had secretly discovered the real thing suddenly realized everyone else had discovered it too. Much of the impetus for this revival has come from the feminist project of transforming the canon, of—echoing the charge of Virginia Woolf—"if we are women," thinking "back through our mothers," but Gaskell has benefited as well from recent work in social history and the social problem novel, from work that stresses the ideological contradictions and social tensions behind the literary text. In the movement of fiction studies away from more purely aesthetic judgments, and in the decline of often equally ahistorical structuralist criticism, the socially dense, narratorially complicated, historically motivated work of a novelist like Gaskell has proven particularly fruitful; to study the transformations in Gaskell scholarship can offer a similarly fruitful understanding of our own critical approaches, of "the way we live now," in Victorian studies.

I begin this essay by discussing the basic scholarly materials (editions, biographies, letters and bibliographies) and then offering a brief history of Gaskell studies, but my central focus here is recent studies of Gaskell, trends and problems, what this tells us about what we are learning about Victorian fiction, and what kind of work we want to read next. A survey of the criticism of even a "neglected writer" calls up more material than can adequately be dealt with in a single essay; hence, I have made two decisions, one slightly less arbitrary, to govern the selection of materials. The first is that, having sketched out the classic critical "inheritance" of Gaskell studies, I will begin in more depth with three "reassessments" attempted in the late 1960s, through which I hope to sketch further the range of critical issues. But following these general statements, I will focus on what seem to me the most influential (and challenging) essays and books, with the double aim of suggesting the best work which has been done, and remains to be done, in Gaskell scholarship and suggesting further the ways that the inclusion of Gaskell in the ever-expanding canon of Victorian literary studies changes the boundaries of that study, the ways in which the inclusion of Elizabeth Gaskell will encourage us in a "reassessment" of our own critical practices.

I

To begin with the material available for teachers and scholars: nowhere has the shift in Gaskell studies been clearer than in the recent availability of scholarly editions of the novels. Penguin English Library has all but two of the novels (*Ruth* and *Sylvia's Lovers*) and *The Life of Charlotte Brontë* in print; they have very fine introductions (particularly Laurence Lerner's of *Wives and Daughters* and Martin Dodsworth's of *North and South*) and generally have more than adequate appendices. Oxford's World Classics series has equally fine editions; in the case of *North and South* and *Cranford*, the notes on revisions and publication history are extremely helpful, and Oxford also has the best available editions of *Ruth* and *Sylvia's Lovers*—the latter is particularly fine. The gap continues to be the reprinting of Gaskell's short work: most of the stories and essays are available in the Knutsford edition edited by A. W. Ward, and there is a very good selection available in an Oxford World Classic (*Cousin Phillis and Other Tales*, which includes such essential works as "Lois the Witch" and "Lizzie Leigh") but there is a real need for a scholarly collection of all of Gaskell's stories, tales, incidental and conversational pieces. This gap suggests some of the inability of the Victorian industry to recognize the range of Gaskell's work: pieces like "The Schah's English Gardener" and "Company Manners" reflect both the variety of her interests, and the difficulty of pigeon-holing something we call "Victorian fiction"; both technically and contextually, these works are of great interest. Such a collection would be of real pedagogical value as well: Gaskell's short fiction is among the most complex and interesting of the period, and given the demands of teaching Victorian fiction on the semester- or quarter-system, we can all benefit from the availability of shorter works.

There are two modern biographies done before the publication of Gaskell's collected letters: Elizabeth Haldane, in *Mrs. Gaskell and Her Friends* (1931; rpt. Freeport, NY: Books for Libraries) gives a range of voices, with occasional gifted insights; A. B. Hopkins in *Elizabeth Gaskell: Her Life and Work* (London: John Lehman, 1952) goes much further, and writes a compelling and often moving biography. Despite the lack of material available to her, she seems to me to have captured much of Gaskell's spirit, without the querulous note of apology that marks so much other criticism of the time. The most recent biography, Winifred Gérin's *Elizabeth Gaskell* (Oxford: Oxford University Press, 1980) is more disappointing; though she uses the letters and a wide range of sources, she lacks a background in industrial England, radical literary culture, Unitarian Manchester—and more, her primary interest does not seem to be Gaskell. Gaskell's daughter Julia is mentioned three times as the daughter who charmed Charlotte Brontë, and the spirit of the Brontës (all of whose biographies Gérin has of course already written) hovers over this book; Brontë is the writer Gaskell did not manage to be, in Gérin's mind, and though Gaskell (she argues) was sweeter and more conventional, she lacked the dark passion the Brontë sisters brought to fiction—and, one almost feels, her life lacks some of that interest for Gérin as well. It is not quite that Gérin is angry at Gaskell; more, that she is quietly (resignedly) disappointed in her, and at some absence in her life. But much of this absence is of Gérin's own making: she seems interested in presenting Gaskell in as conventional and placid a mode as she can, and even where the material suggests otherwise (the notorious example of William Gaskell pocketing his wife's earnings) Gérin wants to silence "negative" critics, and argue away the darker side of this picture. Her Gaskell is a lovely lady, and a talented, if morbid, writer; she is neither a genius nor a neurotic, and Gérin's life accounts neither for Gaskell's best fiction (how did this contented housewife write *Sylvia's Lovers?*) nor for her depressions, headaches, and anxieties. It is not Charlotte Brontë but Virginia Woolf one can imagine hovering near this biography; but that figure is not one that interests Gérin deeply.

For that more ambivalent, angry, riotously funny Gaskell, one must go to her accounts of herself—a difficult task, since Gaskell kept a diary only briefly, and asked her family and friends to destroy much of her correspondence. The journal (entitled *My Diary*) is primarily an account of the birth and growth of her oldest daughter, Marianne, and its few personal moments concern her own anxieties about raising that child; the diary is difficult to find (it was published privately by Clement Shorter, who introduces the volume as well) but it is even more difficult to read—particularly to read as an autobiographical fragment. Gaskell, like so many nineteenth-century women writers, had a deeply ambivalent relationship to her audience (and to what she called their prying eyes); self-revelation is hardly her interest—for all that she has so vibrant and vivid a personality.

In the light of this quiet modesty, and her instinct towards self-protection, at least from the gaze of her reading public, it is hard to find a "private" Gaskell—but if one exists, it must certainly be in her letters. The greatest boon to Gaskell scholars, and one whose usefulness is acknowledged thankfully in all the material published since it became available, is the collection of letters edited by J. A. V. Chapple and Arthur Pollard (Cambridge, Mass.: Harvard UP, 1967). Winifred Gérin, who wrote the first biography after the publication of the collection, describes an earlier biographer as attempting to "make bricks without hay"; the letters are cleanly edited, well indexed, and a pleasure to read. Angus Easson has suggested that they are under-annotated, but the absence of interruption makes them accessible and human; the other failures he notes—the lack of chronology imposed by late additions to the volume, and the general inaccuracy and inadequacy of the index—are more serious obstacles to research. While scholars ought not to assume the letters can be read without skepticism (they are not purely autobiographical or naive, and reflect Gaskell's own sophistication and experience of writing for diverse audiences) they suggest much that is best about her: her slapdash enthusiasms and warmth; the range of her friendship; the variety of her interests. J. A. V. Chapple has edited a *Portrait in Letters*, but the full flavor of the collected letters is hard to reproduce, and the Chapple and Pollard collection is essential for anyone interested in either the richness of Gaskell's voice, or the sense of the culture in which she wrote. A more touching portrait is provided in a collection assembled by Jane Whitehill before the publication of the complete letters of the correspondence of Gaskell and Charles Eliot Norton, the American she met on a trip to Italy, and continued to exchange letters with until her death (*Letters of Mrs. Gaskell and Charles Eliot Norton: 1855–1865*, London: Oxford University Press, 1932). None of her correspondence so movingly suggests both her own passions, and the love she inspired in others; further, it is an interesting conversation between American and English writers who shared Unitarianism, liberalism, and a deep interest in other cultures. The letters they exchange on the American Civil War, no less than the letters on the births of his daughters and the marriages of hers, convey their love for each other, and their concern about politics and culture at mid-century.

Anyone beginning to study Gaskell will appreciate the existence of two guides to research, both following on the bibliographies by Clark S. Northrup (appended to Geraldt deWitt Sanders's *Elizabeth Gaskell* (New Haven: Yale UP for Cornell UP, 1929) and Stanton Whitfield's, in his *Mrs. Gaskell: Her Life and Work* (London: George Routledge & Sons, 1929). The more complete of the two, *Elizabeth Gaskell: A Reference Guide*, by Robert L. Selig (Boston: G. K. Hall, 1977), discusses the limitations of the previous guides, and adds considerable material to them: by his count, where, for the period 1848 to 1886, Northrup has 61 entries and Whitfield 42, Selig includes 367. Jeffrey Welch's *Elizabeth Gaskell: An Annotated Bibliography 1929–1975* (New York: Garland, 1977), in addition to moving one year further into the present (Selig ends in 1974) is able to provide more thorough annotations for the more recent work, though even there he provides fewer references. Selig's *Guide* seems throughout to have a broader sense of the field of Gaskell scholarship, and a genuine interest in changes in critical approach; Welch's entries are more prone to errors, both trivial and serious—of spelling and of emphasis.

II

To trace some of the changes in Gaskell scholarship is to acquire an interesting perspective on larger shifts in Victorian studies and particularly studies of the novel. Some notes sounded early in the criticism resound still: Gaskell is a lovely lady; she is a deeply moral woman; she is, whatever else is said, a "minor writer." One amusing aspect of these persistent generalities is to watch the shifting of other writers around her: variously, Hardy, George Eliot, Trollope, and Gissing appear as "other minor writers," but Gaskell's place remains assured. The less amusing aspect of all this dismissive affection is what one can only perceive as the pervasive sexism of much of it: Gaskell's "charm," to use a word Dickens occasionally used to dismiss her, is so intensely gender-coded as to make it impossible for her ever to acquire "major" status. She seems to fill the slot of "the minister's wife," the loving friend, the gentle story-teller; if the facts of her life (her marriage, her beauty, her generosity,) seem to doom her to a conventionality the Brontës and George Eliot have been spared, they have also led critics, unfortunately, to doom her stylistically as well. No Victorian novelist has suffered more than Gaskell from an unwillingness to look for the *un*conventional ending, or what D. A. Miller has called the "discontents" of narrative. It would, one supposes on reading these critics, have seemed bad manners to probe too deeply into the stylistic or sexual politics of "Mrs. Gaskell"—at least as that figure has been imagined (smiling, gentle, tolerant) on the borders of the (major) Victorian novelists.

Early criticism of Gaskell can be comfortably divided between two views of the novelist, views as polarized as "the two nations." One is the Gaskell of the social novel, the other, the Gaskell of *Cranford*—a division of Hebraic and Hellenic proportions. The first is discussed in volumes like Cazamian's *The Social Novel in England* (London: Routledge & Kegan Paul, 1973; orig. publ. 1904), which place Gaskell in the tradition of prophetic social criticism; the second, a pastoral Gaskell of great sweetness, is enshrined in works like *Mrs. Gaskell: Haunts, Homes and Stories* by Mrs. Ellis H. Chadwick (London: Sir Isaac Pitman & Sons, 1913), which stakes its claim on "the author of *Cranford* and of the *Life of Charlotte Bronte*," and tells its story literally by moving from one place Gaskell lived to another. ("Haunts" is not as fruitful a designation as one might hope; the book does, however, end with a description of "memorials" to Gaskell which, presumably, the reader can also visit.) But if these poles are representative, and I think they are, Gaskell scholarship has found itself poised somewhere between the social pamphlet and the ladylike travel guide; between city and country, prophecy and nostalgia, the ideological and the local.

It is the first of these critical schools that has produced the more polished and useful studies. Most of the best work on Gaskell can be traced to the seminal studies by Kathleen Tillotson and Raymond Williams, which served to place Gaskell specifically within the context of Victorian "social fiction." (Much of the neglect, doubtless, can be ascribed to F. R. Leavis's dismissal of her in *The Great Tradition*, where he firmly places her in the second-tier of minor novelists—along with, of course, Trollope.) Although the chapter on *Mary Barton* is not the best material in *Novels of the Eighteen-Forties* (Oxford: Oxford UP, 1956), Tillotson's study does take for granted that Gaskell played an important part in shaping that thing we familiarly know as "Victorian fiction," and that the novel of social realism (with its attention to its reader, its immediate involvement in the problems of the day) offers something of particular value in understanding shifting Victorian relationships to fiction. But *Mary Barton*, "though a distinguished and memorable novel, is hardly of the scale or the quality of the other three novels here selected," and is somehow relegated by Tillotson to the "kind of novel . . . directly concerned with the social problem." Tillotson further takes the unfortunate out of arguing that "it is also, as befits a woman's novel, more purely compassionate" than the other "novels of purpose," but neither purpose nor femininity seem particularly valorized here, and Tillotson accepts more fully than she might the stories that Gaskell began writing purely out of grief for her son, and with little literary experience. Her reading of *Mary Barton*, like Raymond Williams's in *Culture and Society: 1780–1950* (New York: Columbia UP, 1983), dwells heavily on the failure of Mary's plot, and the ways "her relation to [the narrative's] theme seems too weakly suggested." Williams, who has throughout a more complicated understanding of what he calls "the facts of the new society, and . . . the structure of feeling," has a similar difficulty in reconciling what he regards as the interesting plot of John Barton, and "the familiar and orthodox plot of the Victorian novel of sentiment" that centers around Mary, a plot which is "of little lasting interest." Williams reads the violence of the murder of Harry Carson as rending the novel, making impossible the "deliberately representative novel" Gaskell meant to write. Like Tillotson, and again like most early critics, Williams reads Gaskell as "coming to this life as an observer, a reporter," (as, that is, naive) prepared only with her "flow of sympathy" and a "response to the suffering [that] is deep and genuine." The strength of Williams's account is his own sympathy to that suffering, and his anger at what he reads as the "writing-off, when the misery of the actual situation can no longer be endured"; the limitations of his account stem from his notions of transparent realism and an inability to read the "representative" qualities of the *heroine's* life.

The difficulty of integrating the social with the feminized Gaskell has proven a persistent problem for feminist readings of Gaskell, to which I will return at greater length, but it is important to note that there are earlier studies that attempt to raise the feminist issues even in "Mrs. Gaskell," among the most intriguing (if finally unsatisfying), Aina Rubenius's *The Woman Question in Mrs. Gaskell's Life and Works* (Upsala: A-B Lundequitska; Cambridge, Mass.: Harvard UP, 1950), which blends historical data with a summary of earlier attempts, and offers a useful rebuttal to such assertions as Lord David Cecil's in *Early Victorian Novelists* (1934) that "she looked up to man as her sex's rightful and benevolent master," and a reading of the problem areas of Gaskell's work as arising from cultural difficulties in defining female roles. No such subtlety, unfortunately, enters into the customary discussion of the "social" novel, and the material and discursive realities of women's lives (and the early feminist movement of the 1850s) remain undiscussed.

The critical heritage with which contemporary Gaskell studies begin, then, includes some fairly fixed conceptions about Gaskell's relationship to realism (naive), to politics (sentimental), and to feminism (muted, if any). It will be remarked, of course, that these blind-spots are not limited to views of Elizabeth Gaskell, but she seems to have suffered not only from the positivist conceptions of "the well-made work of art" and the difficulty of reading the social that marks *all* early criticism of the Victorian novel, but from the affectionate neglect that surrounds the "lady novelist." As the earliest revisionists begin to point out, neither the "author of *Mary Barton*" nor the "author of *Cranford*" is well-served by these approaches.

Three books published in the mid- to late-sixties mark the beginning of a reassessment of Gaskell's career, trying to make something more coherent of her oeuvre. Of these, the most successful is Edgar Wright's *Mrs. Gaskell: The Basis for Reassessment* (London: Oxford UP, 1965), which offers a serious explanation of the critical neglect Gaskell has experienced, ranging from a critique of "Jamesian" criticism to the overly biographical references, and the "undertones" they contain. His case for her importance rests largely on her increasing "maturity"—at points, he in fact argues for her success by Jamesian standards—but his readings of the novel are fairly interesting, and the book has an interesting structure: some chapters are organized thematically, and others center on individual works, so that both large and small elements in the novels receive attention. The subtlety of some of his readings is welcome as well: on so hackneyed a subject as Gaskell and community, for instance, he writes that she is "primarily a social novelist, concerned however not with society at large but with small communities in which individual conduct and feeling are important, and which will serve at the same time to illustrate universal standards" (43). But he is less flexible on stylistic questions: he has concluding chapters on "technique" and "style" (the difference is never quite clear) and his interest in unity leads him to suggest cutting one third of "My Lady Ludlow," because it would be a better story without the French Revolution. While he is often astute about the rush others have made to unify Gaskell's works by ignoring contradictions, his case for her importance finally rests on a similar argument: that her growing experience and skill, her move away from social problems, and the increasing harmony of "theme and technique" (all of which he sees most clearly in "Cousin Phillis" and *Wives and Daughters*) make her later works the fulfillment of early promise, and the true development of her natural skills as a story-teller.

At the least, Wright's critical methodology does not lead him to throw out half of Gaskell's literary production, the path taken by other books, most notably Margaret Ganz's *Elizabeth Gaskell: The Artist in Conflict* (New York: Twayne, 1969). Ganz is more dependent on chronology for her argument, though she is less dependent on a developmental model than is Wright; her one disruption of chronology comes in her discussion of Gaskell's "humor," for her thesis is that therein lies Gaskell's "most meaningful achievement," and that the texts it marks are *Cranford* and *Wives and Daughters*. While Ganz admirably insists on the range of Gaskell's work, and the "variety of her literary productions," she insists throughout on her "failure to realize her artistic potential." This failure she locates in Gaskell's lack of "total intellectual commitment to one's art which makes the safeguarding of integrity essential" (one senses that Thackeray, Dickens, and Trollope would fail on these grounds as well!—integrity is an odd word for the Victorian literary marketplace) which leads Gaskell to "fail to carry through the ideas and psychological insights which she undoubtedly had." Ganz can see nothing of interest in these artistic conflicts—nor does she see Gaskell's contradictory impulses as bespeaking larger cultural doubts; artistic failure is rather the keynote of her book. But despite the condescension of tone and the failure on Ganz's part to read these contradictions as contradictions in ideology, she manages some interesting readings—oddly, the material on *Sylvia's Lovers* which (due to her perverse chronology) closes the book (and somewhat abruptly at that), forms one of the better chapters in the book; once Ganz points out that Gaskell is not Emily Brontë, and Sylvia not Catherine Earnshaw, she goes on to give a sympathetic and compelling reading of the novel. But for the most part, she sees only limitations everywhere; and the carelessness and inattention that occasionally mark her own book makes this finally less useful than Wright's.

Arthur Pollard's *Mrs. Gaskell: Novelist and Biographer* (Manchester: Manchester UP, 1965) is the most difficult of these three "reassessments" to assess, in part because his own methodology remains obscure. "Basically," he claims, "Mrs. Gaskell is a simple writer. . . . The most appropriate method of interpretation I suggest therefore should be a simple one." But this simplicity remains undefined: he is trying to show "that Mrs. Gaskell is far more than merely the author of *Cranford*," he wants to "confirm the standing of *Wives and Daughters*, to "raise that of the unjustly neglected *Sylvia's Lovers*," to "mark the importance of *North and South*," to "indicate the ways in which we may profitably read the early novels without feeling it necessary to ignore or apologize for their faults"—all this, by concentrating "more deliberately than previous critics have generally done on matters of plot, character, setting, information and moral purposes." This seems straightforward enough—except for "information," which is glossed in the next sentence as "the use of sheer information in her work," but I am afraid I cannot help my reader here to understand this term—except to say that Gaskell seems very good with information ("sheer information") as far as Pollard is concerned. (Edgar Wright, who has useful information about such things as when trains came to Knutsford—later than the date given in *Cranford*—would seem to have a better grasp of the uses of information in Gaskell's work, but I am not convinced this is a major critical category.) There are some very nice touches throughout the book (Pollard has a surprising gift for noticing changes in verb tense, for instance, and for explaining the structural flaws of a novel—of *Ruth*, for instance, he usefully notes that the story possesses a beginning, a middle, and an end, but that only the middle is convincing) but the chapters are given over to the obvious, to summary, and to essentially conservative readings of the novels; the book seems infinitely more dated than Wright's, or even Ganz's, which at least still has the capacity to annoy.

In the years since, several books focussing exclusively on Gaskell have attempted to follow through on this critical evaluation; they have not, unfortunately, been marked by much new information, or readings that go far in expanding our understandings of the fiction. With one exception, they have done little to explain or mark the relevance of the social structures in which Gaskell wrote; more seriously, they have not far expanded our critical vocabulary, and have taken recourse in the "simplicity" Pollard makes so much of. Coral Lansbury's *Elizabeth Gaskell: The Novel of Social Crisis* (New York: Barnes and Noble, 1975) is highly allusive, attempting to bring in a range of information about Victorian England, but unfortunately remains fairly superficial; Lansbury is prone to generalization, towards plot summary, and towards moralizing, and the book seems rather repetitive, given its small size. The book is marked by a certain breeziness, which does not always do the novels justice, as when Lansbury comments, of *Wives and Daughters*, "When Hyacinth Kirkpatrick moves through the softly carpeted halls of the Towers she can smell the Cumnor money and feel it under her feet." The real sociological point she goes on to make—that "middle-class women of this country society . . . are most affected because they have neither the means nor the opportunity to engage in trade, or undertake a profession"—is lost, first, because the odd metaphor distracts the reader (it is far from a metaphor Gaskell would use) and because the historical point remains ungrounded either in the text (does Gaskell know this about trade and professions?) or by the historical detail that would make more clear the environment for middle class women in the 1860s. As is, this level of generalization remains slightly irritating, certainly when backed up by generalizations about human nature ("like most people who have experienced the life of the city she now feels bound to its problems") and truisms about art ("the ordered reality of art" is a persistent desideratum of the text.) But the most persistent problem of the book is that its thesis (that the narrative voice of the novels is assumed to placate middle-class readers) goes largely unproven, and entirely unproblematized. As in the passage about Hyacinth's profession, we need to know more about the ideology and the lived experience of the Victorian middle-class—and about the contradictions within a "classed" society.

Lansbury published a second book on Gaskell in the Twayne Author Series in 1984, but it offers little that is new—and, surprisingly, makes no more of an attempt to incorporate recent social history or feminist theory, which might help make specific her broader claims. (The book also seems somewhat sloppy, titles and references often inadequate, and quotations occasionally wrong.) Enid Duthie's *The Themes of Elizabeth Gaskell* (Totowa, NJ: Rowman and Littlefield, 1980) which is—as its title would suggest—organized entirely thematically, does little to advance the field; its themes ("the natural scene," "the social scene," "the industrial scene," "the family," "the individual") are the familiar notes we have already heard sounded, and its literary vocabulary conventional and vague. A more useful book for Gaskell scholars and general readers is Angus Easson's *Elizabeth Gaskell* (London: Routledge & Kegan Paul, 1979). Easson's research is impeccable, and wide-ranging: on the sources of *Cranford*, for instance, he cites not only Mary Russell Mitford's *Our Village* but the tradition of the Romantic essay and such writers as Gilbert White; he goes on to comment on the evolution of *Cranford* itself, and then on its influence on George Eliot and Anne Thackeray Ritchie. The material on Unitarianism and Manchester culture alone would make this book worthwhile, but Easson is also a fine reader, and his textual insights are often as subtle as the cultural breadth he brings to the novels. Of the troubled ending of *Ruth*, for instance, a difficult plot turn noted often in Gaskell criticism, he comments that "she couldn't escape the conventional idea that Ruth, the heroic dignified expansive creature, is also a victim, who must have her tragedy." This does not go much beyond what many have said, but what follows does: "She has not yet grasped fully,"

Easson continues, "as she was to in *Sylvia's Lovers*, that to live can be more tragic than to die." Easson avoids the universal "it is" that so many other critics are prone to; he grounds his insight in the specifics of the novels; he is willing to undercut his own point (in a moment he goes on to admit that he may seem to be "carping") and his real gift is in being at once generous to Gaskell, and aware of contradictions in the novel—the contradictions, as he argues in concluding the chapter on *Ruth*, of someone always trying to "extend her own range." But if the strength of the book is his conscientiousness, his thoroughness, his clarity, its weakness is in not having an over-arching argument and—perhaps—in the carefulness of what it claims for its subject: "she has been rightly assessed as amongst the most interesting of the Victorian novelists of second-rank—attempts to place her with Dickens and George Eliot are only like to provide an excessive counter-reaction." Rankings of first- and second-rank are of limited usefulness, obviously, but if one were to judge rank in these post-structuralist days in terms of the kind of criticism a novelist enables, of the enthusiasm her or his work generates, or of the variety and range of her or his literary production, then it seems to me that Gaskell's rank is firmly assured, and the modest praise she has inspired ("among the most interesting of the second-rank") is not really appropriate.

I say this with some confidence, because when we leave the realm of single-author studies, much of the most innovative and curious work being done in Victorian fiction has placed Gaskell at its center; as literary criticism has left the realm of Jamesian non-intrusive narrators, of thematic coherence and psychological realism, and moved towards history, culture, feminism, and materialism, Gaskell's novels have seemed increasingly important, and the variety and tensions present in her work have made her an extremely productive source for critics. From the first, her most sensitive critics have begun with the social realm, and recent work by Marxist and post-Marxist critics has both reasserted both her centrality to the development of the novel, and the range of social voices that enter her texts.

John Lucas has proven one of Gaskell's most sympathetic, if most critical, readers; no critic has gone further in teasing out the contradictions in her political positions and narratorial intrusions, which he discusses under the division of her "official" and her "anarchic" selves. His *Literature of Change: Studies in the Nineteenth Century Provincial Novel* (Sussex: Harvester, 1977) devotes two chapters to her, one to the provincial novels (particularly *Sylvia's Lovers* and "Cousin Phillis," which he terms the most perfect story in the English language), the second, to Gaskell, Engels, and Manchester. What unites the two is his complex sense of the relations of individuals to social change; that "again and again . . . the social process forces choice on individuals, which in turn forces a crisis of identity on them." While he is at times too quick to read Gaskell straight, and insists on reading the "official" as the "intentional" writer (if this is so, why does her "anarchic" reading of John Barton go hand in hand with her claim that it was around him that her sympathies gathered?) he provides both the best portrait of her gentle liberalism, and the sharp critique that she herself provides of the failures of the liberal vision. Indeed, in the chapter on Engels, he gives the best account we have of what is missing from Engels (the individual character of working-class life), refusing to stop at what is missing from Gaskell; as he concludes, in contradiction to critics from Williams to Steven Marcus, the failures of vision that limit Engels's "intimate" knowledge of Manchester are "why we need *Mary Barton*."

In an earlier piece, Lucas gives one of the best social readings of *Mary Barton*, and his essay deserves a longer account. The strength of "Mrs. Gaskell and Brotherhood" (which appeared in the collection *Tradition and Tolerance*, edited by Lucas, John Goode, and David Howard, London: Routledge & Kegan Paul, 1966) is that "failings . . . count for most in this essay." "Its purpose is to suggest that the flaws inherent in the genre of the social-problem novel are a direct result of the novelists' failure to deal really honestly with the social experiences their novels are intended to portray." But Lucas's discussion goes beyond listing the "stock political attitudes" novelists use to "bridge all imaginative lacunae"; he is a very sharp critic of the flaws of *Sybil*, *Alton Locke*, et al. Of the former, he remarks, "*Sybil* is not nearly so good a novel as has been the custom to pretend"; of the latter, that "*Alton Locke's* most interesting moments are ones of muddle rather than achievement"; of both, that the more the novelists try to link the two nations, so increasingly are we made aware of how far apart they are. But of *Mary Barton*, whose reputation he also wants slightly to depreciate, he claims "the real wonder is that it should exist at all," that it escapes the false idealization of workers in Disraeli, or the myth of similar middle- and lower-class interest in Kingsley, offering instead the "disturbing centre" of John Barton's voice. John Barton, Lucas argues, "challenges all the ideas to which, as a middle-class liberal undertaking a social-problem novel, [Gaskell] holds." In *Mary Barton*, as in *North and South*, Gaskell goes beyond the truisms of political economy; the fine comparison of *North and South* and *Hard Times* which closes the essay continues Lucas's argument, that Gaskell went farther in depicting the way workers look to themselves, the "stench of hopelessness," the "dignity" of their lives—and to pointing out in her novels the failures of her own, "liberal" solutions—than any novelist of the time did. While Lucas repeats some truisms—about the publisher's insistence on the inclusion of the Mary Barton love plot—on other, seemingly tired questions he offers some new insights: he is very strong on Margaret Hale's mediation of "north and south," connecting her depiction to the convention of the "not-poor" heroine, and equally strong on the failure of the reconciliation of men and masters at the end of the novel. His is an unusually supple social reading.

The critic who has most successfully continued the work of social criticism of these novels is Catherine Gallagher, whose *Industrial Reformation of English Fiction: Social Discourse and Narrative Form, 1832–1867* (Chicago: University of Chicago Press, 1985) offers splendid chapters on *Mary Barton* and *North and South* that bring new historical research to bear, placing the "failures" and contradiction Lucas and others have identified within contradictory ideological positions in Victorian England. The real strength of Gallagher's work is in the connections she draws between ideological tensions and novelistic form, and it is here that Gaskell plays such an important role. After a stunning chapter on the variety of narrative genres invoked in *Mary Barton*, among them melodrama, tragedy, documentary and the "domestic tale," Gallagher comments that it is not surprising that no one "saw" Gaskell's "idea of a tragic poem," for that tragedy is obscured by "antagonistic intentions," contradictions contained within the "Unitarianism of the 1840s and in certain features of the tradition of industrial criticism that Gaskell inherited." But she goes on to add, "we should also remember that her failure is the foundation of the book's formal significance, for its very generic eclecticism points toward the formal self-consciousness of later British realism." The preparation for this reading—in readings of British pamphlets, of the "providential plot" of novelists like Harriet Martineau, in debates over free will and determinism—pays off not only in a view of one particular novel, but an account of tensions inherent in the development of "the novel," a genre which Gallagher's historically based formalism works to unfix. Her discussion of *North and South* similarly blends social and fictional debates, moving from "didactic domestic fiction" to the social problem novel, taking on the common critical debate on the retreat of the social novel into the "family plot" and reading the "ideological and formal factors" that caused these "contradictions and reversals." But the power of her discussion of the later novel is in its attention to detail—literally, to the way the novel organizes detail, and addresses what she calls an "anarchy of signification" in the social system—and the social novel. As in the discussion of *Mary Barton*, Gallagher's reading of *North and South* moves between the vagaries of representations and the social debates they reflect, comment on, and displace.

Rosemarie Bodenheimer's *The Politics of Story in Victorian Social Fiction* (Ithaca: Cornell UP, 1988) follows through on the insights of *The Industrial Reformation of English Fiction* in the connection between novels and what Bodenheimer calls "public discourse." She sees in the social-problem novel the "display [of] conflict about the nature and diversity of a newly empowered and newly fragmented middle class," conflicts particularly "well-focused" in these novels because "they must bring order and meaning to situations characterized exactly by their lack of established historical meaning, or by acute conflicts about the meanings assigned to them in public discourse." The first section of the book, which focuses on "Women's Fate and Factory Questions," contains a fascinating discussion of *North and South* and "the romance of the female paternalist," but—perhaps because this novel has been the more discussed—this section is less compelling than her discussion of *Ruth* as a "maternal pastoral." The strength of Bodenheimer's approach throughout is the carefulness of her readings, and the clarity of her prose. While she lacks the broad-ranging theoretical and historical material—and some of the sharpness—of Gallagher's approach, her book does seem nonetheless to open up the field further; the broadness of her definition of "social novel," coupled with the clarity of her focus on "plot" as social and fictional organization, makes this book a model, and the use she makes of the literary precedents and inheritances (I am thinking especially of some wonderful pages on Wordsworth and the "blurring of class differences" the Victorians inherited) is truly unique in this field. For Gaskell scholars, in particular, Bodenheimer opens up possibilities of rhetorical studies still informed by and implanted within historical and cultural conflicts; equally, this book would be unimaginable without Gaskell's fiction.

Several other books and essays attempt this blend of literary and social analysis, with varying degrees of success. Deirdre David's *Fictions of Resolution in Three Victorian Novels*, (New York: Columbia UP, 1981) which has chapters on *North and South*, *Our Mutual Friend* and *Daniel Deronda*, argues that "the tension between representation of social actuality and desire for difference is mythically resolved in fictions of one sort or another," but her discussions suffer from being less historically precise, and less critically exact, than Gallagher's or Bodenheimer's. The most successful moments in the book move close to what David wants, "a conjunction of economic situations, class position and sexual being," and David's distinction between the success of the sexual—as opposed to the class—resolution is useful, but the remainder of the section on *North and South* poses less of a challenge to the novel. Ruth Bernard Yeazell, in a wonderful essay entitled "Why Political Novels Have Heroines: *Sybil*, *Mary Barton* and *Felix Holt*" (*Novel*, Winter 1985, 126–44) raises again the question of the "cover" the "innocent heroine" (and her love story) provides, fixing on the heroine's "modesty," and the class violence that her desexualized energy diffuses and "decontaminates." Yeazell dwells usefully on the division between Mary's maidenly passivity and the *permissible* action of saving her lover's life; Rosemarie Bodenheimer, in "Private Griefs, Public Acts in *Mary Barton*" (*Dickens Studies Annual*, 1981, pp. 195–216) similarly reverses some of the critical truisms on the novel, arguing that the book's deepest concern is not with political action, but with the conversion of emotion into action. Although Bodenheimer in some ways slights the political text of the novel—as in her book, one sometimes feels a more explicitly feminist position would advance her beyond some difficulties—the essay is wonderful on the blurrings and confusions of private and public plots in the novel. Terry Eagleton's fine essay "*Sylvia's Lovers* and Legality" (*Essays in Criticism*, 1976, Volume 26 [1], pp. 17–27) similarly avoids the easy dichotomies of public/private, fictional/real, and its strength is in seeing social structures and narrative structures as running along parallel—but not identical—tracks; his reading blends broader historical insights with a real sympathy for the tragedy of the plot, and manages to slight neither critical mode.

That Gaskell has not been as well served by critics who focus on more conventionally literary questions—problems of form, of voice, of allusion, influence, and inter-textuality—has remained a puzzle to me; in general, formal studies of the Victorian novel have been less successful than such studies in other periods, perhaps because there is less of a purely literary realm to debate, but more likely because critical conventions about the naiveté of the Victorian novelist (particularly of the amateur woman writer) have persisted far longer than they should have. Recent studies of Victorian realism (among them George Levine's *The Realistic Imagination* [Chicago: Chicago UP, 1981] and Elizabeth Deeds Ermarth's fine *Realism and Consensus* [Princeton: Princeton UP, 1983]) have gone a ways in dispelling these notions, but neither considers Gaskell. In her case, no doubt the myth of the grieving mother turned author has done particular damage to her claims to literary seriousness, but in general, the subtlety of her effects (I will avoid the word "modesty," which is surely the *most* over-used term critics invoke in her presence) and the lightness with which she wears her learning (literary and otherwise) have led critics astray. In her letters, as well as in the *Life of Charlotte Brontë*, she avoids clever literary chit-chat—though it is worth noting her light comments are invariably spot-on, and sharper than one might expect—and she has not left behind the evidence of her writing method, the construction of plots, and so on, that might feed such critical studies. But the sophistication of her fiction is still largely unexplored.

Jerome Meckier tackles the question of literary influence in *Hidden Rivalries in Victorian Fiction* (Lexington, Kentucky, University of Kentucky Press, 1987), but he never seems to take Gaskell as seriously as he does other novelists, and the rambling qualities of his discussion do not really sustain a thesis. Michael Wheeler's *The Art of Allusion in Victorian Fiction* (New York: Harper, 1979) offers a fine chapter on *Mary Barton* and the "Dives versus Lazarus" reference which runs through the novel; he is particularly strong on the difference between the novel as realism, and as the fable which critics have missed by ignoring the dense allusions that create the text. Like many such treatments, Wheeler's tends to present things as causes that are really effects—that is, the allusions spring from, rather than necessarily create, ideological meanings and conflicts—but the precision of his work, and his attention to questions like class and plot, are welcome; he has a similarly fine essay on biblical allusion in *Ruth* ("The Sinner as Heroine: A Study of Mrs. Gaskell's *Ruth* and the Bible," *Durham University Journal* 68, pp. 148–61), which occasionally follows one half-finished thought on the part of a character through to a whole series of allusions and meanings in the text. A writer like Gaskell would repay more such careful studies; we need to think more deeply about her patterns of reading, references to contemporary writers, her responses to the literary marketplace, the dense questions of intertextuality that have gone unexplored.

One of the better treatments that moves in that direction is Donald Stone's *The Romantic Impulse in Victorian Fiction* (Cambridge: Harvard UP, 1980). Rather than count the Wordsworth allusions in Gaskell's fiction, Stone interestingly connects the woman writer's habit of self-effacement ("modesty" again) to the Romantic (and post-Romantic) debate over egoism and the "creative imagination." Pointing to the methods of "self-censorship" others have noted in Gaskell, Stone goes further, and discusses the patterns of submissiveness in her characters, the move away from economic individualism, and Wordsworth's "mood of reverence for and acquiescence to the eternal forms of power." His discussions of *Mary Barton* and *Ruth* are consistently interesting; further, he makes a more strikingly coherent argument about questions of fiction, romance and "everyday life" than do most critics. While most critics assert Gaskell's "balance" only at the expense of her complexity, he retains both; more, he makes clear not only the range of

her sympathy, but of her intelligence. His Gaskell is a varied—and complicated—writer. One would hope for something similar from Shelagh Hunter's
Victorian Idyllic Fiction: Pastoral Strategies (Atlantic Highlands, NJ: Humanities Press, 1984). As Lucas's *Literature of Change* and Bodenheimer's
chapter on "the pastoral argument" would suggest, and as critics like William
Empson and Fredric Jameson have argued, idyllic literature is both textually
and politically charged. Hunter's "idylls" begins with claims to some political
and literary sophistication, but she winds up fairly firmly in the realist's camp,
and despite the grace of many sections of her chapter (particularly her material
on time in the idyll) the chapter seems choppy, and not entirely coherent. But
more, she seems to take some of the edge away from Gaskell's pastoral: the
novels verge too much on the lyric in her descriptions.

If I have left feminist criticism for last, it is in part because I think we will
see many of these same difficulties I have been tracing throughout this essay
resurface in new ways, and in part because it is to feminist criticism that we
might look for ways out of the tensions between public and private, literary
and political, formalist and historicist questions; the commitment of feminism
to inter-disciplinary studies, and the attention given to questions of the
marketplace, of cultural strictures, of ideological contradiction and divided
consciousness in the best feminist criticism, leads one to hope for the Gaskell
studies we do not yet have from feminist critics; more, the ideological and
cultural density of Gaskell's literary production suggests that attention to her
work might push feminist literary criticism even further.

The complexities of locating "a" "feminist" view in Gaskell has reciprocally pointed out some of the contradictions in contemporary feminist theory.
Gaskell, as most critics note, seems to have lived happily within a conventional "female" role—as one early critic explains, in terms we could hardly
repeat today, she was unique among Victorian women novelists in being
beautiful and happy. More importantly, she was happily married, and was a
great advocate of that state for others, though she recognized the difficulties
of achieving it (she worried often that her own daughters, educated,
cultivated, and sensitive, had in fact been trained out of the marketplace, and
would never marry) and of sustaining it (there are more unhappy marriages in
her novel than critics have tended to notice.) But Gaskell's marriage, and her
ability to sustain both writing and a family, suggest the greater complexity of
Victorian social roles: within her marriage, Gaskell achieved her own separate
income; she travelled widely, visited frequently, and bought a house for her
husband without his knowledge; she also chafed, often, under the routine of

household tasks and the inability to enter a separate and "hidden world of art."

All of this has made the task of feminist critics difficult. Patsy Stoneman, showing the stress more than some, is compelled to add to her own preface the comment that she does not see why her own marriage and the presence of her husband should put her (as a critic) in a situation of oppression; this critical defensiveness is rare, and suspect. But the need of critics to place Gaskell's feminism (and that of her fiction) strictly according to her own concessions to (accommodations within) the cult of domesticity suggest some of the failures of feminist criticism—an over-dependence on generalizations about patriarchal culture and its reproduction in fiction, and (to speak in more literary terms) a tendency towards thematic rather than formal or structural criticism. Feminist criticism of Gaskell has shown itself more naive textually than has social criticism: critics have attended to characters and their motivations, and the reflection we can read of the author's own anger or contentment, rather than remarking on concerns of narration, plot and intertextuality; feminist criticism of Gaskell, motivated primarily by historical over-simplification, has resulted in rather limited and naive readings of the novels themselves.

The heritage of feminist criticism is not on the side of a novelist like Gaskell. Though Ellen Moers's *Literary Women*—still one of the most interesting approaches to women's writing—includes a section on women writers and reform, subsequent critics (particularly Elaine Showalter in *A Literature of Their Own* and Sandra Gilbert and Susan Gubar in *Madwoman in the Attic*) have relegated Gaskell to second place—in the former, she is noted primarily for the *Life of Charlotte Brontë*; in the latter, her headaches get more attention than her fiction. The emphasis of *Madwoman* is away from the political novel, from the social critique and plots of class struggle that motivate Gaskell's fiction; the interiority of Brontë, the patriarchal struggles of Eliot, seem closer to their paradigm. (Here again, we seem in danger of arguing Gaskell was not "angry" enough; I would argue, rather, that the anger has gone unnoticed, and that the formal innovations it creates and subversions it enables need more serious attention.) Judith Newton's *Women, Power and Subversion: Social Strategies in British Fiction, 1778–1860* (Athens, Georgia: The UP of Georgia, 1981) does raise many of these questions, but Gaskell is slightly peripheral to her argument as well. While her discussion of influence and power, of the difficulty of writing within "the ideology of the woman's sphere" does lead her to Gaskell, she too assumes that Gaskell was a more conventional writer than Brontë or Eliot; she dismisses Gaskell with terms like "mystification" and "suppression," and always takes the darkest possible view of Gaskell's accommodation to the systems she depicts. She notices, for instance, that *Villette* and *North and South* raise the same critique of male property, and that while *Villette* kills M. Paul and leaves Lucy his money, *North and South* "keeps the husband" and is silent on the question of property. But silence is not always acquiescence, and the openness of Gaskell's endings seems to escape Newton.

Patsy Stoneman's *Elizabeth Gaskell*, a volume in the Indiana "Key Women Writer" series (Indiana UP, 1987), attempts to argue a more coherent—and indeed, much stronger—case for Gaskell's feminism. She opens with a provocative—and convincing—history of Gaskell criticism, and with a strong sense of what a feminist case for Gaskell would have to argue against. What she argues *for* in the progress from *Mary Barton* to *Wives and Daughters* is a move from "public to private themes, from fatherhood to motherhood, and from a self-conscious use of Romantic or biblical allusion to the language of family life"; what is unique in Stoneman's view of this transformation is her reading of these as a movement towards a focus on "the woman question." Stoneman's readings are informed by her use of feminist theory, particularly Carol Gilligan's notions (in *In a Different Voice*) of female ethical thinking, and Nancy Chodorow's views (in *The Reproduction of Mothering*) of family relations, of the value of "mothering." While Stoneman effectively traces the maternal presence in male and family characters, her work remains a little too programmatic; her individual readings are interesting, but often they seem to serve only to introduce relevant bits of feminist theory, rather than providing more fully-fledged interpretations. She sees Gaskell as coming out of a tradition of Unitarian liberalism that stresses the value of individual rights and individual speech, and connects that with the feminist project (more accurately, with one feminist project) of moving from silence to speech, but her own hostility to Marxist or deconstructionist readings, and her consistent emphasis on character and theme over structure and form leads her, perhaps, to over-emphasize the "truth-telling" qualities of the characters—and the fictions. The book is valuable, but still seems somewhat thin.

Several books that attempt to trace female communities, textual strategies, or themes do slightly better by Gaskell. Nina Auerbach's *Communities of Women* (Cambridge, Mass.: Harvard UP, 1978), though it seems to race through its texts too quickly, is one of the first to note the anger and power of *Cranford*; the irony of the "Amazons" which has been lost on many critics leads her to interesting speculations about the text itself, and about the relationship of *Cranford* to Gaskell's fantasies about the Brontë sisters. (The other essay which points out the hidden violence of *Cranford* is Martin

Dodsworth's notorious and still provocative "Women without Men at Cranford," [*Essays in Criticism*, 1963, pp. 132–45] which is one of the few serious Freudian readings of Gaskell—and which has come in for as much criticism as one would expect, for over-ingenuity, etc.) Two works organized thematically focus attention on "the fallen woman": the earlier of the two, Sally Mitchell's *The Fallen Angel: Chastity, Class and Women's Reading, 1835–1880* (Bowling Green, Ohio: Bowling Green UP, 1981) is a thoroughly researched and well thought-out volume that moves from penny-weekly magazines to high literature, drawing interesting connections between them, and pointing out the relations between theme, form and audience; her reading of *Ruth* is enhanced by her treatment of earlier fiction Gaskell would have read, and an understanding of the ways *Ruth* in turn shaped audiences' expectations of the genre; the book on the whole, however, is too plot- and theme-oriented, and does not give a sense of the richness of the fiction she discusses. George Watt's *The Fallen Woman in the Nineteenth-Century Novel* (London: Croom Helm, 1984) unfortunately limits its scope to "high literature," and indeed, to fairly straightforward literary interpretations, but he has some interesting insights into *Ruth*, particularly when he notes the relation of the fallen woman to the ideal heroine. But the novels in this book suffer from their relative isolation from history—and from the other forms of representation.

A book which manages to be more purely literary and still historically (and theoretically) informed is Joseph Boone's *Tradition Counter Tradition: Love and the Form of Fiction* (Chicago: UP of Chicago, 1987), a splendid book on the marriage plot and its subversion, interruption, dispersal. Boone treats *Cranford* as a "centric" text, disrupting the marriage plot, turning on the power of the single female protagonist, and similarly disrupting "the causality of linear narration." The chapter thus manages both to account for the structural innovation of *Cranford* (and the critical disagreement which he points out has attended its reception) and to make a cultural argument out of its narrative pattern; the book as a whole moves with similar grace between text and tradition, and offers an illuminating view of the evolution of the novel and its "undoing" of its own tradition. While other books attempt to argue for the "female" world of Gaskell's fiction, no other work puts her so squarely at the center of tradition—or of an anti-tradition. Pauline Nestor's *Female Friendships and Communities* (Oxford: Clarendon, 1985) does comment usefully on the connections between Brontë, Eliot, and Gaskell, and does a fine job of placing their fictional imaginings in larger cultural imaginings about "the woman's view of life" and women "banding together," but her readings of the novel do not live up to her material. Robyn Warhol, in an article on direct address in Gaskell, Eliot, and Harriet Beecher Stowe ("Toward a Theory of the Engaging Narrator: Earnest Interventions in Gaskell, Stowe, and Eliot," *PMLA* October 1986, pp. 811–18), suggests that women writers, working within a sense of their own tradition and trying to carve out a voice that would express that difference, had a different view of the role of fiction itself; literary history, formalist criticism, and feminist insights merge here, again to suggest a different lineage for the "realist tradition." The connections between these breaks in the conventions of realism, and the social novel, are worth investigating further.

Two other works which challenge the assumptions about the origins and development of the novel use Gaskell's work to focus a feminist argument: Terry Lovell's *Consuming Fiction* (London: Verso, 1987) raises the problem of a subversive text, which would "be read," would "give pleasure to a female readership while at the same time disturbing the foundations of that pleasure." For Lovell, the novel reproduces the middle-class woman's relationship to a patriarchal capitalism, "but the relationship it reproduced is a deeply ambivalent one, which protested while it submitted. It may be read as conciliatory, reconciling women to their own subordination. It may also be read as reproducing and reinforcing women's characteristic fears of male domination, their resentment against it, and wish to escape it." In this context, she sees Gaskell's concern with middle-class women and a domestic ideology that was at once enabling and constricting, and her focus (on the family plots of *Mary Barton* and "Cousin Phillis," on, again, the private and public plots of the former) actually leads to some interesting insights. The book is quick, schematicized, reductive, but often canny; it reads as if other books should grow out of it. More, in its range of references, and its willingness to be flexible on such potentially ideological questions as female labour, female readership, domestic life, it shows an open-mindedness absent from a book like Julia Swindell's *Victorian Writing and Working Women: The Other Side of Silence* (Cambridge: Polity Press, 1984), which also focuses on the development of literary labor and the novel. The strength of Swindell's book is its comparisons of kinds of labor and kinds of authors—as, for instance, in her discussion of the "different class and gender routes which have their determinations in the lives of the two writers—Gaskell and Thackeray—which dispose and predispose them towards different types of writing career and to different types of writing." But the book tends towards generalization and inaccuracy; she is too quick to assume Gaskell had no literary training, she doesn't note Gaskell's early pseudonym, and mistakenly claims that "Mrs. Gaskell" appeared on the title-page of *Mary Barton*. These would be small mistakes, except that Swindell is claiming that "the significance of pen-names for women, then, seems to be as a temporary defence of a writer attempting to make an entry from a vulnerable position in gender and class," without distinguishing between degrees of vulnerability. She also argues, wrongly, that Gaskell's education at a girls' private school had as its "primary emphasis" "imbuing the girls with those accomplishments thought suitable to feminity," groomed for "what culture has constructed as the peculiarly female positions in the family," the "wife and the mother, whose 'proper duties' are held to be at odds with the pursuit of literary careers;" again, this matters only because Gaskell was, in fact, encouraged to write at school, was quite well-read for a Victorian woman—indeed, for a Victorian novelist; she was certainly better educated and more widely read than Dickens—and her own grooming seems to have trained her for both a "peculiarly female position in the family," and the pursuit of her literary career.

The book that makes the strongest claim for the relationship between women, the middle-class, and the novel is Nancy Armstrong's *Desire and Domestic Fiction: A Political History of the Novel* (New York: Oxford UP, 1987), which argues that as women came to control the means of literary production, they became the administrators of middle-class culture, a kind of domestic police, involved in turning the rest of the world into middle-class women. Armstrong's argument grows out of a strong sense of historical evolution—the confusion after the challenge and defeat of the working class at Peterloo; the growth of the domestic plot and interiority in the novel—but it seems rather rigid; its historical causality is mono-explantory, and it is fiercely optimistic about female power, domestic strategies, and the freedom assigned to these women agents. Its strength is in the Foucauldian analysis, which emphasizes that "literary texts" and "historical events" are not frozen in separate worlds, the one fictional, the other real. As Armstrong rightly stresses, the discursive structures for social change often appear *before* the social structures they ostensibly justify. But her readings of the novels do not always bear out her theses, and she tends to minimize the political complexity, and exaggerate the female power, of the novels she discusses: it is very hard to see where female authority lies in these texts, or even (as in the case of *Jane Eyre*) how women control the tools of culture. Of *Mary Barton* she claims, for instance, that "history virtually disappears from [Gaskell's] novel as class conflict comes to be represented as a matter of sexual misconduct and a family scandal," but that is to reverse the progress of the novel. Harry Carson's death—which had seemed to be a result of his sexual threat to Mary—is in fact an act of political assassination, and it is the question of John Barton's motivation, *not* Mary's romance, that preoccupies everyone at the end of the novel. The book seems often to elide the real politics of the heroine's story, treating everything domestic at once as apolitical, and guilty of the sneakiest political trickery (getting everyone to be middle-class in spite of themselves). In this way its relation to feminism seems questionable, for it needs to reinvent separate spheres to politicize the novel; more, its relation to its fiction seems troubled, often needing to make the novels more monolithic than they are, so as to indict them more thoroughly. The book is densely—and not very gracefully—written, and while its urgency is compelling, and the range of its material intriguing, for all its breadth, it winds up feeling a bit claustrophobic.

If Armstrong finds herself back in the realm of separate spheres for political reasons, Margaret Homans is there for psychoanalytic reasons, and, as with Armstrong, one feels she has written a fascinating book which loses only by adhering too forcefully to a rigid structure. In *Bearing the Word: Language and Female Experience in Nineteenth-Century Women's Writing* (Chicago: UP of Chicago, 1986), Homans offers a blend of Lacanian theories of language and object-relations' view of mothering, to suggest that women in the nineteenth century had a more "literal," more grounded, more translative relationship to language, and hence to the realm of the literal in their fiction. The argument, even more than Armstrong's, seems to duplicate the structures of the thing it sets out to critique: what Homans has written, of course, is a Romantic view of Romantic language theory and Romantic novelists, and there is far too little that is problematic in her account of this. Further, her readings are not always convincing: in her opening discussion of the skull in *To the Lighthouse*, I simply do not believe her on which is a literal, and which a metaphorical description; these terms remain somewhat ill-defined, and hard to locate in the texts; more, they are overly polarized. Still, she offers some wonderful material, and the chapters on Gaskell (along with a lovely chapter on *Romola*) are the finest in the book—and among the most sophisticated Gaskell has received. As with Armstrong, it is hard to tell Homans's relationship to feminist criticism; feminists have profitably used Lacan, but with a slightly more critical edge than Homans offers here. Further, her notions of maternal presence, the mother's body, and so on, desperately need to be historicized and contextualized. But the sense of women writing out of their bodies, in a tradition they perceive as female, is worth developing further, and Homans's use of lesser known texts (Gaskell's diary about her first child, the amazing short story *Lois the Witch*) to illuminate better-known novels (an intriguing discussion of *Wives and Daughters*, for instance) makes this book of value for feminist critics, despite its generalizations and vagaries.

This might suggest some of what we still need from Gaskell studies: I have not mentioned any studies of Gaskell and science; Gaskell and aesthetics; much that is sophisticated on the question of Gaskell and religion. In general, we need a more complicated sense of Victorian feminism; more studies of intertextual influences; more feminist/Freudian approaches that would pursue some of Homans's insights; more specific studies of Gaskell's relationship to the literary marketplace, to literary authority, to both the grit and the ephemera of Victorian culture. While there has been some very fine work on Gaskell, she has yet to receive the range of critical intelligence, careful reading, and cultural shake-up that she deserves; but then, in what way can a review essay of so important a novelist end, but in wishing for still more?

Index

371

Contents of Previous Volumes

Volume 8 (1980)

Volume 9 (1981)

Volume 10 (1982)

Volume 11 (1983)

Volume 12 (1983)

Volume 13 (1984)

Volume 14 (1985)

Volume 15 (1986)

Volume 17 (cont'd)

Volume 18 (1989)